The Dussehra of Kulu

History and Analysis of a Cultural Phenomenon

The more it changes, the more it remains the same.
— French saying

The Dussehra of Kulu

History and Analysis of a Cultural Phenomenon

Karuna Goswamy

Indian Institute of Advanced Study
Shimla

Aryan Books International
New Delhi

THE DUSSEHRA OF KULU

ISBN: 978-81-7305-523-2

Published in **2014** by

Indian Institute of Advanced Study
Rashtrapati Nivas, Shimla - 171 005

and

Aryan Books International
Pooja Apartments, 4B, Ansari Road, New Delhi-110 002 (India)
Tel.: 23287589, 23255799; Fax: 91-11-23270385
E-mail: aryanbooks@gmail.com
www.aryanbooks.co.in

Designed and Printed in India by
ABI Prints & Publishing Co., New Delhi

Cover Illustrations:
front: The images of Raghunathji and Sita being carried back to the *rath* after victory on the battlefield.
back: Narsinghji, formally adorned.

Preface

The present study, dedicated to one of the greatest festivals of the state of Himachal Pradesh, the Kulu Dussehra, was conducted over a sizeable period of time. Four times over the last seven years that I have been engaged in studying the Dussehra, I have stayed in Kulu for long stretches, observing the festival closely from the day it begins—sometimes even before it does—till its very end on the seventh day. I was drawn to the subject early on while working on *Vaishnavism in the Punjab Hills and Pahari Painting,* the subject of my doctoral dissertation. For in the Kulu Dussehra were reflected many cultural processes at once: the role that the Rajas of the hills played in the spread of the 'newly-arrived' faith; the acute thinking that must have gone into the effort; the accommodation in practices that had to be made before any headway could be made by the classical faith; the setting up of a rich and colourful festival that would on the one hand catch the imagination of the people and, on the other, somehow bind them and the outlying areas of the state, together, while allowing the folk to stay within the spaces of the faith that had been theirs long before the wave of Vaishnavism came to the hills in this form. But undertaking field-work, seeing the Dussehra from close, interviewing people ranging from the Raja and the Sanskritic priests to village-centred *gurs* of local *deotas* and common folk drawn to the festival, provided me with different insights into this great cultural phenomenon, leading me to understand a bit better how cultural processes work. The opportunity to put it all together came, however, in the three years that I have spent as a Fellow at the Indian Institute of Advanced Study. These years enabled me to order all the information that I had been collecting, in the form of words and images and sounds, and allowed me the opportunity to examine it against the theoretical frameworks that several scholars have been working with, in India and elsewhere.

In many ways, the Dussehra of Kulu is an 'event' that has few parallels. For more than three hundred and fifty years, the festival, participated in by hundreds of thousands of visitors or 'pilgrims' from all over the hills, has gone on being held, year after year. As a cultural event, it has been written about by many, some of them learned persons who belong to this region and have done much field-work; but as a *cultural phenomenon*, it has only been thinly studied till now. I have been particularly interested in tracing the history of the festival, in trying to understand the complex set of reasons for its being founded as a 'State Festival' in the 17th century, in following the changes that it has undergone over the centuries, and in analyzing the causes behind its uncommon longevity.

To describe the great festival can be engaging. Briefly put, the Dussehra celebrates, like in the rest of India, the victory of Rama; here, in Kulu, however, it was started early in the third quarter of the 17th century as a 'State Festival' by Raja Jagat Singh of Kulu, soon after he became a convert to Vaishnavism, following a dramatic event in his personal life. He is believed to have been instrumental in bringing to Kulu from Ayodhya a small metal image of Rama—widely known locally as 'Raghunath ji'—and installing it in a temple attached to his royal palace. He declared Vaishnavism as the state religion of Kulu, but it could not have been easy, for the area was dominated by shrines raised to local or regional deities, celebrated as 'devis' and 'deotas', to whom the hill folk owed impassioned allegiance. Many of these 'gods and godlings', as they have been called, bore the names of deities and rishis known to classical Hinduism; others seem to have been of purely local, tribal origin; a great many were completely unknown outside the region, as were the ways they practiced their faith. On the one hand, one gets names like Shesh Nag, Parashar Rishi, Tripurasundari, and on the other Hidimba Devi, Jamlu Deota, Phungani Devi. The Raja appears to have conceived the idea of inducing, or forcing, all these local deities to come once a year to Kulu to pay homage to Rama. The Dussehra festival thus got founded, and has been going on ever since. Year after year these *deotas* travel, each accompanied by his or her groups of priests, shamans, devotees, their 'mask'-like images carried by them in *rath*-palanquins on their shoulders to the accompaniment of music. The images arrive in Kulu, pay homage to the Raghunath idol, and then camp on the *chaugan* of the place.

The Kulu Dussehra, however, is not only a religious or cultural event. It has always had dimensions that are equally political and economic, for it turns into a visible sign of the assertion of authority as also a commercial and trading event. Long after Vaishnavism has lost its status as the religion of the state, and the authority of the Rajas of the state of Kulu has gone, the Dussehra festival continues to be held. But great changes have taken place. A new kind of politics comes into play now; new *devis* and *deotas* are being added, some of them founded or invented by low-caste groups or communities; the form remains but rituals have undergone modifications; the quantum and the form of homage is now different than it was before. This study draws attention to these and other matters. It remains an outsider's view of this complex phenomenon, but it is at least a deeply interested, and sympathetic, outsider's view.

If this work has come to fruition, it is because of the help and support that I have received over the years from so many people and institutions. To acknowledge these debts here is a pleasure.

Words are imperfect vehicles of expression and cannot in any way discharge even a fraction of the indebtedness that I feel for all those who helped me reach this point. It was their generosity and understanding that helped me in pursuit of my dream despite all the personal difficulties that came my way.

My sincere thanks go out to Professor Bhuvan Chandel, who was the Director of the Institute when I joined as a Fellow. She both supported and encouraged me in more ways than one. The Chairman, Dr. Mungekar, and, later, the Secretary, Mr. Madhukar Sinha saw me through difficulties of rules and regulations with a graciousness that was soothing.

I feel also greatly indebted to the former Director of the Institute, Professor Peter D'Souza, who took very kind interest in this work, and to the present Director, Professor Chetan Singh, under whom it is now being published. I have always greatly benefited, now as I did in the past, from Prof. Chetan Singh sharing with me, with customary generosity, his insights into the society and the politics of the hills. These have been invaluable to my work.

To Dr. Debarshi Sen, Academic Resource and Publication Officer of the Institute, I remain grateful for his support to this project. The list of my debts is long, and kept growing. I am grateful to Dr. Prabitra Kumar Ray, Dr. Meenu Agarwal, Mr. Ashok Sharma, Mr. Majumdar, Mr. Kundan Lal, Mr. Mela Ram and Mr. Bhrishtu Ram, for help during my stay at the Institute in a manner that was heart warming. I also received extremely valuable support from Smt. Pushpaji, Mr. Bhardwaj and Ms. Neeraj Sharma of the library. Without their alacrity and deep desire to help, I might never have reached this point in my work.

Mr. Narain Dass and his strong and loyal team headed by Manuji, Girdhari ji, Rakesh, Rajesh, Roshan, Soni, Dev Raj and Jeet Ram are never to be forgotten. Devinder from whose canteen flowed tea, delicious, hot and sweet, lifted the soul. Om Prakash and Kesar Singh with their sharp intelligence and quick dispatch saved me valuable time. Vijay shed light in more ways than one and Vijay Lakshmi healed with the balm of medicine. Things took a shape only because of Pinky's vital role of the sustainer. Gopal helped in a very basic way and kept the atmosphere full of good cheer and a spirit of protectiveness. The IT back-up I received was extremely helpful.

Casting my mind back to the point in time when I began my researches, I cannot forget the help extended to me by Dr. Vidya Chand Thakur, Dr. Sita Ram Thakur, and Dr. Vidya Sharma. Their erudition and intimate knowledge of their culture sensitized me to so many issues and nuances that would have otherwise escaped my notice.

My most sincere thanks are due to Raja Maheshwar Singh ji and to the senior functionaries of Raghunath Temple, e.g. Bhatu ji, who spared their time and tried to answer all my queries at a time when they were extremely busy with the organization of the Dussehra on different occasions. My thanks are also due to Mr. Prem Sharma, the then Director, Department of Languages and Culture, to Mr. Garg and Mr. Dev Raj, the Librarian of the Academy, who kept me abreast with the latest publications. For the visuals I owe a great deal to Mr. Birbal Sharma of Mandi and Mr. Kuldeep Chauhan of the *Tribune*. When I needed help with the maps, Professor Swaranjit Mehta and Professor K.D. Sharma of the Department of Geography at the Panjab University were most generous. Their understanding of the area that I have been working in, and the expertise of S. Mohan Singh, proved invaluable in this task. The care and courtesy shown by Mr. Madhav Shyam, Deputy Director of the Census of India at Chandigarh, who located for me vital information, puts me greatly in his debt.

My debts of gratitude would be inadequately discharged if I were not to record my warm thanks to our friends, Dr. Eberhard Fischer and his wife Barbara Fischer, in whose company I first turned my attention to the Dussehra of Kulu. I am equally grateful to another friend, Deepak Sanan, for it was he who helped me access crucial documents having a bearing on my project. From another kind and gracious friend, Mrs. Lakshmi Chetan Singh, I have always received warmth and generosity in rich measure.

At Chandigarh, Professor Mahesh Sharma was always a source of strength and gave unstintingly of his time and expertise whenever I needed it, adding to my understanding his intimate knowledge of the hills.

While Shehnaz Pathania was her giving self in securing for me an important map, the work of giving shape to the manuscript was done not only with efficiency but also the warm and friendly care of Mr. Dharam Vir of Skill Spot at Chandigarh.

Words are not adequate to express my gratitude to my husband, Professor B.N. Goswamy, who was always his patient and generous self. But for his help this work may never have come to fruition. For their understanding, affection, and timely help, I am beholden to my children, Apurva and Malavika, who too were always there for me, not to forget little Damini and Madhav.

And last but definitely not the least, it is for me to acknowledge the great help that the conscientious and strong team at home has been: Bhag Singh, Gurnaib Singh, and Ravinder.

K.G.

Contents

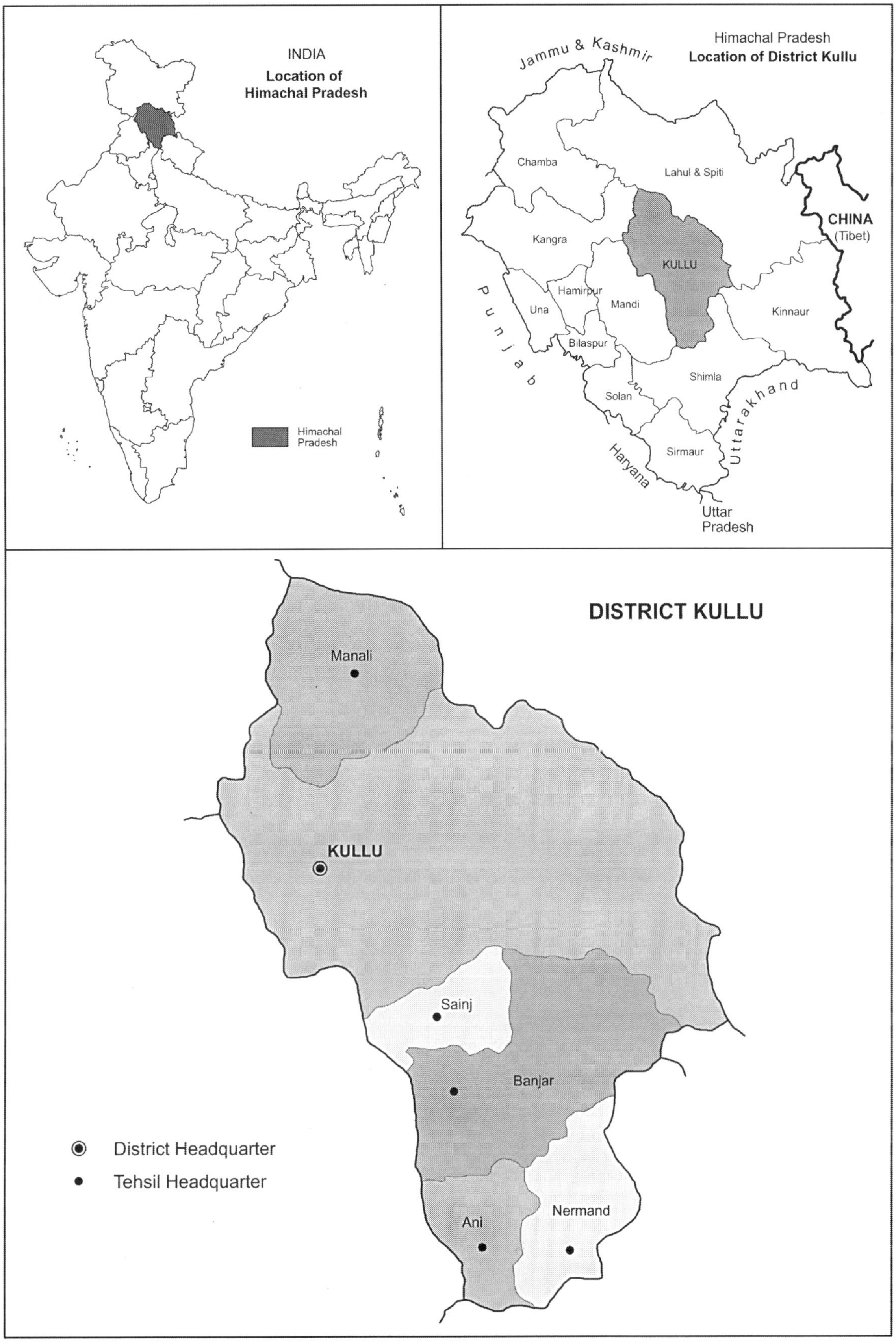

Map 1. Page with three maps locating Kulu, each with added legends in corners above or below; thus (a) Himachal Pradesh; (b) The location of Kulu in Himachal Pradesh; (c) Tehsils of the present district of Kulu.

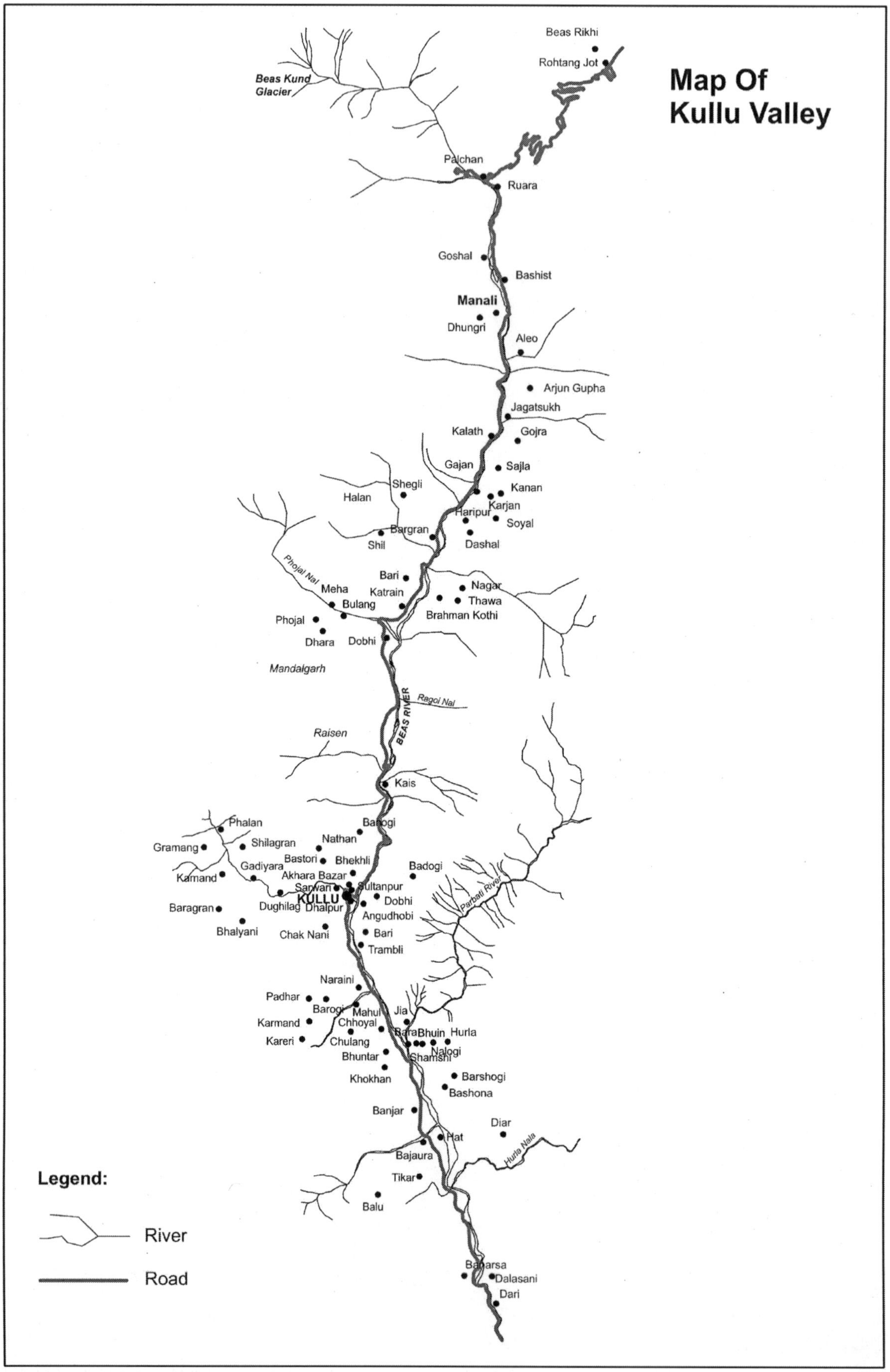

Map 2. Map of Kulu Valley.

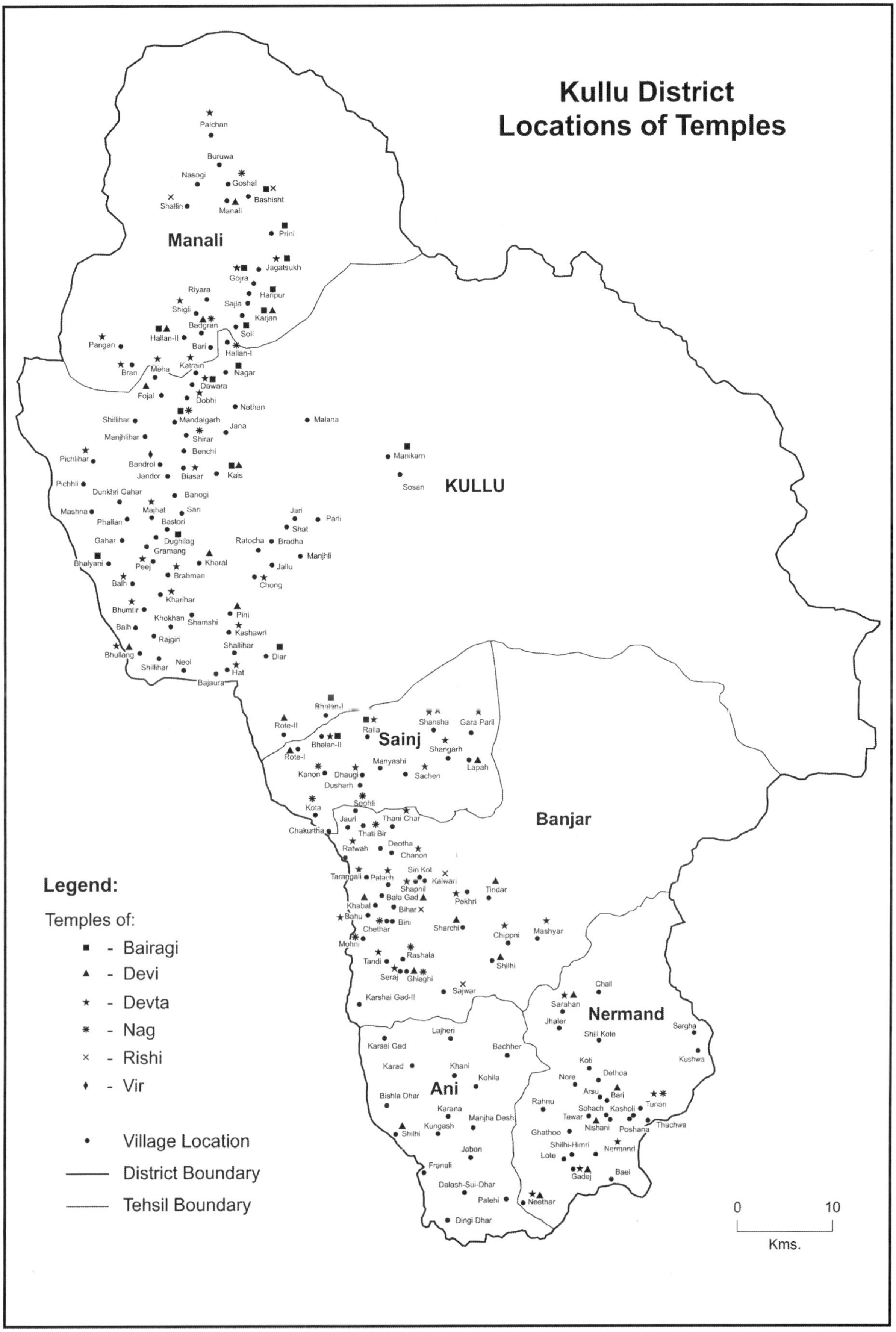

Map 3. Locations of temples in Kulu district.

List of Illustrations

16. Cleaning and preparation of accessories at the Raghunath ji temple.
17. More preparations of that kind; silver vessels being cleaned.
18. The regalia of Raghunath ji: The *nishans* meant for his procession.
19. More *nishans* and other emblems of sovereignty of Raghunath ji.
20. A finely crafted *nishan* presented by a devotee to Raghunath ji.
21. The *chhatra*, or royal parasol, for Raghunath ji's image.
22. *Palki* for Raghunath ji to be carried in.
23. The Rajmata preparing garlands of flowers for Raghunath ji.
24. The Raja waiting in the temple courtyard, ready for the procession.
25. Yuvaraj, the Raja's son, similarly waiting.
26. The Raja's grandson, waiting in the temple courtyard.
27. Raghunath ji's *palki* being taken out of the temple.
28. The small, unpretentious temple of *deota* Bir Baradhi at Kareri.
29. Another view of the same temple.
30. Another small shrine on the Bir Baradhi complex at Kareri.
31. Pujari and other devotees inside the Bir Baradhi temple.
32. *Shastra puja* by the *gur* of Bir Baradhi prior to leaving for Kulu.
33. A *deota* being honoured by villagers during his journey.
34. Traditional musicians – *bajantris* – making preparations.
35. Musicians blowing on their *narsingha* horns.
36. A *deota* temple, with crowds of devotees in the background.
37. Materials for the *shringara* of the goddess Hidimba being taken out.
38. *Mohra*-masks inside their safe boxes at the *bhandar.*
39. Preparations for making the *reerh*-skirt of the goddess.
40. The *reerh*-skirt, ready to be draped.
41. The *reerh*-skirt being transported to the *rath* of the goddess.
42. *Mohra*-masks being mounted on the *rath* of the goddess, and Manu *deota.*
43. Jewellery to be worn by the goddess being selected.
44. The goddess's *rath* in the state of near-readiness, with the *gur* by her side.
45. *Mohalla* day: *Haziri* register. Narsingh ji's *ghori* outside Raghunath temple.
46. *Sair Puja*: The Raja showers walnuts from the fresh crop over the devotees.
47. Devotees wait at the Ram Shila by Beas riverside for Hidimba's arrival.
48. Hidimba's decorated *rath* at Ram Shila with the *kardar* and *gur* by her side.
49. Hidimba's *mohra* in the bottom row of masks, wearing a nose-ring.
50. Hidimba's *rath* making its way to the Raja's palace through the streets.
51. Hidimba's *gur* in front of her *rath*, with his tongue protruding.
52. The *dharach*-ladle belonging to the 18 *karadus.*
53. A view of the Raja's palace known as that of the Rai of Rupi.
54. The visiting *deotas* arriving at the Raja's palace.
55. A *deota* bows in homage to the sacred doorway of the 18 *karadus.*
56. The goddess Hidimba entering the private residence of the Raja.

Chapter ONE

Introductory
Studying the Cultural Field

I

If the aim of history is to try and understand the past, it is necessary to delve into areas that are invisible and inaccessible at the same time, and in doing that the task of the historian becomes extremely complex. For quite some time it has been understood that ploughing the furrows of economic and political history alone does not yield the meaning of many abstract realities. The field of cultural studies has therefore appeared promising as far as the laying bare of the basic structures of society is concerned, and of making the 'invisible', 'visible', so to speak. The words 'culture' and 'society' seem to be interchangeable, if one were to follow Edward Tylor,[1] for he speaks of culture as "...that complex whole which includes knowledge, belief, art, morals, law, custom and any other capability and habits acquired by man as a member of society". In his own manner, Bronislaw Malinowski also stated the same while taking it forward. Culture, according to him, referred to "inherited artifacts, goods, technical processes ideas, habits and values."[2] In any case, it seems no longer necessary to argue the need for cultural history. Some outstanding names, and studies, are by now associated with the field. When Jacob Burckhardt, in his influential if by no means exhaustive writings, addressed the field in the 19th century, he spoke of the relocating of emphases and the desirability of shifting the focus from the simple recording of political and economic events to an intuitive capturing of the 'spirit of the age'.[3] As he drew attention to abstract concepts like individualism, self-consciousness, and competitiveness, and documented them almost for the very first time, cultural history started moving into a different orbit, even as other typical and recurrent trends co-existed with it.

It is of use perhaps to recall here some examples of the manner in which cultural studies grew and developed. For Johan Huizinga, the early 20th century Dutch historian, it was necessary to foreground the portrayal of thoughts and feelings along with other patterns of culture characteristic of the age. Historical writing as he saw it needed to concern itself with decoding symbols, focusing on feelings like a 'sense of decline' or the 'fear of death', and other similar themes, that had entered man's consciousness in that period. Contemporary art and literature was replete with references to the awareness and presence of these and other emotions hitherto not consciously noticed. Standards of ideal behaviour were defined as was an ideal civil society. Academic researches framed new conclusions. By studying the art and literature of that period, Huizinga wrote about the nature of contemporary society with its inevitable shift of emphasis on to thought processes such as values and emotion. Economic changes he saw as being brought about by mindsets influenced by religious thought and values. The culture of self-control and civil behaviour was discerned as a direct outcome of forms of centralized government.[4]

The seminal writings of Sigmund Freud, in which 'civilizing processes' figured prominently, had their own influence. The earlier obsession with the 'elite' was replaced with a new-found interest in the teeming humanity, looming on the peripheries of society.[5] Important studies in 'popular' culture were undertaken. The use of new source materials like painting, folk-tales and folk songs led some academics into newer and innovative areas of research, as for example a study of *The Jazz Scene*, (1959).[6] The discourse here was not only limited to insights and perceptions about jazz as a form of music, but extended itself to reactions and responses of the listening public, to jazz being used as a form of national and class protest and even to jazz as business. It appeared to many then that 'the arid landscape of history had greened and was now blossoming with a myriad human faces'. The common man, the ordinary man with all his cultural extensions, was entering the ken of history.

The landmark publication in 1963 of Edward Thompson's *Making of the English Working Class* signalled the beginning of the writing of a 'history from below'.[7] Writing on the 'discrete' phenomena constituted by the class mostly of weavers and tailors, Thompson used their dialect poetry to provide insight to his scrutiny and interpretation of society. The informal honesty of the dialect poetry of the working class, it could be seen, was both stunning and disarming. Everything about these 'dregs of humanity', their lives, homes, rituals, religious symbolisms of food, iconographies of riots, the importance of fairs to their cultural life, moved silently, surely and with great clarity, into the spotlight. Thomson's poetic lens revealed that the 'class' of workers was neither a 'structure', nor a 'category'. It was, instead, a historical relationship created by the articulation of an identity resting on common interests. Different sets of interests, he maintained, would create separate and different identities, which would naturally be placed in opposition to one another. A consciousness of class was thus created from "the way in which these experiences are handled in cultural terms, embodied in traditions, value systems, ideas and institutional forms". The role of 'popular' culture in the creation of class became visible only when the mind had been weaned away from the usual search for the roots of class formation in economic and political circumstances. Thompson's analysis of the imagery thrown up by Methodist hymns and different styles of Methodist preaching enriched his study enormously. This treatment of those "unsung voices of history" became highly influential. For historians everywhere, search for new source materials yielded fresh insights into the 'mentality of subalternity' as it obtained in the case of already well-documented political events. This led to the production of valuable research more in tune with ideas of socialism and democracy.

In India, subaltern studies also started into focus, with Ramachandra Guha's pioneering work.[8] The classic study by Shahid Amin, one of India's leading subaltern historians, of the image of Gandhi as enshrined in peasant consciousness threw up a prime example of religious beliefs influencing political attitudes.[9] Further subaltern literature revealed how 'pre-existing patterns of popular belief' first transformed Gandhi into a virtual Krishna and then transformed the devotion of his followers into the mode of the Bhakti Cult. Increasingly, studies like these, undertaken in depth, revealed the intersection of the political with the cultural. 'Clothed in political raiments', the historical fact was 'decoded with the key of popular culture'. Literary texts by unknown and common people were dug out and subjected to scrutiny, turning eventually into essential material for piecing together this variant of 'history from below'. A sensitization towards the meaning of symbols coupled with an understanding of the need for collective historical enterprise led to the writing of what could be termed as 'Total History'. The territory of the historian, it can be seen, was enhanced by the incorporation and enlargement of the cultural field.

From the 1960s onwards, the crossing of the trajectories of the historians and the anthropologists fertilized historical studies and gave rise to work that was richer in cultural understanding, whether one called it 'anthropological history', or 'historical anthropology'. Studies on gifts, witchcraft, myths, attitudes and notions of purity enriched an entire generation of historical studies. Cultural histories of virtually every aspect of society were written. Dreams, food, emotions, travel, memory and gesture: everything attracted researchers. The roots of violent political expressions like revolutions were found to have their beginnings in cultural conflicts. In his study of Ireland, F.S.L. Lyons[10] established that political collisions in Ireland were only the superficial reason for conflicts. The essential reasons for these political conflicts were rooted in basic cultural differences between the English, the Ulster Protestants, the Irish and the Anglo-Irish, four culturally distinct communities living in Ireland. These differences made them 'unable to live together' or 'live apart', contributing irrevocably to the generation of an ongoing tension.

The work of the Russian historian, Aron Gurevich,[11] bore the impact of anthropological methodologies, even as it helped in the understanding of medieval society. Writing as he did on beliefs, perception and categories of popular medieval culture, Gurevich was highly influenced by the work of Marcel Mauss on 'gift-giving'.[12]

Writing on Scandinavia, he pointed out the fact of generosity being a hallmark of status. Magical rewards of good harvests and the prevalence of peace were linked by him to 'gift giving', which was to be seen as a moral duty. Extensive documentation was undertaken of the rituals accompanying gifts, the kind of objects used as gifts and the obligation imposed upon the recipients to reciprocate these gifts. Using a Scandinavian poem as the opening for his work on 'gift', Gurevich had cast himself, without fully realizing it, in the role of a historian of 'mentalities'. Skilled in the interpretation of semiotic concepts enshrined in the various literary genres of the medieval period, Gurevich was equally adept and perceptive in picking up and understanding the acculturation processes operative between two cultures when they came face to face.

Clifford Geertz's seminal work on the theory of Culture[13] affirmed, among other things, the functional importance of religion. One of his fundamental assumptions was that any religion, like the wider cultural system that it was a part of, affirms as well as defines what reality is all about, and how the individual has to act within its parameters. He maintained that the underpinnings of cultural patterns of everyday life were visible through religious symbologies and the rituals attached to them. Rituals could be read like any other text, be it a folk tale or a philosophical treatise.

Culture and its study, thus, subsume several areas of human activity: religion, the structure of society, the quality of everyday life, local individual experience, local knowledge, the economic impact of cultural events, material culture, and above all 'mentalities'. Micro-history, now a popular genre, focused on studies of villages, the influence of geography on settlement patterns, local economies, an analysis of the relationship between the community and the outside world, individual families, convents, riots, festivals and the like. Methodologies concerned themselves with interviewing people and looking through new kinds of source materials: for example, account books, inquisition books and the like. In India, in a path-breaking work in 1968, B.N. Goswamy looked at pilgrim registers in the possession of priests to reconstruct the genealogies, and patterns of movement, of painters from the hills of Himachal and from thereon to create a new paradigm about family being the basis of style in painting.[14]

The 1980s, marked the beginning of a new phase in cultural history with Benedict Anderson[15] and his constructivist approach stressing the role of imagination, collective and otherwise, as an important process in making things happen. Anderson examined various 'scenarios' displaying power and unity in political festivals, weddings, coronations, parades, processions and other collective actions and their defining role in the creation of participant identity. Myths, ceremonies, rituals all forming an integral part of these collective actions, contributed significantly to the creation of identities, he said.

Takashi Fujitani,[16] writing on the restoration of imperial power in Japan, observed how "Japan's governing elites invented, revived, manipulated and encouraged national rituals with unprecedented vigour". Pageants and public festivals were supposed to have "produced power simply by their pomp and glitter and not because they communicated any particular myth or ideology". A king's life could be ritualized and theatricalized. Even meals and gestures could turn into performances. Acts of speech, body language, everything added to the performance. The image of the king could be just as much 'created' or 'recreated' through these 'performances' as through 'Imperial Image' paintings, like in the case of the Mughals,[17] and sculptures. It is through these 'performances' that the king gained visibility among the people, the nobility, the neighbouring states and, above all, in posterity.

The theoretical approaches of the *Annales* school,[18] in regard to their responses to problems as also their re-conceptualisation of problems, have wielded enormous influence, even helping the present study by providing appropriate tools for piecing together diverse facts of Kulu's socio-cultural history. Individual as well as collective attitudes, thought-processes as well as feelings of both the elite and the commoners, conscious thoughts, unconscious and unspoken assumptions, as established by the *Annales* school, formed a necessary part of 'mentalities', which came to be of great interest to the scholar. The concern here is as much with the 'structures' of society as with those of belief and its contents. 'Categories' are of importance but then so are 'metaphors' and 'symbols'. The preoccupation is not only with *how* people think as with *what* they think. Handling these basic approaches is not possible within a single discipline, it was demonstrated. Inputs are required from other disciplines, like anthropology, philosophy, psychology, literature, history of art, history of science, and so on. The mapping of both distinctive and indistinctive 'thought communities' thus became possible. The term 'mentalities' remained in vogue for a long time even though it is now being substituted by some scholars with the terms 'representation' and 'collective imagination'.

Three or four streams of theoretical formulations were current in the period in which the *Annales* school was emerging as a major school of thought in the field of cultural history. One of the major influences on cultural theory was the writings of Mikhail Bakhtin,[19] which became accessible to the Western world only after 1965, with the translation into French and English of his book on Rabelais. Bakhtin's basic concepts, with his deep interest in semiotics, have become such an integral part of cultural history that it is difficult to imagine an academic world without these tools. His theory about the subversion and penetration of 'high' culture by 'low' culture, came to be accepted as normative. The effect of 'popular' laughter in the subversion of high culture is one telling instance of his analysis of 'cultural hegemony'. The domination of the elite classes by the lower orders through the medium of popular laughter was, according to Bakhtin, infinitely more effective than any control exerted through 'political hegemony' of the normal kind. Bakhtin drew attention to carnivals and processions being used as instruments of subversion. Depending upon the manner in which they were used by the masses, even 'mock' processions could contribute to a 'de-sacrilysation' of otherwise pious meanings. Bakhtin marked the presence of multiple voices, different voices, within the parameters of a single 'text'. Within these texts, both 'dialogues' and 'voices of coexistence' could be heard. The reader was skilfully made a part of the dramatic oppositions, which existed between the 'playful' and the 'aggressive', the 'high' and the 'low', the 'male' and the 'female'.

The expansion and opening up of the territory of the historian was also achieved by the ideas of Norbert Elias,[20] the German sociologist, writing on civilization, and the art of everyday living. Elias' account of the history of table manners was meant not to be seen simply as an account of the surface things of human existence but as a meaningful documentation of the development of self control over emotions. It is through Elias' work that an awareness of the concept of 'civility' came into focus. Emotions of 'embarrassment' and 'repugnance' were highlighted. Through this, Elias maintained, the tolerance level towards unacceptable emotions was decreased and society unobtrusively propelled towards a civil conduct. Could developments such as these have led towards the formation of a 'civil society'? These were some of the searching questions now being asked. Pierre Bourdieu,[21] a philosopher by training and practice, was identified with four or five theoretical concepts that were influential in the field of cultural theory. These were to do with the notions of 'the Field', which was defined as an independent autonomous domain with its own cultural conventions, its own cultural reproduction, and its own cultural distinction. This notion of a 'Cultural Field' began to open up and greatly attract some historians. The idea of 'cultural reproduction', Bourdieu felt, was contained within a system, through which a social group ensured its position of dominance in society. The system, for example, worked through the kind of qualifications laid down for selections, either to a system of higher education or to positions of power. Most of these qualifications were already inherent in the group or were easily acquirable. The selection, thus, from a particular social group was easy and appeared to be accomplished quite 'naturally'.

Another important aspect of Bourdieu's cultural theory was the notion of 'distinction'. In search of achieving dominance in society, a group would often tap into its 'cultural capital' (i.e. the body of thought processes handed down from a long period in the past) for finding solutions to their problems. In the absence of this skilled use of past knowledge, other strategies had to be worked out to achieve the desired end. This strategy was quite often the strategy of achieving a 'distinction' that would clearly set them, as a class apart, from others classes lower down in the hierarchical scale. 'Distinction' was acquired quickly and effectively by becoming identified in terms of taste, with any classical cultural form, say, for example, with classical music. A quiet unobtrusive departure would have been made from the earlier traditions associated with the group. An awareness of this process would contribute to the historian's understanding of the past. Bourdieu, in his 'theory of practice' (referring to everyday practice) argued against Levi Strauss' theory about the rigidity of cultural rules. He perceived the qualities of remarkable elasticity and a capacity for a 'sustained improvisation' within the framework of the mind-body schemata laid down by a specific culture. Both these qualities vastly enhanced a social group's capacity for success, he asserted.

Michel Foucault,[22] whose writings have been amongst the most influential of our times, uncovered the basic processes operative within a society with great incisiveness. Foucault drew attention to 'ruptures' and 'cultural discontinuities' taking place within society, from time to time. These took place, according to Foucault, whenever a dis-association occurred between words and their meanings. Foucault believed in a kind of cultural construction that occurred through discursive practices that indirectly helped to construct and constitute, shape and mould, the very identity of the objects that they referred to. Quite significantly, Foucault felt that even thought processes could be controlled. This was achieved quite simply and discreetly by the manner in which certain subjects were foregrounded and others were dropped in writing as well as speech. Drawing attention to 'basic' patterns of society, Foucault spoke of the function of institutions like schools, prisons, hospitals, etc. in producing 'docile bodies' and minds, with all capacities to venture out of line having been eliminated. Disciplining through the look or the 'gaze' was seen by him as an expression of a modern disciplinary society. In this and many other ways, Foucault's penetrating insights helped not only in understanding 'Tradition' but also helped in departing from it.

II

The Dussehra of Kulu, the subject of the present study, can be seen as a cultural phenomenon. Now close to 350 years old, this festival can easily be described as a 'performance of magnitude', a 'pilgrimage', or, again, as a display of the splendour of the Rajas of Kulu. Lasting for ten days, this annual cultural event, institutionalising the processes of integration in the society of Kulu, has, despite its importance, received little scholarly treatment till now. There has been a body of vernacular works devoted to the event, but it falls broadly in a very different category of work, more descriptive than analytical. It needs a different treatment, for a lot has grown about and constructed around the event. The Dussehra is not only a 'religious' event but has equally important dimensions of political and economic importance. Besides being a commercial and trading event, it displays visible signs of the assertion of authority. The political and economic aspects of the festival are *at least* as important as the religious. Forms, from the past, whether religious or political, remain, but they have undergone a lot of modification. The process is marked by the willingness to change, if there is a necessity to change. The remarkable vitality and adaptability of Indian culture gets mirrored in many ways in this cultural phenomenon. Change occurs through an intricate and complex web of capillaries spreading out and binding people and societies together into one homogenous mass. Many other issues arise. These involve, among other things, encounters between the classical Vaishnava faith and cults of local gods – the *deotas* –, the integration of disparate linguistic and ethnic groups, the balance struck between the centre and the peripheries, and many other newer balances in the process of being struck. Everything, thus, needs to be subjected to close scrutiny, with the overall aim being to understand *how* these 'structures' of Kulu society functioned. Appropriate theoretical tools, best suited to the nature of the material, have been used. The attempt is to proceed from the specific to the general, recording what lay below the surface, decoding 'mentalities', examining and analysing thought-processes, collective or individual, conscious or unconscious, spoken or unspoken. The similarity or otherwise of a 'mentality' is discerned from the type of reasoning or justification it employed along with its assertions of authority. A careful analysis of symbols, both religious and sociological, the effects of mass processions and their effects on the mentality of the people, is sought to be documented, opening access to many different areas in the study of Kulu society. Rituals, and the power that they wield, are seen as a means of asserting cultural hegemony. The multiple voices within the single text of the Dussehra, thus, all come together as one, in the decoding of the culture code.

With the emergence of an interest in historical psychology, different methodologies adopted by a society, to ensure for itself certain positions of social dominance, are studied. A sensitization to newer tools of research has helped in uncovering strategies used by kings and gods in Kulu to ensure positions of political and religious dominance for themselves, as hierarchies were being fixed and tribute-related issues were being settled. A distinctive culture, composite and multi-layered, especially in the field of its history and its religion, had emerged in Kulu.

Geographical factors play a very special role in our understanding of historical and sociological processes. Lying between 31°20′ and 32°55′ latitude and 76°50′ and 78°35′ longitude, the territory of Kulu is cut across by numerous narrow river valleys, separated from each other by extremely high mountain ridges rising up to a height of 13,000 ft. The impact of environment on human actions, along with the long-standing relationship that develops between man and his surroundings – always worthy of notice – is of special significance in Kulu. Physically separated from one another by natural features and segregated from the rest of the world by the barriers of the mountains, the people of this area developed over time the skill of meeting natural challenges with great flexibility. Peopled as the region was by small yet distinct communities, individualistic, self-contained, self-sufficient, independent, none of these traits acted as hurdles of any kind. Because of their adaptive nature, the people of Kulu were able to arrive at a consensus, quite easily, and also follow a path of interdependence if and when required. Each region was thus "a micro-region, both in geographical and human terms".[23] Economic and cultural distinctiveness developed naturally in the region, something that acted, as has been remarked, as an inhibiting factor and prevented the opening up of the area to the outside world.

The process of gathering materials, on which a cultural study such as the present one can be based, is a matter of absorbing interest. In general, one can say that the conventional source materials for writing a history, cultural or otherwise, of Himachal, and of Kulu in particular, are very limited. One has therefore to fall back upon different methodological tools, some of them of an unorthodox kind. For this study, it was realized, it was a *requirement* to give central importance to rigorous and in-depth field-work. A careful and minute participant-observation of all festivals, rituals and their preparations was undertaken. Personal interviews were conducted along carefully prepared lines. Some of the other sources tapped were records of the erstwhile Kulu state, the archives of the state of Himachal Pradesh, land settlement records of the colonial period, temple account books of the Raghunath temple, *Haziri* registers and *Nazrana* registers from the office of the deputy commissioner, as well as those of the Raghunath temple. Publications in vernacular languages, some of them of very limited circulation, along with modern works in English, have been used to assess the degree of continuity and change in the form, flavour or politicization if any, of the Dussehra festival over the years. A careful study was also made of the more recent official brochures brought out by the state administration at the time of the Dussehra. Pamphlets, invitations, notices of meetings of Kardar unions, even contents of the entertainment programmes sponsored by the government have been analysed. Other accounts that reflect changing norms and patterns of Kulu society, like some publications of the Language and Culture Academy of Himachal, have been analysed in terms of organization of material, different viewpoints, and slants of writing. This is especially so with the writings of important writers from the region, like Pandit Chandra Sekhar 'Bebas', M.R. Thakur, Surat Thakur, and V.C. Thakur. Special care was taken to interview people from different segments of society in terms of status, to gain a fuller insight into the great Dussehra event. Oral evidence thus collected from the 'Raja Sahib' of Kulu and other members of the royal family, the *pujaris* and representatives of the *deotas,* as well as the functionaries of the Raghunath temple, along with interviews of other important as well as unimportant members of Kulu society formed an important body of the material gathered. Through this broad range of people interviewed, one was able to hear multiple voices present within the single 'text' of the Dussehra. Attempts were made to validate oral evidence against available written records wherever possible.

Several queries were thrown up even during initial encounters with functionaries connected with Dussehra. How, for instance, is the framework of officialdom organized? What are the approaches of the official brochures? What are the perceptions of the common man? Efforts to trace the origins of the *deotas* proved to be very rewarding and yielded valuable information at times. Among the questions formulated were, for instance, how far back in time do the *deotas* go? What is their relationship with the classical gods of Hinduism? If they stand in relationship to the classical deities, how did the process of 'sanskritisation' take place? What are the ideological and locational affiliations of the *deotas*? Does a study of the regional distribution of the shrines of the *deotas* reveal any significant pattern or clusters? How have governmental policies as well as programmes of political parties affected the behaviour or economy of the *deotas*? An analysis, done at present or in the future, of all these and many more questions and issues could yield some meaningful answers. It is from complex interactions and relationships between the gods and the people that the cultural and religious hegemonies of a society have sought to be explained. Just as there are many levels to the search, the answers too cannot be simple or monolithic. As one works in the field, one realizes that arriving at the truth could be a little like attempting to hold mercury in the palm of one's hand and keep it still.

In all this, all the published material, containing some information directly or indirectly on Kulu, is naturally of help. A valuable body of literature came into existence after the British, assured of their continued presence in India, commissioned research in various areas in the 19th century. Their prime aim was to understand the 'mentalities' of their Indian subjects, knowledge being seen, rightly, as 'power'. For good governance and therefore effective control of their subjects would be a natural corollary of this knowledge. Towards achieving this end, several extensive surveys were conducted, most useful now in the context of the present study. Landholdings and populations were all quantified and the information thus collected contributed towards the finalisation of revenue settlements. Information regarding people and their beliefs, among other things, was compiled in the shape of census reports and District Gazetteers. Of great value, in this connection, are the land settlement reports of the area. G.C. Barnes in 1850[24] wrote the very first settlement report of the district of Kangra, of which Kulu was then a part. This was later revised and published by Lyall in 1872.[25] Subsequently, a joint report was published in 1875, carrying both their names.[26] Models of scientific enquiry, these reports were extremely valuable as source material because of their near-contemporariness as also the acute nature of their personal observations. Most of the *District Gazetteers*[27] compiled later in point of time, drew upon these settlement reports for their information. Closely allied to the surveys just mentioned, but adding to them, was the work of Col. A.F.P. Harcourt, who was appointed the Assistant Commissioner of Kulu in 1869.[28] Densely researched and carefully written, Harcourt's work, following directions from the administration, drew upon all the "interesting matter" contained in his diaries, and took the form of a report to "be submitted officially to government". Col. Harcourt, however, wished to write a full-fledged history, being acutely conscious that a mere report would not do justice to the subject matter. Trade with Central Asia, passing through Kulu as it did, interested Harcourt just as much as the social customs and manners of the people in this sub-division. But difficulties with figuring out dates and chronologies acted as major hindrances. By Harcourt's own admission, his account of Kulu fell short of being a good historical account in areas that were of great interest to him. Despite these self-admitted flaws, the account is marked by an eye for detail and good descriptions. Displaying his penchant for good administration, Harcourt described the revenue networks in fair detail, highlighting the role of the *Negis, Lambardars* and *Chowkidars* within this system. The appendices in his work contained detailed tables concerning revenue matters, and are of great value. Harcourt's account, though methodically and meticulously compiled, may have some weaknesses, coming as did from a different culture. All the same it has served as an important reference book for later administrators and scholars. Well researched, detailed, precise and relentless in their pursuit of accuracy, these early colonial endeavours were documenting 'reality' as they understood and perceived it. In the use of this material, however, the present researcher is of the opinion that the information provided to British officers by the local pundits or other informants may have been subjective in nature. Answers to queries are not unlikely to have been moulded or coloured by the kind of questions asked and the manner in which they were asked. In addition to this, colonial prejudices – in the section dealing with religion, the *Gazetteer of Kangra and Kulu* (1917), for instance, describes the music of the *deotas* as 'uncouth' and the various rituals followed by the devotees as 'grotesque'– and value judgements inevitably crept into colonial writing, sometimes obscuring the truth from view.

The material contained in the *Gazetteers* goaded, it might be added, some Indian writers towards putting together histories of the hill region and states in vernacular languages, prominent among them being those written by Hardayal Singh,[29] Thakur Kahn Singh Balauria,[30] Diwan Sarbdial,[31] and Kanwar Ranzor Singh.

Early attempts at writing a continuous and comprehensive history of the hills were also made by some scholars connected with the British Raj in India. Prominent among them were J. Hutchison, a missionary stationed at Chamba, and J.Ph. Vogel, who worked as a superintending archaeologist in the Archaeological Survey of India. Their work appeared initially in the form of several short articles in various numbers of the *Journal of the Punjab Historical Society* published from Lahore. These collected essays were finally published in the form of a two volume history in 1933.[32] Still regarded as one of the most detailed and generally reliable narratives of the erstwhile 'Punjab Hill States' (most of them later reorganized and subsumed into the state of Himachal Pradesh), these two volumes are the end product of painstaking and sincere labour. The authors made use of a wide range of source materials, such as vernacular literature and vernacular histories, handwritten manuscripts, royal *vamsavalis* (genealogical tables), travellers' accounts, folk songs and proverbs; some of these they collated with numismatic evidence and archaeological remains. Many other scattered reports as well as accounts by local officials were incorporated by the authors in their narrative even as they struggled with the linguistic nuances and meanings of local words. The final product, however, was a methodical and lucid work, albeit a little short possibly on an understanding of the inner workings of societal thought processes. One might miss in the work the feel of that vital sap of culture, which lends vibrancy to all social and religious forms evolving within any given culture, but these 'drawbacks' notwithstanding, Hutchison and Vogel's work, remains a pioneering work which has inspired several later works.

There is then a body of relatively more recent work written by historians native to Himachal or Himachali by affiliation. Sukhdev Singh Charak,[33] in his multi-volume history published in 1979, devotes the second part of Volume II to the history of the Kulu state along with some of its neighbouring states. This publication along with Mian Govardhan Singh's work published in 1996,[34] covers ground that is almost similar in content and organization to the work of Hutchison and Vogel. Mian Govardhan Singh's work, in particular, having been put together by a scholar located within the culture, presents some meaningful insights into local culture. 1996 also saw the publication of Mahashe Satya Pal Bhatnagar's work.[35] Written along the lines of Hutchison and Vogel's *History of the Punjab Hill States*, it has a few additions and a few variations in the organization of its facts, with an emphasis on the principal events of the Pala and the Singh dynasties of Kulu. Published in 2000, Tobdan's[36] work on Kulu once again departs slightly from the pattern established by colonial historians. The range of themes covered in it includes an account of the *deotas*, temples, Buddhism, sati and sati stones, and Kulu painting along with the basic history of the Pal and Singh dynasty. A valuable addition is the appended translation of relevant portions from Hardayal Singh's vernacular history, *Majmua-i-Tawarikh-i Riyasat-hai Kohistan-i-Panjab*.

Travel accounts by Europeans who came to the region form another valuable source for studying the history and culture of the region. The journals of William Moorcroft and George Trebeck are especially of great interest.[37] Undertaken between 1819 and 1825, Moorcroft's travels primarily aimed at improving trade and commerce relationships between different parts of British India, such as Northern and North Western India, and travel details were of only incidental interest to him. One of his primary interests lay in rural manufactures and economies. Neither an Orientalist nor antiquarian by training, Moorcroft still took sharp interest both in antiquities and different cultural practices. Enterprising, hardy, alert, he seems to have recorded the 'unusual' with great alacrity. His visit to Kulu was only a small part of the larger design of his travels, but Moorcroft noticed and recorded information about *deota* Adi-Brahma as also the *deota* at Doangunu. The *Gur* of the *deota* and his 'prediction' fascinated Moorcroft. His descriptions are colourful and are interspersed with detailed descriptions of local flora, fauna and local agricultural practices. Moorcroft's notings about the local history, religion and culture of Kulu are too general and too few to be of any great value, but the references do serve as confirmatory evidence of information collated from other more rigorous sources. This account, however, does have the advantage of being well written and contemporary with the times.

F. St. J. Gore in his travel account of 1895[38] gives a fairly good description, although with a certain lack of respect, of the temple of a hill *deota* at Jenog. The *deotas* of Jibbi, and Kot Manglaur are mentioned, as are Hidimba, Jamlu of Malana and *deota* Aleo. The Rai of Rupi as also the *ratha* of a *deota* is the subject of a detailed and careful description. No great insights however emerge from this account, which remains just a simple recording of a disciplined observation.

Belonging to more recent times is the travel account of Rahul Sankrityayana. His travelogue in Hindi, collected and published together in two volumes in 1994,[39] contains a brief history of Kulu. The material presented is not vastly different from that in other works, but there are separate sub-sections focusing on the economic, social and cultural aspects of Kulu. Sankrityayana does draw attention to social structures and religious beliefs but does not attempt to establish connections and linkages or look behind the present structures for deeper and sometimes hidden meanings. Possessing a lot of local flavour, this account was perhaps never intended to be more that a travelogue.

Penelope Chetwode's is an important account of her travels[40] through Kulu for it displays the spirit of a true researcher and gets sharply to the heart of the matter. Her writings have flavour and her descriptions are vivid enabling the reader to visualize what she is describing. She notices different architectural systems of the temples of the *deotas*, describes their sacred groves, and points acutely to different styles of *rathas* of the *deotas*. The account is both analytical and full of sharp observations. A couple of unusual facts are recorded by her: for example, the mode and occasion of bathing a *deota* and the presence of a woman *gur* (oracle). Chetwode brings in an evocative description of the mela at Bhuntar, which appears to be very similar to the Dussehra mela in terms of organization and the coming together of religion and trade. Her descriptions of the various events within the Dussehra festival also appear fairly accurate. She tries to look into the economic reasons for the suspension of the Dussehra after independence, and is quick to understand the central importance of various phenomena like *the Narsing Swaroop* and the *Jagatipat*.

Christina Noble's travel account of 1991[41] uses an entirely different framework. The account, however, does contain local flavour, including a closely observed vignette of *pujaris* at prayer. She notices the tone of easy familiarity, of equality between the *deota* and his devotee, and, interestingly, picks up the fact that the *Gur* generally belongs to a lower caste.

The '*deota* system', which seems to be quite unique and representative of Kulu, Kinnaur and the Shimla hill states, has been written about repeatedly by local scholars, steeped in Kulu religion and culture. The *deota* is such an intrinsic part of the lives and thoughts of the people that it is difficult for the believers to conceive of *any* activity being performed outside the consciousness of 'his' presence. An entire range of writing centering on local religious beliefs has therefore issued forth from local scholarship. The tone of these works is different from that of some of the official publications, which were commissioned to support and supplement state-sponsored festivals like the Dussehra of Kulu.

To this body of literature, an important contribution is made by the prolific writings of Pt. Chandra Shekhar *Bebas*.[42] Belonging to the family of *Raj-Purohits* of the Kulu Rajas, Pt. Chandra Shekhar wrote on a wide range of subjects encompassing the history, religion and culture of the area. Cast more in the mould of classical Sanskrit writing, these works reflect the keenness of *Bebas'* intellect and showcase his obsessive concern with detail and his desire to trace every significant fact back to its roots. A lot has been written by him on individual *deotas*, the festival of Dussehra, and other important festivals, the performing (folk theatre, folk entertainment) as well as the visual arts, and their connections with the religious traditions of the area. These writings appear in several collections of essays and even as part of independent publications. The quality of his writing is mature and more research-oriented than is generally seen.

Aware of the importance of documenting their fast changing culture, several Himachal scholars have turned to the task. Prominent mention needs to be made of the work of B.R. Sharma,[43] Sudarshan Vashistha,[44] Maulu Ram Thakur,[45] Vidya Chand Thakur,[46] Surat Thakur[47] and Vidya Sharma.[48] In most of their writings, whether forming part of edited collections of essays or independent publications, they have focused largely on the tradition of the *deotas:* their myths, beliefs and rituals. The body of work amounts to a painstaking collection of mythic as well as ethnographical facts which form an excellent foundation to be built upon. The work of Lal Chand Prarthi[49] and of Dilaram Shabab[50] also deserves serious notice in this connection. Of a different order, however, is the work of Laxman S. Thakur, whose eyes remain firmly trained upon the field of cultural history. His publications, whether on architecture,[51] or on the relationship between text and figure in his study of a Buddhist *sutra*[52] from Tabo, are informed by an understanding of the complexity of modes of expression. Valuable for the purposes of the present study is Postel, Neven and Mankodi's work on the *Antiquities of Himachal*.[53] For, the authors devote a considerable amount of attention to the masks or *mohras* of the Kulu *deotas*, the work having an archaeological and art-historical slant. A lot of information on stone and metal sculptures, architectural styles of classical and indigenous temples has also been brought together in the work. But it is the *mohras* or masks representing the *deota* that have been studied with care, their styles being distinguished and their inscriptions read. Initial notices of inscribed *mohras* of *deotas* from the Kulu region, had been taken by Hirananda Shastri[54] in 1907-1908, and by H.H. Shuttleworth[55] in 1919. But, furthering the scope of these initial studies, Postel, Neven and Mankodi have pulled together an exhaustive account of other *mohras* from the area. Using thermoluminesence method of analysis, carried out in a British laboratory, the authors have rested their dating and subsequent analysis of style on fairly accurate scientific methods.

Chetan Singh's rigorous study of the Himachal region (1998),[56] exemplifies the writing of a new kind of cultural history, using in part the methodology of the *Annales* school. Starting from a notice and an analysis of a host of non-verbal interactions as also a well established relationship between environment, economy and society, Chetan Singh charts out the social response of Himachal society to its physical environment. In the process, he focuses on the continuities and changes as they co-existed within society. In two subsequent articles published in 2004[57] and 2005,[58] Chetan Singh, understanding that myths, folklore and legends are also 'forms' of historical accounts, focuses on them to document political and social change. Considering that most historical accounts in Himachal must necessarily rest on oral traditions and popular memory, Chetan Singh constructs a theory about this evidence with clarity and precision. Using this methodology he speaks in his paper, "Nature, Religion and Politics in the Western Himalaya: Case studies of Keonthal and Kumharsain", of historical facts being inextricably intertwined with religion. There is at times an erasure of distinctions between religion and politics, he states, something that can be seen equally in the larger context of Kulu. Historical facts were often collectively 'experienced' or 'remembered', one knows, and Chetan Singh has studied the indigenous communities of rural Himachal to document what history meant to them.

Along the course set by the *Annales* school, and moving towards newer interpretations and readings of earlier historical evidence, Mahesh Sharma, in his study, "State Formation and Cultural Complex in Western Himalaya: Chamba Geneology and Epigraphs 700-1650 CE", 1994,[59] explores the interface between the cultural complex and state formation in Chamba. Processes of change and transition, linkages between polity and religion as they mutated over 'la longue duree', are studied by him with care. He examines religion and religious symbols as they 'shaped' the situation and were in turn 'shaped' themselves. It is through this process that the consent to rule and legitimization of power were created. Of what he has observed and stated about Chamba, one can hear echoes in Kulu too. Our understanding is being enhanced through the gathering momentum of studies such as these.

The above survey of the materials available for a study of the cultural field in Himachal Pradesh is brief, one realizes, but it prepares one to move towards Kulu, and to the heart of the present study: the great Dussehra festival there.

NOTES AND REFERENCES

1. Edward B. Tylor, *Primitive Culture*, 1871.
2. Bronislaw Malinowski, 'Culture', *Encyclopaedia of the Social Sciences*, Vol. IV, 1931.
3. Jacob Burckhardt, *Kultur der Renaissance in Italian*, 1860.
4. J. Huizinga, *The Waning of the Middle Ages*, 1924.
5. Sigmund Freud, *The Psychopathology of Everyday Life*, 1904.
6. Eric Hobsbawm, *The Jazz Scene*, 1959.
7. Edward P. Thompson, *The Making of the English Working Class*, 1966.
8. See Ranajit Guha and Gayatri Spivak, *Selected Subaltern Studies*, 1988.
9. Shahid Amin, 'Gandhi as Mahatma', in Guha and Spivak, *op. cit.*
10. F.S.L. Lyons, *Culture and Anarchy in Ireland*, 1979.
11. Aaron Gurevich, 'Wealth and Gift-Bestowal among Ancient Scandinavians' in *Historical Anthropology of the Middle Ages*, 1992; *Medieval Popular Culture: Problems of Belief and Perception*, 1988.

12. Marcel Mauss, *Essay on the Gift*, 1924.
13. Clifford Geertz, *The Interpretation of Cultures*, p. 91.
14. B.N. Goswamy, 'The Family as the Basis of Style', in *Marg*, Vol. 21, No. 4, 1968.
15. Anderson Benedict, *Imagined Communities*, 1983.
16. Fujitani Takashi, *Splendid Monarchy; Power and Pageantry in Modern Japan*, 1996.
17. Milo C. Beach, *The Imperial Image*, 1981.
18. See, Maurice Aymard and Harbans Mukhia, *French Studies in History*, 2 vols., 1988.
19. Mikhail Bakhtin, *Rabelais and His World*, 1965.
20. Norbert Elias, *Civilizing Process*, 1939.
21. Pierre Bourdieu, *Outlines of a Theory of Practice*, 1972.
22. Michel Foucault, *The Order of Things*, 1966; *Discipline and Punish*, 1975.
23. Chetan Singh, *Natural Premises: Ecology and Peasant Life in the Western Himalaya, 1800–1950*, 1998.
24. George C. Barnes, *Report on the Kangra Settlement* (Completed in 1850).
25. J.B. Lyall, *Kangra Settlement Report* (Completed in 1872).
26. The Joint Settlement Report of *Kangra* by Barnes and Lyall was completed in 1875 and published in 1889.
27. *Kangra District Gazetteer*, Part II, *Kulu Saraj*; III *Lahul*; IV *Spiti* – 1917 *Mandi State Gazetteer*, 1904. *Suket State Gazetteer*, 1904.
28. A.F.P. Harcourt, *The Himalyan Districts of Kooloo, Lahaul and Spiti*, 1870.
29. Hardayal Singh, *Majmua-i-Tawarikh-i-Riyasat-hai Kohistan-i-Panjab*, 3 vols. (in Urdu), 1885-1888.
30. Kahn Singh Balauria, *Tawarikh-i-Rajputan-i-Mulk-i-Punjab*, (in Urdu), 1912.
31. Diwan Sarbdial, *Tawarikh-i-Rajgan-i-Zillah Kangra*, (in Urdu), n.d.
32. J. Hutchison and J. Ph. Vogel, *History of the Punjab Hill States*, 2 vols., 1933.
33. Sukhdev Singh Charak, *History and Cultures of Himalayan States*, 1979.
34. Govardhan Singh, *Himachal Pradesh Ka Itihas*, (in Hindi), 1996.
35. Mahashe Satya Pal Bhatnagar, *Kulu ka Itihas Aur Sanskriti*, 1996.
36. Tobdan, *Kulu: A Study in History* (From the earliest to AD 1990), 2000.
37. William Moorcroft and George Trebeck, *Travels in the Himaalyan Provinces of Hindustan, and the Punjab in Ladakh and Kashmir; in Peshawar, Kabul, Kunduz and Bokhara, 1819 to 1825, 1837.*
38. F. St. J. Gore, *Light and Shades of Indian Hill Life*, Delhi, 1972.
39. Rahul Sankrityayana, *Himalaya Parichay* (in Hindi,) 1953; *Himachal* 2 vols., (in Hindi), 1994.
40. Penelope Chetwode, *Kulu: The End of the Habitable World*, 1989.
41. Christina Noble, *At Home in the Himalayas*, 1991.
42. A prolific writer on issues which formed a part of his background and cultural milieu, Pt. Chandra Sekhar 'Bebas' wrote regularly for the souvenir brought out at the time of the Kulu Dussehra. An important compilation of some of his writings was published as special issue (*Vishesha Anka*) for the Hindi Patrika *Shrikhanda*, under the title *Bebas Sahitya Sadhana.*
43. B.R. Sharma, *Kinnar Lok Sahitya; Himachal Ki Pauranic Jan Jatiyan.*
44. Sudarshan Vashistha, *Vyas ki Dhara*, n.d.; *Kulu: Dev Samagam*, 1995; *Himachal Meim Dev Sanskriti*, 2006.
45. M.R. Thakur, *Himachal Mein Pujit Devi Devta*, 1981; *Himachal ke Lok Natya aur Lokanuranjana*, 1981; *Pahari Sanskriti Manjusha*, 1996; *Myths, Rituals and Beliefs in Himachal Pradesh*, 1997.
46. Vidya Chand Thakur, *Mandavya Prabha*, 1990.
47. Surat Singh Thakur, *Himachal Ki Dev Sanskriti*, n.d.

48. Vidya Sharma, *Kulanta Darpan*, 2001.
49. Lalchand Prarthi, *Kuluta Desh ki Kahani* (in Hindi), 2000.
50. *Kullu: Himalayan Abode of the Divine*, 1996.
51. *The Architectural Heritage of Himachal Pradesh* (1996).
52. *Visualizing a Buddhist Sutra: Text and Figure in Buddhist Art*, 2006.
53. M. Postel, A. Neven and Kirit Mankodi, *Antiquities of Himachal*, 1985.
54. Hirananda Shastri, *Archaeological Survey Report*, 1907-08, p. 264.
55. H.H. Shuttleworth, 'An Inscribed Metal Mask Discovered on the Occasion of the Bhunda Ceremony at Nirmand', Paper read before the *Dutch Oriental Society*, 21 April 1922.
56. Chetan Singh, *Ibid.*, 1998.
57. Chetan Singh, 'The Place of Myth, Legend and Folklore in Western Himalayan History', Paper read at the Seminar on *Popular Literature and Pre-Colonial Societies in South Asia*, 1st-2nd January 2005, Panjab University Chandigarh.
58. Chetan Singh, 'Nature Religion and Politics in the Himachal (Western) Himalaya: Case Studies of Keonthal and Kumharsain', Paper read at the International Conference of Historical Sciences, Sydney, Australia, 3rd-9th July 2005.
59. Mahesh Sharma, in *The Indian Economic and Social History Review*, 41, 4 (2004); *The realm of faith: subversion, appropriation, and dominance in the Western Himalaya, 2001; Western Himalayan Temple Records: State, Pilgrimage, Ritual and Legality in Chamba*, 2009.

Chapter TWO

Historical and Cultural Background

SOME GENERAL OBSERVATIONS

The 'Punjab Hill States', as they were once called and of which Kulu formed a part, lie between four rivers: some between the Beas and the Sutlej, some between the Sutlej and the Ravi, and some others between the Ravi and the Chenab. They are hemmed in the north by the Himalayan ranges and are separated by the Shiwaliks from the plains of the Punjab. The physical environment of these hill states varies between extremely high mountain ranges cut across by torrential streams as well as broad valleys with large lazy rivers. Segregated and difficult to approach from the plains, the topography and climatic features of the hill states contributed greatly towards the formation of the character as also the shaping of attitudes of the hill folk. The basic personality of the people of the region, certainly including Kulu, is marked by remarkable flexibility and a marked degree of hardiness in facing up to difficult situations and scenarios. Independent in spirit as they are, they still have an unusual capacity for arriving at consensus with the greatest of ease. This quality greatly enhanced their ability to work within the framework of interdependence, especially within the same community. At the same time, one senses that co-existing with this was also a certain inability to identify with the 'other', or act in concert with another community.[1] To ensure even a bare minimum of produce for maintaining adequate subsistence levels, what was required was a hard struggle with the often harsh environment. Resultantly, small, distinctive, self-contained, self sustaining, non-hierarchical communities developed within the 'micro-regions' of each valley. Writing a political or cultural history of the Punjab hill states is therefore not an easy task.

Hutchison and Vogel who, as is widely established, authored the first connected history of these states, saw these states falling into three distinct groups: [a] the Western group, consisting of thirteen states which later adopted Islam under the influence of Kashmir; [b] the Central group referred to as the Duggar circle comprising of twenty-two states; and [c] the Eastern group, also called the Jalandhar circle, which consisted of fourteen states. Prominent among the last were the states of Kangra, Nurpur, Mandi, Suket, and Kulu, all lying to east of the River Ravi and bounded by the River Sutlej on the other side.[2] The country-side consisted of ridges and valleys, which gradually increased in elevation as they receded from the plains. The valleys, especially in the case of Kulu, were 'convulsed till they are no longer distinguishable, from the ridges'.[3] The hill people inhabiting these terrains had a passionate fondness for their land, which in their eyes was 'unrivalled in beauty and richness'. The folk songs of the region endowed the land with even greater beauty.[4] It is another matter that people from the plains often saw them differently. The medieval historian Yazdi, writing about the difficulties presented by the hills, said, for instance, that they are 'so high that no eye could see from the bottom to the top, and the trees so dense that the rays of the sun and the moon could not reach the ground'.[5] The Kulu valley is mountainous but not that unapproachable.

The hills were, in some ways, isolated from the plains but not, as will be seen, from their influences. To take the example of Kulu alone: the style adopted in the legends on the early Kuluta coins, or inscriptions such as on the Copper Plate at Nirmand, shows clearly that the classical styles prevalent in the plains were not only known in the region, but also being emulated.[6] The rugged nature of the countryside made 'invasions' difficult and 'conquests' well nigh impossible to undertake. Hence, despite Islamic conquests, there existed in the hills "Rajput dynasties with pedigrees more ancient and unbroken than can be shown by any other royal families in the world".[7] As far as ruling dynasties are concerned, however, it is of interest that, with just a few exceptions, almost all of them actually came into the hills from outside and took on the name of the territory occupied by them. With striking uniformity, traditional accounts speak of the founders of these families coming in either as pilgrims, or as adventurous scions of royal families in search of new avenues of power. Interestingly, however, connections with the Rajput groups of Rajasthan were not too strong: it is other areas that are spoken of in this context. The Kulu royal house thus is believed to have come from Prayag in UP,[8] although the Haridwar region also finds mention; the Suket royal house came from Bengal and the Rajas of Mandi were a splinter group of Suket.[9] Significantly, this influx into the hills is believed to have taken place between the 6th and 12th centuries, and it is more than likely that it was turmoil in the plains that caused this influx into the hills. According to one view, wave after systematic wave of Hindu immigrant groups came into the hills from the plains following Islamic invasions, the battle of Tarain in 1193 often spoken of in this context as being of pivotal importance. Members of Rajput clans started moving into the 'safe' parts of India. While the hills offered a near perfect refuge, the establishment of new dynasties there was not without struggle. In fact, 'a tremendous internal conflict, sanguine and persistent' was sparked off at some places, and is sometimes reflected in the records of the hills. The 'original inhabitants' put up a remarkable resistance in an area like Mandi, for instance, where this conflict lasted right into the 17th century.[10]

The hill areas had always been inhabited and, long before the coming of these groups from outside, there is evidence of the existence of different tribes there. The coin hordes of the *Kunindas* or *Kulindas,* discovered at Jwalamukhi, not far from Kangra, of the *Audumbaras* at Nurpur, and the *Kulutas* of Kulu, point to these groups having been among the earliest inhabitants of the hills. One among the many views is that the *Kunindas* were perhaps the ancestors of the later *Kanets*, a large group in the hills, who may have initially been located in scattered areas but come to be concentrated at a later date in the areas of Kulu and Mandi.[11]

There are references in early accounts also to a class of petty rulers, the Ranas and the Thakurs, who held sway over large segments of territory in the hills. Known for their pride, intrepidity, and courage, but also their ruthlessness and cruelty, the Ranas are known to have put up resistance to the incoming Rajput clans. There is hardly a state, in fact, in which accounts of such conflict do not live in popular memory. Lasting sometimes for long years this conflict, however, seems to have ended in triumph for the incoming Rajputs. The account of the manner in which Behangmani Pal, the founder of the Pal dynasty of Kulu, overcame the resistance of the local chieftains of this order, is told elsewhere in this study. As far as the entire region is concerned, there was pressure upon the eastern region also from the powerful dynasty ruling in neighbouring Kashmir, which, from the seventh century onwards, had grown in power and influence, and had established its paramountcy over the Central hill states.[12] At the same time, there was pressure from 'below', for the rising power of Islam in the plains led to several sporadic invasions of the hills from the 11th century onwards, which inflicted great damage, both in moral and material terms, on the Punjab hill states in general. It is during this period that the ancient kingdom of Jalandhar-Trigarta, which had extended from the plains into the hills, got dismembered, with the territories lying in the plains getting separated from the hilly areas. Various splinter groups branched off from the parent state of Trigarta or Kangra, among them Datarpur, Jaswan, and Siba.

The establishment of the Mughal rule in India in the 16th century affected the old order in the hills substantively, for the Emperors of Delhi gradually asserted paramountcy over the entire region. The areas lying in the outer hills became theatres of incessant war. The contacts between some of the hill rajas and the Mughals were close but also restrictive in nature. The Mughals were reluctant to concede to the

Rajas their royal status and titles, and almost routinely referred to them as *zamindars* in their correspondence and records. In view of the persistence of pockets of rebellion against them in the hills, the Mughals wished to ensure subjugation, and exacted tribute from most of the hill Rajas. Taking advantage of local rivalries, the Mughals followed a policy of 'divide and rule', always trying to drive a wedge between various rulers of the hills and playing them one against the other. Gaining mastery over the famous, and reputedly impregnable, the fort of Kangra in the time of Jahangir was a major victory for the Mughals. Contemporary records speak of the celebrations at Agra that followed the receipt of "the joy enhancing news of the conquest of the fort of Kangra".[13] This event of single importance in the history of the Punjab hill states marked the ouster from their home of the Katoch rulers of this premier state. The Katoches, however, continued their relentless struggle against the Mughals, even from their places of exile. It appears as if the penetration of Mughal authority in the Kulu region was not deep, however. In general, the tenor of the relationship between the Mughals and the hill Rajas kept changing with time, the kaleidoscope of contact producing varying patterns. The slightest shift and change in the balance of political power in the plains would result in creating new patterns of alliances. This became even more evident when Mughal authority at the centre began to weaken. The period of Aurangzeb (r. 1656-1707) witnessed a gradual loosening of Mughal hold over the hill states. This was followed by a brief interlude of some Afghan adventurers availing themselves of emerging opportunities and stepping into the vacuum of power created by receding Mughal authority.

The 18th century witnessed the rise of a new challenge to Mughal authority, which also impacted the hills. This was the meteoric rise of the Sikhs and the creation of pockets of power by intrepid Sikh chiefs especially in the areas close to the foothills. The uneasiness of the people in dealing with this new and unfamiliar phenomenon, alike in the plains and the adjoining hill areas, was noticed and recorded by Forster in the course of his travels in the hills.[14] Unable to handle the aggression of the Sikhs, the hill chiefs, ambivalent in the their attitude towards them, alternately opposed the Sikhs or joined forces with them.

Within the context of the history of the hill-states, the third quarter of the 18th century witnessed an event of magnitude. The fort of Kangra was reclaimed by Raja Sansar Chand II of the Katoch dynasty who ousted the Mughal governor from his seat of power in the hills. Leaning on the arm of Jai Singh of the Kanhaiya Misl, Sansar Chand, combining bravery with shrewdness, established himself as the dominant power in the hills, subjugating a large number of hill rajas. Interestingly, this dominance is reflected even in paintings, for one of them shows him regally seated with as many as twenty-two hill chiefs in attendance.[15]

Kulu and Mandi were prominent among the states that were subdued by Sansar Chand. But resentment against this aggression started growing among the subordinated hill chiefs. In their despair, they turned to the Gurkha chiefs of Nepal for aid against the Kangra chief. The Gurkhas accepted the invitation to intervene, and came, but left behind a trail of blood and devastation. Unable to resist the Gurkhas who succeeded in investing the fort of Kangra itself, Sansar Chand turned for help to the Sikh Maharaja, Ranjit Singh, who had established himself as the ruler of Lahore by this time. Help was given and the Gurkhas repulsed, but not without a price. The retrieved fort of Kangra was taken over by Ranjit Singh himself who slowly unfolded his plans. Between 1809, when the fort of Kangra passed into his possession, till 1839 when he died, Ranjit Singh made and unmade the map of the hill states as he pleased. Sikh governors were appointed to administer the hill areas; hill rulers were by turn subdued, made subservient, or exiled. Reduced to the position virtually of a vassal, even Sansar Chand retired, broken and drastically reduced in power, to Nadaun and Sujanpur Tira.[16]

After Sansar Chand died, his son and heir, Aniruddha Chand, unable to face the pressure created by Ranjit Singh's dominance, left Kangra and took refuge in Garhwal to save himself and his sisters from a life of humiliation. Ranjit Singh kept ensuring that many of the hill Rajas attended his court in Lahore or Amritsar.[17] His successors, Kharak Singh and later Sher Singh, brought the inner hills of Kulu, Mandi, and Suket under the direct control of the Sikhs. However, a challenge to Sikh hegemony appeared at this time in the form of the rising British power, which had designs of its own. Their hold over the cis-Sutlej areas of the Punjab made them the power to which many hill Rajas, including Sansar Chand and his son, Aniruddha Chand, turned for help. Not wishing to antagonize Ranjit Singh, however, the British did not encourage the hill Rajas nor held out any great hope to them. Embitterment therefore often marked the tone of the correspondence between the hill Rajas and the British.[18] Hope for protection by the British was, however, completely destroyed in the minds of the hill chiefs, for they slowly comprehended the intent of the British to keep the hill states for themselves, and administrate them on their own. After the First Sikh War, most of the areas of the hills passed into the hands of the British. There was some resistance to them, as evidenced in the revolt of the Rajput chiefs in Kulu and Tira at the time of the Mutiny or Great Uprising against them in 1857.[19] But these weak and ineffective protests were of no avail and till the attainment of India's independence in 1947, it was the British that continued to hold all the power in the hills.

THE NATURE OF MUGHAL AND SIKH RULE IN THE HILLS

For all the resistance to them, for nearly 200 years Mughal influences kept steadily permeating into the social fabric of the Punjab hill states. Everyone knew that Mughal authority had been forcibly imposed from above, and was never fully accepted by the hill chiefs in their hearts. But contacts with the Mughal court, and its refined culture, were unavoidable. There was a steady coming and going. From the time of Akbar, young Rajput princes were kept as hostages at the Mughal court, as a guarantee for good behaviour on the part of the rulers. In Jahangir's time there were as many as twenty-two hill chiefs – a conventional number, perhaps – at the court of Agra. All this must naturally have led to exchanges. In this encounter between the two cultures, many ideas, thoughts, and practices must have been exchanged, learnt and adapted. A kind of quiet cultural osmosis must have been at work even as political happenings defined the relationships at the obvious level. To be sure, direct Mughal rule in the hills was confined to a very limited area.[20] The hold of Mughal authority over the people was more in the nature of an acknowledgement of their claims of sophistication in matters of culture, and in the realm of the 'feeling' of fear that their presence induced in the mind of the common man in the hills. At the emotional level, the Mughals were always seen as 'outsiders', intruders in these parts. And the feeling of being subjugated to them never really went away. Interestingly, Thevenot, a 17th century traveller in Mughal India, mentions that there were many Rajas "who own not the authority of the Great Mogul". Cunningham, however, was of the view that this was true only of the states of the inner hills. The Mughals were obviously well aware of the inherent difficulties of maintaining their rule in these far-flung areas and difficult terrains. And it is this awareness that must have accounted for the ridiculously low 'token' amounts that were often levied as tribute upon some of the hill Rajas. The Mandi rulers are known thus to have paid only Rs. 500 per annum as tribute,[21] and the rulers of Sirmur were required to send in only boatloads of ice and some falcons to the Mughal overlord annually in acknowledgement of his sovereignty. This did not rule out thus some informality creeping into relationships at times, as evidenced in the exchange of correspondence between the ruler of Sirmur, Budh Singh, and the princess Jahan Ara, daughter of the emperor Shahjahan.[22] In the *farmans,* translated, edited and annotated by Hirananda Shastri, one notices some complaint by the Mughal overlord addressed to Jagat Singh of Kulu about the inferior quality of precious stones sent as gifts by him.[23] The attitude of the hill chiefs towards the Mughals kept alternating thus between the submissive and the rebellious at times. It was their abject acceptance of Mughal authority that elicited, in the late 18th century, a sharp reproach in the form of a letter addressed to the hill Raja by Guru Gobind Singh, the tenth Guru of the Sikhs, who had taken up arms against the Mughals. This was reflected in the bardic compositions emanating from the courts of the hill Rajas.[24]

In the domain of culture, a very different situation obtained. Even though the Mughals could not establish firm political hold over the hill-states, a very clear cultural hegemony over the hill Rajas was established by them. Cultural influences emanating from the Mughal court filtered down to the Punjab hill-states in substantive ways. Over a period of time, there was emulation in the hills of Mughal sartorial fashions, personal adornment, and art styles: influences in these respects were absorbed as well as adapted with such ease that they became an intrinsic part of 'hill' society.[25] In many subtle ways, the notion of Mughal paramountcy had become firmly established in the popular mind. When the Sikhs took over, it was their style, and their code of behaviour, that became the norm in some circles in the hills.

CONTACTS WITH THE OUTSIDE WORLD

Even though the hills, being somewhat distant and cut-off from the plains, were seen by the outsiders as a refuge, it would be true to say that they were not as isolated as one might initially imagine. Contacts with the outside world were many, and spread over a long period of time. One can therefore visualize many exchanges, and a measure of cross fertilization, in the realm of ideas. How these travelled is not easy to document, but there were many agencies. It is possible, for example, to think of pilgrimages, undertaken by people from the hills in the plains and by outsiders to religious places in the hills; religious personages on proselytising missions kept coming into the hills; Rajput hostages stayed for long terms at the Mughal court. Pilgrimages always create a remarkable cultural network for the dissemination of ideas.[26] Documentary evidence is to be found thus in the *bahis* – pilgrims' registers – of the *pandas* at Haridwar, Kurukshetra, Jagannath Puri and Gaya, of people from the plains, coming on pilgrimage to the hill-shrines of Jwalamukhi, Kangra, Triloknath (Chamba) and Manikaran (Kulu). Similarly, people from the hills went on pilgrimage to Haridwar, Kurukshetra, Badrinath and Kedarnath. The hills continued to register fresh impulses from the plains even though they were seemingly cut off from the plains. At other levels, matrimonial ties between the royal houses of Rajasthan and the princely families of the hills, the import of learned pandits from Benares and Kashmir to hill courts, the movement of religious figures – missionaries and mendicants and sadhus – making the hills their home, all contributed to sustained contacts with the outside world. Krishnadas Payahari who settled in Kulu, and of whom one will hear in detail later in this study, and Bawa Banwari Das Bairagi who made Nahan in Sirmur his home in the 17th century, and who were instrumental in bringing in a new wave of Vaishnavism to the hills, are cases in point.

To the hills also came people from different parts of India and from diverse backgrounds to take up employment with hill Rajas: Gujaratis, Bengalis, Marathas, among them. If one takes into account the clear possibility that men like these must have gone home and returned from time to time, one can see another channel through which ideas and goods must have travelled.

RELATIONS AMONG HILL STATES

The relationships between the states of the hill region were, almost like everywhere else, complex and varied. They bore the imprint of private, sometimes primeval, passions, geographical proximities, and the logic imposed by extremely fluid interstate boundaries. This whole chapter is marked by matrimonial alliances, family feuds, and wars of expansion. The overall impression one gets is that of constant conflicts interspersed with close collaboration and friendships. But the wars between hill states were by nature limited, and the scale was generally small. Despite being at war with one another, it was important for the people of these hill states to maintain working contacts that were often pleasant and affable. The conflict between Kulu and Mandi over border areas, for example, quite sharp as it was at times, did not impede relationships between the people of the two states. Thus, despite hostilities, maintaining a pleasant balance appeared to be the norm of these relationships. Consideration for each other's rights, and the maintenance of an even tenor of life was greatly valued at peoples' level. Even at the political plane, the subjugation of one state by another seldom meant a complete subversion of it. Exacting tribute from the 'enemy', replacing the existing chieftain by a kinsman, was often all that was imposed by the victor. An example from Chamba helps to illustrate the nature of these relationships. The area of Nerti, which lies between the states of Chamba and Kangra, was always a subject of dispute. When, it is recorded, in the course of one of the conflicts over it, the Raja of Chamba, Raj Singh, was killed on the field of battle, the Raja of Kangra instituted a fair at the place to commemorate the valour of the fallen enemy.[27]

There came, however, a time in the 19th century when these conflicts meant nothing, and all the Rajas were reduced to a powerless state. Virtually all control had moved into the hands of the British, and contemporary writers speak with feeling about the pathos of the condition of these hill chiefs. There were now, as was observed, "no worthy outlets for their energies". Though they keenly resented their degradation at the hands of the outsider, their traditions and breeding prevented them from obtruding themselves into the notice of the government, whichever it may have been at a given point of time. Dragging out an existence on such pittances as had been vouchsafed for them, seemed to be their lot. For the most part they lead aimless lives, as Hutchison and Vogel say somewhat sadly, "courting a dignity which they had not the means to maintain, dreaming of a departed glory that could never return".[28]

BRIEF HISTORY OF KULU

The fact that Kulu is surrounded by states and regions that vary considerably in their history and ethnic composition has naturally affected the course of its history. Even within the state, there are visible differences in the geography and the productivity of its different parts: the seven *waziris* into which the state was traditionally divided: Parol, Rupi, Saraj, Lag-Maharaja, Lag Sari, Bangahal, and Lahul.[29]

The general scarcity of historical documents in the hill states has been commented upon. Even among these states, Kulu appears to have been especially bereft of records. The existence of a *vamsavali* of the royal house of Kulu – essentially a record of genealogical descent – is of obvious help, but the document does not go, like other *vamsavalis* elsewhere, much beyond providing lists.[30] Numismatic evidence is of some help: early coins, dating back to the first century CE, refer to a king of "Kuluta" named Virayasas. Brief references to the region occur in some early texts like the

Vishnu Purana, the *Ramayana*, the *Mahabharata*, the *Markandeya Purana*, the *Brihatsamhita*, Bana's Kadambari, and the *Rajatarangini*. Hieun Tsang's 7th century account speaks of Kulu as a kingdom in its own right, which had contacts with Kashmir, Ujjain, and even the Cholas of the South. But no details are given. Because of the Chinese traveller's interest in Buddhism, we do get mention of the presence of Buddhism in the area – something also supported by the occurrence of some early Buddhist images found inside as many as fifteen *deota* temples – but of political history we get to know little. Local records and memory speak not of a central authority, but of the area having been ruled for long periods of time by petty chieftains referred to as the Ranas and the Thakurs.[31]

An early reference to kingly power in Kulu is found in the Nirmand copper-plate grant of the seventh century CE, for it speaks of a *maharaja-mahasamanta* or major feudatory chief, implying the existence of an overlord[32]. A later copper-plate of the 11th century from Chamba again refers to royalty in Kulu and its connection with a Chamba king who is "asked the favour of bestowing royalty in return for services, by his kinsman, the lord of Kuluta, anxious to render him homage".[33] But there are no details: names, affiliations, and the like. From Vishakhadatta's *Mudrarakshasa*, in which the king of Kuluta is spoken of as being from among the *mlechchas*, one is tempted to surmise that power here was in the hands not of the higher castes as one knows them from the northern plains, but of people of local stock.[34]

Early Kulu does not appear to have been insulated from its neighbours. Like a 'low-pressure' area on a climate chart attracting high-pressure winds, it seems to have aroused and attracted the predatory instincts of powers surrounding it. The twelfth and, later, the sixteenth centuries witnessed successful invasions from Ladakh. Tribute was tendered in the form of *dzos* and iron. Ladakhi records speak of these successful campaigns, and we hear of the rulers of Kulu having been "made to feel the weight of his (the Ladakh ruler's) arm. In much the same vein, Zain-ul-abidin of Kashmir claims to have "robbed by his splendour, the glory of the town of Kuluta". Kulu also naturally felt the weight of the Mughal Empire from the 17th century, even though the attitude of the Mughals towards the hill-states in general was more patronizing than stern. Thirteen official letters of the Mughals, many of which are only available as copies, and some of them addressed to Raja Jagat Singh of Kulu – whose period is of great interest to this study – reflect the fact of only peripheral interest having been taken by the Mughal overlords in this area.[35]

The boundaries shared by Kulu with Mandi and Suket appear to have been generally fluid and flexible, changing ever so often. Speaking of the temples of Kulu, it becomes extremely confusing and difficult to remember which temple lay in which state at a particular point of time. There is the case of the Shiva temple of Bajaura, which is now within Kulu territory but was a part of the Mandi kingdom[36] for many years as per available records. When several *deotas* of today decline to join in the

Dussehra procession of Raghunathj ji at Kulu, it may be due to remembered animosities of the past in which these *deotas* might once have been located in Mandi territories. Onwards from the period of Sidh Pal or Sidh Singh, whose dynasty continued to rule for several centuries, a trend towards establishing centralized control over outlying territory begins. Initially, the territory controlled by the Kulu Rajas was not very extensive perhaps, many areas being under the control of the Ranas and Thakurs, but with their subduing, the territory under the Rajas' control steadily expanded.[37]

The coming of Rajput cadets into the hill areas, either as refugees from the plains, or for establishing pockets of new power, is something that one hears of repeatedly. The present royal family of Kulu traces its descent from the Rajput family that originated in Prayag in Uttar Pradesh. The local legend of the goddess Hidimba of Dhungri, Manali – spoken of in this study at different places – and her connection with the establishment of the control of this royal family over local chieftains and to local gods, records perhaps the shrewd and successful processes set into motion by the Rajput rulers of this family: not by conquest alone but through the merging of local religious and political systems into those coming from outside. The oft-repeated legend involves the establishment of his rule by the founder of the dynasty, Behangmani Pal, with the aid and blessings of Hidimba, and points clearly towards the attempts made by the new ruler to legitimize his claims to power in the eyes of the people. The area claimed by him lay between Manali and Jagat Sukh, and the stone slab called *Jagati pat* at Naggar, to which the people of Kulu still resort for finding answers to difficult questions, was not located here without reason.[38]

An analysis and interpretation of local myths, legends and folklore such as this about the goddess Hidimba becomes necessary, for it enables the historian to unravel the tangle of past 'facts', which suddenly come into focus and just as suddenly disappear from the ken of vision. The oft-repeated legend thus of the division of the territory of Kulu between Makkar and Bhot, for example, obviously masks the essential cultural differences between the people of Kulu and those who were 'Bhots', meaning essentially those from Lahaul.[39] There are some attempts at establishing a relationship between these culturally diverse areas, as hinted at in reports about family ties brought about through matrimony, but the facts remain thin and vague.

With the establishment of the dynasty founded by Behangmani Pal, backed by the considerable support of Hidimba, sustained progress is made towards gaining control over the scattered possessions of 'unruly and oppressive' local chieftains. Tributes were sought to be exacted, and for many turbulent years the pendulum of power must have swung back and forth. Because of the extension of territories under direct control, the capital of the state kept shifting. It was at the now abandoned place earlier called Makrahar for some time. By the time one arrives at the reign of Visuddh Pal, however, we come across statements about Naggar turning into the capital town. There are statements that one comes upon about Naggar in records. Thus, *Nagar Rajai Sri ka*, i.e. "the town of the illustrious Raja", or *Nagar Tripura*

Sundari abad hua, i.e. "the town of Tripura Sundari was inhabited", this goddess being the tutelary deity of the royal family. Naggar had obviously, by this time, replaced Jagat Sukh which also served as a capital town, after Makrahar, for some time.[40]

In this early period of Kulu's history, one also comes upon attempts at gaining control over the tribal area of Spiti. Local folklore in Kulu refers negatively many a time to someone called *Piti Thakur*, a title that is synonymous today with cruelty in the mind of the common man. This appellation probably refers to 'Spiti Thakur' or the Lord of Spiti. Spiti made efforts of its own to gain control over Kulu. Infighting amongst the members of the royal family of Kulu weakened their resistance and defence against Spiti. As a result, one reads about Kulu having been forced to pay, for a length of time, a tribute of six annas in a rupee as yearly revenue to the Spiti overlords. Taking advantage of a Ladakh invasion of Spiti, Raja Parsidh Pal, however, managed to free Kulu from the domination of Spiti. Spiti itself passed into the hands of Ladakh, and Kulu gained from its contact with the Ladakh rulers, who bestowed a jagir of three villages on Sansar Pal of Kulu, according to one account.[41]

Many times in the ensuing years, Kulu was caught in the vortex of events that unfolded on its borders, or around it. At times we read about the royal houses of Chamba, Ladakh, Suket, Bushahr, Kangra and Bangahal coming together to ensure the continuity of Kulu's efforts to control and possess power; at others the same powers sought to expand themselves at the expense of Kulu.[42] For example, Kulu succumbed in the seventh and eighth centuries sometimes to the onslaughts of the fast expanding, ascendant state of Chamba.[43] Suket too made similar inroads in the early 10th century into the territory and power of Kulu, leading to uneasy peace being bought by Kulu after paying a tribute, and accepting tributary status. Kulu was even annexed by Suket at one time in retribution for its having joined hands with rivals opposed to the stability of Suket. Freedom followed by subjugation, then freedom again, appears to have been the cyclical nature of the relationship between Kulu, Suket and Mandi.[44] In this process Kulu lost at one point the *waziris* Rupi, Lag, and Saraj and a portion of *waziri* Parol to Suket. The patterns and grouping of power between Kulu and its neighbours can thus be seen to have been constantly shifting and changing. Areas as far as Tibet and Baltistan, and as close as Suket, Mandi, Kangra and Bangahal were involved. But much of this, one reminds oneself, was in the period when the territory of Kulu was mostly under the control of scattered Ranas and Thakurs.[45]

At one point, Kulu besieged as it was on sides, added to its problems by developing ambitions, and invading Tibet. The campaign failed, however, and retribution came soon enough in the face of a joint military expedition mounted against the land by Tibet and Baltistan around 1125-50. After many trials, Kulu got back its lost territories but not without the help of the sovereign power in Delhi, according to local tradition. An occasional favourable wind also blew in the direction of Kulu, like when the neighbouring state of Suket added to its territories by gifting the *waziris* of Lag Maharaja and Lag Sari to a purohit from Kulu, in grateful recognition of favours received from him. These *waziris* formed the nucleus of the growth of the kingdom, the area round Lag being consolidated and later brought under his control by Raja Jagat Singh of Kulu.[46]

In the dynasty founded by Behangmani Pal it is the figure of Raja Sidh Pal, later called Sidh Singh, that stands out in popular memory. The legend about the expansion of his power is not dissimilar to that associated with Behangmani Pal himself. Once again, one gets the feeling that need must have been felt to legitimize the authority that Sidh Pal/Singh was acquiring. There are continuities that were possibly being aimed at in the narration and growing popularity of these legends.[47]

Coming to power with popular support, Sidh Singh appears to have begun his career as the chief of the Waziri of Parol. Slowly but surely, pursuing a policy of firmness combined with shrewd manipulation of the situation, Sidh Singh is believed to have reclaimed areas from the Piti Thakurs as well as from Suket. The growing resources of Kulu owed themselves also to its location. From very early times, Kulu had lay on ancient trade-routes connecting Yarkand, Tibet and other Central Asian destinations important for trade, with the plains of Northern India. Some large flat areas, like the Dhalpur *chaugan*, where the Dussehra is now held, enabled the holding of large *mandis* or *bazaars* where traders would meet and exchanges took place. Salt, wool, borax and other precious goods came for the Indian markets from Central Asia: for Tibet, wheat from the plains of India and barley from Lahul was of great value.[48] The normal trade routes going through Kulu were not free from hazards, however. Rivers had to be crossed, tracks kept in shape, and marauders avoided. Safe routes were thus sought in favourable seasons: crossing the Baralacha Pass, down the left bank of the Chandra River, passing through the Kanawari plains, avoiding thereby the Hamta and Rohtang passes, thus.[49]

In Kulu, Raja Bahadur Singh succeeded Sidh Singh to the throne in the year 1532. Taking advantage of the insult meted out to the Thakurs of Rupi by Suket rulers who were their allies once, Bahadur Singh forged a durable alliance with them. Gradually many pockets of resistance in the *kothis* of Harkandhi, Chung, Kot-Kandhi, Chanwar, Bhulan and Sainsar was curbed and a much stronger Bahadur Singh established himself at Makarsa opposite Bajaura. The identity of Makarsa as a capital of Kulu was so strong that for a long time, the name Makarsa stood for the entirety of the state of Kulu. The capital later, however, shifted: first to Naggar, and then to Sultanpur a few generations later. Bahadur Singh gradually acquired the Parbati Valley, Saraj, Waziri Parol, Waziri Rupi, Waziri Lag Sari, and Waziri Lag Maharaja, inner and outer Saraj, as also a portion of Chhota Bangahal. Peace was further ensured by forging a matrimonial alliance between the royal houses of Chamba and Kulu[50].

Four reigns after Bahadur Singh, Raja Jagat Singh ascended the throne in the year 1637. This was a period of great importance for the state of Kulu, especially with reference to the current study of the Dussehra. In this period, what has been called 'ardent Vaishnavism' came into the state, setting into motion developments that remain in the forefront of this study and will be drawn attention to in detail later. This is the period when grants of land in the village Bhuin were made to the family of priests who came over with the image of Raghunath ji from the Treta Nath temple of Ayodhya. Decisions were also taken at this time to start sending to Ayodhya, one third of the offerings at Raghunath temple, as *Tirhara,* the share of the Treta Nath temple. Jagat Singh was one of the most notable of the Kulu chiefs and it is during his reign that the kingdom became further enlarged and consolidated. In the initial period, Jagat Singh continued to retain his association with the old capital of Makaraha. But other events unfolded, as will be seen later: the sin of *brahma hatya* and the subsequent events leading to the coming of Vaishnavism to Kulu.[51]

The Mughal presence in the hills had always varied from the negligible to the palpable. These were times when it started being acutely felt. Jagat Singh attempted in his own politic ways to keep the powers in the plains happy through acknowledging their sovereign status. Regularly, he sent presents of hawks and falcons – traditional symbols of sovereign power to the Mughal overlord – following an understanding arrived at. At the same time, he shrewdly disregarded Mughal commands to surrender certain tracts of territory. This 'resistance' on his part was however ignored, and his help was sought by the Mughals from time to time to strengthen their hold over the hills.[52] One has to recall that at this time Jagat Singh was involved in the series of events at the centre of which was the figure of the Vaishnava missionary-saint, Krishnadas Payahari, who had come from the northern plains into the hills and was instrumental in persuading the Raja to bring the idol of Raghunath ji from Ayodhya, and thus launch 'ardent Vaishnavism' in the Kulu domains.[53]

During the period of Bidhi Singh, Jagat Singh's successor, the boundaries of the state expanded in all directions. Some of the Shimla hill-states were subdued and the Sutlej became the boundary for the Kulu state. Lahul was freed from Ladakh. The main Chandrabhaga valley was acquired right up to the boundaries of Chamba.[54] But it was under Man Singh who came to the throne in 1688 that the power of Kulu reached its zenith. According to popular accounts, Man Singh ran over Mandi, even though that control was later relinquished. The conquest of Saraj was also completed by Man Singh. This period was marked by intrigue and treachery, especially on the part of Mandi. Man Singh was, however, in the process of freeing Bangahal from the hold of Mandi, and succeeded later in annexing it to Kulu. Spiti and Shangri too were annexed. Man Singh also built new forts at several places of strategic importance. Kulu thus acquired an entirely new importance under Man Singh[55].

His reign was followed by a period in which power relations in these parts were in a state of flux. The Sikhs had arrived on the scene, and the Tenth Guru, Gobind Singh, is believed to have sought the assistance of Kulu against the Mughals. In the eighteenth century, especially during the period of Raj Singh, Sikh power started being increasingly felt in the region. After him, repeated attempts were made by them to gain a foothold in the hills.[56]

After Raj Singh, the period is marked by further attempts made by Sikh power to establish itself in the hills. The Mughals too were eager to retain their hold over the region. Mandi remained a constant threat to Kulu, perpetually trying to make inroads into territories along the border, a bone of contention between the two states being the salt mines of Drang and Guma.[57] The reign of Raja Pritam Singh in the end of the 18th century remained generally uneventful, however. There was a threat from the agreement that Mandi, Kangra and Chamba reached upon attacking Kulu, and seizing some of its territories, but these plans did not materialize. Some instability did result from this; however, the real threat at this time came from the invasion of the hills by the Gurkha forces of Nepal.[58] Like some other states in the hills, Kulu was also forced to seek help from the Sikhs against their determined advance. In return, the Sikhs demanded heavy sums of money from the Raja. Unable to pay these, they themselves attacked Kulu, and the Raja had to flee into the mountains for some time. The states of Mandi, Kangra and Chamba had not abandoned their plans, and were still eyeing portions of the Kulu territories.[59] The real trouble for Kulu at this time continued to come from the Sikhs against whose depredations a community revolt, traditionally called 'Dum' or 'Dhoom', took place, spearheaded by Kapuru, the Wazir of Saraj.[60] Repenting his decision of having earlier called upon the Sikhs for help, Kapuru tried to rescue the royal family of Kulu, which had been captured by Sikh forces. Through clever and intelligent moves, and attacking the Sikh forces from positions of advantage, he was able to rescue the Raja, Ajit Singh, who was safely conveyed to Shangri, and placed under the protection of the British who had by this time moved with authority into the hills.

On their part, the Sikhs re-grouped: they attacked Kulu and plundered it, and even 'sold' it to Mandi for the sume of Rs. 32,000. When the Kulu Raja, Ajit Singh, died, the Sikhs even laid claim to the *gaddi* of Kulu, even as the Ranis did. Eventually Thakur Singh, a first cousin of the late Raja, was declared the 'Raja' and given Rupi as a *jagir*.[61] Following their victory in the first Sikh war, the hill country between the Sutlej and the Indus was ceded to the British. Kulu fell within this territory, and the British now wielded real power over the state. They confirmed Thakur Singh in his *jagir* of Rupi. The rest of the state, including Lahul, was attached to Kangra, which became a district under the direct rule of the British. Kulu became a sub-division of the Kangra disrict. Spiti was separated from Ladakh and joined to Kulu.[62]

The *jagir* of Rupi was re-confirmed upon the royal house of Kulu, but the title of the ruler was changed from 'Raja' to 'Rai'.[63] It is this family of the Rais of Rupi that plays such an important role in the Dussehra of Kulu to this day, as will be seen later, the descendant of the line still referred to by everyone as the 'Raja Sahib' of Kulu.

KULU SOCIETY AND SOCIAL STRUCTURES

The enduring image conjured up by the very mention of Kulu is of hill villages with nucleated settlement areas, set jewel-like in the midst of verdant agricultural fields. Bonded with its village, in an environment of nature, lives a community of simple hill folk. Joint and collaborative efforts involving the worship of their gods, the resolution of their disputes, the holding of their properties, all contribute to an atmosphere of emotional security. Functioning within each Pahari community are various kinship and family groups that are sub-sets of particular castes. It is ties of kinship and family that continue to receive precedence.

Traditionally, primacy went according to an order: it was given first to the family, then to caste, then to community, and then to the village. The family was a patrilocal residential unit that was the basis of all economic, social and religious activities. It is this unit that participated in life-cycle rites and applied all kinds of safeguards to enhance and protect the family and its image[64]. Many of its customs such as *pahurna*, i.e. visiting a sister in her husband's home every spring, or attaching a new bride in a relationship of *dharmachara* to a member of the family, were designed as strategies to cement relationships.[65] They were reflective of the thought, care and importance given to the family as a social unit.

In the region of Kulu, caste – within which the kinship units are placed – has always been marked by many striking features. Hereditary, endogamous, creative of group identity, it has served as an unalterable bond. Caste not only cut across, but transcended, all boundaries of community. There was a clear division between the dominant, high or twice-born castes and the 'untouchable' or lower castes. In the society were, at the top levels, Brahmins and Rajputs, who were landowning agriculturists by profession, and they stood apart from the 'service classes' comprised of blacksmiths, carpenters, weavers, musicians, shoemakers and the like.[66] While lines of hierarchy were sharply etched within each division of society, they did not affect interactive relationships between these two broad social divisions of society.

The range of castes in the hills is much smaller than in the plains. To take an example: traditional castes that figure in the broad Hindu society in the plains – such as *Vaishya* and *Shudra* – are conspicuous by their absence in the hills: they are not spoken of, and do not figure in people's thoughts.[67] The nature of the interaction between various castes and local groups is essentially affected by environmental factors, in many indirect and unobtrusive ways. Cultivable areas being small and scattered, and villages also being small and isolated, certain patterns of interaction are imposed upon the people. Resultantly, rules of behaviour between castes, communities and kinship groups have perforce had to be flexible and somewhat lax in nature. Travel and communication between one point and the other being slow and difficult, isolation has always been a factor to live with. This has led to developments of an inward-looking and self-contained nature.[68] For all these reasons and more, caste groups in the hills manifest less cultural differences than do caste groups of the plains. Here, there is an interesting dichotomy in the display of social taboos, too. While distinctions of purity and pollution are well and clearly understood and lead to a social segregation between the dwellings of the higher and the lower castes, there is, at one level, a toning down of distinction between the high and the low, especially when it comes to occupational mobility.[69] Occupations such as agriculture and the practice of crafts were not mutually exclusive. Hereditary caste positions may generally indicate the following of a particular kind of profession, but it is the occupation actually pursued that matters, even if it belongs traditionally to a completely different caste. This lack of rigidity has led to the coming into existence of a simpler, less stratified social order. To take an example: the *Kolis*, the *Dagis* and the *Chanals* of the region, belonging as they did to the lower castes, did not only pursue professions followed by outcastes, but also took on the professions of artisans belonging to higher castes. Positions of the poor peasants, agricultural labourers and artisans, again, were interchangeable between themselves.[70] Thus, oppositions that appear to be seemingly incongruous elsewhere, were present in this society. Higher castes while avoiding the touch of the outcaste, had absolutely no qualms about eating out of the leaf platter made by him.[71] Chetan Singh attempts to explain this spirit of egalitarianism in terms of the average Pahari's ability to move away to another village, if life became difficult for him at a particular place. This aspect of mobility militated against the prospects of an oppressive control by dominant social sections.[72]

The position in the social hierarchy of the Rajputs and the Brahmins of the hills is also of quite special interest. Here in Kulu the word Rajput does not necessarily refer to racial descent. Very often it was only a status marker taken on by the rulers. Sometimes even persons of the Brahmin castes would take on the 'caste' of Rajputs, when they acquired temporal and royal power.[73] In popular lore this interchangeability of the two upper castes survives in different ways, and people point to the unusual fact of a family of Bharadwaj Brahmins and Rajputs of the royal house of Rampur being the descendants of two real brothers.[74] As a distinct 'caste', Rajputs appear to have come into the hills from the northern plains. The success they achieved in these regions they owed often to the support they received from erudite and skilled Brahmins who travelled with them in search of new opportunities.

A large number of Rajput landowners here actively pursued agriculture despite the existence of the usual caste taboos, which discourage them from taking to ploughing. At many places the Rajputs who were the overlords of the *Kanets*, owned less land than the *Kanets*. On their part, the *Kanets* instead of acknowledging their expected subordination to the Rajputs chose to by-pass them and expressed their loyalty directly to the Raja instead.[75]

As a caste, Brahmins too were not natives of the hills. Pahari Brahmins were often looked down upon by the Brahmins of the plains because of their having taken to the plough in defiance of extant taboos: sacerdotal duties should have ideally been their preferred activity. In more ways than one, the Brahmins stepped into 'forbidden territory' by following other professions like money lending. Here in the hills, the dietary rules followed by the Brahmins were also different. There was no interdict on the consumption of flesh and intoxicating drinks. Many a times the Brahmins were unfamiliar with 'high languages' and spoke only a hill dialect, making them different in the eyes of the outsiders.[76]

The *Kanets* were the dominant caste in terms of sheer numbers in the Kulu region. Their caste was low, but they formed a major part of the population. Equated with the *Kulindas* by Cunningham, they were described as the original inhabitants of the hills who were subdued by immigrant Rajputs. This identification has not been accepted however by all authorities. On their own part, the *Kanets* regard themselves as having descended from the offspring of a Rajput from a local hill woman. They are an influential peasant community. Predominantly located in Kulu, Suket and Mandi, in Kulu the *Kanets* are known to have held about two-thirds of the land. The strength of the Kulu *kanet* lay possibly in the fact of his having freed himself from the traditional hold of the Brahmin orthodoxy. In respect of personal faith, the *Kanets* professed a much freer belief-pattern than the other castes in Kulu.[77]

Analyzing the basis of the caste system, one of the more influential models relating to Indian social structures speaks of the hierarchical opposition that appears to exist between the pure and the impure. Each society is known to attach primary importance to a particular aspect of its social life, which then, in turn, is seen to encompass other less significant aspects of life. Presenting an example from Nuer society, it has been observed that everything in their society is articulated with reference to the lineage system. In the case of India, it has been established that it is the Indian religious language that overshadows everything else. This permeates the institution of caste also. Religious concepts are what caste is based on, and it is this which most affects everyday behaviour.[78]

Even though the rules of caste do not appear to be strict within hill societies, yet whenever there was an expulsion from caste, forgiveness was granted to the offender with marked difficulty. Within a caste, thus, there existed very strict rules, and infringements of laid down norms were not taken lightly at all. Expulsion from caste, or even the threat of it, was greatly dreaded.[79]

In the region, caste was generally perceived as not being rigid: it was in fact seen as mutable. People were always seen making the effort to rise in the social scale. The Raja as the head of the state had the right, by royal promulgation, to change the caste of an appellant, if he thought it fit. This upward change in caste could be achieved through a skilful system of arranged marriages with the partner belonging to a higher caste. In the course of time, the caste of the offspring could change in accordance with ancient laws. This could happen over a period of seven generations: a saying often quoted is from Kangra where the Ghirths form a large group. There it is said: *satvin peerhi, Ghirathni Rani ho jave*, meaning "In the seventh generation a Ghirth woman can become a Rani".[80] A lot of fluidity resulted from the absence of rigid rules in the enforcement of caste in hill societies. By allowing flexibility in occupational specializations that could be followed within the framework of caste, the caste status of a person was not jeopardized, but his economic security certainly got reduced. This is so because certain castes traditionally held monopolies in the matter of practising certain crafts. Any new entrant to that craft specialization had therefore to compete hard with others to whom the trade really belonged. In this the new entrant remained, at least initially, at a considerable disadvantage.

All these factors notwithstanding, the character of caste in the hills was still quite remarkable. One notices that by laying down 'strict' boundaries of an invisible kind around the basic caste groups, society managed to stay predominantly Hindu and remained practically untouched by the coming of Islam and Muslim influence.[81]

Deviations from traditional occupation, earlier followed, were many and are not easy to define or enumerate. Problems arising out of the presence of differences in caste status created by comparatively new ways of dealing with the monopolies and privileges of those following certain occupation were, however, handled with remarkable sophistication and ease in the hills. There was easy communication between people of different castes and groups. Even as the higher castes were addressed with reverence by persons from the lower castes, thus, a high-caste Rajput or Brahmin would stop to enquire after the health of a man of a lower caste with a rare sense of ease and humour. Bitterness between the different castes seems simply not to have existed in the hills. This attitude may have something to do with an easy acceptance of authority, and submission to it: these being the 'twin pillars of a stable society'. The only distance that was really not bridged was the one that existed between the concept of the clean and the unclean.[82]

Turning to rules and customs that governed the average man's life, marriage customs would be important to focus on. The most noticeable feature about these customs in the hills, was the lack of ceremonies and rituals rooted in Sanskritic ethos. The form of marriage generally observed in society was one which involved the payment of a price for the bride. Practiced widely, as compared to the plains, were the customs of polyandry, levirate, divorce by mutual consent, and the remarriage of widows. Both inter-caste marriages as well as marriage between the highest and the lowest of castes were viewed with tolerance. There was also a fair amount of post-marital freedom among the sexes. Among brothers, relationships with one another's wives were also sanctioned by customary law. Marriage, however, was prohibited within the clan from the mother's side.[83]

Among the other noticeable features of social life in Kulu was the absence of the wearing of sacred thread even by males belonging to high caste families.[84] Society placed a great deal of reliance upon the prophecies of *gurs* (mediums) and diviners. They were consulted for nearly every problem faced, small or big. In Kulu society, the Brahmin priest occupied a position of much less importance compared to what it was in the plains.[85] Ritual purification rites too were of little importance in the minds and the thoughts of the people. Animal sacrifice was extremely common. In fact, at the end of virtually every religious ceremony – either as an act of thanksgiving or for the removal of taboos imposed by purity-pollution rules – at every stage connected with the worship of the *deota*, or his visit to the homes of the faithful, a goat was sacrificed.[86] Some of the important festivals in Kulu include the spectacular ceremony of the *Bhunda* sacrifice at Nirmand, which contains remembered traces of a human sacrifice, that may well have existed in the distant past.[87]

In the hills of Kulu, life in general meant hardship and struggle against the elements. In his general demeanour, the Kulu peasant might appear lazy and disinterested in work; in fact, however, looking at the range of his activities, one is struck by his capacity for labouring hard. Looking at the annual cycle of life – whether it is working in the fields, planting, hoeing, reaping, or building temples and homes, cutting timber, picking herbs, grazing their flocks of goat and sheep, importing salt and other raw materials – the life of the average man in Kulu remained more than full, at least in the past.[88]

The position of the woman in Kulu is very different from that of her counterpart in the plains. Possessed of an unusual amount of freedom, women participate in almost every aspect of life. The woman in the hills is a major participant in and contributor to the economy, by her labours in the forest as well as the field. Valued as a full-fledged member of the family, contributing actively to the prosperity and needs of the home, she is treated with the care and circumspection due to an important member of the family, and the society. The hill women are not shy of mixing with men.[89]

In their manner, the people of Kulu can be observed in general to be courteous and sociable, but suspicious of strangers. The average person is ignorant of many issues that would have something to do with 'high' culture and refinement. The people are, however, more earth-bound and pragmatic, and are possessed of a high degree of rooted-ness. Because their lives are full of hardship, the people of Kulu continue to value the simple pleasures of life: like song, dance, and colourful attire. Most of the celebratory aspects of life are connected to the people's belief and closeness to their *deotas* at whose shrines festivals and fairs are held, and with whom their universe begins, exists, and ends. Their beliefs are complete in themselves, satisfying, as well as supportive of their system of life.

In the *Settlement Report* of Kangra and Kulu that Barnes wrote in the nineteenth century, there is this engaging passage about the society and the people of Kulu. "They (the people)," he wrote,

> are good humoured among themselves but rough and inhospitable to strangers, very shy and distrustful of any new officer but almost fond of one they know well, very submissive to constituted authority if exercised with any tact, not given to theft, and not much to falsehood, but this is partly the result of a simplicity or want of cunning which does not see how a fact perfectly well known to the questioned person can be concealed from the questioners. On the other hand they are not so industrious, so frugal, or so enterprising as the Kangra people, and they are still more superstitious. That they have imagination is proved by many of their legends and fairy tales which contain as much of that quality as any in the world. Their sense of the picturesque is proved by the situation they chose for their temples, by the wild stories they attach to

each cave, lake, frowning cliff, rugged rock, or water-fall, to explain the impression which its form produces on their minds. They are very fond of music; the tunes, which are quick and lively, remind one of Irish jigs or Scotch reels. The women sing a great deal, and rhyming songs are made at each marriage or funeral, or in commemoration of any remarkable event. As a general rule, one line in each couplet is not original and has no reference to the subject in hand.... Their heads are full of strange fancies about things spiritual; for instance, they believe in the soul leaving the body during sleep, and account in this way for dreams: in these wanderings they say the soul can hold converse with the spirits of deceased persons, and communications are often received in this way. Both men and women are very susceptible of the passion of love, and do wild things under its influence. They will run off and live together in a cave in the mountains till forced down by the pangs of starvation. Men of the best families constantly incur imprisonment or loss of office for breaches of marriage laws, or social outlawry for the sake of some low caste woman. They are not manly or martial in manner, but I doubt if they can be called a cowardly race. I have seen them attack bears and leopards without fire-arms in a rather courageous way.[90]

There is a quaint air in the passage, but, as far as this description of the character of the people of Kulu goes, one notices that not much has changed in the century and a half that has gone by.

NOTES AND REFERENCES

1. Chetan Singh, *Natural Premises: Ecology and Peasant life in the Western Himalaya 1800-1950*, pp. 207-25.
2. J. Hutchison and J. Ph. Vogel, *History of the Punjab Hill States*, Vol. I, p. 59.
3. George C. Barnes, *Report of the Land Revenue Settlement of the Kangra District*, pp. 1-2, 4.
4. M.S. Randhawa, *Kangra ke Lok Geet*, p. 7.
5. Sharaf-u-Din Yazdi, Maulana, *Zafar Nama*, in Elliot and Dawson, III, p. 154.
6. For details of these, see Chapter Five, *infra*.
7. Hutchison and Vogel, *op. cit.*, I, p. 70.
8. *Ibid.*, II, pp. 430-31.
9. Man Mohan, *A History of the Mandi State*, p. 7.
10. Hutchison and Vogel, *op. cit.*, II, p. 385.
11. V.A. Smith, *Catalogue of Coins in the Indian Museum*, I, p. 167; Cunningham, *Coins of Ancient India*, pp. 67-70. For more recent notices of these coins see P.L. Gupta, *Numismatic History of Himachal Pradesh*, as also Devendra Handa, *Tribal Coins of Ancient India*, pp. 42-43.
12. M.A. Stein (ed.), *Rajatarangini*, I, Text, p. 138.
13. *Tuzuk-i-Jehangiri*, II, pp. 183-88.
14. George Forster, *A Journey from Bengal to England*, pp. 227-29, 231-32, 236, 242, 257, 258-59, 262-63.
15. The painting is reproduced in B.N. Goswamy and E. Fischer, *Pahari Masters: Court Painters of Northern India*, Plate 116. There are twenty-two doors leading to the Darbar Hall at Tira-Sujanpur. Eleven on each side, symbolically assigned to each ruling chief on the occasion of their attendance at Sansar Chand's court. This probably indicated Sansar Chand's paramountcy over the twenty two states of the hills.

16. Hutchison and Vogel, I, p. 187-93. The accounts of the hills as pieced together more recently by Sukhdev Singh Charak, *History and Cultures of Himalayan States,* or Mian Govardhan Singh, *Himachal Pradesh Ka Itihas,* (in Hindi) paint more or less the same picture.
17. Sohan Lal Suri, *Umdat-ut-Tawarikh,* IV, p. 17.
18. When the Rajas learnt that "we intended our conquests for ourselves it turned them into desperate and discontented subjects", Barnes, *Settlement Report,* p. 12.
19. This fact is recorded in British official correspondence. See, *Lake to Montgomery,* No. 6, dated 5 Jan., 1858 in *P.G.R.,* VIII, Pt. I. p. 145.
20. Barnes, *Settlement Report,* pp. 8-9.
21. Cunningham, *Ancient Geography of India,* p. 160.
22. See Ranzor Singh Kunwar, *Tarikh-I Riyasat Sirmaur,* for this correspondence.
23. Hiranand Shastri, "Historical Documents of Kulu", *A.S.I.A.R.,* 1907-08 II, pp. 270-71.
24. M.A. Macauliffe, *The Sikh Religion,* V, p. 100
25. Hermann Goetz, "The Coming of Muslim Cultural Influence in the Punjab Himalaya", *India Antique,* pp. 164-65.
26. The fact of many Sikhs coming to Jwalamukhi on pilgrimage as also visits by the Rajas of Phagwara are clearly reflected in the entries in the *bahis* of Pt. Shiv Lal of Jwalamukhi.
27. A.F.P. Harcourt, *The Himalyan Districts of Kooloo, Lahoul and Spiti,* p. 322, contains notice of learned Pandits from Benares at Nirmand. The colophon of the *Dilipranjani,* an account of the political history of Guler written in Braj Bhasa, mentions in the colophon, that the author Uttam Kavi was a learned Brahmin from Kashi. This text has been translated by me as part of a Civilization Project from the IIAS and is awaiting publication.
28. Hutchison and Vogel, *op. cit.,* I, p. 98.
29. *Kulu and Saraj: Kangra District Gazetteers,* 1917, p. 5.
30. J.B. Lyall, *Kangra Settlement Report,* p. 109, 1872; A.F.P. Harcourt, *The Himalayan Districts of Kooloo, Lahul and Spiti,* pp. 113-15, 1972; Hiranand Shastri, "Historical documents of Kulu", *A.S.I.A.R, 1907-08,* pp. 260-76.
31. Hutchison and Vogel, *op. cit.,* Vol. II, p. 425.
32. *Corpus Inscriptionum Indicarum,* Vol. III, pp. 280-91.
33. Hutchison and Vogel, *op. cit.,* p. 419.
34. *Ibid.,* p. 419.
35. *Ibid.,* pp. 422, 460-61.
36. Mandi and Kulu, exact neighbours, shared a troubled relationship. The boundaries between them changed many times. *Kulu and Saraj: Kangra District Gazetteers,* 1917, p. 29.
37. *Ibid.,* p. 25.
38. Hutchison and Vogel, *op. cit.,* p. 430.
39. A.F.P. Harcourt, *op. cit.,* p. 35.
40. Hutchison and Vogel, *op. cit.,* p. 432.
41. *Ibid.,* p. 434.
42. *Ibid.,* p. 434.
43. *Ibid.,* p. 435.
44. *Ibid.,* p. 428.
45. *Kulu and Saraj: Kangra District Gazetteers,* 1917, p. 26.
46. Hutchison and Vogel, *op. cit.,* p. 456.
47. *Ibid.,* p. 442.

48. A clear visual memory survives in the minds of the people like Pt. Chandra Shekhar "Bebas" of mules coming in from Central Asia with exotic goods. *Ibid.*, 448.
49. Poonam Minhas, *Traditional Trade and Trading Centres in Himachal Pradesh,* 1998.
50. The reign of Bahadur Singh was important for the significant step taken by the royalty binding the *deotas* to themselves by gifting *muafi* lands to each of them.
51. The coming of Vaishnavism to Kulu is well documented in Karuna Goswamy, *Vaishnavism in the Punjab Hills and Pahari Painting,* 1968, Doctoral dissertation, Panjab University Library.
52. Hutchison and Vogel, *op. cit.,* p. 461.
53. *Ibid.*, p. 461.
54. *Ibid.*, p. 462.
55. *Ibid.*, pp. 463-64.
56. *Ibid.*, p. 464.
57. *Ibid.*, pp. 466-67.
58. *Kulu and Saraj: Kangra District Gazetteer,* 1917, p. 31
59. *Ibid.*, p. 31.
60. Chetan Singh, "The Dhoom in Himachal Pradesh, Community Consciousness, Peasant Resistance or Political Intrigue", in Laxman S. Thakur, *Where Mortals and Mountain Gods Meet: Society and Culture in Himachal Pradesh,* pp. 107-16.
61. *Kulu and Saraj: Kangra District Gazetteer,* 1917, p. 35.
62. *Kulu and Saraj: Kangra District Gazetteers,* 1917, p. 35.
63. *Ibid.*, p. 35.
64. Gerald D. Berreman, *Hindus of the Himalayas,* p. 339.
65. *Kulu and Saraj: Kangra District Gazetteers,* 1917, p. 58.
66. Berreman, "Cultural Variability and Drift in the Himalayan Hills", *American Anthropologist,* Vol. 62, pp. 774-94.
67. Berreman, *op. cit.,* p. 202.
68. *Ibid.*, p. 351.
69. Chetan Singh, *Natural Premises: Ecology and Peasant Life in the western Himalaya,* 1800–1950, pp. 208, 216.
70. *Ibid.*, pp. 207-08.
71. Participant–observation during field work; also, B.N. Goswamy, *The Social Background of Kangra Valley Painting,* p. 176, 1961; doctoral dissertation, P.U. Library, Chandigarh.
72. Chetan Singh, *op. cit.,* p. 208.
73. B.N. Goswamy, *op. cit.,* p. 151.
74. *Ibid.*, p. 142.
75. Chetan Singh, *op. cit.,* p. 208.
76. B.N. Goswamy, *op. cit.,* p. 159.
77. *Kulu and Saraj: Kangra District Gazetteer,* 1917, pp. 54-55.
78. Jonathan Parry, "Egalitarian Values in a Hierarchical Society", in *South Asian Review,* Vol. 7, No. 2, Jan, 1974, pp. 95-119.
79. B.N. Goswamy, *op. cit.,* p. 172.
80. This is a popular saying in the Kangra area, illustrative of the potential of upward mobility within the caste of the hills, See H.A. Rose, *A Glossary of the Tribes and Castes of the Punjab and North West Frontier Provinces,* I, p. 42.
81. B.N. Goswamy, *op. cit.,* p. 148

82. "The concept of pollution governs relations between different castes. This concept is absolutely fundamental to the caste system and along with the concepts of Karma and Dharma it contributes to make caste the unique institution it is", M.N. Srinivas, *Religion and Society Among the Coorgs of South India*, 1952.
83. *Kulu and Saraj: Kangra District Gazetteer*, 1917, pp. 50-51.
84. *Ibid.*, p. 49.
85. Participant-observation during field work in Kulu
86. Participant-observation during field-work in Kulu.
87. Sudarshan Vashishta, *Himachal mein Dev Sanskriti*, pp. 218-19.
88. Participant observation during field work in Kulu.
89. Berreman, *op. cit.*, pp. 76, 176.
90. Barnes and Lyall, *Kangra Settlement Report*, 1872, p. 154.

Chapter THREE

Historical and Cultural Context (contd.)

I

EARLY RELIGIOUS BELIEFS AND PRACTICES

Society in the hills is easily described as Hindu. Even though there are indications in some areas of early pockets of Buddhism[1] in the hills, as also faint traces of Jainism,[2] by and large the faith of the people was Hindu all over the hills from the very early times.[3] Frequently described as "Hinduism of the Himalayas",[4] it is a somewhat unorthodox kind of Hinduism that obtained in these regions. It may not be wholly true of all parts of the hills, but as one gets into the inner part of the Himalayas, the faith of the people starts getting more and more complex to understand. It becomes permeated with practices, some of which which are no longer encountered in the plains of the Punjab, and the description that: "the religion of the people of Kulu is a species of Demon worship, upon which a certain form of Hinduism has been grafted"[5] has a measure of truth in it. It was once noted that: "They hold in honour the greater names of the Hindu mythology and reverence the temples that contain statues of the noticeable God but their affections are more particularly concentrated on their own local deities (*deotas*), whose help they invoke in trouble, and by whom they swear when taking an oath. The temples erected to these local deities are to be found in every village and hamlet of the valley and are supported by grants of land assigned for the purpose in former days by the native Rajas."[6] Well-informed writers described the faith of this region as one which is essentially "syncretic", that is, one in which an animistic religion has been merged with the Brahmanical faith which arrived from the plains.[7] Even though this gives it a peculiar character, this kind of Hinduism might, in a sense, be described as a truer kind of

Hinduism. This is so because it is more ancient and probably preserves practices that were followed at an earlier time rather than those that evolved in later periods.

Among the people of the hills, which naturally includes the people of Kulu, the most popular deities from the very early period appear to have been the Goddess, under her different names, and Shiva, also under many different names. Vogel, writing a long time ago, stated simply but emphatically: "Devi is indeed the deity most widely worshipped by the rural population of the Punjab Himalayas."[8] Rose said much the same when he spoke of the popularity of the "malignant and terrible Kali Devi", as he described her.[9] From neighbouring Chamba, evidence pointed again to the fact that the two deities most widely worshipped were Shiva and Devi.[10] In fact, in popular belief these hills were the very home of Shiva.[11]

The popularity of the Devi Cults, together with those of the Nagas – snake gods – has not only been commented upon by several observers; they are also described as being "the oldest in the hills" and as worthy of "being regarded as, in part at least, of aboriginal origin".[12] There seems little doubt that Shiva, Devi, and the Naga are the ones that the people of the hills identified themselves most with and appear to have received worship for the longest period of time as far as local memory goes.

In his pioneering work on the *Early Wooden Temples of Chamba*, Dr. Goetz referred once to the religious situation in Chamba as "abnormal", for here in this region, the antecedents of a host of "curious godlings" such as Sindhu Bir, Mundlikha, Mahasu, Jamlu, Narsingh, and Sidhas were difficult to trace.[13] To an outsider the situation would indeed appear to be slightly confusing because many of these names are entirely unknown outside the areas of the Punjab hills and do not form a part of the orthodox Brahmanical pantheon.

As far as the Puranic *rupas* of the Devi are concerned, the favourite mode in which devotees offer her their adoration in the hills till today is the singing of *bhents* – community singing – in words that not only speak of the boons that the Goddess confers but also the forms, almost reminiscent of Bengali prayers, that she takes: *Because you love the burning ground, I have made a burning ground of my heart – so that you, dark one, haunter of the burning ground may dance your eternal dance.*[14]

She may be Tripurasundari too – the one that is the most beauteous in the three worlds – but very often she worshipped in her fierce or *tamasic* aspect. Propitiated and worshipped so that she confers prosperity upon her devotees, she is resorted to in hours of distress and of need. She is the all-powerful force, terrible in aspect, supreme and without peer. She is celebrated under various names: as Durga or Mahisasuramardini, as Kali or Bhadrakali, as Chandi or Chandika, as Jawalamukhi or Jalpa, as Shakti or Bagulamukhi, and as Shyama or Chamunda. Repeatedly, she appears as the one who is possessed alike of power and the capacity to inflict harm upon her enemy.

In her normal aspect, the Devi does not only appear as a *pindi* or stone emblem; she also takes on an anthropromorphic form. She is often four armed, three eyed, aged and terrible, wearing a necklace of skulls around her neck, carrying a *khadaga* in her hand. Because of its *tamasic* aspect it is not a matter of surprise that the cult of the Devi became associated with sacrifice in the hills. The goddess not only passively accepts, but actually "demands". In the Puranic tradition, she sacrifices her own body in the *yajna* ceremony of her father out of annoyance with the ill-treatment meted out to her husband, Shiva.[15] The local devis (who go under the generic name of *deotas* in the Kulu region) apart, sacrifices even in the hill temples of pan-Indian significance – like Vajreshwari and Jwalamukhi in the Kangra region – are not uncommon. There are ceremonies which are reminiscent of the human sacrifices of earlier days. Even now the occasion or the rituals of sacrifices have a sanguine aspect. The *ashtabali yajna*, or the eight-sacrifices ceremony, held once in 20 years in the temple at Kothi, even today, can be a chilling spectacle.[16] The full details of the ceremony have to be observed for one to gain a complete idea of its fierce nature.

In the hills the temples of the Devi – one speaks here not of the devi-*deotas* of Kulu – are innumerable. It is virtually impossible to describe fully the strength and the extent of belief in her, in the hills. It is commonly believed that among the forms that she assumed in this region were those of sisters establishing a close linkage between the forms. There are conventional ways of referring to her numerous forms: as the 'seven sisters' as spoken of in by some areas,[17] as the nine Durgas in others, or the 360 forms assumed by the Devi at the time of installation of the temple inside the Kangra fort.[18] There is clear evidence also of Tantric worship in the hills. The presence of large collections of handwritten Tantric *mss*[19] in private hands in the hills suggests an intimate connection of the goddess with these Tantric beliefs.[20] Closely linked with Tantric worship was the wide prevalence of *vama-marga*, "the left handed ways of worship". This curious, and according to some, "debased", development in the religious beliefs of the country, gave license to the devotee in the matter of eating and drinking and promiscuity. *Vama-Marga* appears to have been not only intimately known in the hills but also actually practiced. The forms of the goddess as Matangi, Dhumavati, Baglamukhi or Bala Sundari are all associated with "indulgence in meat, drinks and debauchery" and are known in the region. The nature of *Vama Marga* being what it is – secret and esoteric – it is not possible to know the precise extent of its spread but one might not be wrong if one guesses that it was, in general, fairly widespread. For long lists of Devi temples in the hills, one can refer to Rose's *Glossary*.[21] A brief survey in one *Gazetteer* mentions the worship of Shakti under the names of Bhangani Devi, Sai Devi, Devi Nagarkoti, Devi Jwalamukhi, Naina Devi, a new goddess called Shakuria Devi, Doodham Devi, Lagasan Devi, Katasan Devi, Bala Sundari, among others.[22] Among the local devis that one encounters in the 'official' lists of *deotas* prepared from time to time in Kulu figure the devis Hidimba, Mahamai, Bhaga Siddh, Docha-Mocha, Tripurasundari, among others[23].

As with the Devi, so with Shiva. Kulu is dotted with shrines raised in honour of the great god. James Tod's description of the situation in Rajasthan might well apply to the entire hill region in fact: "Whenever there is a deep glen, a natural fountain, or a cascade", he wrote, "the traveller will infallibly discover some traces of the great God of the Hindus, the Creator and Destroyer of life". With the hills, Shiva is especially firmly associated, for he, as the texts and popular belief say, is the dweller of mountains. The Gaddis of neighbouring Chamba refer to Shiva in fact as a 'native', to their mountain peaks as "Shiva Bhumi".

The worship of Shiva, apart from being very ancient, assumed forms at least as numerous as those of the Devi. The suffix 'Mahadeo' or 'Nath' preceded by the name of a place are always certain signs that the a temple is dedicated to Shiva. Among the many *deotas* in Kulu carrying the name of Shiva, for instance, are Bijli Mahadeo, Siyali Mahadeo.[24] Different legends are conncted with each temple. A belief connected with the prominent shrine of Bijli Mahadeo is that the *lingam* – Shiva's emblem – enshrined there is struck by lightning every two years and has to be put together again.[25] The spot thus becomes sacred to Shiva, ever renewed and eternal.

The third major deity in the hills is the Naga: sacred serpent. The fact was noticed as long ago as in the times of the emperor Akbar, when Abu'l Fazl wrote of about 700 places in the hills, which had "graven images of snakes, which they (the people of the hills) worship and regarding which wonderful legends are told".[26] Enquiring into the religion of the hills, Emerson felt a long time ago that the majority of the gods of Mandi, Kulu's neighbouring state, belonged to the serpent group.[27] The conclusions of Vogel about the extent of Naga worship in the hills were not very different.[28] In the list of *deotas* of Kulu, Nagas figure prominently: thus 'Kali Nag', 'Basu Nag', 'Dhumal Nag'. Their temples are unpretentious, like those of the other *deotas*, but are located generally inside a clump of trees. The proliferation of Naga worship especially in the region, which includes neighbouring Mandi and Suket, is preserved in an interesting early legend.[29] The village of Ghoshal in Kulu is where the legend is often told and relates to the group of Kanets living in the area. According to it, a Kanet woman fell in love with Basuki Nag and bore him 18 naga children. Kept inside a pot, the Nagas were nearly burnt by an incense fire accidental dropping into it. To save their lives, they escaped in all directions. In some ways, the number 18 in this legend reminds one of the 18 *karadus*-legend so often told about the *deotas* of Kulu, as will be seen later. Of the Nagas here, two are believed to have gone to Mandi and Suket, and two to Lahul. Allied to the worship of the Naga, is the cult of Gugga, which has its devotees in the hills too. Folk songs are sung in honour of this deified hero: Gugga Pir as he is often called.[30]

In saintly men or semi-divine beings, the hills are rich, and there is widespread worship of them as *siddhas.* Often associated with one major deity or the other as they are, they are revered in their own right also. Sprinkled all over the countryside one can see stones, called *siddha*-stones, which are worshipped. On these are carved, rudely, a *chhari* or staff and two imprints of feet which become the symbols of the Baba or *siddha*. These stand in the courtyard of a house or by the roadside and women worship them by pouring water or milk over them. The *siddha* is thus honoured at a level of immediacy.

More than *siddhas*, however, it is Birs – from Veer, meaning a hero – whom one encounters in the region. They are sometimes counted among 'minor deities', but that is somewhat misleading, for belief in them is strong and extensive. In the regions neighbouring upon Kulu, one of the most often encountered deities is *Sindu Bir*, "the whistling demon"[31]: a splenetic deity who gets annoyed very soon, but is generous to true devotees. The Bir who needs most prominently to be mentioned, as far as Kulu is concerned, however, is Narsingh Bir, for he figures prominently in the ceremonies of Rama-worship in Kulu and will be spoken of in some detail later in this study.[32] There is a measure of confusion caused by the fact that the name belongs to a locally worshipped Bir, as also to the fourth incarnation of Vishnu. But how the worship offered to the two different deities gets coalesced in the ceremonies around the Dussehra is fascinating, and is dealt with later in this study.

VILLAGE DEOTAS IN THE HILLS IN GENERAL

The generic term *deota* is used to refer to a special class of 'godlings', as some scholars have described them, peculiar to the hills. Much will be seen of them in the next section of this chapter, for their presence and participation is so critical to the holding of the Kulu Dussehra. But it is necessary to notice here, in this general account of early beliefs, that they are everywhere. There are countless accounts of *deotas* and some of these afforded amusement to early researchers and outsiders who could not help noticing that there were *deotas* who fell ill, whose houses were occupied by their opponents, or who in a fight with their rivals lost an eye or who even died.[33] Gore was a little puzzled and then amused at "these stones smeared with vermillion"[34] that stood for them, and so perhaps would be others if they were not familiar with the power held by the *deotas* in the hills. The names of the *deotas*, again, are diverse. Endlessly long lists have been tabulated of their temples.[35] What is important is the intense faith of the people in them. The *gurs* and *pujaris* who are invariably attached to their temples are enormously important individuals in their small communities, and the *deotas* command almost total obedience. What is important is to note that while one particular *deota* in a village may not be very ancient, the *deotas* as a class appear to have been worshipped from very remote times. Individual *deotas* are heard as having been replaced, expelled, or introduced, but the faith of the people seems always to have been centred around the *deotas*, especially in the areas of Kulu and the close-by Shimla hills states. There are *deotas* like Parasuram whose worship is extensive; others like Jamlu who are whimsical and splenetic; still others like Junga, whose jurisdiction or power cuts across state boundaries. It is to these deities that the people of the village turn in times of crisis. When an epidemic disease breaks out, or a crop fails, or when draught strikes, or when a wife craves the boon of a male child, it is the *deota* who is a approached to grant the boon. What has to be emphasized in the context of the present study is that the worship of the *deotas* is not a new phenomenon: much like minor goddesses like *Maha-mai* or Sitala, the *deotas*, associated with one miracle or the other, or spoken of in one legend or the next, seem to go back a very long time in antiquity.

For gaining a firmer grasp of what the situation in Kulu was, or is, it is of use briefly to cast a look at the entire region for ascertaining which of the gods and goddesses were either the most ancient or the most popular in different states. One can begin with Kangra, the principality which is believed to be the most ancient in this region[36]. A folk song relating to Kangra and praising Kangra begins by saying: "O mother, this Kangra made by you is a Vaikuntha". The address to the mother is not without significance because she *is* the deity whose name occurs first of all to a person living in this region. This, because the Devi or the Mother Goddess is the tutelary deity of the Katoch dynasty which ruled Kangra for countless centuries.[37] The founder of this family, the first Raja, Bhumi Chand, is believed to have sprung to life "in full proportion, like Minerva from the brow of Jove, created from the perspiration of the brow of the Goddess" enshrined at Kangra. The Katoches even to this day consider themselves the children of the Devi[38] and when a Rajput of Kangra is believed to be especially favoured by the Goddess, it is said that "the Goddess always walks by his side". The temple of the Devi Ambika, inside the fort of Kangra, is believed to have been established by Raja Susharma Chand, in the days of the Mahabharata.[39] In the days of Raja Dharam Chand, a contemporary of Akbar, the Goddess is said to have appeared to him in a dream and asked him to build a temple in her honour inside the Kangra Fort again.[40] In the temple at Tira above Sujanpur, which was the capital of Sansar Chand II, the highest point is occupied by the temple of the Devi.[41] Throughout the historical accounts of Kangra we get numerous references[42] to the temple of Vajreshwari Devi at Kangra itself, one of the most celebrated shrines not only in these parts but in the whole of northern India. Countless pilgrims travel to this shrine and there are records which speak of this from early times.[43] The Muslim historian Ferishta refers to the relation of the Kangra Rajas with the Goddess.[44] Abu'l Fazl on the subject writes: "Nagarkot is a city situated upon a mountain with a fort called Kangra. In the vicinity of this city upon a lofty mountain is a place, *Mahamai*, which they consider as one of the works of divinity, and in groups pilgrimage to it from great distances..."[45] There are also interesting references to the great shrine in William Finch.

Another great religious establishment dedicated to the Goddess in the hills is the temple at Jwalamukhi, "the goddess of the flaming mouth". Numerous references to this temple are found in histories[46] and in travel accounts[47]. Many princes who came and established themselves in the hills are said to have come originally with a view to pay homage at the temple of Jwalamukhi. In a sense this temple becomes central to the faith of the hills. An elaborate legend speaks of Sati, the wife of Shiva, immolating herself in the fire of her father's *yajna*. She was then carried by Shiva, distracted in

1. The river Beas on the banks of which the present town of Kulu is located.

2. A view of the habitations along the banks of the Beas.

3. The pagoda style temple of Adi Brahma at Khokhan.

4. Carved façade of the bhandar of Hidimba Devi at Dungri, Manali.

5. A view of the 'Rupi Palace': residence of the royal family of Kulu.

6. The approach of the Raghunath ji temple, adjacent to the royal palace.

7. Flag atop the Raghunath ji temple.

8. Preparations for the worship of Kali Devi inside the royal palace.

9. The Raja as a devotee inside the shrine of Kali Devi.

10. The Raja making adjustments to the throne of Kali Devi.

11. The Raja rendering homage to Kali Devi.

12. The installed image of Kali Devi.

13. Inside the Raghunath temple, royal turbans are daubed with sacred marks.

14. Further floral adornment for the ceremonial turbans.

15. Morning puja of Raghunath ji by the Raja.

16. Cleaning and preparation of accessories at the Raghunath ji temple.

17. More preparations of that kind; silver vessels being cleaned.

18. The regalia of Raghunath ji: the nishans meant for his procession.

19. More nishans and other emblems of sovereignty of Raghunath ji.

20. A finely crafted nishan presented by a devotee to Raghunath ji.

21. The chhatra, or royal parasol, for Raghunath ji's image.

22. Palki for Raghunath ji to be carried in.

23. The Rajmata preparing garlands of flowers for Raghunath ji.

24. The Raja waiting in the temple courtyard, ready for the procession.

25. Yuvaraj, the Raja's son, similarly waiting.

26. The Raja's grandson, waiting in the temple courtyard.

27. Raghunath ji's palki being taken out of the temple.

28. The small, unpretentious temple of deota Bir Baradhi at Kareri.

29. Another view of the same temple.

30. Another small shrine on the Bir Baradhi complex at Kareri.

31. Pujari and other devotees inside the Bir Baradhi temple.

32. Shastra puja by the gur of Bir Baradhi prior to leaving for Kulu.

33. A deota being honoured by villagers during his journey.

34. Traditional musicians – bajantris – making preparations.

35. Musicians blowing on their narsingha horns.

36. A deota temple, with crowds of devotees in the background.

37. Materials for the shringara of the goddess Hidimba being taken out.

38. Mohra-masks inside their safe boxes at the bhandar.

39. Preparations for making the reerh-skirt of the goddess.

40. The reerh-skirt, ready to be draped.

41. The reerh-skirt being transported to the rath of the goddess.

42. Mohra-masks being mounted on the rath of the goddess, and Manu deota.

43. Jewellery to be worn by the goddess being selected.

44. The goddess's rath in the state of near-readiness, with the gur by her side.

45. Mohalla day: haziri register. Narsingh ji's ghori outside Raghunath temple.

46. Sair Puja: the Raja showers walnuts from the fresh crop over the devotees.

47. Devotees wait at the Ram Shila by Beas riverside for Hidimba's arrival.

48. Hidimba's decorated rath at Ram Shila with the kardar and gur by her side.

49. Hidimba's mohra in the bottom row of masks, wearing a nose-ring.

50. Hidimba's rath making its way to the Raja's palace through the streets.

51. Hidimba's gur in front of her rath, with his tongue protruding.

52. The dharach-ladle belonging to the 18 karadus.

53. A view of the Raja's palace known as that of the Rai of Rupi.

54. The visiting deotas arriving at the Raja's palace.

55. A deota bows in homage to the sacred doorway of the 18 karadus.

56. The goddess Hidimba entering the private residence of the Raja.

57. The goddess Hidimba occupying the inner apartments of the palace.

58. Hidimba leaving the palace while her gur cries out for the Raja.

59. The Raja and his family humbly greet the goddess.

60. The goddess Hidimba's rath proceeds to the Dussehra ground in Dhalpur.

61. The Raja's chhari-staff bearer, as the Raja leaves with Raghunath ji.

62. The Raja and Raghunath ji's procession passes through Sultanpur streets.

63. The Raja's family at the head of the procession.

64. The priests in front of Raghunath ji's palki pass through the streets.

65. The raths of different deotas pass through the streets on way to Dhalpur.

66. The old rath of Raghunath ji lying at Manikaran.

67. Raghunath ji's rath at Dhalpur Dussehra grougs, fully covered.

68. Deota raths flanking Raghuath ji's rath at one side.

69. Other deota raths flanking Raghunath ji's rath on the other side.

70. The Raja enters the grounds preceded by Narsingh ji's chhari-staff.

71. Raghunath ji's image being carried to his rath at the Dussehra ground.

72. The Raja and his family stand respectfully facing Raghunath ji's rath.

73. Group of priests performing a purifying ritual in front of Raghunath ji.

74. A view of Raghunath ji's rath as it stands ready to move with followers.

75. The Raja and his family do the parikrama-circumambulation of the rath.

76. Raghunath ji's rath being pulled by devotees with ropes.

77. Raghunath ji's rath on its way to the 'camp' on the 'battle-field'.

78. A view of Raghunath ji's camp, his temporary abode.

79. In his new abode, Raghunath ji and Narsingh ji after their morning bath.

80. Sita ji's dressed-up image being brought out to the 'darbar'.

81. Rituals being performed before installation on the throne.

82. As the Raja waits, Narsingh ji's idol-stone/ shaligrama being prepared.

83. Narsingh ji's face being painted by the priest.

84. Narsingh ji, duly adorned, placed on a sacred sheet.

85. The Raja waves a morchhal-whisk over the idols as a sewak.

86. Bhog-thalis for Raghunath ji, Sita ji, Hanuman ji, Narsingh ji and the 'abhyagat'.

87. Evening puja of the sacred idols by priests.

88. The idols are taken for retiring for the night-shayan.

89. The Raja, in his Rai of Rupi camp, being greeted by a deota.

90. A deota bends in greeting before the Raja.

91. 'Rasa lila' by men dressed as women at the Rai of Rupi camp.

92. The Raja as a sewak-dvarapala at Raghunath ji's portal in the evening.

93. The Rasa lila performers arrive at the Raghunath ji's camp.

94. Enactment of devi Tripursundari as she arrives at Raghuath ji's camp.

95. The devi Tripursundari places her shield on her lion-mount.

96. The Raja honours devi Tripursundari.

97. The deotas start settling in at the Dhalpur chaugan.

98. Devi Nava-Durga's rath waits to settle in.

99. A deota with a devotee inside the tent, his temporary abode at Dhalpur.

100. The Raja in a sukhpal-palanquin sets out for the jaleb, visiting deotas.

101. The Raja in his jaleb procession accompanied by some deotas.

102. More deotas join the Raja's jaleb procession.

103. The deo-khel evening entertainment at the Rai of Rupi camp.

104. A view of the crowds that gather for the bali-sacrifice ceremony.

105. Consultations by the Raja's family members before the bali-ceremony.

106. The buffalo sacrifice.

107. Devi Hidimba's gur claims his share of the sacrificed buffalo's flesh.

108. Sacred images being carried back to the rath after victory on the battlefield.

109. The images enter the Raghunath temple after their triumph in battle.

110. A view of Raghunath ji's rath surrounded by crowds of devotees.

his sorrow, who went about with her half-burnt corpse on his shoulder from place to place. It is said that her head fell here at Jwalamukhi. When Shiva saw this he ordered that fire spring here from the earth. The third major religious establishment of antiquity in Kangra is the famous temple of Vaidyanath, now called Baijnath.[48] A well known *prasasti* of the early 13th century gives us some indication of the antiquity of this noble monument.[49] It appears to have been regarded as one of the twelve *jyotirlingas* or great phallic monuments in the country and the rulers of Kangra paid great devotion to Baijnath.[50] The devotion that the people of these parts had for Shiva apparently found expression in the homage that was paid to the temple of Baijnath.

In the state of Chamba, where a great many ancient inscriptions have survived, we have clear evidence that early faith centred round the cults of Shiva and the Devi. The most significant evidence comes from the reign of King Meruvarman, of the 7th century AD. This is related to the famous temple of Brahmaur, the ancient capital of Chamba, and the temple of Chhatrarhi.[51] At Chhatrarhi, the Devi is called Shakti, and hers is one of the most magnificent images found in Himachal Pradesh; another image is that of a life-size standing bull in bronze – the great Nandi – clearly related to the faith of Shiva. The temple facing which the Nandi image stands bears the name Manimahesh: it appears to have been dedicated to Shiva from very early times even though the structure which now exists at that place is rather recent.[52] The Devi image is *in situ* and the inscriptions on the Shakti Devi idol and the Nandi image leave little doubt that Meruvarman himself was a devotee of Shiva and the Goddess. The temple at Chhatrarhi is even to this day a place of pilgrimage.[53] Three centuries after Meru-Verman, Raja Sahila-Varman is said to have been a devotee of Shiva also and many legends are connected with him, the foremost among them being that he constantly moved about in the company of a group of 84 Jogis, worshippers of Shiva, led by Charpat Nath.[54] Sahila Varman is said to have founded many Shaiva temples and his name is preserved in several inscriptions inside Chamba. The rulers that came after Sahilavarman, like Soma Varman, or Jasata, have also left behind inscriptions which clearly state that they were worshippers of the same deity whom their ancestors had so clearly and devoutly adored.[55]

From Nurpur we have early interesting numismatic evidence in the form of "Audumbara" coins. The Audumbara people, of whom "the national god was Mahadeva or Siva", are said to have inhabited the region of Nurpur.[56] This leads one to believe that the early faith of the people in the region of Nurpur, was Shaiva, even though there is some indication that there was a fusion of Shaivism with Buddhism and possibly even Vaishnavism among them. Later indications also point to the fact that the most popular shrines in and around Nurpur were Shaiva. The oldest temple in the town of Nurpur is of Dharmeshwar, where a *linga* is installed. The Trilokanath temple, about 15 miles from Nurpur, again, is one of the most popular in this region.[57] A huge Nandi image here, standing in the midst of a stream, is venerated by the people. The family deity of the Pathania Rajas of Nurpur, however, is not Shiva, but

Naga, the serpent. An elaborate legend about the founder of the Nurpur dynasty, Kailash Pal, whose Rani gave birth to a snake-child named Naga-Pala. This serpent was put in a *bauli* called Nagabari and was designated the *kulaj* or the family deity of the Pathanias. It is revered to this day by the members of the Pathania family.[58]

In Kulu itself, an early association with the Devi is evident from the fact that Naggar, one of the ancient capitals of the state, was known formally as the "town of Tripura-Sundari".[59] Reflective of the situation inside Kulu accurately, the two most important temples in Kulu again were those of the Devi: those at Jagatsukh, 8 miles from Naggar, and Doongri near Manali. The temple at Jagat Sukh was dedicated to the goddess Sandhya Devi, "goddess of twilight". Dated AD 1528, this temple is among the early classical temples in Kulu.[60] The other temple at Doongri is wooden – one of the best of its class – and is dedicated to the goddess Hidimba, who is seen as belonging to the *deota* class, and is intimately associated with the royal family of Kulu [61] as mentioned elsewhere in this study. Her great power in those parts can be gauged from the fact that she continued to maintain her authority even after the introduction of Vaishnavism in the 17th century by Raja Jagat Singh.

The most ancient of temples devoted to an orthodox Brahmanical deity in Kulu is the celebrated temple at Bajaura. Called Bashesar or Vishveshvar Mahadeva, it is one of the finest ancient monuments in the Kulu valley. Going back to the 11th century, it enshrines a large *lingam*, and has within its precints several minor images that got damaged badly in the earthquake of 1905.[62]

In the neighbouring state of Mandi, the situation is very similar to that in Kulu. The Bhut Nath temple at Mandi, with a Sadashiva image installed in it, is the most ancient temple in the town. Founded by Raja Ajbar Sen in the first quarter of the 16th century, it is not without significance that the town of Mandi was founded by this very Raja and this temple was the first structure raised by the Raja here.[63] The story connected with the Bhut Nath temple is the usual one of a cow pouring her milk over a particular spot which, when dug up, revealed an enormous Shivalinga over which a temple was raised under the orders of the Raja. The story, which has parallels from other parts of the country, only emphasises the antiquity of the sacred image. The Shiva idol apart, the ruling family of Mandi believed in the Devi as its family deity under the name of Rajeshwari. A temple of Rajeshwari, or Sri Vidya as she is also called, is located inside the Mandi royal palace. She is depicted as having four arms and holding the top of a man's skull (*munda*), an elephant goad (*ankusa*), a bow (*dhanush*), and an arrow (*bana*) Wearing red garments and a half moon on her forehead, she is believed to grant the twin boons of health and happiness. Her bedstead is supported by Brahma, Vishnu, Indra and Shiva.[64] Inspite of the later leanings of some other rulers towards Vaishnavism, the most popular temple in Mandi remains the temple of Shyama-Kali built on the hill called Tarna, overlooking Mandi town. This temple was built by Raja Shyam Sen in the end of the 17th century, in fulfillment of a vow.[65]

Looking at the evidence from the state of Suket, the situation in terms of religious beliefs is much the same as in the neighboring state of Mandi. Situated in the Balh tehsil is the most ancient temple of Suket: dedicated to Shiva Mahadev, with a huge *lingam* enshrined in it. The priests of the temple maintain that their forefathers came with the ancestors of the rulers of Suket when they migrated to these parts from Bengal.[66] It is of interest that the very same legend that is narrated about the Bhut Nath temple at Mandi is told about this temple.

Evidence from the Western group of hill states is very similar to that from the Eastern States. The state of Basohli has an early tradition of Shaiva and Shakta worship, with the Bilvikeshwar temple, the temple of Bhagwati Sukral,[67] and the temples of Chamunda Bhagwati and Nilkantha Mahadwa in Basohli town[68] still in worship. There are other temples in the vicinity: those of Trilochan Mahadeo and Jatajuta Maharaja. The sheer number of these Shaiva and Shakta points to the strength of these faiths in the area.

At Bhadrawah, it is the Naga cult that is most in evidence, with Basuki Naga as the deity most worshipped. Significantly, however, legend has it that Vasuki Naga came and settled here after having sought the permission of the local deity, the Devi.[69] A fusion between the Naga and Devi cults is obviously what the legend points towards. In Jammu, the worship of the Devi goes back to early times. The worship of Kali under the name of Bhagwati is extensive in this region and the Rajputs of the Jamwal clan believe in the Devi as their family or tutelary deity.[70] There are also temples of the goddess Kalika inside most forts in the Jammu region, and fairs are held virtually everywhere in the temples of the Devi during the Navaratras.[71]

II

THE DEOTAS OF KULU

Kulu with its narrow river valleys separated by steep, difficult-to-negotiate mountain ridges, each dotted with its own precariously perched *deota* temple, presents to the world glimpses of a society unique in its social organization, influenced deeply by the Sacred. Here, in 'Kuluta', as it was called in olden times, people lived hard lives, separated yet inextricably bound to each other by mutual need, and the *diktat* of the *deota*. Strong bonds, intra-personal and intra-group in nature, developed, leading in turn to equally strong territorial affinities. Subtle but strong identities located in the bedrock of shared values and shared beliefs were summoned forth in times of social need. When necessary, people could be seen as, and function in the manner of, a seamless whole.

The vibrancy and immediacy of folk beliefs dominates the lives of common men in the region. The *deotas* are present everywhere in Kulu society, as stated before: at fairs and festivals, participating in all social customs, helping in performances of rituals and *samskaras*. The comforting immediacy of their presence has been felt, since early times, in every aspect of social and religious life, be it that of a *kul-deota*, a *griha-deota* or a *gram-deota*. Easy to please and equally easy to offend, the *deotas* were bound in relationships of intimacy and familiarity with their *hariyan* [believers]. What was projected was a faith, both visceral and close to the soil, just as much as it was close to the heart. Unquestioned belief in the *deota* was of the essence here. Other beliefs of a classical nature seemed like overlays, secondary in nature.

Careful scrutiny and analysis of the names of various *deotas* reveals three distinct categories among them. One knows that, within the fold of Hinduism, names like Indra, Surya, Usha, Rudra and Narayan are Vedic in origin, while Brahma, Vishnu, Mahesh, Narsingh, Vaman, Parushuram, Rama and Krishna are evidently Pauranic. But *deotas* with names like Phungani Devi, Bhekhli Devi, Kali Ori, Jamlu, Mahdeo and Gohri are clearly of autochthonous origin. There are still other *deotas* – like Jeevanu Narain, Katrusi Narain – who may be of purely local origin but in whose names the addition of the suffix *Narain* indicates that they are possibly in the process of being upwardly mobile in their aspirations towards a classical Vaishnava status. That the Hinduism of the Himalayas is syncretistic in nature is a fact only too well recorded and understood. Presenting an unusual amalgam between the autochthonous and the classical, this syncretism set into motion trends of absorption, adjustment, even reinvention, where the *margi* fed into the *desi*, and vice versa. This circular process changed local customs, rituals and patterns of worship. Tripura Sundari, the goddess whose name is classical, is worshipped with the help of a *puja-paddhati* of local origin; she is represented by a *mohra*-mask and undertakes journeys among her faithful in exactly the same manner as the local *deotas* do.[72] It becomes difficult to disentangle the classical from the autochthonous.

Temples to the *deotas* are located in almost every hamlet in Kulu. Nestling against steep hill-sides or in secluded valleys, these temples vary in size, from simple one-room structures to all-imposing 27 meter high structures that are difficult even to enter. The height of the tower temple is an indication of the position of the *deota* within the divine hierarchy of the sacred pantheon. A host of charming legends and tales are narrated in connection with prevalent architectural prescriptions regarding heights and locations of temples.[73] These indigenous architectural styles of Pahari temples are very different from the North Indian *Nagara* temples with their distinctive *shikharas*.

A simple Pahari temple is generally a wooden structure typical in its use of local rocks and stone to build its walls with a method known as *kath-kuni*: the rough equivalent of *fachwerk* structures in the mountainous parts of Europe.[74] In this technique rocks are tightly packed between two horizontal wooden beams. These temple styles appear to be influenced as much by ecological factors as the availability of local materials. They appear also to be influenced by life styles of autochthonous people. As has been observed, these Pahari temple architectural styles may well be "...a subtle response of indigenous talent to the challenge of recreating the classical stone temple in a regional diction".[75]

Visible all around in Kulu are these simple one-room structures, as, for example, the temple of the *deota* Bir Baradhi at Kareri. Referred to as a pent-roof temple in architectural terms, many of these temples consist of a small cella on a square plinth of heavy timber. A sloping roof of slate slabs is supported by wooden pillars creating a verandah all around. This serves as a *pradakshina-path* also. A low doorway provides access to the interior of the shrine, establishing an atmosphere of sacrality and aesthetics that is enhanced by the intricate carvings on the wood-work.[76] The interior of the *garbhagriha*, unlike the classical Nagara temple, houses very few objects. A *ghanta* [bell], a *shankha* [conch shell], some *shastras* [weapons], and a *pindi* with features of the *deota* painted on it, is about all that lies within the temple. The cella may sometimes also have an installation of an anthropomorphic image of Shaiva, Shakta or Vaishnava affiliation. Nagas and Rishis too have temples of their own and are worshipped like local *deotas*. Within the *garbhagriha* lies sometimes a hand-written *bahi* [register], which contains the *bhartha* [legend] describing the legendary origins of the *deota*, information concerning the relationships of the *deota* with other *deotas* of the neighbourhood, the customs and *pujas* connected with his worship, the factors causing the *deota* to locate himself at this particular site, the difficulties and oppositions faced by him and how he solved them. This is all noted down in the *bahi*. Also present within the temple are records of money loaned out by the *deota* to various people in the locality. The *bahi* is thus an important document constantly used as a guide on just about every matter concerning the *deota*.[77]

A variation of the pent-roof temple is also fairly commonly come across among architectural types. Here too the cella is built on a floor plan that is square. Verandahs encircle the cella on all four sides. The temple has three or four storeys, which decrease in circumference and size as they proceed upwards, creating the impression of a pagoda-like structure. The interior space of these multiple storeys is used quite differently than in the simpler variety of the pent-roofed temple. The first storey houses some musical instruments and weapons of the *deota*; the second storey keeps securely the flour, grains, clothes and *mohras* belonging to the *deota*. On the third storey lies the *deo-rath*, or palanquin in which the *deota* rides out. The *shirsha* [roof] at the very top slopes on all four sides from a central *shahtir* [beam] on top of which are fixed three *chhatras*.[78] Functionalism and aesthetics come together in these simple but attractive structures. Important examples of this style at Kulu are the Bijli Mahadev temple at Mathan, the Raghunath temple at Sultanpur, the Narad Muni temple at Neenu, the Devi Madasana temple at Nigna-Kamand, the Sandhya-Gayatri temple at Jagatsukh, the Chaugasan Devi temple at Chaung, and the Jamadagni or Jamlu temple at Malana.

A Pahari style of temple building, believed to have stylistic links with a temple style of Nepal, was popular in Kulu and the neighbouring areas, between the 14th and 19th centuries. Popularly referred to as the pagoda-style, temples of this style are predominantly wooden ones. Constructed out of deodar wood, they are generally located within picturesque forests of *deodar*. This temple has three to five roofs successively decreasing in size, creating the impression of a pagoda. At the very top is fixed a *kalasha* made of wood, brass or silver. These temples also use the time-honoured technique of *kath-kuni* to build the walls of the cella. All around, below the edge of the lowest roof, there is a fringe of vertical wooden *pattikas* [bars]. This is referred to as a *chanani* to which are attached bells referred to as *chunanis*.[79] The forest breeze rustling through these wooden leafs produces a soothing musical sound. Prominent examples of this architectural style in Kulu are the Hidimba temple at Doongri, Tripura Sundari temple at Naggar, Manu Rishi temple at Shainshar, Adi Brahma temple at Khokhan, Trijugi Narain temple at Diyar, Parashar Rishi temple at Kamand, and the Shringa Rishi temple at Plaich.

A striking and dramatic structure in Pahari temple styles is what is the tower temple or the *kota* or *kothi* temple as it is referred to in the local dialect. These are very high temples going up to a height of 27 meters or more at times. An important example is the Kot Rupi temple of the village Chanehni in Kulu. Often used as a *bhandar* of the *deota*, in which was stored his wealth in terms of silver, gold, precious objects and cash, this kind of a temple also served as a fort at times for the defence of the local Raja. The design of the temple inhibits easy access to an outsider. Built on a square ground plan, the temple rises to a height of 15 to 20 storeys. At the very top there is a storey that projects out and away from the tall tower in the form of a 4-ft. wide covered verandah with *jharokha* windows here and there, making it difficult for the outsider to look inside. This houses the cella. The roof at the top slopes away gently on either side of the *kurada* [central beam], which is made out of the trunk of a single tree. The main entrance door lies sometimes in the middle of the tower, or even at the very top. Outside the tower, against the main tower wall, is set the staircase leading to the uppermost storey, where the cella is located. Made out of the trunk of a single deodar tree, steps carved inside the tree-trunk provide an extremely precarious foot-hold into the temple.[80] In Kulu, tower-temples of this kind are the Devi Kot of Chanehni, the Asha Puri temple of Diyar, and the temple of Jamadagni Rishi of Hawai.

Referring to a world and a reality very different from the one that we are part of and experience, the philosopher Santayana said once that "Religion provides another world to live in". Yet it is this 'other' world that becomes the present concrete reality for the *hariyan* in their interaction with their *deota* and as they participate in tasks connected with the *deota*. The world as 'imagined' and the world as 'lived' coalesce, making it difficult for them to be perceived as separate worlds. Each individual is bound to his *deota* with ties that are invisible, and are fostered by common beliefs and common values. Socially unifying, belief in the *deotas* produced a commonness of purpose that can be witnessed in the *hariyan* as they come together to collaborate in the procedure of building a temple for their *deota*.[81] The 'cultural performance' of temple building becomes productive of a certain 'social order', 'social stability' and 'social cohesion'. The very essence of the relationship between the *deota* and his *hariyan* is encapsulated in these 'discrete performances' of rituals, prescribed and followed most devotedly by the faithful. The *deota*, his rituals, his worship, his wishes, his commands, virtually take over the mind of the devotee. Milton Singer perhaps rightly perceived religious ceremonies as being of the nature of cultural performances.[82] Rituals, ceremonies, customs, connected with the worship of the *deota*, the construction or renovation of his temple, all are treated with great seriousness and with a consciousness of their importance as cultural performances. They have been likened by sociologists to social events of a secular world. Geertz, in his seminal work, finds religion sociologically interesting not only because it appears to describe the social order, but because it sets into motion certain processes and performances which by shaping popular behaviour both affect and shape the social order.[83] More than the consensus generated, it is tasks performed with a collective involvement that were seen to be productive of social integration. It has been observed that religious experiences, intense and visceral like the *khel* of a *gur*, or the recitation of the *bhartha* of a *deota,* change both the performer and the spectator irrevocably. The realities of everyday life are transcended, as the world of the believer and his *deota* come together in a state of complete identification. This sense of identification was difficult to match by the less demanding and controllable universe of classical faith.

Procedures adopted during the construction or even renovation of a *deota's* temple are interesting, revealing, and at the same time extremely stringent. The total involvement of the community, the monitoring of every single detail by the *deota,* underscores the fact that this relationship between the believer and his god was not one that was taken lightly. Temple building, like everything else in the religious domain, was a collective enterprise for the community. From the selection of the site, to the architectural plan, every little thing was decided upon and revealed by the *deota*. This was done through the medium of the *khel* of the *gur,* who during the entire process of temple construction is required to lead with complete rigour, a life of chastity and restraint. During this period, the craftsmen eat only once a day and sleep on the temple premises. The craftsmen along with their tools are worshipped at the very beginning of the enterprise. The daily functioning of the lives of the villagers is also suspended. Even marriages, let alone other festivities, all have to wait. Everything else comes to a complete halt. After the putting up of the roof and the doors, the *deota* embarks upon a friendly visit to a neighbourhood *deota*. Thereafter, he goes to a *tirtha sthana* to take a purificatory bath after which the *pratishtha* of the temple is performed. On this occasion while the *kalash* is being fixed on the top of the roof, a goat is sacrificed on the roof itself. This is followed by a *bhandaaraa* [community feast]. The occasion is one of great importance. Sometimes people from an entire *waziri* or *pargana* come to bear witness to the events. Several *bharthas* speak of instances of generous rewards like one *maund* of gold that was given to a craftsman. A raised platform constructed in the centre of the courtyard of the temple forms an important architectural feature. This is referred to as the *deota ri sauh*. The *deo-rath* is placed on this platform during festivals and other ritual occasions, and forms the focal point for the singing of *bharthas* on important occasions.[84]

It is in these *bharthas* that the origins of the innumerable *deotas* of Kulu lie embedded. The *deotas* are described as being 365, sometimes 33 crores, in number. Just as the numbers, 7, 84 and 108 are magical, having reference to the original number of *rishis* being seven, or to the sum of the days of the week multiplied by the number of months in a year, or again the sum of the number of months in a year multiplied with the number of planets, the number 365 may well be a reference to the days in a year. Similarly, 33 crores may well be a reference to the notion of th population of India at a particular point of time.[85] Whatever be the origins of these figures, in 1961 the documented number of *deotas* with *muafi* land-grants was listed by the sub-divisional office in Kulu and came to number 401 at that time.[86] This list is reproduced as Appendix E to this study.

To arrive at the exact number of *deotas* in Kulu is not an easy task. Apart from the fact that the lists – being a part of official records – are not easy to access for a researcher, and much persuasion or influence is needed, there are differences in the lists prepared from time to time by official agencies. This, as much because the situation remains fluid and changes over a period of time as because the ends with which these lists were prepared vary. There could be a list enumerating the number of *deotas* who attended the Dussehra in a given year; another which is based on the holdings of each *deota*, whether in cash or kind; one that records the *muafi* lands enjoyed by the *deota* shrines; yet another that records the *nazrana* offerings made by each *deota* to the preseiding deity of Dussehra, Raghunath ji. And so on. One of the most useful lists that have been accessed in the course of the present study is reproduced in Appendix E. It goes back to the settlement made in the years immediately following Indian independence. It contains occasional notes relating to some *deotas* that are of great interest to this study of the Dussehra of Kulu. The list was not possible to photograph, and is made in hand from the official records accessed. Some entries in it, relating to revenues, etc. are in Persian numerals, using *pucca hindasas* as they were called, following the practice followed in British India, and some had to be condensed in view of the short time for which access to it was possible. But these reservations notwithstanding, there is great value in the record. To take an example, this is how the gist of the first entry in the register runs, relating to the temple named Arjun Gupha, which is located in the Mandir Gupha, village Shoru in the mauza of Jagatsukh. It states that the initial grant (by the British Government apparently) to the temple was made on the 21st of Nov. 1847 (when the British took over these parts); this was revised in 1869, and further amendments were made in 1890 and 1912. In each settlement, minor amendments and adjustments were made in the cultivable and non-cultivable area. Further that the grant was confirmed in 1951 on the ground that the temple was intact, and people held the *deota* in reverence. The *muafi* was maintained on the condition of the good character of the kardar, during the pleasure of the state, and till the temple is intact. The *muafi*, the entry states clearly, is not transferable. There is a note that this *deota* makes a *nazrana* of eight *annas* per year to Thakur Raghunath ji as per previous practice.

This, as can be seen, is valuable information. Not every entry is detailed, many of them being copied from the one preceding it, directly above, except of course in respect of the figures of revenue exempted, and the location apart from the name of the *deota's* temple. The list contains 224 entries all of which are reproduced in Appendix E.

Numbers and locations apart, the obvious but all-important question relating to the *deotas* is: Who are they? How did they reveal themselves? How did their worship spread and proliferate? Several questions like these rise to the surface and become a part of the larger debate on the religion of simpler societies. In terms of this debate, the *deotas* could have had their origins in the psychic, in 'the invisible, immeasurable powers of the mind, in conscious will... in an intelligence analogous to our own'.[1] Man is in communication with all of these. It is not possible here to participate in the debate between LeFebvre's anthropism where, for worship of gods, it would be "the endeavour of men to attribute to all surrounding beings, objects and phenomena, forces and abilities analogous to our own",[2] and Tylor's animism which "includes the belief in souls and in a future state in controlling deities and subordinate spirits... resulting in some kind of active worship".[3] But the economic conditions of men in simple rural hill societies are bound to have affected their belief patterns. Life in the villages of Kulu centred around the basic satisfaction of temporal needs and in the care of the villager's own personal life. He had complete faith in the *deotas* because he felt that the *deota* would protect his seeds and his bullocks and save him from the perils of the tiger as well as the snake.[4] Most of the legends explaining the emergence of *deotas* follow a standard format and are structured around conventional archetypes. Similar stories and similar legends are encountered elsewhere throughout India, adding to a sense of the *deja-vu*. Associated with the arrival of the *deota* in a particular location are various miracles like cows pouring their milk over a certain bush or rock day after day leading to the excavation of the site, which reveals a miraculous source of water along side *pindis*, *Shiv-lingas* or an image. All of this is accompanied by an announcement made in a state of trance by the man who excavated the site, revealing that the discovered object is a *deota* who has come to stay at this location for good[5].

A variation in these legends speaks of an accidental turning up of a *mohra* at a particular spot, helping a desperate mother to locate a source of water for her thirsting son. Innocent of the arrival of a *deota* in that area, the *mohra* [mask] is carelessly stored away in the granary of her home. The quantity of stored grains miraculously doubles as a result of this. Any disbelief voiced regarding the divine nature of the chance discovery leads, on the other hand, to a cycle of misfortunes for the disbeliever. A person in a trance reveals the true nature of the *mohra* that had come to stay in the form of a *deota*.[6]

Also recorded are occasions when the edge of a ploughshare strikes against a buried *murti* [icon] or a *pindi* [aniconic form, generally a stone]. This event is sometimes accompanied by the miracle of a dumb man finding his speech.[7] A sense of wonder and worship follows. A *deota* comes into being. There is also the legend of the mustard plant [*brassica indica*], which kept growing despite being plucked constantly. Careful scrutiny revealed that this was so because a *mohra* lay buried under the bush. Like in the earlier legend, the *mohra* is what brought prosperity to the granary where it was stored.[8] A *deota* has emerged.

And then there is the miraculous tale of a girl vanishing from the midst of her human family. Revealing herself in a dream to her father, she predicts that her divine presence could be located at a spot where one found a fire burning next to a source of water.[9] *Deotas* are also known to have appeared in the form of birds. Some were discovered in the shape of a *dharach* [ladle] that is used by the *gur* for burning incense. Sometimes rocks splitting into two revealed the presence of a *deota*.

Inventive and different was the legend about the *deotas* Arji Pal, Rupan Pal and Kshetra Pal, who, as the legend records, were washed away during a cloud burst caused by the *joginis* venting their anger against them. The Pals, however, turned into *murtis* [icons] after this deluge. They were subsequently worshipped as *deotas*.[10]

In addition to the mode of his origin, the *bhartha* of any *deota* also contains an account of his growth and spread in a particular *kshetra*. Also given in fair detail are the reasons for the *deota's* staying on permanently in that territory.

Illuminating in this context also is the *bhartha* of the *deota* Gilhru Than or Than Narayan of village Bhutti. The *mohra* of the *deota* was discovered while working in the fields by a woman whose family holds the right till today to be the principal performers of worship for this *deota*. After being discovered he was kept in a container meant for the storage of grains, the quantity inside which kept miraculously doubling. The woman was transfixed by the multiple miracles seen after the discovery of the *mohra*. Challenged to produce proof of his miraculous powers, the *deota* did not disappoint. Unusual happenings like milk converting into yoghurt at his command, even as it was being milked from the cow, provided proof enough of his being no ordinary person. Other deeds attributed to this *deota* were the curbing of the cruel Thakurs of the area. Longish accounts mentions how Buddhists settled in the area were permanently banished by the *deota* to Lahaul, leaving the area free for the spread of his own influence. In a righting of wrongs, a cowherd boy ill treated by the Buddhists was transformed into a divine subsidiary or a *sahayak deota* by Gilhru Than who has been attending the Dussehra at Kulu from early times onwards.[11]

A slightly different *bhartha*, that of Kaila Bir, talks about his capacity to tie up within a small bundle all the sins of, and imprecations uttered, by the evil ones. In his context, an account is narrated of how Raja Jagat Singh of Kulu forced the short-tempered Parashar Rishi to attend the Kulu Dussehra against his will. Resultantly, when the *rath* of Parashar Rishi approached the royal palace at Kulu, the palace was damaged by the sound of the angry beats of the rishi's drums. Seeing this, wise counsel prevailed, and the Raja permitted Parashar Rishi to turn back. However, not to dishonour the Raja or the event being celebrated, Parashar Rishi sent Kaila Bir to represent him at the Dussehra in his capacity as a *sahayak deota*.[12] This situation remains unchanged till today.

Deo-bharthas, one notices, often have their origins in Vedic or Pauranic tales. These classical strands are recognizable in them, despite the regional twists in plot given to the tale, and the language used. The *bhartha* placing the origin of the 33 crore *deotas* (*taintis kror deota*), the 84 *siddhas* (*chaurasi sidhs*), the 64 *Joginis* (*chaunsath yoginis*), the 52 *viras* (*bawan virs*), and the nine *Naths* (*nau nath*) born from the rubbings of dirt coming off from different parts of Narayan's body is one such example.[13] This kind of a legend with slight variations exists in other classical tales, too.

In the *deota* temples, the *bharthas* are sung or recited by the *gur* sitting on a *jagti* stone, as he is surrounded by crowds of devotees. The occasion could be the celebration of the birthday of the *deota*, or some other festival associated with him.

A particularly interesting legend is the one referring to the origins of the very first *deotas*, eighteen in number, coming into Kulu, carried as they were in a wicker basket [*karadu*] by Rishi Jamadagni. A strong wind blew the *deotas* out of the basket as he was crossing the Chandrakhani pass and scattered them in various directions, particularly on to the Dhalpur Maidan, which is referred to as the *athara karadu ri sauh*.[14] The importance of the *deotas* of the eighteen *karadu* is underscored by the fact of their *dharach* [incense ladle] being held in safe-keeping at the royal palace of Kulu even today. It is this very *dharach* that is used by the Raja of Kulu at the time of the *Jagti Puchch* at Nagar, when critical decisions concerning the region need to be made, or great moral dilemmas arise.[15]

It is observed that a *deota's sthan* or seat often spreads and proliferates, and the story of this is always encapsulated in the legends about him. Thus, *deota* Virnath's spread into different areas is contained in the story of the flowers of Virnath being scattered in various directions leading to the establishment of *mandirs* in all these areas.[16] The legend about the eighteen *Nagas* escaping and settling in various places in different geographical locations hints at how Naga worship spread in those areas. The very first temple to be established to a *deota* is referred to as his *jetha sthana*, senior seat, in other words. Primacy in all matters, however, is given to the original *deota* established in a particular locality over any newcomers. Stories about d*eotas* travelling in *kiltas* [baskets] of salt, or moving with newly married brides to the family of their husband as their *ishta-deota*, and other similar tales point obviously to the means through which *deotas* multiplied.[17] The establishment of multiple Jamlu temples, or multiple Virnath temples, would necessarily explain tales regarding their proliferation.

The *deotas* of Kulu are bound together in a system that has been more or less institutionalized, even though they belong to different categories, if one can call them these: thus, *devis, deotas, rishis, nags, birs, sidhs, narayans,* and *mahadeos*. It is not easy to map their distribution over the Kulu region, either. One could hesitantly say that in the waziris of Sainj and Banjar, there is a concentration of *Naga* temples, or there are more *devis* in the Lag Sari and Rupi *waziris* than elsewhere.[18] But nothing can conclusively be stated. What is of the greatest interest, however, is the general fact that customs, conventions and rituals centring round the worship of *deotas* in nearly all these temples have evolved together, or so it appears. This seems to have happened through a slow process of accretion, in a manner that is complex and absorbing at the same time. Several scholars from the region have written about these issues, and concluded that they come from the fact that these form an integral part of the belief system themselves.[19] Sourced as they are from the rich matrix of local folk tales, legends, songs, ballads, as well as personal experiences, in most accounts there seems to be an attempt to locate the origins of these gods within Vedic times, or at least to connect them with Vedic and/or Paurnic gods. The *bharthas* of the *deotas* – which, one might add, grow with time – remain full of references of this nature, almost as if the interpreters of their divinity were seeking a validation through this for their *ishta*, who was the focus of their world of prayer and worship.

The *deotas* have been intensely humanized in their *bharthas*. Possessed of endearingly human traits of character, they laugh, talk, walk, dance, lose their tempers, rebel, display human weaknesses like fears and ambitions, the desire for recognition and importance and primacy. Many of them are bound to one another through a web of family relationships. Known to have sons and daughters, sisters and brothers, *deotas* have left their temples many a times in a fit of anger or displeasure or pique with their *hariyan*, to go and stay with another *deota* connected to them through a relationship. Like any sovereign, *deotas* guard their territory, defined as *har* and *hargi*, with an energy and commitment worthy of praise. They were not willing to surrender even an inch of territory belonging to them as spiritual or titular heads. In an exceptional case, they might agree to divide their territory – amounting to their 'sovereignty – and share it with others, as is the case with Jamlu *deota*'s temples which have multiplied twelve-fold over time. There existed, however, a clear understanding that there would be no territorial transgressions between them. There are instances of violent disputes when these understandings were infringed and the sovereignty of a *deota* was endangered. Though completely sovereign in their own territories the Jamlus came together in a bond of unity, when they went together to visit and honour their guru Trijugi Narain on a particular day and occasion.[20] The *deota* system mirrors quite faithfully, the complexities of the human mind, both in its elevated and vulnerable aspects. Along with this mirror image of society, what does get underscored and expressed are the normative values of the hill society. If analyzed with care, these belief patterns would necessarily reveal just which traits of character, which modes of behaviour, were meant to be emulated, just as much as which codes were to be held up as ideals among all the codes of social behaviour. Running through this fabric of belief as a recurrent pattern, was the capacity of simple hill folk to be immersed completely in their beliefs. The nature of the relationship between the *deota* and devotee was underscored in the process. The *deota* was bound to his *hariyan*, in an equation of familiarity and trust, as also an understanding of one another's needs. The rules and codes of conduct towards the *deota* were extremely clear. There was no scope for ambivalence. Despite these strict codes of conduct the believer saw in his *deota*, a close personal friend whom he could question or even shout at for the non-performance of a promise.[21] As stated earlier, the ties of devotion rested on the foundation of complete understanding and ease with each other. Belief in the *deota* was not an issue in which there was space for any doubts. It was simply an area that was central to the very fabric of the devotee's being.

The modes of *pujas* conducted at the *deota* temples are contained in the *puja-paddhatis* or *bahis* maintained there.[22] In these is reflected a certain informality and flexibility, which allows for the introduction of change in the set patterns of worship germane to more rigid and classical forms of worship. The sociological reasons behind these accommodations would be fascinating to go into. As a case in point, there is clear integrative intent in the fact that the *puja-paddhati* of the *deota* of the Tahuk village, Virnath, in the Manikaran valley, incorporates within its prayer for daily worship, a basic veneration for *all* the *deotas* located in that valley.[23] The words of the prayer are couched in the local dialect leading to a sense of immediacy and emotional closeness. The Pahari *deota* is a *sakha*, friend, and not a formal deity in a temple, who has to be venerated and appeased with a certain element of fear in the mind. As has been stated earlier, even classical gods and goddesses in the Kulu area are treated with less formality, and less fear, than they would be in the plains.[24] Modes of worship change sometimes to incorporate local practices, and local forms of worship. But what still emerges is the fact that the style of offering puja is not truly formal.

Many temples do not have a formal routine of rituals overseen and conducted by a *pujari* who is present at all times. The temple remains open, people may come and go, but there is no one present at all times to help conduct a ritual of worship in the temple. In some temples, *puja* is conducted both in the morning and the evening. In others, however, *puja* may be performed only once a day. Routines vary and at some places *pujas* may be performed only on a few fixed days of a year. But there are times when *pujas* are obligatory, and are *definitely* performed in *all* temples. This, for example, is the case when the *deo-rath* is decorated and placed outside on the platform of the *deota-ri-sauh* on certain festivals. This is a time when a defined cycle of rituals is necessarily performed. *Bharthas* are sung in the presence of the *deota* who, after coming out in the *ratha*, performs a *parikrama* of the temple, listens to his *bhartha* for a while and then proceeds to visit each household that forms a part of his *hargi*. Worship begins with an offering at the temple, of incense in a *dharach*; lamps are lit and waved, while bells ring and conches are blown. Against this background and with the *hingarna* [going into a trance] by the *gur*, the *deo-rath* goes and settles down on a heap of corn, which is given to the *deota* as an offering by an individual household. The lady of the household performs the worship with *arti* and *dhup* in this case. As the *deota* leaves the temple, a small lamb or goat is sacrificed and the body thrown over and across the *deo-rath*, so as to fall at the door of the temple. This is a sacrifice for protecting the emptied temple from evil spirits. In fact, the entire system of worship of the *deota* is marked by sacrifices at every stage, made in thanksgiving or in appeasement of the *deota*.[25]

A striking feature of the *deota's* worship is the simplicity and pragmatism with which all rituals and *pujas* are carried out. All materials and objects used are such as are easily available. Thus, the incense used is made from local herbs. Other materials required for the *pujas* are routine household items, like *akshat* (unbroken rice), corn, whole wheat, walnuts. Being a predominantly agricultural community, produce from the fields is used in all the rituals, both to be blessed and to be given as gifts to the *deota*.[26] In a refreshingly simple, way the entire system of the *deotas* was woven into the lifestyles of the people. Its pragmatic and simple nature ensures its observation in perpetuity. Difficult terrains, a scarcity in terms of easy facilities, may well have contributed to the development of this distinctive pattern of *deota* worship in the hill area.

The *deotas* are brought from long distances, carried on the shoulders of their devotees, in palanquins that are sedan-chair-like structures supported on poles (*argalas*). The other kind of transportation used by the *deotas* were baskets (*karadus*) carried in the right hand or as they were generally supported on the top of the head of the devotee. These vehicles of the gods, referred to as *rathas*, carry the *deotas* who take the form of *mohras.* Made of silver, gold or an alloy of different metals [*ashtadhatu*], these *mohras* were generally six to eight in number. Kept inside the *karadu,* along with flowers or arranged in horizontal tiers along the back of the chair-like palanquin, the original and the oldest *mohra* is generally placed at the very top. The shape of the *ratha* would dictate the positioning of the *chhatras* on top of the *mohras*. Generally five to seven in number, the *chhatras* are placed in the order of their decreasing sizes. The *rathas* are beautifully decorated with many different colourful pieces of cloth which are a part of the *deota's* prized possessions.[27] *Kimkhwab*, pieces of brocades, presented by rajas to their deities, were kept in storage along with the *mohras* in the *bhandars* of the *deota*, to be taken out for purposes of decoration of the *deota*, on every important festival. The preparation is elaborate and detailed. It takes an entire day, for instance, for the preparation and decoration of Hidimba's *rath* which takes place at the Manu Mandir in Manali. The skirt of the goddess is prepared exquisitely with all the colourful textiles attached to a rope-like coil of cloth.[28] Bedecked with jewellery and flowers, many hours later, Hidimba is ready to take her place besides

Raghunathji's *ratha* along with the other *deotas*. In a quaint re-living of reality, Tripura Sundari's *natth* (nose ring) and gold bangles are recast every Dussehra, as part of her preparation for the Dussehra.[29]

The *karadu* style of *ratha* is the earliest in point of chronology as also perhaps the most historic with its reference to Rishi Jamadagni bringing in the first eighteen *deotas* to Dhalpur, Kulu. Panchvira of Kota Kandi and Jeevnarain of Jana are among the Kulu *deotas* who come to the Dussehra in a *karadu* even today.

Seen in greater numbers at the Dussehra than the *karadu ratha*, is what can be described as the *chhatra* type of the *khara* or *pheta ratha*. When decorated and covered with colourful cloths, the impression received is one of a man in a sitting position, with both his arms spread outwards. Of a length of 6 ft., a height of 3 ft. and a breadth of 2 ft., this *ratha* is picked up by devotees with the help of two poles known as the *jamana* or *argala*. The *ratha* is surmounted by a large, 2 ft. diameter, single canopy-like *chhatra*. This is covered with a rich looking cloth that is referred to as *shiv*. Placed above this are silver *chhatras* that are smaller in size. To keep them in place, *mohras,* which may be from 8 to 15 in number, are tied to the different parts of the *ratha* with a cotton string [*sutri*]. Two of these *mohras* could well be of the *ashtadhatu* material. These would represent the original *mohras* that were dug out of the ground and are referred to as *mooli mukh* or *jiyumukh*. The front part of the body is decorated with necklaces in silver and gold. The waist is covered with a *kanchua* or a *ghagra* (skirt). Also tied to the *ratha* are 2-yard. long *dupattas*, pieces of colouful cloth.[30] The *ratha* of Devi Tundi of Bhulang, Kothi Khokhan, is an example of this style of a *deoratha*.

The *khara* or *pheta ratha* has two variant style: (a) the dome style, and (b) the *dhalwan* or sloping style. The dome style is more popular in Mandi, though there are some *rathas* of this style in Kulu also. The *jamanas* or *argalas* are about 20 ft. in length. This *ratha* differs from the *chhatra* type in as much as that, in place of the member referred to as *shiv,* there is a dome-shaped portion that extends from the *gala* (neck) to the *chhatra* at the top. The dome is generally covered with a beautiful, rich looking cloth around which is wrapped a scarf-like cloth that lends it further attractiveness. The number of *mohras* may be the same as in the case of the *chhatra* type of the *khara pheta ratha*. The lower portion of the *ratha* is covered with a fitted cloth, over which a *lungi* or a *kanchua* is wrapped. These sloping *rathas,* without a covering for the face of the *deota,* are present in great numbers in Kulu. Their general measurement is 3 ft. in length, 4 ft. in breadth and 3.5 ft. in height. The main board of the *ratha* is sloping and it is on this slanting portion that all the *mohras* are fitted. Two or three silver *chhatras* are fitted at the top end, the larger one is in the centre and is surrounded by smaller *chhatras* on either side. The *mohras* are all fitted on the front of the *ratha* in horizontal tiers. The back of the *ratha* has vertical rows of *dupattas* hanging close together in parallel lines. Along with them is fixed a *paranda,* a black cotton thread accessory used by women to plait their hair.[31] On the lower half of the body is fitted a skirt. A clear example of this kind of a *ratha* can be seen in that of Devi Chamunda from village Nashala in Kothi Nagar.

Also in existence is a much smaller version of the *pheta ratha*. Designed to be carried on the head of a devotee it can display only eleven *mohras*.[32] Gohri *deota* of Dhalpur and Lakshmi Narain of Kamand come to the Dussehra in this style of a *ratha*.

Interviews with people in Kulu and its neighbouring areas have revealed the exact nature of the belief of the people in their *deotas*. That this belief was very central to their beings, has already been established. In multiple ways, whether it was the social, the economic or the cultural aspects of Kulu society, the *deotas* dominated every area in a substantive way. If the *deota* was the money-lender to his people, he was also their account keeper. Keeper of a virtual archives of the historical and cultural records contained in his *bahis*, he was the landowner, the executive head, the judge who gave judicious judgements in difficult and acrimonious disputes; above all, he was the framer of laws.[33] The process started by Raja Bahadur Singh, of giving *muafi* lands to the *deotas*, was carried forward by Raja Jagat Singh.[34] In the relinquishing of all personal claims to the lands of the state, in favour of Thakur Raghunathji, it is the *deotas* who stood to gain as assignees. The *deotas* gave their services to the shrine and not to the Raja. Thakur Raghunath ji had distributed his lands among the *deotas*, taking on the role of a feudal lord between them.[35] The *deotas* distributed their lands further, amongst the members of their *hariyan*, and to their *sahayak deotas*, casting them in the role of tenant cultivators in relationship to themselves. A certain percentage of the produce from the lands of these tenant-cultivators was deposited in the *deota's* treasury as his share. Like any other feudal ford, at least in this limited aspect, the *deota* could requisition the services of these people for the repair and the building of the temple or any other services connected with the temple. This help was willingly extended with a sense of deep devotion. The forest lands or *dev-bans* belonging to the temple were governed by strict rules regarding the use of their timber and other produce. Clear distinctions were made in the matter of the use of the wood belonging to the *dev-ban*, whether it was in with regard to its use for cooking or for the repair work in the temple. Women and low castes were not permitted entry into the *dev-ban*, nor was the use of liquor allowed inside the forest. These rules, as has been established, have helped in saving the forests from denudation, keeping them clean, and in preserving the ecological balance of the terrain.[36]

A well thought out administrative system was put into place in connection with matters concerning the *deota*. Duties and responsibilities were defined unambiguously. Transgression of rules laid down by the *deota* was punished with an alacrity and sternness befitting a tightly controlled regime. No external institution was needed to enforce the law. At the apex of the team of functionaries connected with the administration of the *deota* was the *kardar*. A hereditary post, the *kardar* was very often selected by the Raja but at times also by the *deota* himself. In the event of his death, the Kardar's successor was chosen either on the basis of primogeniture, or that of seniority. The range of duties performed by the *kardar* included collection of land tax from the tenant cultivators of the *deota's* lands, and the management of his *jatras, jagarans* and other festivals. Taking care or at least overseeing the care of the *deota's* material possessions along with other important issues, like the building or renovation of the *deota's* temple, is seen as a part of the responsibilities of the *kardar*. These services are generally performed without any remuneration: the prestige of the post was considerable. The *kardar* was generally selected from among the upper castes. The *kardar* many a time received a portion of the *deota's* land to cultivate, as also double the share of *prasada*. The closeness of his relationship with the *deota* can be likened to that of a family member. On the death of a *kardar*, the last rites and related *samskaras* are performed by the *deota* himself who, after observing a period of mourning, goes through purificatory rites to enable his participation in events that demanded absolute purity.[37]

The *gur*, the *shaman* or the oracle is the other all-important functionary of the *deota*. In many ways he is the closest to the *deota* because he is the medium through which the *deota* expresses and communicates his views and prophecies. Distinctive in his outward appearance with long hair and a bared torso, which were mandatory in his functioning as a *gur*, he can be spotted easily because he leads the *deota's* procession, holding a *dharach* with smoking incense in one hand and a bell in the other. *Gurs* generally belong to the lower caste of *kolis* and *harijans*, though at times they could be selected from the upper castes also. Women are also known to have been selected as *gurs* under specific conditions. A *gur* is selected in a variety of ways. The feature common to most *gurs* is the sudden uncontrollable shivering of the body and the falling of the cap from his head. Despite no earlier tutoring, the *gur*-elect confirms the fact of his being a medium by being able to recite the entire *bhartha* of the *deota* when he is made to sit on the *jagti* in front of the *deota-ri-sauh*. The selection of a *gur* is ratified by the *deota*, and by unusual happenings that sometimes accompany the event. The *gur* is not allowed to function till his *pratishtha* takes place. On this occasion, after many rituals, a goat is sacrificed on his behalf; the blood of the sacrificed animal is sprinkled on the *gur*, and the ceremony is complete. The head of the sacrificed animal is given to the *gur* as his share of the *prasada*. Highly respected by the community, the *gur* is gifted a regular share of 2/3 kgs of grains by each household that forms a part of the *hariyan*. After his selection, the *gur* is honoured through the gift of a turban by the *deota* and he is given, regularly, a small percentage of money from the *deota's* treasury. Money offered at the time of prophesies by the devotees also ordinarily belongs to the *gur*.[38]

The list of functionaries attached to a *deota* is long. What is striking is the detailed thinking that has gone into ensuring the division of work. People are selected from certain hereditary castes, and there is a great deal of clarity regarding the tasks they have to perform. Thus, even though they may not be present constantly in the temple, not one functionary forgets to arrive at the appointed hour to discharge his duties with a sense of responsibility. Briefly, the *pujari's* task is to perform the *puja* at the *deota's* temple. He decorates and cleans the image of the *deota*, performs the *arti*, lights the incense, performs the necessary purificatory rites needed for an impure place, god, or man. The *pujari* also distributes flowers from the *ratha* as blessings to the *hariyan*. In the matter of the performance of the daily puja, each *pujari* takes on this responsibility as per rotation. During this period, he will sleep in the temple and lead a life of total chastity. The *pujari* is generally chosen from a Rajput or a Brahmin family. His source of income comes from his right to a small portion of the money-offerings at the shrine, as also from a small piece of land that may be allotted to him by the *deota*. In the more routine and mechanical tasks be is assisted by the *dhami*. The *bhandari* is in charge of the wealth of the *deota* in the form of *mohras*, money, grains, other objects of clothing, or precious metals belonging to the *deota*. The *bhandari* also dictates the accounts of the temple to the *kayatha*. The *jathera* or the *pogaldar* is responsible for the maintenance of discipline to look into matters of purity and pollution at the shrine of the *deota*, as also to ensure that all the tasks to be performed for the *deota* at the time of a festival are properly performed. The *kuthiala's* main function is to collect the *deota's* share of rations from each household. The *nishandar* is in charge of the symbols of authority such as flags and banners, *chhatras* and fly-whisks. The *palsara* is in charge of the gifts made to the *deota*. This would include the live goats which are for him to tend and present at the time that they are needed. Then there are the *banth* [the cook], the *bajantris* or *bajgis* [musicians], the men in charge of the musical instruments [the *dhaunsis*]. At the spiritual level, at the *deota's* temple, at the apex is the *Baradeo* or the principal *deota* who has under him *sahayak deotas* who act as his *wazirs*. They occupy smaller temples close to the temple of the main *deota*. From among this category are also the *birs* or bodyguards and the *bhors*, who function in the manner of the *deotas's* servants.[39]

The worship of the *deotas* appears on the surface to belong to a faith that is both informal and popular. It possesses nothing of the formal prescriptions and rigid rules of classical Hinduism. In effect, however, this popular faith was organized on a fairly regulated basis. It appears to have changed very little and stays based on clear prescriptions that may have had their remote beginnings in *shastric* injunctions. In its present form, this mode of worship has got so intertwined with local practices that it takes on the form of popular worship.

It is these *deotas* that come to Kulu at Dussehra time to pay homage to Thakur Raghunath ji. After their customary visit to the Raghunath temple and then to the palace of the Raja, the *deotas* come and settle down on the *athara kardu ri sauh* at the Dhalpur *maidan/chaugan* where their 'seats' are clearly marked out and known to everyone, for grave matters of precedence and prestige are involved in this. The tents of the *deotas* are pitched behind and around Raghunath ji's camp, which in turn is pitched along side the Raja's camp. The entire contingent waits in this *maidan*, waiting to go to battle for the rescue of Sita on the final day of the Dussehra. The Dhalpur *maidan* was a spot that was traditionally used for the holding of fairs even before the Dussehra came to be celebrated there. This is also the place where the first eighteen *deotas* who came to Kulu are believed to have been landed after being blown out of Rishi Jamadagni's *karadu* on the Chandrakhani pass. Two different lists, giving names of these gods, have been published. There is a popular saying in the region: *Thara Naga, Thara Narayan*, meaning there are eighteen Nagas, and eighteen Narayans. The legend of the eighteen *Nagas* escaping from the *bhandal* to avoid being burnt may be seen as the beginning of *Naga* worship in the Kulu area. The legend of the *Thara Narayan*, on the other hand, may well contain a reference to a righting of the balance by supporting the gods who were aspiring to a Vaishnava status. The eighteen *deotas* that first to came to Kulu have been listed as[40]:

1. Shamshiri Mahadev of Ani
2. Sukirni of Banjar
3. Trijugi Narain of Diyar,
4. Kasoli Narain of Kasol
5. Jagtham of Barshaini
6. Bhaga Sidh of Pini, Kayas
7. Sinha Mal of Gahar, Kayas
8. Girmal of Banogi
9. Thirmal of Dhara, Kayas
10. Ishwari Narain of Ajimal, Soyal
11. Jeev Narain of Jana, Nagar
12. Jamlu of Malana
13. Ambala of Chachogi
14. Shub Narain of Rumsu
15. Harshu Narain of Halan
16. Shandila of Shaleen
17. Manu Rishi of Manali
18. Gautam Rishi of Goshal

An important fact to be noticed is that, despite being invited, not all *deotas* come to participate in the Dussehra, even though they may have been the recipients of land-grants. The list of those who do not come is short, but several names figure in it. Prominent among these are Jamlu of Malana, Bhekhli Devi, and Parashar Rishi. Even though they do not come to the Dussehra – for reasons that lie embedded in local legends and history – they do make some gestures towards demonstrating their acknowledgement of Raghunath ji's supremacy. Some of them come and station themselves on the left bank of the river Beas, within sight of the Dhalpur *maidan*. Jamlu's *nishan*, *dharach*, and bell are brought by the *gur* to Angu Dobhi where they remain throughout the duration of the Dussehra festival.[41] Others send their *ghanta* and *dharach* along with their *gur* to the Raghunath temple with their share of the *trihara*, i.e. their share of offering to be sent from Raghunath temple to the *Treta Nath* Mandir in Ayodhya. Traditionally, Bhekhli Devi comes out of her temple at Dussehra time, and makes a *parikrama* of her temple, symbolizing her participation in the festival.[42] One wonders if these silent but rebellious assertions have something to do with events in the past or with the fact that a different form of governance prevailed among them: like the republican form that is practiced in Malana. *Deota* Parashar Rishi's refusal to go to the Dussehra may have had something to do with the fact that, at one time, this *deota* was located in a territory that once belonged to Mandi and only later was incorporated in Kulu.[43] Are basic antagonisms rooted in material causes expressed in this manner, one wonders again.

An overview of the faith in the *deotas* of Kulu, and the practices followed at their temples, reveals a curious mixture. Knowledge of Sanskritic *shastras* as disseminated by travellers and *pandits* coming into the hills appears to have become intertwined inextricably with the local beliefs in magic, ghosts, spirits and lesser beings that were the reality of the Pahari world. The complex faith that resulted has been described as 'animism' by some scholars and as 'primitive belief' by others. Locally, however, the conviction that it was the malevolent machinations of supernatural beings that led to the spread of crippling diseases and death contributed to the growth of an obsessive concern with finding solutions designed to soften the curse of evil spirits. Money, time and effort was spent unhesitatingly. It is against this background that belief in the *deota* provided a different level of comfort, marked by emotional security. The *deota* is a friend who provides succour. One is reminded of a statement of Turner: "Religion was made up of a series of facts and observances, the correct performance of which was necessary or desirable to secure the favour of the gods... religion did not exist for the saving of souls, but for the preservation of the welfare of society...'[44]

Appended below is one of the many lists/tables that seek to simplify the multitude of facts available about the different *deotas* of Kulu. The focus in these tables appears to be to document the various festivals held at the shrines of the listed *deotas*. Limited as the information it contains in its scope, it is based on a document compiled by the Department of Language and Culture, Government of Himachal Pradesh, Shimla. The information that this list contains may not be definitive on all counts, but it is undoubtedly full of interest.[45]

NOTES

A. The numbers given in the column titled 'source' in the table indicate the work/s used for compiling the information it contains. The numbers stand for the following works:

1. Sudarshan Vashisht, *Himalaya Mein Dev Sanskriti* (Delhi, 2006).
2. Sudarshan Vashisht (ed.), *Kulu Dev Samagam* (Shimla, n.d.).
3. Vidya Sharma, *Kulant Darpan* (Dobhi Kharahal, Kulu, 2001).
4. Surat Thakur (ed.), *Kullu ki Rishi Parampara* (Kulu, 2005).

B. The term 'Mool Sthan' has been used as supplied by informants and indicates the principal or original place where the temple of the *deota* was located from the beginning.

Sl. No.	Name of Deota/ Alternate Name	Cate-gory	Location Village Valley	Relation-ships	At Dussehra Since	Source	Remarks
1.	Vasuki Nag	Nag	Mool Sthan Thati Beed: Village: Gopalpur Tehsil: Banjaar		From the beginning	1 & 2	Main festivals held: Lohri, Phagli, Naga Panchami, Nahuli
2.	Dhumbal Nag	Nag	Mool Sthan: Goshaal Village: Halaan Kothi: Badagarh Tehsil: Kulu	Said to be son of Vasuki Nag	From the beginning	1 & 2	
3.	Kali Nag	Nag	Mool Sthan: Himbri Village: Karaal Kothi: Mandalgarh Tehsil: Kulu		From the beginning	1 & 2	Local legend claims Kali Nag and *Deota* Bir Nath manifested themselves at the same time:
4.	Ayadu Nag	Nag	Mool Sthan: Kanon Village: Dehuri Kothi: Bunga Sub-Tehsil: Sainj		Since 1971	1 & 2	Main festival held: Shoiri

Sl. No.	Name of Deota/ Alternate Name	Cate-gory	Location Village Valley	Relation-ships	At Dussehra Since	Source	Remarks
5.	Karath Nag	Nag	Mool Sthan: Kandi Village: Kandi Tehsil: Banjar		From the beginning	1 & 2	
6.	Chotru Nag	Nag	Mool Sthan: Shodha Village: Shodha Kothi: Raghupur Tehsil: Ani		From the beginning	1 & 2	Main festivals held: Sisri, Kathadhar and Rani Kot. Locally is believed to be the same as Shesh Naga
7.	Chham-ahun Nag	Nag	Mool Sthan: Badagran Village: Badagran (Paudhli) Tehsil: Banjar		From the beginning	1 & 2	Main festivals held: Garh jatra, Baisakhi, Shoiri and Nahuli
8.	Chham-ahun Nag	Nag	Mool Sthan: Daliyada Village: Daliyada (Kotla) Kothi: Bunga Tehsil: Banjar		Since olden times	1 & 2	Main festivals held: 10 in number throughout the year. The *deota* is believed to be a manifestation of Karttikeya Swami
9.	Tarunoon Nag	Nag	Mool Sthan: Bhagona Village: Bhagona Tehsil: Banjar		Since 1980	1 & 2	Main festivals held: The sankranti of Phalguna and Bhadrapada months
10.	Nag Dev	Nag	Mool Sthan: Suchehan Village: Suchehan Kothi: Banogi Tehsil: Banjar		From the beginning	1 & 2	Main festivals held: Phagli, Baisakh, Homa, and Bhadon vrata

Sl. No.	Name of Deota/ Alternate Name	Cate-gory	Location Village Valley	Relation-ships	At Dussehra Since	Source	Remarks
11.	Patrunu Nag	Naga	Mool Sthan: Padyona Village: Padyona Kothi: Bunga		Since 1981	1 & 2	Main festivals held: Bali mela, Banjar mela, Sainj mela and the beginning of Samvat year
12.	Boodhi Nagan	Naga	Mool Sthan: Shrekul Sar Village: Dhiyagi Kothi: Khadagadh Tehsil: Banjar		Since olden times	1 & 2	Main festival held: On the 7th of the month of Vaishakha. This devi is believed to be the mother of 18 nagas.
13.	Hidimba Devi	Shakti	Mool Sthan: Dhungri Village: Manali	Said to be sister of Jamlu and Ghepad; also sister of the demon, Tandi	From the beginning	1 & 2	Main festivals held: Dhungri Jach, in the month of Jyeshtha. At this temple regular puja is held according to classical prescriptions.
14.	Docha Mocha Devi	Shakti	Mool Sthan: Gajan Village: Gajan-Karjan		From the beginning	1, 2 & 3	Main festivals held: Chachohli mela on the full moon night of Chaitra. The devis are said to be the same as the Pauranik devis, Jaya and Vijaya
15.	Asha Puri	Shakti	Mool Sthan: Dhalyara		From the beginning	1 & 2	

Sl. No.	Name of Deota/ Alternate Name	Cate-gory	Location Village Valley	Relation-ships	At Dussehra Since	Source	Remarks
			Village: Dhalyara				
16.	Jwala Devi	Shakti	Mool Sthan: Fojal Village: Fojal Kothi: Hurang Tehsil: Kulu		From the beginning	1 & 2	Main festivals held: Birshu, Kapu and Kajeli
17.	Jwala-mukhi	Shakti	Mool Sthan: Shamshi Village: Shamshi Khoti: Khokhan Tehsil: Kulu		From the beginning of Dussehra	1 & 2	Main festivals held: Somashi Birshu of the goddess
18.	Dashmi Varda	Shakti	Mool Sthan: Kais Village: Kais		From the beginning	1 & 2	Main festivals held: Birshu, Shauna, Phagli, Shanhu, Diyali of the month of Pausha, and Konha Birshu
19.	Tundi Devi	Shakti	Mool Sthan: Bhulang Village: Bhulang Kothi: Khokhan Tehsil: Kulu		From the beginning	1 & 2	Main festivals held: Mahul Jach, Dhara Jach, Shanhu Jach, Shanauhli and Mundhar Punu. This devi is also known as Naina Devi.
20.	Chamunda	Shakti	Mool Sthan: Nashala Village: Nashala Kothi: Naggar Tehsil: Kulu		From the beginning	1 & 2	Main festivals held: Bishu and Shaun Jach. The devi is believed to have sprung from the joint energies of Brahma, Shiva and Vishnu

Sl. No.	Name of Deota/ Alternate Name	Cate-gory	Location Village Valley	Relation-ships	At Dussehra Since	Source	Remarks
21.	Neyitra Devi	Shakti	Mool Sthan: Khasambhali Village: Khasambhali Dhar Kothi: Khokhan Tehsil: Kulu		From the beginning	1 & 2	Main festivals held: Baisakhi, Paanju, Nauhli and Birshu
22.	Naina Devi	Shakti	Mool Sthan: Bhuntar Village: Sundar Nagar		Since 1995	2	Main festivals held: Baisakhi, Nalbad, and Mahadev. The image of the devi was first at Bhuntar, and then taken to Sundar Nagar
23.	Panchali Devi	Shakti	Mool Sthan: Panjaali Village: Panjaali Kothi: Fatehpur Tehsil: Banjar		From the beginning	1 & 2	Main festivals held: Tuar, Hum, Phariaut, Bagi and Navaratri
24.	Devi Phungani	Shakti	Mool Sthan: Shiradh Village: Shiradh Kothi: Raisan Tehsil: Kulu	Said to be close to Kali Nag	From the beginning	1 & 2	Main festivals held: Konha, Birshu, Shanohli and Kahika
25.	Bala Tripura Sundari	Shakti	Mool Sthan: Naggar Village: Naggar Tehsil: Kulu		From the beginning	1 & 2	Main festivals held: Sharhi Jach in the month of Jyeshtha
26.	Bhaga Sidh	Shakti	Mool Sthan: Peeni Village: Peeni Tehsil: Kulu		From the beginning	1 & 2	Main festivals held: Shanhu, Shaun, Mundhar Punu, Paush Diyali, Kahika, Phagli,

Sl. No.	Name of Deota/ Alternate Name	Cate-gory	Location Village Valley	Relation-ships	At Dussehra Since	Source	Remarks
							Birshu and Jyeshtha puja
27.	Bhaga Sidh	Shakti	Mool Sthan: Narogi Village: Narogi Kothi: Kotkandi Tehsil: Kulu		From the beginning	1 & 2	Main festivals held: Baisakhi, Kathachi, Shaun and Punu
28.	Bhatanti	Shakti	Mool Sthan: Naggar Village: Naggar Tehsil: Kulu		Since 1976	1 & 2	Main festivals held: Sharhi Jach, Shauiri, Birshu and Dei ri Jach
29.	Bharatha Devi	Shakti	Mool Sthan: Galchhet Village: Galchhet Kothi: Mandalgarh Tehsil: Kulu		From the beginning	1 & 2	Main festival held: Kapu Mela
30.	Mahamai	Shakti	Mool Sthan: Kachhaini Village: Kachhaini Sub-Tehsil: Sainj	Is the Shakti of Brahma	Since 1990. At first a single *mohra;* later devi comes in her own rath	1 & 2	Main festivals held: Hum, Sajabashad, Shauiri, and Dewali. This devi is also worshipped in village Kanaun in Sainj tehsil
31.	Shabari	Shakti	Mool Sthan: Shuroo Village: Shuroo		From the beginning	1 & 2	Main festivals held: Sita Navami in the month of Vaishakha
32.	Shyama Kali	Shakti	Mool Sthan: Dalasani Village: Dalasani Kothi:		From the beginning	1 & 2	Main festivals held: Hum, Birshu, Shauj and Magh Mela

Sl. No.	Name of Deota/ Alternate Name	Cate-gory	Location Village Valley	Relation-ships	At Dussehra Since	Source	Remarks
			Bhalahan Phati: Rot Tehsil: Kulu				
33.	Varahi	Shakti	Mool Sthan: Maueel Village: Maueel Kothi: Shainshar Sub-Tehsil: Sainj		Since olden times		
34.	Bijli Mahadev	Shaiv	Mool Sthan: Mathan Village: Mathan		From the beginning of Dussehra	1 & 2	
35.	Mangale-shwar Mahadev	Shaiv	Mool Sthan: Chheyaunr Village: Chheyaunr Kothi: Kotkandi		Approx. for 300 years	1 & 2	Main festivals held: Makhshari, Kahika and Baisakhi
36.	Khodu Mahadev	Shaiv	Mool Sthan: Trehan Village: Trehan Kothi: Kotkandi		Since 1961	2	Main festivals held: Makhshar Chaitra and Narogi Jach
37.	Khodu Mahadev	Shaiv	Mool Sthan: Dhara Village: Dhara Kothi: Chaihni Tehsil: Banjar		From the beginning	2	Main festivals held: Banjar mela, Shairi, new Samvat and 8th of Magh mela. The *deota* is a sahayak of Shringi rishi
38.	Trijugi Naraian Diyaar	Vishnu	Mool Sthan: Diyaar Village: Diyaar	Said to be born out of the combined powers of Brahma, Vishnu and Shiva	'From ancient times'	1 & 2	Main festivals held: Kahika in the month of Shravana

Sl. No.	Name of Deota/ Alternate Name	Cate-gory	Location Village Valley	Relation-ships	At Dussehra Since	Source	Remarks
39.	Kali Narain	Vishnu	Mool Sthan: Hurang Village: Jonga Kothi: Maharaja Tehsil: Kulu		From the beginning	1 & 2	Main festivals held: Mundhar Punu mela in the month of Margashirsha. Having been brought from Hurang, the *deota* is also called Hurang Narain sometimes
40.	Chhamani Narain	Vishnu	Mool Sthan: Chamaan Village: Chamaan Kothi: Kayas Phatis: Khashauri Tehsil: Kulu		From the beginning	1 & 2	Main festivals held: Shanhu, Birshu, Mundhar Punu and Janmashtami
41.	Juaanu Mahadev	Shaiv	Mool Sthan: Juani Village: Juani Kothi: Kayas Tehsil: Kulu		From the beginning	1 & 2	Main festivals held: New Samvat, Birshu and Shaun mela
42.	Thaan Narain	Vishnu	Mool Sthan: Bhutthi Village: Bhutthi		From the beginning	1 & 2	Main festivals held: Jetha Birshu, New Samvat, Konha Birshu, Salahar, Shanohli, and Shoiri
43.	Narain	Vishnu	Mool Sthan: Badi Shilh Village: Badi Shilh Kothi: Raisan		From the beginning	1 & 2	Main festivals held: Phagli and Paruin

Sl. No.	Name of Deota/ Alternate Name	Category	Location Village Valley	Relationships	At Dussehra Since	Source	Remarks
44.	Narain	Vishnu	Mool Sthan: Ardaar Jot Village: Meha Kothi: Badagarh	Related to Narain of Meh are: Hurang Narain of Daral, Dev Brahma of Brahan, and Hari Narain of Kathi. Devi Jwala of Fojal also appeared with him.	From the beginning	1 & 2	
45.	Bali Narain	Vishnu	Mool Sthan: Barakola Kothi: Badagarh		From the beginning	1 & 2	
46.	Laxmi Narain	Vishnu	Mool Sthan: Koliberh Village: Koliberh		Since 1966	1 & 2	Main festivals held: Nahuli in the month of Asharh
47.	Laxmi Narain	Vishnu	Mool Sthan: Raayla Village: Raayla Sud-Tehsil: Sainj		From the beginning	1 & 2	
48.	Shaprada Narain	Vishnu	Mool Sthan: Aashani Village: Aashani		From the beginning	1 & 2	Main festivals held: Shaun mela, Shoiri in Ashwin, and Baisakhi
49.	Shaprada Narain	Vishnu	Mool Sthan: Bhadogi Village: Bhadogi Kothi: Kotkandi			1 & 2	Main festivals held: Melas in the months of Jyeshtha, Shravana, and Margashirsha
50.	Hari Narain	Vishnu	Mool Sthan: Kathi Village: Kathi		From the beginning	1 & 2	Main festivals held: Kajeli, Shanauhla and Phagli

Sl. No.	Name of Deota/ Alternate Name	Cate-gory	Location Village Valley	Relation-ships	At Dussehra Since	Source	Remarks
51.	Hurang Narain	Vishnu	Mool Sthan: Daraal Village: Daraal Kothi: Hurang		From the beginning	1 & 2	Main festivals held: Phagli, Thandor and Kolu
52.	Hurang Narain	Vishnu	Mool Sthan: Hurang Village: Gadiyaada		From olden times	1 & 2	Main festival held: Mandhar ka Phera
53.	Adi Brahma	Brahma	Mool Sthan: Khokhan Village: Khokhan & Rohlagi		From the beginning	1 & 2	Main festivals held: Birshu, Shanhu, Shoiri, Mlahul Jach, Dhara Jach and Pun
54.	Brahma	Brahma	Mool Sthan: Kanon Village: Kanon Kothi: Bunga Sub-Tehsil: Sianj		From the beginning	1 & 2	Main festivals held: Chhoom, Shoiri and Baisakhi
55.	Parashar Rishi	Rishi	Mool Sthan: Kamaand Kothi: Kathaun	Close to Jamlu son of Shakti Rishi and grandson of Vashisht		1 & 3	Main festivals held: Pur in Magh, Shalohni in Shravan, and Jachu in the month of Bhadrapada. Women are not allowed to enter the premises of this *deota*. The *deota* is considered the elder brother of

Sl. No.	Name of Deota/ Alternate Name	Cate-gory	Location Village Valley	Relation-ships	At Dussehra Since	Source	Remarks
							many other *deotas* including Narain of Buai, Narain of Lot, Sharpal of Ligar Bonasu, Bir Kaila of Khalogi and Bir Baradhi of Kareri
56.	Shringi Rishi	Rishi	Mool Sthan: Sakoran Village: Baagi Tehsil: Banjar	Is son of Vibhandak Rishi, grandson of Kashyap Rishi	'From olden times'	1,2 & 3	Main festivals held: Banjar mela in Jyeshta. The *deota* goes out on appointed days to perform different functions. The rishi is said to have been given birth to by a female deer.
57.	Beas Rishi	Rishi	(i) Mool Sthan: Kueenr Village: Kueenr Kothi: Raghupur Tehsil: Aani (ii) Mool Sthan: Goshaal Kothi: Manali Tehsil:	Manifested with Gautam Rishi and Kanchan Nag	From the beginning	1, 2, 3, 4	Main festivals held: Sisari, Balh, Dagali, Bhares, Bashaul, Michun and Bhadera. The *gur* of the *deota* performs Shogal Katara as a part of Deu Khel. Other melas

Sl. No.	Name of Deota/ Alternate Name	Cate-gory	Location Village Valley	Relation-ships	At Dussehra Since	Source	Remarks
			Kulu				held are: Baisakhi, Dhungri, Shauri, Chhota Sarani, Kulang Barua
58.	Gautam Rishi	Rishi	Mool Sthan: Manihaar Village: Manihaar Kothi: Kotkandi		From the beginning	1, 2 & 3	Main festivals held: Kaundha, Phagli and Baisakhi
59.	Gautam Rishi, Vedvyas and Kanchan Nag	Rishi	Mool Sthan: Goshaal Village: Goshaal Kothi: Manali		From the beginning	1, 2 & 3	Main festivals held: Sarani, Shoiri, and Phagli. The rishis Gautam, Vyas, and Kanchan Nag share the same *rath*. Also shared are the *bhandar*, and the *bajantri*-musicians.
60.	Chaman (Chyavan) Rishi	Rishi	Mool Sthan: Najaan Village: Najaan Kothi: Kotkandi Tehsil: Kulu	Has Jehar Jaraal as his *sahayak deota*	From the beginning	1, 2 & 3	Main festivals held: Konha Birshu in Vaishakh; Pachauhla Jach in Jyeshtha also; killing of witches in Bhadrapada is celebrated. On the sankranti of Phalguna, the *gur* narrates the *bharatha*

Sl. No.	Name of Deota/ Alternate Name	Cate-gory	Location Village Valley	Relation-ships	At Dussehra Since	Source	Remarks
							of the *deota*. Deukar is held in Chaitra.
61.	Durvaasa Rishi	Rishi	Mool Sthan: Paalagi Village: Paalagi Kothi: Bhalahan	Said to be close to Narad muni	From the beginning	1, 2 & 3	
62.	Narad Muni	Rishi	Mool Sthan: Neenu Village: Neenu Kothi: Kotkandi	Has Jaraal *deota*, Jehar, and Khodu deo and Banshira as his sahayak *deotas*	From the beginning	1, 2 & 3	Main festivals held: Bittha and Neenu Laman; Pandhar Jach on a peak near Gadasa is held.
63.	Pandir Rishi	Rishi	Mool Sthan: Kaithaugi Village: Kaithaugi	Said to be living along with Lakshmi Narain of Rehla	From the beginning	1, 2 & 3	Main festivals held: Hum in the month of Ashwin. Also Dehuri mela in Vaishakh.
64.	Markandey Rishi	Rishi	Mool Sthan: Balagarh Village: Balagarh Kothi: Shikari Tehsil: Banjar	Devi Tripur Sundari Bala is said to reside with him	From the beginning	1, 2 & 3	Main festival held on the Sankranti of Phalgun in honour of Tripurasundari. Hum is held in Vaishakha. Inharu in Vaishakha also; Banjar mela in Jyeshtha. There are other villages where temples to this rishi have been

Sl. No.	Name of Deota/ Alternate Name	Cate-gory	Location Village Valley	Relation-ships	At Dussehra Since	Source	Remarks
							raised. Thus, Sajwar, Tharas, and Shikarigarh.
65.	Markandey Rishi	Rishi	Mool Sthan: Mangalor Village: Mangalor Kothi: Mangalor	Multiplied through striking of lightning at Bajhad village of Lahul	From olden times	1, 2 & 3	Main festivals held: Phag and Bittha.
66.	Lomash Rishi	Rishi	Mool Sthan: Pekhadi Village: Pekhadi Kothi: Nuhanda Tehsil: Banjar	Has Thamat and Maryadu *deotas* as his sahayak *deotas*	Since 1956	1, 2 & 3	Main festivals held: Phagli, Shanyaj, Gushaini, and Banjar mela. Also Baisakhi and Diyali.
67.	Garg Rishi (Rot) Garg Acharya Risha Khanargi	Rishi	Mool Sthan: Rot Village: Rot Mool Sthan: Talada Other seat: Khanargi	Has Varangu, Tushala and Banshir *deotas* as his *sahayak* as his *sahayak* Also Bugadu, Varangu, Tuchhala, Righu, and Banshira, Danavargadu and Tunga Bir as his *sahayaks*	From the beginning	1, 2 & 3	Main Festivals held: Dhansar Vaishakh and Krishna Janmashtami. Also Khangari Bittha, and Saja Jeth. This *deota* is believed to be the same Gargacharya who was Krishna's *purohit*.
68.	Garg Acharya	Rishi	Mool Sthan: Lashani Village: Lashani		From olden times	1, 2 & 3	Main festivals held: Bhadon Shoiri, and Chaitra sankranti
69.	Gauhri Deu	Brahma	Mool Sthan: Khokhan		From the beginning	1 & 2	Main festivals held: Mahul

Sl. No.	Name of Deota/ Alternate Name	Cate- gory	Location Village Valley	Relation- ships	At Dussehra Since	Source	Remarks
			Village: Janaahal				Jach, Shanhu Jach, and Mundhar Punu
70.	Gauhri Deu	Brahma	Mool Sthan: Thacha Mashan Village: Pangaan		From the beginning	1 & 2	Main festivals held: Kapu, Shoiri, Rani ri Jach, Jetha Birshu, and Mehan
71.	Gauhri Deu	Brahma	Mool Sthan: Damcheen Village: Damcheen Kothi: Hurang		From the beginning	1 & 2	Main festivals held: Shaun mela, Phagli, and Bhala Jatra. The *deota* is identified also with Bir Nath
72.	Gauhri Deu	Brahma	Mool Sthan: Hurla Village: Hurla Kothi: Kotkandi	Also known as Bir Nath, guru of the Raja	From the beginning	1 & 2	Main festivals held: Shoiri, Mandhar ka dhup, and others in the months of Chaitra, Vaishakha, and Bhadrapada.
73.	Gauhri Deu	Brahma	Mool Sthan: Thacha Mashan Village: Bagan		Since 1980	1 & 2	Main festivals held: Shoiri, Birshu and Makhashar.
74.	Gauhri Deu	Brahma	Mool Sthan: Thacha Mashan Village: Fojal Kothi: Hurang	Another form of Bir Nath *deota*	From the beginning	1 & 2	Main festivals held: Kapu, Shaun, Punu and Shoiri.

Sl. No.	Name of Deota/ Alternate Name	Cate-gory	Location Village Valley	Relation-ships	At Dussehra Since	Source	Remarks
75.	Gauhri Deu	Brahma	Mool Sthan: Dehri Dhar Village: Buayi Kothi: Maharaja		From the beginning	1 & 2	Main festival held: Shauj. This *deota* is also worshipped under the name of Mahadeo.
76.	Gauhri Deu	Brahma	Mool Sthan: Dachani Village: Dachani Kothi: Badagarh		Approx. since 1960	1 & 2	Main festivals held: Shoiri, Punu and Baisakhi.
77.	Gauhri Deu	Brahma	Mool Sthan: Dhalpur Village: Dhalpur Tehsil: Kulu		From the beginning	1 & 2	Main festivals held: Pippal Jatra, and sankrantis of Vaishakha, Bhadrapad and Ashwin.
78.	Gauhri Daiu	Brahma	Mool Sthan: Bari Tuni Village: Bari Tuni Kothi: Kais		From the beginning	1 & 2	Main festivals held: Birshu, Shaun, Shoiri and Janmashtami. Also new Samvat in Chaitra.
79.	Paunj Bir	Bir	Mool Sthan: Bakhali Village: Bakhali Kothi: Khokhan Phatis: Shilihar		Since 1985	1 & 2	Main festival held: Punu.
80.	Kaila Bir	Bir	Mool Sthan: Kamaand Village: Kamaand		Hundred of years	1 & 2	Main festival held: Shaun. This *deota* represents

Sl. No.	Name of Deota/ Alternate Name	Cate-gory	Location Village Valley	Relation-ships	At Dussehra Since	Source	Remarks
			Kothi: Maharaja Phati: Khadihaar				Parashar rishi at Dussehra.
81.	Paunj Bir	Bir	Mool Sthan: Laut Village: Laut Kothi: Maharaja Phatis: Barahaar		Since 1988	1 & 2	Main festivals held: Birshu, Shanohli and Mundahr Punu.
82.	Tundi Bir	Bir	Mool Sthan: Dalasani Village: Dalasani		Since 1985	1 & 2	Main festivals held: Birshu and Shoiri.
83.	Maha Bir	Bir	Mool Sthan: Manglaur Village: Manglaur Tehsil: Banjar		Since 1985	1 & 2	Main festivals held: Tateri in the month of Magh; Bitth and Holi in Phalguna.
84.	Aiyadu Maha Bir	Bir	Mool Sthan: Trilok Nath Village: Shohul Kothi: Bunga Sub-Tehsil: Sainj		Since 1964	1 & 2	Main festivals held: Shoiri, Mahabharath in the month of Magh; also Janmashtami and Diyali.
85.	Bir Baradhi	Bir	Mool Sthan: Kareri Village: Kareri Kothi: Maharaja			1 & 2	The *deota* is also known by the name of Paunch Bir.
86.	Banshira	Bir	Mool Sthan: Kanon Village: Kanon Kothi: Bunga		Since 1971	1 & 2	Main festivals held: Shoiri, Shanhu and Bitth.
87.	Rupan Pal	Village *Deota*	Mool Sthan: Paha		Since 1977	1 & 2	Main festivals held: Nahuli

Sl. No.	Name of Deota/ Alternate Name	Cate-gory	Location Village Valley	Relation-ships	At Dussehra Since	Source	Remarks
			Village: Paha Kothi: Maharaja				and Shadhi.
88.	Rupanu Pal	Village *Deota*	Mool Sthan: Mandi Village: Tari Ra Gran Kothi: Khokhan		Since 1976	1 & 2	Main festivals held: Shauni Jach.
89.	Ran Pal	Village *Deota*	Mool Sthan: Mauhl Village: Mauhl Kothi: Khokhan		From the beginning	1 & 2	Main festivals held: Mahul Jach, Shanhu and Punu.
90.	Bhuhani	Village *Deota*	Mool Sthan: Baula Village: Baula Kothi: Shikari Tehsil: Banjar		Since Sixty Years	1 & 2	Main festivals held: Banjar mela and the new samvat. Also a mela in Magh.
91.	Balindu Deu	Village *Deota*	Mool Sthan: Kayas Village: Kayas	Was allowed to stay with her by Devi Dashmi Varda	Since a hundred years	1 & 2	Main festivals held: Bhungra in the months of Pausha and Magh.
92.	Banshira	Village *Deota*	Mool Sthan: Sidhwa Village: Sidhwa Kothi: Manglaur	Is a *sahayak deota* of Jamlu	Since 1986	1 & 2	Main festivals held: Banjar mela; also *jagrata* in the month of Magh.
93.	Piradu Thaan	Shaiva	Mool Sthan: Piradi Village: Piradi Kothi: Maharaja	Is said to be the grandfather of Bijli Mahadeo	From the beginning	1 & 2	Main festivals held: Piradi and Shanhu.

Sl. No.	Name of Deota/ Alternate Name	Cate-gory	Location Village Valley	Relation-ships	At Dussehra Since	Source	Remarks
94.	Painari	Vishnu	Mool Sthan: Bahu Village: Bahu Tehsil: Banjar		From the beginning	1 & 2	Main festivals held: melas in the months of Phalguna, Vaishakha, Shravana and Agrahayan.
95.	Jehar		Mool Sthan: Nijan Village: Nijan Kothi: Kotkandi	Is said to be *sahayak deota* of Jamlu	From the beginning	1 & 2	Main festivals held: Kaunda and Choha. The *deota* is so named because in anger his effect is like that of poison (*zehr*).
96.	Janaasar		Mool Sthan: Rainh Village: Rainh Kothi: Banogi Phati: Maneshi Sub-Tehsil: Sainj		Since hundred years	1 & 2	Main festivals held: melas on the ekadashi of Bhadrapada and Chaitra. Also one on the 15th of Magh.
97.	Pasha Kot	Village *Deota*	Mool Sthan: Chota Bangahal Village: Sheladi Kothi: Mandalgarh		Since 1966	1 & 2	Main festivals held: Shoiri and Shaun.
98.	Chambhu	Village *Deota*	Mool Sthan: Kasholi Village: Kasholi Kothi: Daul Tehsil: Nirmand		From the beginning	1 & 2	Main festivals held: Birshu and Diyali.

Sl. No.	Name of Deota/ Alternate Name	Cate-gory	Location Village Valley	Relation-ships	At Dussehra Since	Source	Remarks
99.	Ghatot-kach	Village *Deota*	Mool Sthan: Sidhma Village: Sidhma Kothi: Manglaur Tehsil: Banjar		From the beginning	1 & 2	Main festivals held: Hum and Banjar mela.
100.	Kali Audi	Shakti	Mool Sthan: Archhandi Village: Archhandi Kothi: Naggar		From the beginning	1 & 2	Main festivals held: Birshu and Shaun.
101.	Arji Pal	Village *Deota*	Mool Sthan: Bir Bangahal Village: Nargi Kothi: Maharaja		Since 1984	1 & 2	Main festivals held: Shaun Jach and Maukhshar.
102.	Arji Pal	Village *Deota*	Mool Sthan: Bangahal Village: Jhokadi Kothi: Hurang			1 & 2	
103.	Suraj Pal	Village *Deota*	Mool Sthan: Bada Bhuin (Bhuntar) Village: Bada Bhuin Kothi: Kotkandi		From the beginning	1 & 2	Main festival held: Bhuntar mela.
104.	Shar Pal	Village *Deota*	Mool Sthan: Bonasu Village: Bonasu Kothi: Maharaja		From the beginning	1 & 2	Main festivals held: Birshu and Maukhshar.
105.	Rishi Vashisht	Rishi	Mool Sthan: Vashisht	Was grand-father of		3 & 4	

Sl. No.	Name of Deota/ Alternate Name	Cate-gory	Location Village Valley	Relation-ships	At Dussehra Since	Source	Remarks
			Village: Mathiyana and Koshala	Parashar Rishi			
106.	Jamadagni Rishi	Rishi	Installed at 12 different places: Mool Sthan: Peeni Hamta; Other locations: Malana Halana; Karja; Kulang; Boorua; Majhach; Shangchar; Dephari; Baragran; Chhani; and Khumarati	Said to be brother of Ghepan Rishi. Father of Parashuram Other *deotas* like Banshira, Jehar, Banasur are his *sahayak deotas*. Diyari Thakur is said to be the Guru of Jamlu		3 & 4	Main festivals held at Malana: Malana Shauni; Devi Chechai ri Phagli; Kapu; and the sankaranti of Ashwin. This *deota* is believed to be very close to Parashar Rishi.
107.	Mahrishi Shandilya	Rishi	Mool Sthan: Shaleen Tehsil: Manali	Son of Brahma		3 & 4	
108.	Kapil Muni	Rishi	Mool Sthan: Bashauna Other Villages: Bagicha, Tunhiseri, Jarad, Piplog, Ropaseri, Khaulahog			3 & 4	Main festivals held: Kahika every third year; sankrantis of the months of Vaishakha, Bhadrapada, and Magh. *Jagratas* are held on Shivratri.
109.	Kapil Muni	Rishi	Mool Village: Klath			Surat Thakur	This *deota* does not permit its followers from six

Sl. No.	Name of Deota/ Alternate Name	Cate-gory	Location Village Valley	Relation-ships	At Dussehra Since	Source	Remarks
							designated villages to observe any *japa* or path.
110.	Bhrigu Rishi	Rishi	Mool Sthan: Ashani villages of Gadsa Ghati			3	No local festival is held; but the classical festivals like Ram Navami, Janmashtami, Annakut, and Deepavali are observed.
112.	Gautam Rishi	Rishi	Mool Sthan: Gumbal			4	The rishi's birthday is celebrated in the month of Phalguna.
113.	Manu Rishi	Rishi	Mool Sthan: Manali			3 & 4	The rishi's birthday is celebrated in the month of Vaishakha. Every twelve years there is a kahika festival. The *rath* is shared by Manu rishi and Hidimba.
114.	Manu Rishi of Dhara, Dehra, Shainshar	Rishi	Mool Sthan: Patahara Other seats: from Shakti Maraur upto Shainshar, followers live in several villages			3 & 4	The rishi's birthday is celebrated in Vaishakha. Dhara Dehura mela is also held in Asharh. Every few years, the

Sl. No.	Name of Deota/ Alternate Name	Cate- gory	Location Village Valley	Relation- ships	At Dussehra Since	Source	Remarks
							deota goes to visit his followers.
115.	Vashisht Brahma- rishi		Mool Sthan: Shakati Village: temples also in Shakati Maraud. Kothis Shainshar, Rehla, Bhalahan has a large number of followers in several villages	Dhruv Rishi is said to be his *sahayak deota*		4	The *deota* visits, every eight or ten years, his followers; this is called Chaliyara Hargi. Also travels to Sainj valley. Many *deotas* of Kulu and Mandi regard this *deota* as their guru.
116.	Shakt Rishi (Shakti Rishi)		Mool Sthan: Thanthal Tehsil: Nirmand Other seats: several, where there is following of the *deota*, including: Tirmidhar, Kushain, Thans, Dungru, Jahan, Dhadhsa	Father of Parashar Rishi		4	In Chaitra, happenings in the new setting in samvat are prophesied. The *deota* visits Bhadrah to the accompani- ment of much music and pomp. Chanyal Nirsh is observed in Vaishakh.

NOTES AND REFERENCES

1. There are references in Hiuen-Tsang to Buddhist stupas and monasteries at many places in the hills. The inscriptions at Chari and Kanhiara afford clear evidence of the existence of Buddhism at an early date. There are even the remains of a stupa at Chetru near Kangra. But by the time we speak of, nearly every vestige of Buddhism had vanished from this area except where it survived in a vestigial form.
2. The existence of many Jaina images from the hills points to this. Even as late as the 15th century, a party of Jainas undertook a pilgrimage to Kangra. See, Mul Raj Jain, "A Jaina Pilgrimage to Nagarkot in S. 1484", *Procs. Of the 13th A.I. Oriental Conf.*, 1946, p. 399.
3. In the Kangra district, e.g., the Muslims formed not more than five percent of the population in 1833-84. *Kangra D.G.*, I, p. 1.
4. H.A. Rose wrote several articles under this title in the *Indian Antiquary* between 1903 and 1907.
5. *Kangra District Gazetteer*, 1883-84, II, pp. 27-28. *Cf.* "Throughout Kulu ... the faith is Hinduism; but it is not the religion of the orthodox ..." A.F.P. Harcourt, *The Himalayan districts of Kooloo, Lahoul and Spiti*, p. 192.
6. *Kangra D.G.*, 1883–84, II, pp. 27-28.
7. C.F. Oldham has, in a penetrating note in the *Punjab Notes and Queries*, II, Sept. 1885, pp. 199-200, described the process of the absorption of non-Brahmanic Hinduism in the Hills. Gore, *Lights and Shades of Hill Life, Lights and Shades of Hill Life*, pp. 11-12. "... though Hindus in name, and honouring the name of the Hindu divinities, they are practically demon – worshippers whose religious zeal is in proportion to their superstition."
8. Goetz, *Early Wooden Temples of Chamba*, vii. The words are of Dr. Vogel who has written the foreword to this volume.
9. Rose, *A Glossary of the Tribes and Castes of the Punjab and North – West Frontier Province*, I, p. 401.
10. *Chamba State Gazetteer*, 1904, Pt. A, p. 181.
11. Kahn Singh Balauria, *Tawarikh -i-Rajputan-i Mulk-i Punjab*, p. 455.
12. *Chamba S.G.*, 1904, Pt. A, 184. "...Devi and Naga worship undoubtedly represent the primitive cult of the Punjab Hills." Vogel, *Archaeological Survey of India (Pb. And U.P.) Annual Report*, 1904, p. 67.
13. Goetz, *Early Wooden Temples of Chamba*, pp. 45-48.
14. Coomaraswamy, *The Dance of Shiva*, p. 90.
15. This story is often repeated to justify sacrifices. The goddess herself, the priests tell the devotees, become sati and thus sanctified sacrifice.
16. *Census of India*, 1961, XX, Village Survey Report for Kothi.
17. *Census of India*, 1961, XX, Village Survey Report for Chhatrarhi.
18. Rose, *Glossary*, I, pp. 318-319.
19. Among the principal collections of manuscripts seen were those of Shri Bhu Dev of Sujanpur, Pt. Mohan Lal of Samloti, Pt. Ayodha Prasad of Al- hilal, and Pt. Agya Ram of Bani Lodi.
20. Rose, *Glossary*, I, 329; *Mandi State Gazetteer*, 1904, pp. 37-38.
21. Rose, *Glossary*, I, 318-19, pp. 320-23.
22. *Sirmur State Gazetteer*, Pt. A, 1904, p. 48.
23. The registers prepared in Kulu in 1947-49 listing the holdings of the *deotas*. These official registers could be referred to through the courtesy of the revenue officials at Kulu in the course of field-work.
24. *Ibid*.
25. See Harcourt, p. 198; Rose, *Glossary*, I, p. 275.

26. Quoted in Vogel, *Indian Serpent Lore*, p. 231
27. *Ibid.*, pp. 261-62.
28. *Ibid.*, p. 250.
29. As quoted in Vogel, *Indian Serpent Lore*, pp. 256-57.
30. R.C. Temple, "Some Hindu Folk-songs from the Panjab", *Journal of the Asiatic Society of Bengal*, LI, i, p. 186.
31. *Punjab Notes & Queries*, I, No. 4, p. 37; Rose, "The Song of Sindhu Bir", *Indian Antiquary*, XXXVIII, pp. 295-96.
32. Rose, *Glossary*, I, 378; *Pb. Notes & Queries*, I, VII, p. 73.
33. Pt. Sukhchain of Kumharsain collected a large number of legends about these *deotas*. See, his 'Legends of the Godlings of the Simla Hills", *Indian Antiquary*, LIV, June 1925 & July 1925.
34. Gore, *Lights and Shades*, II.
35. Different lists of *deotas*, as far as Kulu is concerned, have been drawn up from time to time, especially in post-independence India when the State took over many of the powers and functions of the Rajas who ruled these areas. These lists are taken note of in this study, having been either drawn upon or reproduced. Scholars belonging to the region have also drawn up lists. Useful information is also to be found in the district *Gazetteers* and the recently conducted *Village Survey Report*.
36. Of the antiquity of the ruling dynasty of Kangra, D. Ibbetson wrote (*Punjab Castes*, p. 160): "There (Kangra Hills) a peaceful race with no ambition ... may have quietly lived for thousands of years, and their royal dynasties may have been already ancient when Moses was leading the Isarelites out of Egypt and the Greeks were steering their swift ships to Troy".
37. See, Alexander Gunningham, *A.S.R.*, V, 1872-73, pp. 147-51, for a brief account of the Katoch family.
38. *Kangra D.G.*, 1904, I, p. 25.
39. Thakur Shamsher Chand of Bijapur, Interviewed.
40. Diwan Sarbdial, *Tawarikh-i Rajgun-i Zillah Kangra*, p. 54.
41. This temple occupies a corner, but is at the highest point in the Tira palace and fort.
42. For these, see, Hutchison & Vogel, *History of the Punjab Hill States*, I, p. 108.
43. Many of these references can be found in Hutchison & Vogel. The priests at the temple have also in their possession numerous early documents.
44. Farishta, *Tarikh*, trans. by Maulvi Fida Ali Talib, pp. 160-62.
45. Abul Fazl, *Ain-i-Akbari*, II, p. 317.
46. *See*, *Kangra*, *D.G.*, 1883-84, I, pp. 255-56, for some details. Also, *A.S.R.*, V, 1872-73, pp. 169-70.
47. Among the travellers who referred to the temple were George Forster, William Moorcroft, Baron Hugel, Vigne and Honigberger.
48. For a full description of the temple, see *Archaeological Survey Reports*, V, pp. 178-82.
49. See, G. Buhler, "An Additional Note on the Baijanth Prasastis", *Epigraphia Indica*, Vol. II. Dr. Buhler had first read the date as AD 804 which was corrected later by Dr. Vogel to AD 1204– in his "Ancient Monuments of Kangra", *Archaeological Survey of India, Annual Report*, 1905-1906, II, p. 16.
50. The temple is said to have been restored, in part, by Maharaja Sansar Chand in the early years of the 19th century.
51. Vogel, *Antiquities*, I, pp. 138-40; Goetz, *Early Wooden Temples of Chamba*, viii; A.S.R., XIV, p. 110.

52. *Chamba State Gazetteer*, 1904, Pt. A, p. 43.
53. *Census of India*, 1961, XX, Village Survey Report of Chhatrarhi.
54. Hutchison and Vogel, I, p. 283, Goetz, *Early Wooden Temples*, p. 33.
55. Vogel, *Antiquities*, pp. 105, 181, 205, 206.
56. Alexander Cunningham, *Coins of Ancient India*, pp. 67-70; S.K. Chakraborty, *A Study of Ancient Indian Numismatics*, p. 164; P.L. Gupta, *Numismatic History of Himachal Pradesh*, p. 14
57. *Revised List of Objects of Archeological Interests in the Panjab*
58. Hutchison and Vogel, I, p. 221.
59. *Ibid.*, II, p. 32.
60. *A.S.I., A.R.*, 1903-04, pp. 261-69; Harcourt, p. 202.
61. Vogel, "A copper plate grant of Bahadur Singh of Kullu", *A.S.I, A.R.*, 1903-04, p. 264; Harcourt, p. 203; Rose, *Glossary*, I, p. 350.
62. Harcourt, pp. 356, 357; Rodgers, *Revised List*, p. 45.
63. Man Mohan, *History of the Mandi State*, p. 11; Hutchison & Vogel, II, p. 379.
64. *Mandi State Gazetteer*, Pt. A, 1904, p. 37.
65. Manmohan, p. 38.
66. *Gazetteer of the Suket State*, 1904, Pt. A, XXIII.
67. Kahn Singh Balauria, p. 57.
68. Kahn Singh, pp. 9, 37, 50, Hutchison & Vogel, II, p. 652; Narsingh Das, pp. 135-36.
69. Vogel, *Indian Serpent Lore*, p. 250; Kahn Singh, pp. 264-65; Hutchison & Vogel, II, pp. 622-23.
70. Narsingh Das, p. 210.
71. The presence of the Devi Temples inside the forts is of special significance because the deity principally worshipped was always close to the residence of the Rajas.
72. Participant observation at Naggar, Kulu, 2002. Also, M. Postel, A. Neven and K. Mankodi, *Antiquities of Himachal*, pp. 179-235.
73. Surat Thakur, *Himachal ki Dev Sanskriti: Mandir Mele va Tyohara*, pp. v, 167.
74. O.C. Handa, "Wooden Temples of the Western Himalaya", in Laxman Thakur (ed.), *Where Mortals and Mountain Gods Meet: Society and Culture in Himachal Pradesh*, pp. 248, 2002.
75. *Ibid.*, p. 254.
76. S.L.Nagar, *The Temples of Himachal Pradesh*, p. 31.
77. Participant observation during field work at the Bir Baradhi temple, Kareri, Kulu. Also, interview with Shri Kundan Lal Sharma, I.I.A.S., Shimla, 2007.
78. Surat Thakur, *op. cit.*, pp. 172-73.
79. Nagar, *op. cit.*, p. 31; Surat Thakur, *op. cit.*, p. 174.
80. B.S. Malhans, "Reconstructing the Himachali Lower temple of Nanahal Devata, (Mahu Nag) at village Kogi according to Traditional Archetype and and Ritual", pp. 256-77, in Laxman Thakur (ed.), *Where Mortals and Mountain Gods Meet*.
81. Surat Thakur, *op. cit.*, pp. 167-70.
82. Clifford Geertz, "Religion as a Cultural System", in *The Interpretation of Cultures*, pp. 63-64, 82.
83. Geertz, *op. cit.*, p. 64.
84. Surat Thakur, *op. cit.*, pp. iii, iv; M.R. Thakur, *Himachal Mein Pujit Devi-Devta*, p. 13.
85. I am grateful to Prof. B.N. Goswamy for providing this insight into sacred numbers.
86. List dated 1961, of *deotas* with *muafi* land-grants was provided by the Sub- divisional office in Kulu. This has been reproduced in the form of an appendix.

87. See, Roy A. Rappaport, "The Sacred in Human Evolution", in *The Annual Review of Ecology and Systematics*", 2, pp. 23-44, 1971, also, Charles Henning, "On the Origin of Religion", pp. 373-82, in *The American Anthropologist*, Vol. xi, Dec. 1898.
88. Henning, *op. cit.*, pp. 373-82.
89. *Ibid.*, pp. 373-82.
90. Participant-observation at Bir-Baradhi temple, Kareri, Kulu, 2002, and personal interviews conducted.
91. Happenings of this nature are referred to repeatedly in the writings of M.R. Thakur, Chandra Shekhar Bebas, Dr. Vidya Chand Thakur, Dr. Sudarshan Vashistha, Dr. Surat Thakur, Dr. Vidya Sharma and Dr. Sita Ram Thakur.
92. Surat Thakur, *op. cit.*, pp. 12-19.
93. *Ibid.*, pp. 12-19.
94. *Ibid.*, pp. 12-19.
95. *Ibid.*, pp. 12-19.
96. *Ibid.*, pp. 12-19.
97. *Souvenir of the Kulu Dussehra*, 2002.
98. Dr. V.C. Thakur, "Maharishi Parashar, Deo Parashar, Kamand", pp. 53-62 in Surat Thakur, *Kulu ki Rishi Parampara.*)
99. M.R. Thakur, *Himachal Mein Pujit Devi-Devta*, pp. 13-55.
100. Chandra Shekhar 'Bebas', *Thara kardu: ek drishtikon*, pp. 18-22 in *Bebas Sahitya Sadhna, Visheshank* of the journal *Srikhanda*, pp. 8-23.
101. Interview with Shri Kamal Kishore, Raghunath Temple, Kulu, 2002
102. Vashhistha, *Kulu Dev-Samagam* p. 53. Virnath is in essence none other than Gohri Deo.
103. M.R. Thakur, "Some Cultural legends and Traditions of the Kulu valley" pp. 321-33, in Laxman Thakur (ed.), *Where Mortals and Mountain Gods Meet.*
104. This tentative conclusion has been arrived at after attempts at plotting the various *deota* temples on maps showing the villages of Kulu. Village locations are based on information provided by the Village Survey of the Census of 1971.
105. Serious work has been done in collating information on the *deotas* by a dedicated group of local scholars who have been already named in end-note 91 above. This endeavour has been spearheaded by the Department of Languages and Culture in Himachal Pradesh based at Shimla.
106. For detailed information on Jamlu see, Narendra Kumar Sharma, *Malana; Puratan Sanskriti ka Prateek*, 1988.
107. The writer has witnessed an endearing emotional out-burst of a devotee against his *deota* Bir-Baradhi in 2002 at Kulu.
108. Surat Thakur, *op. cit.*, pp. 149-64. Also, interview with Shri Kundan Lal Sharma, Shimla.
109. *Ibid.*, pp. 151-52.
110. Participant observation during field work 2002.
111. These rituals were observed personally at the house of a Zaildar at Kareri, Kulu in 2002.
112. Interview with Dr. Sita Ram Thakur and Dr. Vidya Chand Thakur of the Academy of Language and Culture, Shimla
113. Witnessed the preparations for going to the Dussehra, of Devi Tripura Sundari at Naggar. Field-Notes, 2002.
114. This was witnessed in a day- long preparation at the *bhandara* of Hidimba at Manali. The skirt or *Rihr* as it is called, combines in itself beauty, skill and piety, as they say.

115. Participant-Observation at Naggar in 2002.
116. Surat Thakur, *op. cit.*, pp. 180-93.
117. *Ibid.*, pp. 180-93.
118. *Ibid.*, pp. 180-93.
119. *Ibid.*, pp. 132-48.
120. Hutchison and Vogel, Vol. II, pp. 450-62.
121. *Ibid.*, pp. 450-62.
122. Sudha Vasan, "Community Forest Management: Historical Legacy of Himachal Pradesh" pp. 39-51, in Laxman Thakur (ed.), *Where Mortals and Mountain gods Meet*. Also, Alex Anderson, *Report on the demarcation and settlement of Kulu Forests*, rep. in 1975 by the Himachal Pradesh Forest Department, Shimla.
123. Surat Thakur, *op. cit.*, pp. 138-42, 2004. Also, interview with Amar Singh Jamwal, kardar of the *deota*, Bijli Mahadev.
124. *Ibid.*, pp. 138-42. Also interview with the *gur of* Devi Hidimba and Shri Om Prakash, IIAS, Shimla, who is awaiting his *prathistha* as *gur*.
125. *Ibid.*, pp. 138-42.
126. M.R. Thakur, "Some Cultural Legends and Traditions of the Kulu valley", pp. 321-33, in Laxman Thakur, *Where Mortals and Mountain Gods Meet*2.
127. Vidya Sharma, *Kulanta Darpan*, pp. 53-74; Also, Participant observation, during field work, Dussehra, 2002.
128. Chandra Shekhara Bebas, *Bebas Sahitya Sadhana*, Visheshank, pp. 1-2.
129. Vidya Chand Thakur, "Maharishi Prashar-Deo Parashar Kamand", in Surat Thakur (ed.), *Kulu ki Rishi Parampara*, pp. 53-61.
130. W.R. Smith, *Lectures in the religion of the Semites*, pp. 29-33.
131. Sudarshan Vashishtha, *Kulu Dev Samagam*, n.d.

Chapter FOUR

Vaishnavism in Kulu and the Hills

I

THE SITUATION IN GENERAL

Much has been written about the Vaishnava faith in general, and not much can be added here. Different views are held by different scholars. It is widely held, however, that it may have evolved out of a gradual accretion of several different traditions centering around the cults of Vishnu, Narayana, and Krishna-Vasudeva.[1] Set apart by the distinctive doctrine of *bhakti*, often described as an "intense theism marked by a fervent devotion to a personal God", the Vaishnava movement had, by the 12th century, divided itself into four major schools of thought (*sampradayas*), each connected with a separate name: Ramanuja, Madhava, Vishnuswami and Nimbarka. Each *sampradaya* has as the focus of its devotion one or the other incarnation of Vishnu. For example, for the Ramanuja sect, the worship of Srivishnu or the incarnation of Rama was central. The chief inspiration for the spread of the Rama cult in the north came from the teachings of the great Ramananda, the 16th century saint, who is credited with the foundation of the sect of the *Bairagis*. In an environment where the emphasis was more on Krishna worship, Ramananda had given Vaishnavism a new turn.

As in the rest of India, so in these hills, there are some indications or traces of the existence of Vaishnava belief prior to that time, however. The information is thin, and comes essentially from stray images and a few laconic inscriptions, in which the faith of the donors is only peripherally mentioned.[2] Early Vaishnava temples in the hills are extremely rare and those that are extant may not have been dedicated to Vaishnava worship to begin with. In its early phase in the hills, Vaishnavism could to referred to perhaps as Bhagavatism. The names of Vishnu and Krishna occur in many inscriptions, but this appears to be an echo of the situation existing in the plains of North India in corresponding periods of time. From the different hill states some evidence to this effect can be gleaned.

At the Kanhiara slate quarries, 12 miles north of Kangra, are two massive blocks of granite inscribed with characters as old as the 1st century BC[3] mentioning the name of the place as *Krishnayasyaarama*. Scholars are in disagreement over the date being 1st century BC or 1st century AD[4] as also whether this is actually a place with Buddhist affiliations because of the use of the word *aarama*. The name Kanhiara however may well have been derived from *Kahn* or *Kanhayia*, one of the names by which Krishna is known. Inside the Kangra fort also there is a much-damaged inscription, believed to be of a 6th century date. The inscription begins with an invocation to Vishnu.[5]

One of the most important but little known early temples is the unfinished rock-cut temple at Masrur, close to Haripur in Guler. In popular parlance it is referred to as a *thakurdwara*, a name which in the hills is clearly reserved for shrines of Vishnu or one of his incarnations. Ascribed to the 8th century AD on grounds of style, there is some difference of opinion among scholars about it being a Vaishnava shrine. There is however reasonable indication that if Vishnu was not the principal deity here, there was at least one image of his in the unfinished temple.[6]

Following his work on the Masrur temple, Michael Meister drew up a diagram of the iconography at Masrur in which figure the images of Vaikuntha Vishnu, Vishnu, and Surya, apart from Vaishnavi in a group of Shaktis.[7]

In the neighbouring region of Chamba, several traces of the early existence of Vaishnavism are to be found.[8] The names of Vishnu and Krishna occur in many inscriptions. The Suryavamshi Rajas of Chamba traced their descent from, and related their genealogies back to, Vishnu or Narayana. In their domains, it was during the late Gupta age that the worship of Vishnu seems to have found its feet. For a long period of time the hills had maintained contacts with Kashmir as also with the plains, but the Bhagavatism of the Chamba royal dynasty is likely to have been an importation from the plains, according to Goetz.[9] The great 8th century temples of the reign of Meruvaraman at Brahmaur are associated for the most part with the worship of the Devi or Shiva, but even here, in the temple which houses the great image of Lakshanadevi, a representation of Vishnu in his multiple-headed form - Vaikunthanatha – can be seen in relief on one of the gables.[10] The most important of Vaishnava images at Brahmaur – a magnificent rendering in brass – however, is that of Narasimha which is generally dated to the end of the 8th century.[11] In Chamba again, in the town itself, there is the splendid image known as 'Hari Rai' – Vishnu Chaturanana, in classical terms – which is dateable to the 9th century. The most important temple, however, "the glory of Chamba", is the temple of Lakshmi Narayana which goes back to the period of Raja Sahilavarman and his sons, and is generally placed in the period between the mid-10th and mid-11th centuries. From the 12th to the 14th century onwards, there are repeated references to the rulers of Chamba endowing land "for pleasing Lord Krishna".[12] Inscriptions in which the powers of the rulers are compared to those of Rama, Parashurama and Balarama[13] make strong statements about the presence of Vaishnavism in the area and go right into the 17th century with almost unbroken continuity. Gifts of land keep being recorded.[14]

To the situation in Kulu, one will turn later in some detail, but early traces of Vaishnavism in that region need to be spoken of here. There is evidence – archaeological and sculptural – that points not only to an awareness of the Vaishnava faith but active presence of it. One of the "largest among the few surviving nagara type temples in the entire valley", as Ohri puts it,[15] is at Bajaura, a few kilometers short of Kulu on the main road to it from Mandi. Views about its date vary but it is no later than the first half of the ninth century. Normally the temple is associated with the worship of Shiva – it bears the name Basheshar or Vishweshwar Mahadeva – but both on it and a nearby place called Hat one encounters Vaishnava images. The temple/s that once stood at Hat are now in ruins, but some images have survived, including those of Chakrapurusha – personification of one of the ayudhas borne by Vishnu, the chakra or discus – carved in a style that bears the clear imprint of late Gupta work. Two other images seen at Bajaura and Hat are "almost of life size in dimensions" and both are representation of different aspects of Vishnu associated with the concept of Vaikuntha. An isolated figure of Garuda, Vishnu's bird-vehicle, found at some place near by, now also lies in the temple at Bajaura.To the Vaishnava group of deities belongs Surya, and at Hat again a large image of Surya, carved in high relief, was found. The most important of discoveries relating to the worship of Surya in the Kulu valley was however that of six large, life-size sculptures in wood that Helene Diserens found at Gajan not far from Jagatsukh and Naggar, in a small hill-type temple generally known as Docha Mocha.[16] Related clearly to the late Gupta style as practiced in the plains, the sculptures are remarkable and are generally dated now to between the 6th and 7th centuries. While four of the figures are female and now referred to as *Yakshis*, from the elegant manners in which they stand, the main figure in the group of six is undoubtedly that of Surya. The Gajan sculptures remain the subject of lively discussion among scholars[17] but that they point to Surya worship at an early point of time in the region is not questioned. At Jagatsukh again, in a stone temple, the figure of Surya in high relief is seen in a niche along with those of Vishnu and Brahma. At Nirmand, while the famous copper-plate grant refers to Shiva, one finds the presence of Surya yet again. At a place close to Nirmand, from the ruins of a temple, were found three sculptures, all representing Vishnu. Clearly Vaishnavism had had an early foothold in the Kulu area even if it was not the principal faith of the people there.

What one speaks of however in the context of the Dussehra of Kulu, and the coming of a fresh Vaishnava wave in the hills, belongs to a later date. In the northern and eastern plains Vaishnavism, with its emphasis on *bhakti*, had started gathering fresh force from the 15th century onwards, but it took a little more time before it started making its presence felt in the hills. One is reminded of the time-gap theory that Goetz held: that whatever happened in the plains also happened in the hills, only a little later.[18] In any case, echoes of the increasingly powerful and popular movement of Vaishnavism in the northern plains began being heard in the hills, it seems, from the 16th century onwards.

The channels, through which these influences travelled, were many, as has been said before. An important route of dissemination of ideas was the institution of pilgrimage. To recall, pilgrimages from the hills to sacred centres like Haridwar, Kurukshetra and Gaya were not uncommon throughout these periods of history.[19] Pilgrims came long distances from the plains to temples in the hills also, like to the Vajreshwari Devi at Kangra and the shrine at Jawalamukhi[20] establishing an active channel of contact with the outside world.

Specific religious impulses must have travelled to the hills in other ways, too. During the Mughal period, the hill Rajas maintained an active contact with the Imperial court, where hill princes were kept as hostages at the Mughal court.[21] Hill Rajas were also sent for by the Mughal overlords to be present at Agra, Delhi and Lahore from time to time.[22] Pahari Rajas who served thus in Rajasthan, in the North-West, in Garhwal or in Bengal, are likely to have exposed themselves to many influences. It is also not unlikely that during these visits to other parts of India, the Rajas brought back with them people of talent, known skill, or devotion. There is evidence, for example, of a family of Gujerati *tarkhans* in Chamba[23] and another family of Gujerati *Pandits* at Basohli.[24] Then again, by going back occasionally to places of their origin, like Rajasthan, Bengal or Bihar, the hill Rajas – while renewing contacts which were several hundred years old – must undoubtedly have also picked up ideas, and religious trends prevalent in those areas.

Seen in this light, the hills do not appear to be in the kind of isolation which has been claimed or imagined for them. People from the plains might have been escaping into the hills,[25] but the hills were neither unapproachable nor closed to new ideas brought in by those who sought refuge there.

Vaishnavism appears, thus, to have travelled, almost unnoticed sometimes, through the agency of Rajas on political missions, devout pilgrims, or through the conscious efforts of proselytizing missionaries spreading the sacred word of their faith. The Vaishnavism of the Ramanandi Bairagis, a proselytizing cult,[26] it turned out, came to play a major role in the hills, especially in Kulu, for their efforts were resolute and very conscious.

From Gurdaspur, lying at the foot of the hills, comes the evidence of a number of religious centres established by the Ramanandis obviously with a view to turning them into bases for further operations into the hill areas.[27] Flourishing even today, the most important of these centres is the Vaishnava *math* of Pindori, eight miles east of Gurdaspur town.[28] A large number of local traditions are preserved about Bhagwanji, the founder of this shrine, who is said to have met at Galta in Rajasthan, the Vaishnava missionary, Krishnadas Payahari ("one who survives on water or milk"), who figures prominently in the story of the spread of Vaishnavism in Kulu. After founding his *math* at Pindori, Bhagwanji converted many people but the convert who turned out to be the most important for the future development of Vaishnavism in these parts was Narayanji, his foremost disciple. Narayanji came to be widely known during his lifetime and acquired fame for his *bhakti* among the populace of these parts. Preserved at the Bathu *math* in the adjoining Guler region is a bound volume containing a selection of his compositions, which are of some literary merit. Many of these compositions are in intense praise of the Vaishnava faith.[29] Along with the Vaishnava *math* that he established at Damtal close to Pathankot, the activities of the maths at Pindori and Bathu were so organized as to materially influence the development and spread of Vaishnavism in the hills.

What is of great interest, in the context of Vaishnavism, is the role that several Rajas of hill states played in the spread of the faith in the region. Commenting on the role of the Rajas, Vogel observed: "... at least I found this with regard to the Kangra and Nurpur Rajas, who may be considered to be the most important ones. It seems that while the more popular religion was the grosser Shaivism, the Rajas took to the higher form of Vishnuism. This seems to be the most obvious explanation, though it is quite possible that there were other causes and the Rajas perhaps introduced Vishnuism from the Plains".[30] Not only did some of the Rajas embrace Vaishnavism themselves, but they founded temples and dedicated them to one or the other *avatara* of Vishnu. At Nurpur, the popular tradition is that it was Raja Jagat Singh who introduced Vaishnavism in the state. This is not entirely accurate because the temple built by Raja Basu, his predecessor, inside the Nurpur Fort, also has undeniable Vaishnava associations. Carvings on the surviving plinth depict Vaishnava themes and stylistically the temple is related to the Govind Dev Temple of Mathura.[31] But it is Raja Jagat Singh, Raja Basu's son, who is most commonly associated with Vaishnavaism in the popular mind. The personal faith of Raja Jagat Singh is referred to by his poet, the bard Gambhir Rai[32] whose *Rhapsodies* were sung till the late sixties of the 20th century, by Banka Rai, one of his descendents at Nurpur.[33] Referring to Jagat Singh, Gambhir Rai mentions him as having strong faith in Vishnu. Jagat Singh is also credited with having brought back the idol of Krishna in black marble, known as Brij Raj Swami, from Chittor and installed it in another temple inside the fort.[34]

The state of Guler is also associated with Vaishnavaism as is evidenced by the presence of the Vaishnava *math* at Bathu. Uttam Kavi, the chronicler of the Guler state in his history, *Diliparanjani*,[35] refers to Raja Man Singh, an ancestor of his patron, Raja Dalip Singh, as having brought back from Bangahal the idol of *Rai Dalip* whom he refers to as *Thakur*, clearly indicating the Vaishnava affilation of the idol. During the reign of Bikram Singh of Guler, his mother Kalyan Dei built the temple of Kalyan

Rai within which is housed the idol of *Ashtabhuji Narayan*. This fact is also celebrated in local folk songs.[36] Another Vaishnava temple, with a 17th century inscription dedicated to Gopal Rai, stands at Haripur near Guler.[37]

A similar trend towards Vaishnava *bhakti* is witnessed in Kangra. The Sita Ram temple at Bijapur was founded by Raja Bijai Ram Chand in the middle of the 17th century. The location of this premier Vaishnava temple in a comparatively unimportant area of the Kangra state may have been caused by the state of exile that the Katoch rulers found themselves in after the coming into power of the Mughals.[38]

Moving to the state of Chamba, the Vaishnava affiliations of the Chamba rulers have already been noticed. Raja Prithvi Singh of Chamba, in the mid 17th century, is said to have brought back from Delhi, an image of Raghuvira, i.e. Rama, and installed it inside the Chamba place. This became the family idol of the Chamba royal family.[39]

From Sirmur comes the legend of the establishment of the capital of the Sirmur state with the advice and the blessings of Baba Banwari Das Bairagi early in the 17th century. Maharaja Karam Prakash installed an image of Jagannath in a temple after he had a dream (*suninder)* instructing him about the presence of the idol buried beneath the ground.[40]

The conclusion to be drawn from this scattered but related evidence is fairly obvious. From the manner in which many Rajas of the hills – from Basu of Nurpur to Man singh of Guler, from Bijai Ram Chand of Kangra to Jagat Singh of Kulu, (as will be seen later), from Suraj Sen of Mandi to Karam Prakash of Sirmur – responded, one can say that the true beginnings of this fresh wave of Vaishnavism can be placed between AD 1625 and 1660.

The arrival of this wave of Vaishnavism in the hills was one matter; its spread an entirely different one. Arriving in an area strong in its faith in the cults of Shiva, the Devi and numerous local gods and godlings, Vaishnavism, from the very beginning, had to proceed with tact and circumspection. In a sense the faith had to fight its way through the resistance of a people strongly entrenched in their earlier, or local, religious affiliations. The Vaishnava Bairagis probably had to grope to find ways in which their faith could win the affection of the people of the hills, and hold their attention. It was not an easy task, for the possibilities of conflict were many.

What happened in the hills was probably not very different from what had happened elsewhere and at several periods of time in India. The emergence of the orthodox Hindu faith itself had not been a simple matter. Numerous elements, diverse and conflicting, had gone into the making of what is generally designated as Hindusim.[41] For one thing, several elements of an animistic or demonic kind which prevailed earlier had to be absorbed. C.F. Oldham has, in a very perceptive note,[42] described this process of the absorption of the non Brahmanic cults into orthodox Hinduism in the hill areas. As a result of a prolonged contact, both sides had to yield ground to an extent, and what came into being was an amalgam of opposites.

Even in the plains Vaishnavaism had also aroused strong reactions. With the Shaivas being strongly entrenched, the Vaishnavas had to wage many a grim battle to gain ground. Numerous instances are on record pointing to the strong animosity between the two sects. 'When the Faqirs meet with Baragis, ... they fight desperately,' wrote the traveller Careri.[43] There are references to militant Bairagis in Rajasthan, and later also in Kulu.[44] Jadunath Sarkar also records a decisive victory won by the Naga Sanyasis over Bairagi ascetics at Haridwar in AD 1266.[45]

Fortunately, the conflict between the Shaivas and the Vaishnavas seems not to have been as sharp in the hills. Rose states that the differences between the two sects in the Punjab, were "much less marked" than elsewhere in the United Provinces and Rajasthan, "where the mutual jealousy of the two sects is often very acute".[46] The strong feeling of animosity between the Shaivas and the Vaishnavas in the south is also well-known. In the hills, however, there appears to have been no armed conflict or sanguine hostility. There are clear indications, at the same time, that somewhere deep beneath the surface Vaishnavism had to struggle long and hard to make headway in these parts. The conversion of the Rajas or the importation of small groups of Pandits from Banaras or Gaya was not sufficient guarantee that the people would easily take to the new faith. One has to read between the lines for ascertaining the situation as it might have been in the hills. Legends told about some temples are, however, of great help in this regard.[47] Many of these stories, however quaint and fanciful, often conceal a hard core of facts. There is, for example, the legend about the hot springs of Manikaran in Kulu. The story is that the Goddess Parvati, while bathing with Mahadeva in the river, had taken off her jewelled earrings (*manikarnika*) and placed them on the bank. When she came out, she found that these had been stolen and carried off to *patala*, the regions below the earth, by the serpent, Sesha. This made Mahadeva very angry and before his anger could take a disastrous turn for the whole world, the Gods intervened and pressed the Naga to restore his plunder. He refused, claiming the earrings as his own property, but even as he snorted with indignation, the earrings, which were the subject of the dispute, were released with a tremendous force from his nostrils in which they had been hidden and flew back to the goddess, Parvati, to whom they belonged. It is locally narrated that through the opening made by the hot passage of the jewels to the surface of the earth, boiling water came out, and has continued to flow in Manikaran ever since. It is interesting that the dispute here is between Parvati who is associated with Shiva, and Shesha who is always associated with Vishnu. One is able to detect in this legend an oblique reference to a dispute or a conflict between the Shaiva and Vaishnava faiths.

The Lakshmi Narayana temple at Chamba, one of the early Vaishnava temples in the hills as has been seen, must also have excited varying responses in the popular mind. Vigne, the 19th century traveller, cites a tradition[48] heard by him at Chamba about how the new god who had arrived in Chamba made himself "most obnoxious", by "obtruding into the Chamba Zenanas". The husbands of the town sought the help of a saint who helped them by enlisting the aid of Garuda who, according to the story, let out a cry to warn the ladies when the idol next came out of his shrine. At this the God, it is said, pierced Garuda with an arrow. This strange legend contains a veiled reference possibly to the initial prejudice against the newly arrived Vaishnava idol in Chamba and also to the supposed moral laxity often associated with the new cult.

The presence of recurrent and subterranean conflicts and tensions are mirrored also in a group of paintings which take the form of caricatures of Vaishnava saints and devotees.[49] The depiction of these saints and devotees in undignified and compromising positions, with misshapen bodies, vacant expressions, meaningless gestures, leave no doubt that the intention of the artist in making them was caustic. The caricatures were undoubtedly intended to be pictorial comments on men of religion whom the painter appears to have regarded as charlatans deserving of derision rather than reverence.

Keeping in view some ascertainable facts, it appears that Vaishnavism had to make numerous concessions in the hills before it could gain ground. One major concession was the permission to eat flesh. In the plains, in the popular mind Vaishnavism is quite distinctly associated with vegetarianism.[50] It is inconceivable that a devout Vaishnava should be permitted by his faith to consume flesh of any kind. In fact, in the plains, this appears to be the chief distinction between a Shaiva and a Vaishnava.[51] 'He who eats meat is not a Vaishnava.' This is clearly not so in the hills. In general, the hill people were more enthusiastically the followers of Shiva or the Devi than of Vishnu because there was a great deal of liberty within those cults. One could consume, if one liked, meat, fish and wine, things that were normally taboo in the Vaishnava faith. For a Rajput, who could not do without these things, it was more convenient, in a sense, or more natural, to be a devotee of Shiva or the Devi.

Local customs and folklore mask as well as seek to explain the confusion arising out of the processes of synthesis and adaptation that are at work constantly in society. There is the fascinating, but from the point of view of Vaishnaism in Kulu, an all-important, or at least all-revealing, example of a classical Vaishnava figure coalescing with a local god. This is the case of Narsingh, the fourth incarnation of Vishnu, and Narsingh, the local *deota* who belongs to the Bir category,[52] something which will be treated in some detail later. One has to recall in this connection that Narsingh, as Vishnu's incarnation, was not unknown in the hills, as evidenced at least by the existence of the great Narsingh image in Chamba.[53] Narsingh *Bir* on the other hand bears a wholly local character.[54] But one sees that in a dramatic performance like the one staged at the Brij Raj Swami temple, clearly a Krishna-ite shrine, at Nurpur,[55] the viewers or devotees would not be able to tell the difference. The performance consists of a little niche behind two pillars being covered with painted paper and behind it a priest sitting, dressed up as Narsingh; when the devotees are gathered, at an appropriate moment, the priest who is dressed as Narsingh, the man-lion, pierces the paper screen and emerges with a roar. Pieces of the paper thus pierced by the "emergence" of the "deity" are then taken by women to their own homes, as they would a token of a local *deota's* grace. The belief is that this token is auspicious and would lead to the birth of a son in the family.

Things happen in a like fashion at Chanehni, located within the western group of states,[56] where there is a temple called Sudh Mahadev. The place is sacred to Shiva because it is believed that it is here that Himachal gave his daughter Parvati in marriage to Shiva. At this place there is an enormous *trisula* or trident of Shiva, which is struck into the ground opposite a tank. The story about the *trisula,* in fact about the shrine, is interesting. It is said that Raja Ramchand of Chanehni once made an attempt to measure the extent of the depth of the trident into the earth. He ordered digging operations to be carried out so that the *trisula* could be taken out and measured, but its lower end could not be reached even after digging had been going on for two days and nights. That night, it is said, Raja Ramchand had a dream that on the next morning a small piece of iron from the top of the *trisula* would fall of itself. Out of this, it was stated in the dream, would emerge an image of Shaligram, the ammonite stone emblem of Vishnu. The Raja was exhorted in the dream by the deity to worship this *murti* and to use the iron for forging a sword. In the dream the Raja also "heard" that at the bottom of the pit would be found a Shiva-linga, which should also be installed at that place. The next morning events transpired exactly as they had been dreamt of by the Raja. The Raja installed the Shiva-linga in a temple and took the Shaligram stone with him to his palace in Chanehni for worship by his family. This tradition is widely believed in the Chanehni area and in it we have once again a story which only barely manages to cloak the basic fact that the Raja is here made to divide his attention equally between Shaiva and Vaishnava beliefs.

Suggestive of fusion between Vaishnava and Shakta beliefs, likewise, is the uncommon manifestation of the goddess Vaishno Devi, who is located in the Jammu hills and is widely worshipped in the northern plains. Clearly, the name itself – Vaishno Devi – suggests that Vaishnava and Shakta elements have come together in the persona of the goddess.

By the 17th century, it appears, the new wave of Vaishnavism had come to acquire a significant presence in the hills. But this was not to the exclusion of other beliefs. Very rarely does one come upon an emphatic statement about a Raja, a Rani, or a commoner, paying attention exclusively to a Vaishnava deity. Clearly, there was adherence to Vaishnavism on the part of the Rajas who introduced it in their domains, or on the part of the Pandits who came from the plains. But other faiths continued to flourish at the same time.

For understanding the situation as far as faiths in the hills goes, it is of use to take into account some sections of society and try to examine their attitudes. Beginning with the Raja, the pivot of hill society and the complete master of the state, one can see that at times he gave direction to the development of religion within his domains, for his subjects looked up to him. However even in the case of the Rajas, we do not get any sharply defined position as far as their personal faith is concerned. Since the evidence is not conclusive, for understanding the situation one might with profit turn to a different source: the paintings commissioned and executed in these hill states under the patronage of the Rajas. But here again no clear picture emerges

Looking at the body of royal portraits done in the hill states we can take the example of Raja Kirpal Pal of Basohli, A reference to the Vaishnava faith of Kripal Pal occurs in the colophon of a book written for him, even though no Vaishnava idol or temple is associated with his name at Basohli. It has been suggested that Kripal Pal was urged by his faith to express his feelings for Krishna "in a novel and personal manner".[57] As a result, not only a new style of painting but a special choice of subject matter was introduced. Isolated pictures from Basohli apart, one of the principal set of illustrations produced either under or for Kirpal Pal was that of Bhanudatta's *Rasamanjari*. In W.G. Archer's opinion, Raja Kripal Pal "had directed his artists to do for Sanskrit what Keshavdas had done for Hindi poetry, to celebrate Krishna as the most varied and skilled of lovers and, as a corollary, show him in a whole variety of romantic and poetic situations". One would expect Kripal Pal thus to have been a fervent Vaishnava in terms of his personal faith. Yet, clearly, a portrait of Kripal Pal in the Chandigarh Museum[58] shows him wearing a prominent Shaiva *tilak* mark on his forehead. Whatever be the occasion for this *tilak*, it must have been sufficiently strongly associated with him for the artist to paint the Raja wearing it. In Kripal Pal's mind, there seems to have been no special ardour for Vaishnavism. He may have brought two or three faiths together in his own person, but to describe Kripal Pal emphatically as a Vaishnava would be inaccurate and an over-simplification.

The rulers coming after Kripal Pal at Basohli are also portrayed wearing prominent Shaiva *tilaks*.[59] On the face of it, it appears that adherence to Shaivism was strong among the Basohli Rajas even after "popular Vaishnavism" had come to the hills. Nilakantha Mahadev,[60] the presiding deity of Basohli, appears to have commanded powerful allegiance. The artists, well aware of this, show very accurately the Rajas wearing the Shaiva *tripundra tilaks*.

Another interesting case is that of Sansar Chand of Kangra. Regarding Sansar Chand's personal inclination towards religion, Moorcroft documents the recitation of 'Brijbhakha' songs at his court.[61] From the presence of paintings dealing with themes of the *Mahabharata*, which were done for him as a patron, as Moorcroft records, one can infer that Sansar Chand took a fair interest in Vaishnavism. It has been stated in fact that Sansar Chand was "not only successful in politics and war but from his early manhood was devout to Krishna as lover God..... Under Sansar Chand's stimulus artists began to portray every situation involving Krishna the cowherd".[62] In the light of this, one would expect the faith of Sansar Chand to have been ardently Vaishnava, and directed towards the worship of Krishna. But evidence from other sources indicates otherwise. At Tira, where Sansar Chand lived after losing his power to the Sikhs, there was a temple of Gauri Shankar dedicated to Shiva located inside the fort.[63] The standing *ashtadhatu* image of Shiva in the temple is supposed to have been cast in fact in the Raja's mould.[64] The only other temple inside the fort is a temple of the Devi.[65] Apart from these two, there is a tiny little shrine devoted to Rama, but this is outside the fort and is said to have been built to commemorate a Brahmin who committed suicide at this particular spot.[66] At Sujanpur, below Tira, the principal temple is that of Narbadeshwar, once again dedicated to Shiva. There are many temples at Sujanpur but this is the only one which has frescoes on its walls. The construction of this temple is ascribed to "the Suketi Rani" of Sansar Chand,[67] but it is the Maharaja himself who seems to have been actively associated with it. There is, in one of the panels of frescoes inside the temple, the figure of Sansar Chand himself.

Sansar Chand's adhesion to the worship of the Devi also does not seem to have diminished at all. Like all Katoches before him, who revere the Devi as their *Kulaj* or family deity, he continued to worship and pay homage to her. In one of his engagements with the Gurkhas, Sansar Chand was required by them to take an oath, at the shrine of the Devi at Malkara as a proof of his sincerity.[68] A solemn oath is taken of a deity whom one holds in the highest esteem. Thus, when a pact had to be sealed between Sansar Chand and Ranjit Singh, it was over the sacred fire at the shrine of the goddess Jwalamukh that the parties swore. It becomes clear, thus, that in his personal faith Sansar Chand brought, within his ambit, faith, alike in the Devi, Shiva and Krishna. There is no exclusion in his personal system of belief. What is being argued here is not that Sansar Chand did not take Krishna into account. Some grants of land by him are described in the documents as *Krishna-arpana*, dedicated to Krishna.[69] Other instances of Sansar Chand's Vaishnava affiliations are the construction of the Murli Manohar temple at Sujanpur by one of his Ranis.[70] There are paintings which show him celebrating the birthday festival of Krishna, the Janmashtmi. This evidence is also not without significance, but it leaves the picture of his faith not particularly clear.

The son and successor of Sansar Chand, Aniruddha Chand, is also seen in paintings as celebrating a Vaishnava festival.[71] At the same time, we have an account in some detail referring to his last years spent near Haridwar[72] where he died amidst the chanting of Vedic hymns and Shaiva recitations, wearing *rudraksha* beads associated with the worship of Shiva. All this leaves no doubt about the Shaiva leanings of Aniruddha Chand.

The situation that we have seen regarding the faith of the Rajas of Kangra is quite typical of the situation concerning the faith of the Rajas of other principalities. Belief in the temple of Lakshmi Narayana at Chamba was considerable. "Such is the reverence in which the idol is held," wrote Vigne, "that I have been present when the Raja and every person in his court ceased their conversation, arose from their seats, and muttered a prayer, whilst the bell was ringing at the shrine..."[73] There is other evidence that the idol of Lakshmi Narayana was held in high esteem. The 16th century Chamba plate of Pratap Singh records the co-existence of different faiths. This plate while recording a gift of land mentions the Raja as being equal in powers to "Rama, Parashurama and Balarama" and in the same breath mentions him as one "who has his heart entirely devoted to worshipping Shiva".[74] The situation becomes even more confused because the grant of land is made "out of devotion to the illustrious Ramachandra". Of special significance is the faith of Prithvi Singh of Chamba who is said to have introduced popular Vaishnavism at this stage of Chamba history by having brought the idol of Raghuvira from Delhi. From his reign itself there is a plate from Mindhal with an inscription, which belongs to a Devi temple – that of the goddess Chamunda.[75] There is again the temple of Mulasan Devi with its quaint wood carvings, which bear an inscription of Raja Prithvi Singh of the year 1661.[76] Quite clearly, while Prithvi Singh was paying public homage to the idol of Raghuvira, he was also endowing Devi temples all over the kingdom over which he presided. The faith of Raj Singh of Chamba is reflected in the treaty which he signed between himself and Sansar Chand in the year 1788.[77] The treaty begins with an invocation to Rama. Yet, when Raj Singh was killed, in his memory was raised at Nerti a temple in which is installed a Shiva-linga.[78] Raj Singh's personal faith is underlined and stated, in the treaty, between him and Sansar Chand again, in which it is said that "whosoever violates this agreement will be answerable to the holy Lakshmi Narayana, Manimahesh, the holy Goddesses Chamunda and Champavati".[79] Here, once again, we have the bringing in of all the three major deities who were receiving worship in the hills: Vishnu, Shiva and the Devi.

In Mandi, the position is again somewhat similar, even though here the balance is tilted more or less against Vaishnavism despite its introduction by Raja Suraj Sen in the middle of the 17th century. A portrait of Suraj Sen, contrary to expectations, however, shows him as wearing a Shakta *tilak* mark on his forehead.[80] It is also significant that the name of Suraj Sen is associated with the foundation of the Naina Devi temple.[81] But the most interesting evidence comes from the reign of Raja Shyam Sen who succeeded him. Shyam Sen is supposed to have been a devout Vaishnava, having undertaken pilgrimages to Jagannath and Banaras. And yet, when he was proceeding for a battle, he vowed to the Goddess Kali that if he triumphed, he would build a magnificent temple and dedicate it to her.[82] The Raja was successful and the temple, which is now called the temple of Shyama Kali on the Tarna hill above Mandi town, bears testimony to his gratitude to the Goddess for having conferred upon him the boon of victory.

From Mandi we have some other interesting evidence also. The fact that one Raja adopts Vaishnavism, or tries to promote it, was no guarantee that his successor would take similar interest in the Vaishnava faith. This results in a quick shifting of allegiance between Vaishnavism and non-Vaishnava faiths in the family. Suraj Sen, "the Vaishnava", is followed by Shyam Sen who is only partially a Vaishnava devotee and raises a temple to the Devi. He is followed by Gaur Sen who is a Vaishnava.[83] Then follows Sidh Sen who was a great devotee of Shiva and a resolute Tantric. A large number of paintings show him wearing a prominent Tantric *tilak* mark.[84] There are indications, occasionally, of his having taken interest in other faiths also. The temples of Sidh Ganesha and Sidha Bhadra which he founded show his adherence to the worship of Shiva. Sidh Bhairava is yet another temple that is connected with his name[85] but no Vaishnava shrine is ascribed to him. In a fanciful legend, it is said that when Raja Sidh Sen was victorious in a great battle, he brought the heads of 380 men and made a necklace for the idol of Bhutnath Mahadeva out of these.[86] Sidh Sen was convinced that whenever he raised a new temple, he achieved a great victory on the field of battle. With the powers, as is believed, of flying through the air, which his magical *gutka* conferred upon him, Sidh Sen seems to have leaned quite heavily upon his tantric faith and powers in ruling his state.

There are instructive instances from other States. When we hear of a Raja of Sirmur paying equal homage to the Devi on the one hand and the Jagannath temple on the other,[87] or Jagat Singh of Nurpur being described as a great devotee of the goddess Bhawani who 'resided in his steel blade', and at the same time was an ardent Vaishnava,[88] we are reminded quite sharply of the fact that the faith of the Rajas was often composite. They did not always favour one sect at the cost of another; on the other hand, they often tried to bring different strands together. This could be done either through their own personal faith or in the manner in which they distributed their patronage to various temples or religious establishments.

One other possible index of the extent to which Vaishnavism permeated society in the hills could be the faith practiced by the *purohits* or priests, especially those who were attached to the royal family. This, because the *purohits*, especially those who were attached to the royal family, wielded a tremendous influence over the royal household. This was especially true about their influence on the women of the royal households who were often of deeply religious bents of mind. The *purohits* also presided invariably over religious ceremonies, like *yajnas, pujas,* or *prastishthas*. Hence, the faith of the *purohits*, wherever we can ascertain it, assumes importance.

While it is not so easy to ascertain this faith, we do occasionally get clear statements like "The *purohits* of the ruling family (of Mandi) are followers of this Goddess (Bagulamukhi)".[89] Bagulamukhi Devi is a Tantric deity widely worshipped throughout the hills, and there is clear assertion in the statement that she was the deity of the *purohits* of the Rajas of Mandi. One can see through this the connection between the Tantric *tilak* mark on the foreheads of Mandi rulers and the *purohits* of the royal family, both being Tantric devotees themselves.

From Sirmur we have another indication of the faith of the Raja's *purohits*. Kunwar Ranzor Singh, who wrote the vernacular history of the Sirmur state, has quite sharply contested the statements of Balgobind Kaistha, who wrote a history in

English of the reign of Raja Shamsher Prakash of Sirmur. The Kunwar, scion of the royal family of Sirmur, dismisses Balgobind Kaistha as irresponsible and ill informed, because he was after all, we are told, "a mere clerk". This angry response was to Kaistha's statement at one point in his work that the Rajguru of Sirmur was the mahant of the Jagannath temple. This would make him a Vaishnava. This was questioned so firmly by Kanwar Ranzor Singh.[90] because "the Rajas are Shaiva and the mahant of Jagannath is a Bairagi". On this point one is inclined to believe Ranzor Singh because he, as a member of the royal family himself, must have been familiar with the situation personally.

The faith of the *Rajpurohits* attached to the royal family can also be assessed by looking at the range and the religious content of the collections of manuscripts, which were built up over several generations, in their families. From this point of view one of the most interesting collections was once with Pandit Bhu Dev Shastri whose ancestors were the *purohits* of Maharaja Sansar Chand and to one of whose ancestors, the lands attached to the Gauri Shankar temple were gifted by the Maharaja.[91] Among these manuscripts were a *Bhasha* of the 10th *Skanda* of the *Bhagavata Purana*, a *tika* of the *Vishnusmriti*, the *Devi Mahatamya*, a *Nitya Puja Paddhati, a Trailokya Mangal Kavacha*, a *Sahasranamstotra*, a *Rudrakshamala Sanskar vidhi* and a large number of *mantras*. The *Medini Kosa*, the *Vishvakosha* the *Amarkosha*, a text on *Jyotisha*, and a *Svapna Tattva Prakash* were among some of the other texts in the possession of the family. The co-existence of many beliefs is clearly reflected in the range of these manuscripts, which range from the Vaishnava to the Shaiva and Tantric.

The *purohits* of the Katoch family of Bijapur, to which one of the Maharanis of Kashmir belonged, residing now in a small village, Alhilal near Palampur, had with them a collection of manuscripts in which could be found, among others, the text of the *Rudrayamala tantra*, the *tika* of *Ghatkhappar* written by Tara Chand, a Tantric manuscript with several *mantras* for the Devi, the *Tara Sahasranam*, the *Narsingh Kavacha*, the *Hanumat Kavacha* and the *Mahakali stotra.*

Interestingly enough, even in the collection of manuscripts with the Vaishnava *mahants* of Bathu or Damtal, there are texts which are non-Vaishnava. There was, thus, with the *mahant* of Bathu, on the one hand, a text of the *Samasta Purana*,[92] which ends with the praise of the Jagannath deity, and at the same time a text containing the sayings of Guru Gorakhnath, one of the greatest Shaiva ascetics who ever lived. At the same time, the now dispersed Bathu book, which contains Narayanji's compositions, has on one of the leaves, apparently in a late hand, a hymn in praise of the Sindu Bir, a *deota* popular in the hills.

At another level, which might have been revealing, there is very little evidence available of the personal faith of the artists who painted for their royal patrons in the hills. There is an interesting painting of Mola Ram of Garhwal seen worshipping the goddess Bhuvaneshwari.[93] The evidence of painting is of great importance, because the artist is seen here quite clearly in immediate relationship with the deity whom he adored. One of the descendants of Mola Ram, Jwala Ram by name, is said to have been a Shaiva by belief, and a follower of Gorakhnath. Artists belonging to the famed family of Pandit Seu and Nainsukh of Guler speak of how close their ancestors were to the Devi who always guided their hand on paper. And yet, quite clearly, the artist of the hills must not only have had thorough familiarity with Vaishnava themes, but also a feeling for them. For without these feelings the great series of paintings they turned out – the *Bhagavata Purana*, the *Gita Govinda*, and the like – would not have come about.

In sum it can be stated perhaps that the genius of the common people of the hills lay in their ability to reconcile different faiths within their personal belief. When Kunal Chakrabarti speaks of "the cultural matrix that governed the relationship of reciprocity, contestation and domination... not always being sharply defined",[94] he might as well be speaking of the situation obtaining in the hills in general. Apart from the fact that the Hindu mind is generally eclectic, a working arrangement, an easy balance, seems to have been struck in the hills, which left room for all faiths and all sects, and made it possible for people to bring in more and more deities into their belief-system without pushing any one of them out. The situation continues to be very much the same to this day. In the *Village Survey Reports*[95] that were prepared out at the time of the Census of India of 1961, there are profuse details about the religion of the people. And as far as the hills are concerned, throughout these surveys is reflected a faith which is all-absorbing. Again and again one comes upon the names of Vishnu, Rama, Krishna, Shiva and the Devi, the Naga, the Bir, and the Siddhas as objects of veneration. And it is not as if a certain section of society resorted to some gods while others believed in other deities. All people seem to have visited different temples and paid equal homage. The *ishta* of a family is a personal matter but in their public faith, in the religion that they outwardly and generally profess, there is virtually no exclusion of any deities.

The arrangement worked out by the people is reflected very neatly in the religious practices of the Ghirths, a large group in the Kangra district, for instance. These were recorded by Mr. O'Brien more than a hundred years ago.[96] From evidence, which was then collected, it was seen that the Ghirths did not have any "special" faith as such, although all of them worshipped Ganesh and the Devi. But, among other deities worshipped by them was 'Thakur' which is another name for Krishna, as also Shiva, Hanuman, Bhairon, Naga, Gugga, Sidh, Ajai Pal and even a Musalman pir. Even more interesting than the practices of the Ghirths were those of the people of Churah in Chamba[97]. They are recorded as having specially divided their worship over the week. Different days of the week were set apart for different deities in their scheme of things: Shiva, for example, is worshipped on Sundays, Mondays and Thursdays; Kailu on Thursdays and Tuesdays. The Gaddis of Chamba[98] are generally great Shiva worshippers but on Sundays and Thursdays they worshipped the Naga. The Devis are worshipped on Tuesdays, the Sidhs on Thursday, and so on.

The situation, in a sense, is very similar to that found in the early coins from the hills. In the Kuninda coins from the Jwalamukhi area, some mention the name of King Amoghabhuti and others, which are anonymous, mention the titles of Shiva, while indicating the faiths of the people through the motifs carved on the coins.[99] Among these are a deer, Lakshmi holding a lotus in her hand, the symbol of the river, and *swastika;* on the obverse, Shiva with a trident in his hand and the legend: *Bhagavata Chitreshwara Mahatmanah.*[100] After hundreds of years, it seems that the situation in the hills had not materially altered.

The Rajas seem to have been aware of this, and with this inside knowledge and understanding they instituted State festivals in which one can see reflected this catholicity of the faith of the people. Illustrative thus is the manner in which public worship is carried out at Sirmur. While many festivals and fairs are celebrated here, the most important is the Dussehra festival which consists of celebrations throughout the Navratras of Asuj, culminating on the tenth day in Dusshera, and is different from the Dussehra of Kulu to which the present study is devoted. On this day in Sirmur, all the castes worship their own tools of trade and the instruments of their crafts. According to an account going back to the last century,[101] many people go out of the town on horse or elephant back to see the *garuda* bird and when they spot one they reward their grooms. On the first Navaratra, at the appropriate *mahurat*, the Raja goes to the Kali temple called *Kalisthan* and worships there. This is followed by several ceremonies. A *yajña* continues for many days to the accompaniment of the worship of the Devi. On the ninth day, the Raja again goes with his entire entourage and family to the temple. Great celebrations are held there and a musical performance is organised in which the Nath Mahant of the *Kalisthan* participates. Afterwards the Nath Jogi gives a *nad* (small whistle) to the Raja and all those present as symbols of the blessings of Shiva. The Raja and the other people then offer *nazars* or offerings to the Rajguru. This is followed by sacrifice of buffaloes and goats. In the evening there are sports and on the tenth day, Dussehra is celebrated. On that evening the Raja goes to the temple of Jagannatha with his family, on elephant back. Afterwards the Mahant of Jagannath accompanies the Raja on the Raja's elephant and the procession goes to Ramkandi where there are *samadhis* of the former Bairagi Mahants of this temple. The *garuda* bird is seen there. And in this manner the celebrations, which last for ten days, come to a close. It is easy to see that this festival was organized in a manner so carefully planned that all the principal faiths of the people were honoured by the Raja.

II

DEVELOPMENTS AT KULU

The beginnings of Rama worship in Kulu, from which the institution of the Dussehra – the core of this study – almost naturally grew, go back, both in history and in popular memory, to the reign of Raja Jagat Singh (ca. 1637-1672). Vaishnavism, with its focus upon the worship of the two great incarnations of Vishnu in 'human' form – Rama, the seventh, and Krishna, the eighth – was not unknown before this in the hills, and – to recall what has been stated before – one finds scattered traces of it everywhere from early times. It has also been pointed out before that what is sometimes referred to as "ardent Vaishnavism", consisting of intense personal devotion to an *ishta-deity*, appears to have started coming in like a wave only from the early years of the 17th century. It is then that major Vaishnava stirrings in the hill areas are felt, and major temples in Nurpur, Guler, Mandi and Sirmur, among others, came to be built.

Kulu, too, did not remain untouched by this Vaishnava surge. There, however, its coming is inextricably linked with an event/legend that is recounted each time, for it is till today etched in popular memory.[102] The then ruling chief, Raja Jagat Singh, according to this legend, once became grievously ill, as a result of a curse cast upon him by a Brahmin who, oppressed by an action of the Raja and unable to bear the indignity, killed himself. There are slightly varying versions of the story, but the substance of it remains: a royal misdeed, a Brahmin's rage, and the Raja's illness. When nothing availed, and the Raja continued not being able to eat – he saw blood and worms in every food that was laid before him – someone suggested that he take recourse to a holy man, an austere Vaishnava Bairagi by the name of Krishnadasa Payahari – the name has come up before in connection with the establishment by him of several Vaishnava shrines, including that at Pindori in Gurdaspur district in the foothills – who was then living in a cave at the edge of a stream not far from Naggar, then the capital town of Kulu. As a dedicated Vaishnava, Krishnadas Payahari – he is often referred to by the people of Kulu as 'Phuari ji', and the cave in which he lived as 'Phuari ji ki gupha' – was a devotee of Rama, who had come to live in these parts as a 'missionary', bringing the message of his faith to these remote parts. When approached, he remarked to the Raja that his salvation could come only through bringing to Kulu an image of Rama from 'Awadh' in Uttar Pradesh where it was in worship. Only after he would drink water in which the image was ritually bathed each day could his affliction be cured, the Raja was told. At this, according to the story, a team was formed to leave for Awadh for securing the Rama image. It was not easy, for the idol was in worship and the priests of that temple would not dream of parting with it: a stratagem was then worked out and, stealthily, in the middle of the night, the Kulu team lifted the idol – it was a small bronze image, no taller that four inches in height – and took off. When the theft was discovered, there was panic and pursuit, but, somehow, the Kulu team succeeded in eluding their pursuers and reached the safety of the hills, going first to Kot Kandi where a *deota* temple – the Panchvir – already stood. From there, the idol was taken to different places, including Manikaran, where it 'resided' for some time even though surreptitiously each time, till it finally reached the Raja at Naggar. There the course of action that had been prescribed by Krishnadasa Payahari was duly followed, and, slowly, the Raja recovered. There was great jubilation and the grateful Raja recognized

Payahari ji as his preceptor, vowing to install the Rama image – it was known by the name of Raghunath ji – as the state deity of Kulu and assuming for himself the subordinate role of a Dewan – minister or administrator – of the deity who was now officially designated as the true ruler of Kulu. Clearly, Vaishnavism had triumphed in this relatively remote state.

The veracity of this story, at least of its details, is almost impossible to establish, for no records exist. But it has a firm place in the popular imagination. A saying, using the name Makarhara, which was possibly the old name of the region, is still current among the people of Kulu:

Makarahar Ajodhyapuri manohem Braj ki reet
Jagat Singh maharaj ki Sri Ragho ji saun preet.

[Meaning that, with the coming of Rama's idol, it is as if Makarahar had turned into Ayodhya itself, and that Maharaja Jagat Singh was completely devoted to the illustrious Raghava, i.e. Rama.]

About the prime mover in this whole course of events, Krishnadasa Payahari, not much else is known from Kulu sources. There is not even a *gaddi* or seat bearing his name in the Kulu region. One knows from other sources, like Nahbaji's *Bhaktamal* and similar hagiographical accounts of great devotees, that Payahari ji belonged to the Ramanandi order of Vaishnavas and was, in fact, only two generations removed from the great Ramanand himself. His spiritual guru, Anantananda, was, together with the saint-poet Kabir, and eleven others, one of the immediate disciples of Ramanand. He is spoken of as being of an ascetic, self-denying nature – the honorific Payahari means "one who subsists only on water/milk" – eager to spread the true word. In Rajasthani records, he is associated with having founded the celebrated Vaishnava *math* or *gaddi* at Galta, not far from Jaipur, bringing to the royal house of that state the worship of Rama. A little later, however, one finds him linked as seen before, through his disciple Bhagwan ji, with founding the Vaishnava seat at Pindori. Clearly it must have been with the intent of carrying Vaishanvism, especially the worship of Rama, high and deep into the hills that Krishnadas Payahari moved to Naggar in Kulu, but when exactly did he do that is not known. At Naggar itself there is nothing – no monument, or institution – that serves as a reminder of him except when one is led by some local person to the 'cave' at the edge of the hill-stream where his *padukas* or wooden sandals, betokening his presence once, are pointed out.

To an outsider, some part of the story involving the person of Krishnadasa Payahari, and the conversion of Raja Jagat Singh to Vaishnavism, might read like a legend. But then one has to recall, as David Lorenzen does,[103] that legends, like myths, contain ideological messages, but "they require, and permit, less 'depth' analysis than myths do". The messages that they carry are often subtle ones; at the same time many of their "social, political and psychological implications" are simply "beyond the grasp of imaginative reconstruction" that outsiders tend to bring to them. Whatever the case, the outlines of the developments at Kulu emerge fairly clearly from the 'legend' of Payahari ji and the restoration of the Raja's health. The time was right for a shift in the faith of the Raja, bringing it into line with what was happening in the mainstream culture of the north, and now in the surrounding hill states; the new, devotional message gained in power through its association with a miracle, or miraculous cure; the need for a central religious authority was perhaps being felt for knitting the far-flung areas of the state together and for limiting the extent of local controls even if they were mostly in the religious sphere.

Much must have followed the establishment of Vaishnava worship in Kulu, as epitomized in the image of Raghunath ji, and the Raja's definition of his role as only a Dewan of the deity, but the steps are difficult to trace. One can therefore only try and reconstruct the course of developments. What is almost certain is that at the functional level, to begin with, an entire apparatus of worship – the appointment of *pujaris* or priests, the set of rituals and ceremonies to be observed, the daily routine to be followed at the central shrine – needed to be set up, either under the advice of the preceptor, Payahari ji, or that of a priestly group who are believed to have either accompanied the image from Ayodhya to Kulu or followed soon thereafter: the group called the Ajudhia-basis whose descendants still live in Kulu and have significant roles to play in the Raghunath temple. Under that guidance, whatever the earlier devotional practices were – whether they related to the worship of the goddess who was from earlier times the *kula-devi* of the royal house, or of a *deota* like Narsingh Bir – must have had either to be discarded or superimposed upon. For one thing, Vaishnavism enjoins upon its followers strict vegetarian practice, meaning no sacrifices, no use of meat or other *tamasik* substances: something that must have meant a clear departure from earlier usages, for in the worship of the goddess or of the Bir sacrifices and meat-offerings figure prominently. It is possible to imagine the discussions that must have taken place, and the positions that must have been taken. But eventually the practices that prevailed must have been essentially Sanskritic in nature, modelled probably on those followed in the worship of Rama in Ayodhya. A break with the past needed not only to be made but also demonstrated as having been done. At the same time, it might have been considered prudent to proceed cautiously as far as spreading the message of Vaishnavism among the local populace was concerned, used as people were to earlier, and different, ways. There must have been resistance, whether openly expressed or inwardly harboured, to the drastic changes that were taking place not only in the personal faith of the Raja but in the entire region as such, with Raghunath ji having been declared as the state-deity. It is possible, therefore, that some accommodations might have been thought of as necessary to make. One prominent deviation from strictly Vasihnava practice that one knows of – this comes up repeatedly in all accounts of Vaishnavism in Kulu – is that in the royal shrine, among the offerings made to the deities was included the flesh of a pheasant, the *chakor* bird. Whether this flesh used to be offered from earlier times to the Narsingh Bir icon, or to the Goddess, and the practice had therefore to be retained, or whether the discarding of that practice met with stout resistance, remains difficult to establish. But traditionally this offering continued to be made. However, tradition also records a popular belief that after the *chakor* bird was sacrificed, its bones and feathers were gathered each time and, through the sprinkling of some holy water upon them and the chanting of some sacred *mantras*, the bird would become whole again and come back to life. Clearly, the story of the bird coming back to life was an invention, a myth that served the useful purpose of reconciling two opposites. But such must have been the nature of the polity, or of faith, that it was needed.

The worship of Raghunath ji is *sattvik* in all other respects and stays close, it seems, to the practice followed in most Vaishnava temples in the northern plains. The memory of the rituals and ceremonies followed at Ayodhya is very likely to have travelled with the image to Kulu, and the presence of Payahari ji, as the flag-bearer of the faith in these parts, must have ensured that everything was done in proper order and in accordance with classical, Sanskritic percepts. To this day, the *pooja paddhati* that is followed at the Raghunath temple, and that seems to have been established more that three hundred and fifty years ago, bears the breath of time upon itself. It is all written down in chaste Sanskrit – the use of the language itself invests the temple with great prestige – and everything is spelt out in it with great precision.[104] The day at the temple begins with *mantras* recited in the hour of waking up: "*uttishtha uttishtha govinda, uttishtha garuda-dhvaja* ...", and so on. These are followed by the *mritika mantras*, *mantras* related to *arati*; the sacred conchshell is offered homage through the *shankhodaka mantra*, and the Earth Goddess through *prithvi pooja*. The *dvar devatas* are invoked, *sankalpa* is made identifying the exact space and time at which worship is offered; *mandalas* are drawn on the floor; the whole routine of *nyasa, kavacha*, and *dhyanas* is followed. Then comes the elaborate ritual of bathing the deity and dressing him up: *snana, vastra, yajnopavita, bhushana, chandana, akshata, tulasi, durva, argha, pushpa* offerings. The whole Rama group – Sita and Lakshmana, Hanumana and Sugriva, Vashishtha and Vibhishana – is remembered and invoked. Long and elaborate *dhyanas* and prayers are offered, each time in the most elegant of terms and invested with intense fervour. Most of the recitation and preparation is done in private, by the priests alone; other prayers are open to the devotees who keep coming in. There is sacredness everywhere: the *paddhati* helps create a clear, aesthetic environment even as it bonds the devotee and the deity together.

In the context of the resistance that Vaishnavism might have met initially in Kulu, and the accommodation in its practices that it might have had to make, it may be useful at this point of time to pause and take a look at the kind of cultural processes that might have been set in motion at this point of time. One can take, only as an instructive example, how a complex case is handled: that of Narsingh, a name shared by a classical incarnation of Vishnu and a *deota* of the Bir category of purely local origin that has been mentioned earlier.

Before one does that, however, it is time perhaps to turn, briefly, to some theoretical formulations. One recalls, while speaking of this, Martin Heidegger's formulation of the concept of 'Deep History', in which the environment is formed by multiple layers of traditions, interpretations and embedded meanings, for it strikes a familiar chord.[105] It evokes both response and recognition. The search for 'Aletheia' is however not easy, as has been said.[106]

The present study, empirical[107] and fieldwork-based as it is – with the Dussehra of Kulu at its heart – requires something like the practice of an 'archaeology of culture'.[108] It is essentially societal processes around the Kulu Dussehra that need to be understood, for it is these that would lead to the creation of a space for the emergence of multiple scenarios, possibilities, and their interpretations. Even an initial observation of the large Dussehra event reveals the existence of these multiple layers and strands. The lines of demarcation between different layers, entities, personae and religious forms are indistinct and extremely blurred, making it virtually impossible to separate them. Consequently, many interpretations might be left open-ended to allow for a space to accommodate other inputs of a more scholarly nature.

Issues concerning the Kulu Dussehra can be addressed at many different levels. If studied as a carefully crafted and colourful spectacle, it would invite the viewer to participate in a 'journey through the mythopoetic space of Epic India', that is both multilayered, and richly nuanced. Seen as a 'performance', the Dussehra would display that 'heightened behaviour', a publicly displayed 'behaviour', twice over, inhering in that particular art form.[109] Classical Gods, local godlings or *deotas*, priests, shamans, functionaries and above all royalty form the *dramatis personae* of this theatre and public space gets completely covered with congeries of people welded into a markedly distinctive identity despite the mosaic of different identities issuing from difference of region, caste, occupation or the 'following', that is the *hariyan*, of a particular *deota*.[110] Seen as a 'religious' festival it would stand analysis as a cultural system of symbols representing '...concrete embodiments of ideas, attitudes, judgments, longings or beliefs'.[111] As a 'religious' festival, the Kulu Dussehra would equally be a dramatized symbolic expression of social processes with meanings not expressed elsewhere coming to the fore. Issues of caste, kinship and economics get displayed in this festival and its rituals. And then, the Kulu Dussehra can also be seen as a carefully thought-out political device: a strategy worked out to ensure the harnessing of local godlings into the service of the newly arrived Vaishnava faith. Questions present themselves, however. Does this performative excess also serve to mask the strategic uses of 'culture' in advancing a political agenda? Has the event been structured after being viewed through the cultural lens of politics and history? This may not be the place for them, but what is clear is that political control, protest, even rebellion is expressed through 'the notion of theatre' that is the Kulu Dussehra. There is space as well as accommodation for the dissenting *deotas* on the one hand, and on the other for the rulers who acted out 'their theatre of majesty, superstition, power'.[112] Symbols legitimating royal authority are used with intelligence and this public reminder of royal authority, as Lutgendorf said in another context, serves well to compensate for its loss of status.[113] Transformation, reconciliation, synthesization, a bringing together of opposites, marks the cultural processes set into motion. Silent, invisible and long drawn out as they were, these processes encapsulated cultural forms that mutated and adapted, in response to external stimuli.

In this 'site of convergence between anthropology and history', the concern is with the local, the common and the small in scale. The available texts and codified oral traditions are read not to establish chronologies, not to sift historical fact from mythical fancy, but to try to grasp the meanings of the forms and contents of these texts in their own cultural terms.[114] Documenting all this, Malinowski's observation that 'sources lie in the behaviours and the memory of the living'[115] have directed the present study towards close observation and analysis of various *pujas* and other rituals. *Pujaris, gurs, kardars,* members of the royal family, district language officers and a large segment of the 'devoted' were interviewed.[116] Persistent strains of memory, buried deep beneath the sediments of time, were recorded. Surviving memories had already validated themselves by undergoing '... the process of disputation, transformation and inclusion into a narrative that society [or social section} deems appropriate and worth preserving'.[117]

To return to the case of Narsingh,[118] however. It might form a relatively small area within the larger context of the Kulu Dussehra but it has an important bearing on much larger issues lying encoded in the cultural processes at work in the regional tradition. The late entry of Vaishnavism in Kulu, and the conversion of Raja Jagat Singh to the 'new' faith, have already been referred to, but there is need to go into somewhat greater detail. It is not unlikely that, at the instance of Krishnadas Payahari,[119] Jagat Singh first installed, as the ruler of Kulu, an emblem in stone [a *shaligram* or a *shila* ?] representing *Narasimha* – literally, 'man-lion' – the fourth *avatara* of Vishnu in the classical tradition, while he chose for himself the role of a servitor.[120] According to local informants, the Raja's suffering was controlled, but not eradicated; accordingly, a mission was sent to bring the idol of Raghunath, Rama in other words, then in worship at Ayodhya for gaining final deliverance from the malady. The image once brought, Rama was formally installed as the supreme ruler in Kulu, with Jagat Singh acting as his *Diwan*. The journey of Rama to Kulu, through conscious intent, appears to have been made in a quiet, gradual and phased-out manner, punctuated as it was by periods of temporary residence at Kotkandi, Makarsa and Manikaran till the final *pratishtha* of the image at Naggar, and then in the Raghunath temple in Kulu town. Sharing now this 'stable' centre of the complex universe of belief were Sita, Hanuman and, above all, *Narsingh* in the form of a stone emblem: a *shaligram* perhaps.[121] At Dussehra time, all interest centres around Raghunath ji, but one quickly becomes aware of the other focus of interest which is *Narsingh*. In what manner and at what junctures of the festival *Narsingh* becomes visible to the spectator is of relevance to this study.[122]

The first glimpse of *Narsingh* is on the sixth *navaratra*, the day of the *Sair Puja*, when after the worship of the *kulajas* and Raghunath ji, the first fruit of the winter crop of walnuts is offered to Raghunath ji, other visiting *deotas*, and, above all, alongwith a token homage in money, to a colourfully caparisoned white mare known as *Narsinghji ki ghodi*. On the Dussehra day, along with the worship of weapons, in keeping with Rajput tradition, the Raja worships, before he embarks on the *shobha yatra* of Raghunath, *Narsinghji ki Ghori* at his palace, even as *Hidimba* sits in assertive possession of it inside. Then *Narsinghji ki Ghori*, ostensibly and significantly, leads the *shobha yatra* to the Dhalpur *chaugan* where the military camps of Raghunath ji and the Kulu Raja are pitched. There is another presence quietly felt in this epic theatre. This is of the *gur* of the *deota Panchavir*of Kot Kandi, who is worshipped along with the royal weapons and then also given a place of importance on the *rath* of Raghunath ji, by being seated alongside the chief priest of the deity. To be noticed is that it is the *bajantris* or musicians of Kot Kandi who also serve *Narsingh* of Raghunath temple. Once more, *Narsingh* acquires prominence when, along with Raghunath ji, an *abhishek* and morning *puja* is performed for him, by the chief priest of the Raghunath temple. The Raja of Kulu attends to Raghunath ji, while the chief priest delineates with great sensitivity, the features of *Narsingh* on to the black stone emblem with saffron and sandalwood paste, worships it, and adds the final touch by painting a *Shri Yantra* with saffron on to a silver salver, which is included in the worship. At the time of the mid-day *bhoga*, *Narsingh* still remains in sharp focus – perhaps even sharper than before. He is taken out of the Raghunath camp over to the Raja's camp for his *bhoga* of meat, which has come from the temple of Devi Tripurasundari of Naggar. Then, inexplicably, *Narsingh* is brought back for a vegetarian *bhoga* along with Raghunath ji at his camp. Here, two *thalis* instead of one are placed before him. One *thali* is said to be there for *abhyagat ji*.[123] The *chhari* or the staff of the Raja's authority at the temple is referred to as *Narsinghji ki chhari*. The Kulu kingdom is referred to as *Narsinghji ki gaddi*. The *Bhatu* or chief priest, when interviewed, keeps referring to Narsingh, inadvertently as *Narsingh Bir*, who is also the *kula-devta* of the Kulu Rajas.[124] With *Narsingh's* visibility and importance being more than established, the other quiet and unobtrusive presence that keeps reappearing along side *Narsingh*, is of the *deota Pancavira* of Kot Kandi, whose *gur* is invoked for a *pucch* on the day of the *bali* in the event of any impediment in the ritual. Each day in the afternoon the Raja of Kulu, referred to and recognized as *Narsingh Swarup*, sits in a *sukhpal* palanquin, and is carried around the encampment of the *deotas*. His procession is led by a horse referred to, again, as *Narsinghji ki ghori*.

Many elements of the above narrative, involving Narsingh, do not appear to be in accord with the classical *avatara* of Vishnu. Is this Narsingh then *deota*

Narsingh Bir– folk-hero, warrior, protector of the *kshetra* – one begins to wonder? One does notice the primacy given to the *ghodi* (mare), ordinarily not associated with Narsingh *avatara*, in the Dussehra festival. The *bhoga* of meat also strikes a discordant note in the context of a Vaishnava *deity*. To be noticed also is the fact that the *deota* Panchavir of Kot Kandi is also constantly around. But the question really is about the *Narsingh* of Raghunath temple: is he the classical *avatara* of Vishnu or is he the local folk hero, a *Bir*? A closer examination and contextualization of the religious and philosophical concepts of the *Bir* and of *Narsingh avatara* seem to be needed.

The aspect of the *Bir*,[125] simply as the 'protective' spirit of a realm or a town, is much more complex, multifaceted and fascinating than meets the eye initially. Hero par excellence, royal protector of *kshetra, kshatra* and Brahmins, he was also a guardian of cattle herds, an agent of the powers of nature and a provider of fertility to women through his personal intervention. Initially, *Bir*-worship may have grown simply from the commemoration of an ancestor. He soon got elevated, however, to the status of a demi-god on account of some supremely heroic deed involving the protection of a vital regional interest. His '*virya* has immediate access to God', they say. Loyalty to a cause, complete sacrifice of self, an integrity combined with an exceptional and spectacular daring, upgraded these 'heroes' of the 'Little Tradition' to the position of semi-divine godlings. Associated with hilly and forested regions, *Birs* had linkages with *yakshas* on the one hand and with *siddhas* and *yogis* on the other. Like the former, they guarded livestock and gave the boon of sons and, like the latter, they controlled the energies of the *bavan-viras*, (the fifty-two heroes). There is, thus, the coming together of the concepts of the *yogi* and the 'hero'. This heroism gets commemorated in a cult and its oldest manifestation is in the cult of the *Pancaviras*, the *Vrishni* heroes. Popularly, as befits a hero, with a *Bir* is associated a horse and a sword. Though basically benevolent, *Birs* are quick to take offence and need to be propitiated. The mode of worship of a *Bir* consists of the offering of a coconut with incense, lights and flowers. The *Bir* represented as a *pindi* is propitiated by the sacrifice of a goat. In his role as protector of kings, he is venerated by many ruling families. Several attempts to connect the *Birs* with the Great Tradition through their identification with a *swarup* (form) of one or the other classical deity are visible in popular accounts. But the *Birs*, with their strong strain of tribal individualism, sturdily remained distinct and separate from the mainstream, neither affecting it nor being influenced by it.[126] The two currents of belief appeared to flow side by side as parallel streams. Spatial spread of the cult of the *Birs* was extensive in the hills, as was the practice of their active worship. Inclusive of all its regional variations and expressions, belief in the *Birs* seems to have been a pan-Indian phenomenon, spread over the tribal areas of Madhya Pradesh, Rajasthan, Gujarat, Maharashtra, Goa, Karnataka, Andhra, Tamil Nadu, Kerala and, above all, in the Western Himalayas, the last fact of obvious relevance to the present study.

At the level of popular belief, the veneration of the *Bir* is fairly widespread in the Western Himalayas. The total quantum of information, published or otherwise, being scant, one necessarily enters the area of speculation, seeking affirmation or denial from local legends, vernacular writings and interviews, both with functionaries and devotees. The poor visibility and elusive nature of the inner workings of the societal process entails a certain circumspection in its documentation, since many a times the 'unusual' gets recorded and the 'ordinary' or the 'usual', which may be of import, completely escapes notices.

One knows that as an 'upholder of the socio-moral order', *deota* Bir Baradhi of Tandi, Kothi Bhalan, Kulu, used to command the devotion of the Rajas of Kulu. Occupying a central place in matters of the personal faith of the Rajas, the *Bir* transmitted a sense of well-being and security, creating thus a world full of stable meanings. Local accounts speak of the gift of 500 *bighas* of land made by Raja Bahadur Singh to *deota Bir Baradhi,* in gratitude for a 'wish fulfillment'.[127] A recent consensus worked out between the functionaries and *hariyan* of different regional manifestations of the *deota,* at Peej, Kareri, Bhuntar and Kot Kandi, established, conclusively, the primacy of *deota* Pancavira of Kotkandi as being the original form, from which the rest of his manifestations had emerged and been established, through the diasporic mode, over wider areas. Kot Kandi, then, was the *moolsthana* of *Pancavira,* the *deota* who occupied a position of centrality in matters of faith for the Kulu Rajas.[128] This also puts into proper perspective the reason for Jagat Singh ordering that the image of Rama from Ayodhya be brought, upon arrival in his domains, first to Kot Kandi before bringing it to his capital for installation. It can easily be seen simply as an act acknowledging the primacy of the *deota,* a homage: the seeking of blessings and approval from him.

In local memory, a prominent aspect of the persona of *deota Pancavira* is that he is a solver of problems. Cast in the role of advisor to deities of both the Little and the Great Traditions, he is constantly approached by one and all for help, cutting across barriers imposed by hierarchy. Residing with him and also constantly present with him is *deota Narsingh Bir*, who may well be the executor and implementer of actions, independently or in the name of *deota* Pancavira.

With the name Narsingh being common to the classical *avatara* of Vishnu and a Bir, some confusion, or mixing of identities would be natural. But, if attention were to be paid, a distinction clearly emerges. In this context, it is of interest to go back to the register containing the list of the holdings of *deotas* that was drawn up in 1947-49 and has been noticed before.[129] In that list, a number of temples are referred to as Thakurs – thus, Thakur Ram Chander ji, Thakur Sita Ram, Thakur Murali Dhar – and not as *deotas*. The meaning is obvious: these are Vaishnava deities of the classical order, their temples always being referred to as *thakurdwaras* all over the northern parts of India. In that list also figure several temples that are designated as 'Thakur Narsingh' – thus those at Dhalpur, Baroh, Akhara, Karjan, Jhiri, Dashal – but also one as *deota* Narsingh, that at Mohal in mauza Khokhan. With the former clearly must have been associated the classical *avatara,* and with the latter, the one at Mohal, a locally revered hero: a Bir in other words.[130] Interestingly, in the lists found in Rose's Glossary, out of the temples dedicated to *Narsingh,* the majority in Kulu and even in Kangra are spoken of as belonging to the classical *avatara, Narsingh.*[131] In the popular mind, things however must have overlapped.

As the fourth *avatara* of Vishnu, interestingly enough, Narsingh was among the earliest of the *avataras* to be venerated in the Western Himalayas. Half-man, half-lion, composite in form, possessed of forcefulness, great energy and an *ugra* nature, he somehow held a great appeal for the Pahari mind because of these very qualities and because of his association with deep forests and mountain tops.[132] Of appeal also to tribal sensibilities,[133] the ferocious and sanguinary form of Narsingh is associated with cataclysmic but controlled destruction.[134] Born out of the 'intersecting territories of reality and fantasy,'[135] the man-lion, or lion amongst men, had a raw and immediate appeal with his *pralayic* and 'Sivaesque' image.[136] Linked on the one hand with the Shakti cult through the *Sapta matrikas,* and the Vaishnava cult on the other as an *avatara* of Vishnu, Narsingh bridged the distance between the Shakta and Vaishnava cults by his association with the ten *Mahavidyas,* who in turn are linked with the *Dasavataras.*[137] *Narsingh avatara's* linkage with Tripurasundari of Naggar hinted at or established in this manner, it becomes easy to understand why in his worship at Kulu the *shri yantra* is brought in. All these linkages of the avatara, with Shiva and Devi on the one hand, and the reference to his duality of nature as *nara* and *simha*[138] seem somehow to have made it possible for the *Narasimha avatara* open to different adaptive processes.[139]

To go back to Kulu, and to the establishment of the Vaishnavism to which Jagat Singh had been converted, one can see that the Raja might have decided, on his own or with the advice of his mentor, Payahari ji, to turn to the figure of the Narasimha *avatara* also. The deity was of course known in the hills – the presence of a great image like the one in bronze at Brahmour or as a part of the Vaikuntha-murti images ensured that – and it might have occurred to the Raja to use him to transmit the potent message of hegemony, for the rulers always sought, as has been stated 'fresh instruments of legitimation in new symbols' like *Narasimha*'.[140]

We are clearly in an area of speculation. But it is not unlikely that Payahari ji – who might personally have been a devotee of Narasimha, considering that there is still a "Thakur Narsingh" temple in Jhiri[141] where he lived – noticed that Kulu was part of an 'animistic zone' of religion, and within that the figure of Narasimha, the man-lion, would be easy to accommodate. The 'amusing tradition' of which Hutchison and Vogel speak in which a "Brahman sadhu", after having shown his magical powers to the Raja made him his disciple ends with the sadhu – almost certainly Payahari ji – placing a garland round the neck of the Raja, "at the same time giving him the god Narsingh to worship".[142] Narsingh, Payahari ji must have known, was widely known in the area even as a *Bir* or a *kula-devata.*[143] Therefore, anticipating difficulty in replacing the local peoples' earlier, more visceral forms of worship with Vaishnavism coming from the plains as such, Payahari ji may well have suggested to the Raja to devise the strategy of coalescing the two figures: Narasimha as an *avatara* and *Narsingh Bir*, the local *deota*. They could be seen simply as twin aspects of a single spiritual reality. As a corollary of this, a departure from the Vaishnava norms of vegetarianism might have been made to accommodate and incorporate the need of the *Bir* as well as of the local people's non-vegetarian habits. If this is the way it happened, and these strategies had been thought out with care, it would certainly have helped ease the situation for the Raja, Jagat Singh, torn as he might have been between old and new loyalties.

Lowering the level of resistance to the introduction of a new god may also have been made easy by the persona of the Vaishnava deity selected for royal worship in the initial stages. There is a near-parallel to the situation which one might recall with interest. Eschmann, in the course of her researches in Orissa and neighbouring Andhra, postulated that *Narasimha* was the perfect deity in helping the accommodation of tribal deities within the Vaishnava pantheon of the 'Great Tradition'.[144] In Kulu, Payahari ji might have thought the situation out quite clearly. And by accepting *Narsingh avatara* as an intermediate stage between the worship of the tribal *Narsingh Bir* and that of Rama, the 'Lord of the world,'[145] Jagat Singh also might have been helped in successfully establishing his hegemonic control over the sacred space within his dominions, ensuring legitimation of his authority and control over the mental space of his people. The people of the area as well as members of the royal family could thus have been transformed 'into a seamless collectivity' with the realization that the incorporative nature of the worship actually underscored the fact of there being 'no binary oppositions in real life'.[146]

The 'levels of socio-cultural complexity'[147] in Indian society being well established, it becomes difficult to disentangle the strands because most processes exist so far back in memory that it is difficult to find an accurate response to one's questions. Answers are very often invented quite spontaneously, very little thought being given to the question asked. Societal processes of absorption, assimilation, accommodation, co-existence, adaptiveness, are all simultaneously at work. 'Change is a continuously adaptive process' as has been remarked, "in which the ends are never immanent'[148]. The boundaries separating different forms within society are extremely porous, with no hard-edged categories emerging. Within this continuous process, an absorption and rejection of elements is going on. Tell-tale traces (which have already been mentioned) of the original form remain, firmly enshrined within the new configurations that come into being. Even within the transformations, societal memory lingers on as a constant reminder. All these processes are natural, *sahaja* and subtle. It is these processes that must have been set into motion in the encounter between Little Tradition's *Narsingh Bir* and the Great Tradition's *Narsingh avatara*, as they were inadvertently placed in a contest for primacy. Describing the process of the absorption of the non-Brahmanic cults into orthodox Hinduism in the Western Himalayas, C.F. Oldham spoke once of a prolonged contact in which both sides had to yield ground to the extent that an amalgam of opposites came into being.[149] There is no denial of earlier loyalties, no turning back from anything: the whole attitude is one of inclusiveness. The 'belief of the masses' was 'incorporative of the worship of all gods' with perfect ease.[150] No antagonism between the two entities of *Narsingh Bir* and *Narasimha avatara* eventually survived.

The more one goes over the matter, the more one finds that rooted as the common man is in his local belief patterns, his admiration for the gods of the Great Tradition is curbed and restricted by his strong and tenacious belief in the local gods of the Little Tradition. Higher classical beliefs do not ordinarily find a space in his system of beliefs, despite his admiration for refined philosophical ideas. His attempts, even in the case of his conversion to classical beliefs, do not allow these beliefs to completely integrate with his local beliefs. Nothing, in other words, can overshadow the importance of the *kuldevta*[151] in hill societies. In the eventuality of classical religion achieving a dominance in society, local beliefs still manage to '...find adequate space in it as a ceremonial, subversive, cathartic subidentity....'[152]

The actual relationship between the Great and Little Tradition can be said to be a cyclical one, a sort of a *Marg* and *Desi* continuum, with each tradition fertilizing the other. This contributes to the growth and the strength of both the traditions. The Folk Tradition gets gradually 'transformed' and Classical Tradition gets 'vulgarized' in this exchange. The entire process is extremely slow. The 'Little Tradition' needs to 'simmer', as has been stated, before the process of its upward mobility begins, and the 'Great Tradition' needs to 'integrate and rework' as it filters down.[153] It is against the backdrop of these theoretical formulations, combined with participant-observation, that the processes involving *Narsingh Bir* and *Narsingh avatara* have to be viewed.

One can restate the position very briefly. With his personal belief centered firmly in his *kuldevta, Narsingh Bir,* Jagat Singh appears to have been convinced by Krishna Das Payahari to accept the new faith of Vaishnavism, with *Narsingh*, the classical *avatara*, at the centre of his belief, if not in absolute terms, then at least in conjunction with *Narsingh Bir*. With Jagat Singh's conversion, Vaishnavism became and was declared as the state religion. Raghunath ji, along with *Narsingh,* were to be seen as joint rulers of the state of Kulu, so to speak. Using a masterly strategy, Jagat Singh instituted the Dussehra as a state festival in honour of the Vaishnava deity, Raghunath ji, along with *Narsingh avatara,* whom he served both as *diwan*, and servitor. Kulu is referred to even today as *Narsingh Gaddi* and the 'sceptre' of authority being wielded by the Raja is termed *Narsingh ji ki chhari*. To the public, it represented sovereignty and as authority emanating from the ruler of Kulu. While *Narasimha avatara* occupies almost equal space with Raghunath ji in terms of importance, there are other elements that attach to his persona too: those of the *deota Narsingh Bir* who enter this space too, quietly, unobtrusively, on his own terms and in his own right. This, first as the *kuldevta* of the king, and then as the 'hero', the protector of the ruler's territory and his sovereignty.

Visible signs of his presence in the Dussehra ceremonies have already been referred to, and it is through ritual and prayer that *Narsingh Bir's* primacy at the Dussehra is clearly established. This is not simply a case of a local godling becoming 'Sanskritised', or 'Universalized' or' Classicized', whichever of the terms one may want to accept or use. Nomenclatures could be faulty and therefore open to criticism. They may also be in the process of changing within this fluid situation. The possibility of a slightly different model than what already exists in the field thus needs to be considered. What we see in Kulu in terms of *Narsingh* is perhaps the dual persona of *Narsingh Bir* and *Narsimha avatara* in a state of coexistence. In his pioneering work on Kishangarh, Marriott observed a phenomenon that he described as a process of '...accretion, transmutation in form, without apparent replacement, without rationalization of the accumulated and transformed elements'.[154] In his opinion, what transpires is not a replacement of a Little Tradition form. It is in fact a new form, durable and possessed of more authority along with a significant presence, that comes to stay.

The Brahmanical tradition, according to Marriott, recreates but never supplants the 'Little Tradition'. 'Coexistence' and not just a 'merger' of identities is the adaptive strategy that comes into play. These options are consciously and unconsciously exercised to bring about the much desired state of religious and cultural homogeneity. Thus is assured the continuation and parallel existence of two belief systems, independent yet bound together by the strange inner logic of two parallel streams flowing towards the same goal.[155] It is in this very fashion that concessions were made to adjust and incorporate *deota Narsingh Bir* into the religious landscape of classical Vaishnavism. The acceptance of the Universal tradition and the continuance of the Parochial tradition are thus ensured.

The entire cultural process taking place within Kulu does not conform strictly to one theoretical model or the other. There exist both several similarities and differences. One senses, therefore, that there is a pressing need for viewing the process *in its own terms*. The essence of the Indian identity lies in its ability to contain within itself, a capacity for integration. The manner in which diverse cultural elements get synthesized, displays with sharpness and clarity the nature of the forces at work. This integrative nature of Indian culture is on display during Dussehra time, when hierarchy in the arrangement, in the positioning of the *deotas,* on either side of Raghunath's *rath,* allows us a glimpse into the workings of complex societal processes. Human emotions, political motivations, a hunger for empowerment, are on view in the attitudes of the *deotas* much like those of any social grouping in modern day societies.[156] Rituals have been carefully worked out as tools of integration, to be used with care and precision. All these have been woven into what constitutes the rich fabric and the dynamics of cultural processes in action, displaying and carrying within themselves a host of coded meanings and messages. Examining the presence and role of the principal *deotas* involved in the important task of setting up the Dussehra, one realizes that in the distribution of various functions of the *deotas*, the importance and centrality of different cultic aspects of Hinduism have been paid attention to. There is, for example, the high visibility of *Tripurasundari* of Naggar representing the Shaktas; of *Hidimba*, seen many a times as a *Yakshi*, a semi-divine being; of *Narsingh Bir*, the hero, the protector and the warrior; of *Bijli Mahadeo* representing the Shaiva cult; and of *Gohri Devta*, representing Brahma, whose principal responsibility is to be present around Raghunath ji on the day of the first Navaratra.[157] Is this, one asks, pure chance that a whole range of *deotas*, cutting across different cultic affiliations, come together in the ceremony thus? Or, is this a part of a carefully thought out design, intended to quietly and unobtrusively weld disparate elements together, and create the necessary social harmony? Questions like these come up, as each segment, each nuance, of the Dussehra is submitted to careful examination.

For the man in the hills, it needs to be realized, religion was the very essence of his existence. Divorced from it, life was inconceivable. Strengthened with it he entered the trials and tribulations and fray of life with cheer. Hinduism of the hills was in many ways different, as we have seen, from the Hinduism of the plains. The difference became more pronounced as one penetrated deeper into the hills. The demonistic faith of the inner hills reflected the composition of the population. The immigrants were few as were the contacts with the plains and the outer world. The fear of the forces of nature was great. People took a highly 'practical' view of religion. While not rejecting Vaishnavism with its intense humanism, they also did not allow it to become their principal faith. In times of need when the common man thought of a superior power, he did not think of Rama or Krishna but of the *Naga*, the *Siddha*, the *Devi* and the *deota*. It is they who met his immediate needs and gave him the limited protection that he sought. Most of these gods and godlings had a local character. From his own observation of the religion of Kulu as practiced, Harcourt saw it as a religion which inculcates attendance at *melas*, and such like 'orgies'. It is a creed that does not fail to recommend itself to the simple peasant, for it costs him nothing to keep up the worship in the temples endowed with rent-free grants. Where the tenets of orthodox Hinduism cross his core beliefs, he treats them as if they had no existence. '... the inner voice was moved more perhaps by a deep seated faith than by the form that religion took. He did not question, he believed.'[158]

Seeing the situation that was worked out in Kulu, one realizes that what is remarkable about Hinduism as a cultural force is its elasticity and its capacity to borrow diverse elements, and rework them to produce a completely transformed entity. This process, like any organic process, is slow and cannot be hurried, or made to omit the logical stages through, which it must necessarily pass. Adopting for the moment nomenclatures that are popularly in use, a recognizable characteristic of the Great Tradition, appears to be its inability to accept with ease, doctrines that are outside its ken of understanding. By contrast, in many ways and on many issues, the Little Tradition has much more acceptance of newer ideas, except when they stand in contradiction to the essential core of a belief pattern that is durable, comforting and reassuring. As already stated, the boundaries between the two traditions are porous and within this complex process of interaction, both Traditions are not only aware of each other, but do not attempt to exclude each other. They even affect each other profoundly.[159] This is an ongoing process. Forms of social complexity are thus created as Sanskritic and non-Sanskritic motifs combine. This necessarily leads to a certain amount of confusion. There are times when two dramatically different deities appear to coalesce only to be viewed as if they were different forms of the same godhead: such clearly appears to be the case with *Narsingh Avatara* and *Narsingh Bir*, in Kulu, The two entities seem virtually indistinguishable on the surface.

The inflexibility that marks the Sanskritic tradition is not applicable to the non-Sanskritic Tradition, which demonstrates a capacity to modify both itself and the Sanskritic form in response to a challenge. In one sense, the 'Little Tradition' retains its dominance.[160] This is exemplified to an extent in the manner in which the Kulu Dussehra as celebrated at Dhalpur is structured, differing at several points from the festival as it is celebrated elsewhere in India. The presence of a large number of elements displays a highly innovative regional profile, lending strength to the form of the Dussehra as observed at Haripur, Vashishta, Manikaran, and Naggar, all in the Kulu region.

Keeping the manifest traits of the hill character in mind, one is able to reiterate that the genius of the people of the hills seems to have been in reconciling different faiths within their personal belief. An easy balance is struck which leaves room for all faiths and all sects to bring in many more deities into their belief, without pushing anyone out. Categories do not appear to be hard-edged and fixed. The situation continues to be the same today, and this is exactly what seems to have transpired with *Narsingh avatara* and *Narsingh Bir* in Kulu in the era gone by.

NOTES AND REFERENCES

1. See, R.G. Bhandarkar, *Vaishnavism, Saivisim and Minor Religious Systems.*
2. See, Vogel, *Antiquities*, for a detailed account of these inscriptions.
3. *Archaeological Survey Reports*, V, p. 176.
4. *Ibid.*, V, p. 176. Also see, *Kangra District Gazetteer*, Pt. A, 1904, p. 258.
5. *A.S.R.*, V, pp. 155, 164. The inscription is possibly of the 6th century AD.
6. H. Hargreaves, "The Monolithic Temples of Masrur", *A.S.I., Annual Report*, 1915-16, pp. 46-47.
7. Michael Meister, "Mountain Temples and Temple-Mountains: Masrur", in *Journal of the Society of Architectural Historians*, Vol. 65, no. 1, 2006, pp. 26-49.
8. This evidence has been preserved here because of the remoteness of the Valley rather than to the clemency of the invaders.

9. See his *Early Wooden Temples of Chamba*, p. 84.
10. *Ibid.*, p. 68.
11. For a very informed and useful account, see V.C. Ohri, *Sculptures of the Western Himalayas: History and Stylistic Development*, 1991.
12. See, B. Ch. Chhabra, *Antiquities*, pp. 22, 25, 28.
13. *Ibid.*, p. 28.
14. *Ibid.*, pp. 41, 43, 51, 61, 71, 77, 81, 83 *et. Seq.*
15. See Ohri, *op. cit.*, pp. 33-52 for a detailed account of sculptures at Bajaura and Hat, and at Jagatsukh and Nirmand.
16. Helene Diserens, "Six Unpublished Anthropomorphic Wooden Sculptures at Gajan (Kulu), in *Central Asiatic Journal*, Vol. XXV, nos. 3-4, pp. 163-73. Also see her "Two Images of Surya worshipped as village Goddesses in the Kulu Valley", *SARAS Bulletin*, 3, 1983, pp. 37-47.
17. See, thus, Laxman S. Thakur, "An Iconographic Study of Six Wooden Sculptures from Gajan, Kulu District, and Some Connected Problems", *South Asian Studies*, Vol. 7, 1991, pp. 83 ff.
18. Goetz, "The coming of Muslim cultural influence in the Punjab Himalayas", *Indian Antiquary*, 157. Goetz has treated at some length of this process of cultural assimilation in the Panjab Hill States. He believes that "the whole of contemporary Rajput civilization" was absorbed by the Panjab Hills between the end of the 16th and the middle of the 17th century.
19. An idea of the extent of pilgrimages can be formed from the entries made by persons from the hills in the *bahis*, kept by the priests of these pilgrim centres. See, B.N. Goswamy, "The Records Kept by Priests at Centres of Pilgrimage as a Source of Social and Economic History", *Indian Economic and Social History Review*, III, No. 2.
20. It is significant that a large number of Hill States were founded by royal cadets who came on pilgrimages to the Hills in the 10th century and after. The registers with the Bhojakis of these temples contain long lists of people who came from outside.
21. Hutchison & Vogel, I, p. 74.
22. See, B.N. Goswamy, *The Social Background of Kangra Valley Painting*, pp. 60–67.
23. There are entries from the 17th century in the *bahis* of the priests, listing names of members of the Gujerati Tarkhan families. See, for example, *bahi* of Pandit Sansar Chand at Pehowa.
24. Kahn Singh, p. 68.
25. There are many references to Rajas, especially in the Muslim period, escaping into the hills. Thus, Sikander Sur, who retreated into the Shiwaliks at the approach of Akbar's armies. Hutchison & Vogel, I, p. 73.
26. Ghurye, *Indian Sadhus*, pp. 188, 201; Rose, *Glossary*, II, p. 306; Wilson, *Religious Sects of the Hindus*, pp. 23-38.
27. Something similar seems to happened in Assam. The Vaishnava religious centres called the *Satras* appear to have been founded in Assam, mostly in the 16th century. The great Sankaradeva, "the fountain head of the neo-Vaishnavite movement in Assam, lived from 1499-1569. See, B.K. Barua & H.J. Sreenivasa Murthy, *Temples and Legends of Assam*, 92.
28. See, *Gazetteer of the Gurdaspur District*, 1891 – 92, 61 – 63; also see, B.N. Goswamy & J.S. Grewal, *The Mughal and Sikh Rulers and the Vaishnavas of Pindori*. The authors have reconstructed the history of the Pindori establishment from many sources. The Pindori *gaddi* has published its own brief history entitled *Pindori-Dham-ka-Itihas*, by Pritam Ziyai.
29. Among the manuscripts in this volume are texts like *Sri Ekonkar sat – qur Bija Prasada Granth; Guhya Prakash; Shri tattva Gita* etc. The volume was till lately in the possession of Sri Purushottam Dass, the Mahant of Bathu.

30. Quoted in Rose, *Glossary*, I, p. 261.
31. Hirananda Shastri, "The Ruined Temple in the Nurpur Fort", *A.S.I., A.R.*, 1904-05, II, pp. 119-20. Dr. Shastri believed that the temple was demolished when Suraj Mal's rebellion was suppressed by Jahangir in 1618.
32. John Beames, "The Rhapsodies of Gambhir Rai", *Journal of the Asiatic Society of Benga*, XLIV, 1875, I, p. 212.
33. Sri Banka Rai, bard, as interviewed by Dr. B.N. Goswamy; Dr. Om Prakash and the Pujari of Brij Raj Swami temple, also similarly interviewed.
34. The pujari of Brij Raj Swami temple, interviewed. According to a different account the idol goes back to the time of the invasion of Mahmud of Ghazni. But there seems to be little reason to believe this, considering the style in which the image is carved.
35. *Diliparanjani*, pp. 49-50. The manuscript of the *Diliparanjani* was composed in S. 1760 (AD 1703) by the poet Uttam for Raja Dalip Singh. This has been translated by me into English and is under publication.
36. Pt. Jagan Nath Raina of Haripur, interviewed. The temple of Kalyan Rai occupies a central place in the Haripur town.
37. The date of the temple is recorded in the slab as S. 1719 (AD 1662).The temple is dedicated to Krishna and was probably constructed by a Rani.
38. Thakur Shamsher Chand and the Pujari of Sita Ram temple interviewed at Bijapur. This story was also narrated at Sujanpur by Sri Bhu Dev Shastri, when interviewed long back by Dr. B.N. Goswamy.
39. Goetz, "History of Chamba State", *Journal of Indian History*, XXXI, ii, pp. 138-39; Vogel, *Catalogue*, 28. The figures of Rama, Sita and Lakshmana and of Lakshmi and Vishnu are carved in the wooden porch of the state Kothi at Brahmour, which is said to date back to Prithvi Singh's reign.
40. *Sirmur State Gazetteer*, 1904, p. 12; Ranzor Singh, pp. 196-99.
41. This process was spread over several centuries, but it is possible to see it actually in operation in given areas like the Punjab Hills and Assam. An interesting parallel to the developments in the Punjab Hills is to be seen in Assam, for example. See, Barua and Murthy, *Temples & Legends of Assam*.
42. Oldham, "Non Brahmanic Hinduism in the Himalayas", *Panjab Notes and Queries*, II, No. 24, Sept 1885, Note 1046, pp. 199-200. An example that Mr. Oldham gives is of the Bhagsu Naga temple which, from a Naga temple became transformed into a Shaiva temple and took the name of Bhagsu Nath.
43. Careri, in S.N. Sen, *Indian Travels of Thevenot & Careri*, p. 258.
44. Col. Tod (II, p. 134) speaks of "a brigade of those monastic militants, the Bishen Swamis", in Marwar. Numerous Bairagis appear to have come and settled down in Kulu under Raja Tedhi Singh. See, Hardayal Singh III, pp. 57-58; Hutchison & Vogel, II, p. 465.
45. See, Ghurye, *Indian Sadhus*, p. 166.
46. Rose, *Glossary*, I, p. 366.
47. Moorcroft, *Travels in the Himalayan Provinces etc.*, I, p. 178; Gore, *Light and Shades of Indian Hill Life*, p. 69.
48. Vigne, *Travels*, I, pp. 158-59.
49. Paintings of these themes are scattered with some of them being in the collection of the Chandigarh Museum.

50. Thus an eating establishment which serves only vegetarian food is often called a Vaishnava *dhaba* or restaurant.
51. Rose, *Glossary*, I, p. 259, says that "the grand distinction" between the Shaivas and the Vaishnavas is that the latter are strict vegetarians.
52. The Pujari of the Raghunath temple at Kulu spoke of this distinction in great detail when interviewed.
53. Hutchison & Vogel, I, p. 280.
54. Rose, *Glossary*, I, pp. 376-78; *Simla Hill States Gazetteer*, 1910-11. There is a long list in Rose, of Narsingh temples in some the hill areas.
55. The full account of this ceremony was given a long time ago by Dr. Om Prakash of Nurpur to Dr. B.N. Goswamy, something that he kindly shared with me.
56. Narsingh Das Nargis, 243-245; Kahn Singh, 378-379.
57. W.G. Archer, *Loves of Krishna*, p. 105.
58. Chandigarh Museum, No. 1350.
59. Chandigarh Museum, No. D-138. This appears to be a portrait of Dhiraj Pal.
60. The temple is in the *chaugan* at Basohli, at the point from where the ascent to the palace of the Raja begins. Belief in Nilakantha Mahadev in Basohli is still very strong.
61. Moorcroft, *Travels*, I, p. 191.
62. Archer, *Loves of Krishna*, p. 9.
63. The Gauri Shankar temple has a standing, anthropomorphic image of Shiva. The temple is ascribed to Sansar Chand who is said to have paid personal homage to the deities. The present priest of the temple is descended from the first purohit who was appointed by Sansar Chand.
64. Shri Bhu Dev Shastri and Pt. Narain Dutt, interviewed at Sujanpur.
65. The Devi temple occupies the highest point of eminence in the Tira Fort and palace.
66. This temple is outside the Fort at Tira. There is a little pond around it. It is said to have been built by a descendant of the Brahmin who committed suicide here in protest at the breaking of a promise by Raja Sansar Chand. In addition to the images, there is a stone tablet with Vishnu's feet carved on it, outside the shrine.
67. The priest of the temple, interviewed. The Suketi Rani who built the temple was probably the daughter of Mian Kishen Singh of Suket. For the temple, see, Dewan Sarbdial, p. 97. Also see, Karuna Goswamy, *The Wall Paintings of Sujanpur-Tira*, Portfolio of the Lalit Kala Akademi, New Delhi.
68. Hutchison and Vogel, I, p, 186, Vigne, *Travels*, I, pp. 139-40.
69. One of these documents is in the possession of Shri Bhu Dev Shastri.
70. Sarabdial, p. 97; The *Vamsavali* of Katoch Rajas (in the possession of Pt. Narain Dutt), p. 22.
71. Chandigarh Museum, No. 348.
72. This account is by Kanwar Mohan Singh, a descendant of the Raja of Baghal, and is in a file of correspondence in the Panjab Government record office.
73. Vigne, *Travels*, I, 159.
74. Chhabra, *Antiquities*, II, p. 39.
75. *Ibid.*, p. 149.
76. Vogel, *Antiquities*, I, p. 16.
77. Chhabra, *Antiquities*, II, p. 165.
78. A great mela is held here to commemorate the death of Raj Singh who died fighting like a hero.

79. Chhabra, *Antiquities*, 165.
80. Chandigarh Museum, No. 2745.
81. This Naina Devi is different from the better known Naina Devi temple in Bilaspur.
82. Hardayal Singh, II, p. 19, Hutchison & Vogel, II, p. 387, Manmohan, p. 38.
83. National Museum, No. 63.1050. Also see, the painting reproduced in Manmohan, opposite p. 44.
84. See, e.g. Chandigarh Museum Nos. 2726, 2727, 2734, 2792.
85. Hutchison and Vogel, II, p. 394; Manmohan, p. 57.
86. Manmohan, p. 52.
87. Ranzor Singh, pp. 157-59.
88. The bard Gambhir Rai draws pointed attention to these two aspects of the Raja's faith in his *Rhapsodies*; see, *J.A.S.B.*, XLIV, i, p. 209.
89. *Mandi and Suket Gazetteer*, 1904, p. 37.
90. Ranzor Singh, p. 292.
91. The name of the priest mentioned in the grant is Zorawar Dikshit. The document was once in the possession of Pandit Bhu Dev Shastri of Sujanpur.
92. Shri Purushottam Das. One of the manuscripts is on palm leaf.
93. Rep. in *Rupam*, No. 8, October 1921, 27.
94. See his *Religious Process: The Puranas and the Making of a Regional Tradition*, p. 32.
95. A large number of these reports have been consulted. These contain very valuable information on the social, religious, and economic conditions prevalent at the time of the preparation of these.
96. O'Brien, *The Kangra Ghirths*, p. 7; Rose *Glossary*, II, p. 295.
97. *Chamba State Gazetteer*, Pt. A, 1904, p. 155.
98. *Chamba S.G.*, Pt. A, 1904, p. 149; Rose, *Glossary*, II, p. 271.
99. See, Allan, *Catalogue of the Coins of Ancient India in the British Museum*, pp. ci-cii, Nos. 159-168, 288.
100. Cf. *A.S.R.*, XIV, p. 136. See also Devendra Handa, "History and Coinage of the Kunindas" in Laxman S. Thakur (ed.), *Where Mortals and Mountain Gods Meet...*, p. 205.
101. Ranzor Singh, pp. 157-59.
102. See Appendix C below, in which the legend as given in Hutchison and Vogel, II, pp. 458-59, is reproduced in full.
103. *Kabir Legends and Anant-dasa's Kabir Parichai*, p. 5: State University of New York Press, 1991, p. 5.
104. I am extremely grateful to Shri Gupt Ram Negi, popularly known as Batuji, and to Shri Poshu Ram, both old functionaries at the Raghunath ji temple, for sharing information with me on this and other matters.
105. Timothy Clark, pp. 27-39.
106. The Greek word for 'Truth' signifying 'unconcealments' or 'self-enfolding emergence' in which individual things come forth from obscurity.
107. Arguing for the necessity of empirical studies, Durkheim stated, 'Social reality cannot be grasped by anyone who refuses to plunge into the detailed investigation of social life'. See A. Giddens, p. 35.
108. The obvious reference here is to Michael Foucault's concept of 'archaeology of knowledge'. This phrase emerged from a discussion with Pabitra Kumar Roy, to whom I remain grateful.

109. For the performative aspects of festivals see, Sandra Freitag (ed.), pp. 23-33; Philip Lutgendorf in Freitag, pp. 34-61; Anuradha Kapur, 1990; Richard Schechner, pp. 1-23, 131-83; Raminder Kaur, pp. 1-30.
110. Participant-observation during field work.
111. Geertz, p. 91.
112. Raminder Kaur, pp. 1-30.
113. Lutgendorf, in Freitag, p. 42.
114. Bernard Cohn, p. 69.
115. Bronislaw Malinowski, p. 3.
116. Interviews, among others, with:-
    (a) Chandra Sekhar Bebas, from the family of Royal *purohits* to the Rajas of Kulu.
    (b) *Gur* of Devi Hidimba, Manali.
    (c) Kardar of Bijli Mahadev, Shri Amar Singh Jamwal
    (d) Raja Maheshwar Singh, Rai of Rupi.
    (e) Dr. Vidya Chand Thakur, Himachal Academy of Language and Culture, Shimla.
    (f) Dr. Sita Ram Thakur, formerly District Languages Officer, Kulu,
    (g) Shri Amar Palshar, belonging to a family that served as bearers of the *deota's rath.*
117. Chetan Singh, 2004, p. 3.
118. The local spellings and pronunciation of the Sanskrit *Narasimha.*
119. Karuna Goswamy, 1968, pp. 103, 122; also Hardayal Singh, III, 32-35.
120. The *Shaligram* (black ammonite stone), found only in the waters of the River Gandak and the River Narmada, is the aniconic representation of Vishnu and his *avataras.* The *deotas* (godlings) are represented in their *achal* (immovable) form by a *shila* (flat stone) just as the Devi is represented by a *pindi* (a rounded stone). In their *bhera* or moveable form the *deotas* in Kulu are represented by *ashtadhatu* masks or *mohras* carried in palanquins.
121. Different types of *shaligrams* are categorized on the basis of the *chakras* visible within the stone. Fashioned by an insect., there are as many as 108 varieties, of *shaligrams* each carrying a different name. One out of these is called the *Nrisimha* Shaligram. See, Nagendranath Vasu, 1919, reprint 1986: Vol. 22, 737-739; Siddheswar Jena, 1987, pp. 309-10.
122. The survival of traces betokening *Narsingh's* presence are referred to in the following account.
123. *Bhoga* or food offering to the Gods. *Abhyagat* is defined as someone who has come or arrived uninvited as opposed to an *atithi* as one who has come by invitation. See, Monier Williams, 1974, p. 77. Here it probably signifies *Narsingh Bir*, as the only 'outsider' from the classical fold.
124. Interview with the chief priest (Bhatu-ji) of the Raghunath Temple, Kulu; also see Kamal Kishore Sharma 'Kaushik', p. 1.
125. See, S. Settar and Gunther Sontheimer, 1982, pp. 273-74; also Sontheimer, 1995, pp. 133, 135, and 1997, pp. 32, 47.
126. *Ibid.*, 1982, p. 74.
127. Surat Thakur, p. 110; Vashishtha, 2006, pp. 95-98.
128. Interview with Dr. Vidya Chand Thakur.
129. See Appendix for a complete listing.
130. See also Vidya Sharma, p. 5, who also refers to the Narsingh Bir temple at Mohal.
131. For further information on the *Birs* in Himachal, see, Rose, Glossary, pp. 179, 186, 377, 427, 469.

132. See Siddheswar Jena, 1987; Popular verses speak of *Narasimha's* residence in the forests as Pabitra Kumar Ray reminded me: *'Ausadhe cintayeit Vishnum... kanane Narasimhca....'*
133. Ann-Charlott Eschmann &c., pp. 99-117.
134. Deborah A. Soifer, 1991, pp. 75-90.
135. Wendy Donniger O' Flaherty, 1980, pp. 93-125.
136. Soifer, *op. cit.*, pp. 106-07.
137. The *Guhyatiguhya* Tantra quite clearly establishes the relationship between the Vaishnava *avataras* and the 10 *Mahavidyas. Tripura Sundari* being one of the *Mahavidyas,* explains the worship of the *Sri Yantra* at Kulu in the Puja of *Narsingh* as also the *Bhoga* of meat for *Narsingh* coming from *Tripura Sundari.* See, David Kinsley 1986.
138. *Narasimha* is seen as an example of *Sandhi* i.e. junction, combination, meeting point. This implies the combination of two elements, thereby underlining the duality of *Narsimha's* nature. Both elements undergo transformation while still retaining their identity. See, Bettina Baumer, 1992, pp. 275-77.
139. The *Mayamata* states that the *ghora,* cruel and terrible form of *Narsingh* is to be installed on mountain tops, caves, forests and within the enemy territory when the enemy has to be destroyed. Thus, the form and nature of *Narsingh* encourages the proliferation of his cult in difficult and unapproachable regions and amongst tribal people. The cult, one knows, proliferated in the tribal belts of Orissa and Andhra and acquired a following amongst the Brahmins and non-Brahmins of the deep south.
140. Mahesh Sharma, 2004, p. 398.
141. See Appendix in which the temple is listed under the mauza of Naggar.
142. Hutchison and Vogel, II, p. 461.
143. The worship of *Nar Singh,* Berreman noted, is widespread throughout the Western Himalayas. In some regions he seems to be the incarnation of Vishnu and in others, simply a household God (*kul-devta*). See, Gerald Berreman, p. 107; also Subodh Kapoor, pp. 133-34.
144. Eschmann *et al.*, pp. 79-118.
145. Georg Berkemer, in Hans Bakker (ed.), p. 129.
146. Mahesh Sharma, 2001.
147. Julian Steward, in Robert McCadam, 1966, p. 6.
148. Robert McCadam, p. 7.
149. C.F. Oldham, *op. cit.,* pp. 199-200.
150. Mahesh Sharma, 2001.
151. Interviews and participant-observation.
152. Mahesh Sharma, 2001.
153. George M. Foster, pp. 55, 159-73.
154. Mckim Marriott, p. 196.
155. *Ibid.,* pp. 197-218.
156. Participant observation during field-work.
157. Participant-observation.
158. Harcourt, p. 59.
159. Marriott, pp. 197-206.
160. *Ibid.,* pp. 199-201.

Chapter FIVE

Dussehra
The State, the Raja, and the Event

I

STATE FORMATION AND THE STATE OF KULU

Since the Dussehra of Kulu is often spoken of as a 'State Festival', it may be of interest to cast first a brief look at the whole concept of the state in general, and of the state in India in particular, with an eye upon understanding the process by which the state of Kulu might have come to be formed.

In its discourse, classical western political theory defines the state as "a form of human association distinguished from other social groups by it *purpose*, the establishment of order and security; *its methods*, the laws and their enforcement; *its territory*, the area of jurisdiction or geographic boundaries, and finally its sovereignty".[1] Not just a simple political institution or entity, the western state comes across as possessed of a certain degree of transcendence. As an embodiment of political and civic values, the state bears the aspect of being static, self-centred, unitary, homogenous and, above all, a permanent body. By contrast, the Indian state [the Hindu state] is seen as being a simple, unitary, neutral agent of an agency that lies beyond it, that of a Hindu society or caste.[2] Issues involving the emergence of an early state from pre-state societies have been of continuing interest to anthropologists, historians, sociologists and political scientists.[3] The early state was perceived to be a social phenomenon emerging out of existing social relations. Inden prefers to replace the word 'polity' in discussions on the theme by the word 'society' for this reason.[4] Expression was provided by the early state to existing ideas on power, authority, force, justice, property and so on. Pre-state societies were supposed to have transformed into state societies in response to the challenges and needs presented by their societies.[5] The existence of well-defined territorial boundaries and the presence of a sufficient number of people living within them, was a basic requirement for the complex institution called the state,[6] as it organized itself to regulate the existing social structures with some degree of efficiency.[7] As 'sovereignty' emerged out of a lineage-based society, a *'sovereign'* state implied that it now had a 'will' and could issue 'commands'. As early society matured,[8] in terms of consciousness of hierarchies as also of caste and class, society changed from an egalitarian into a rank society and further still into a stratified society till it reached its final form and emerged as a state society.[9] Differences between "bands, ranked societies, stratified societies, chiefships and state systems" have been emphasized.

The rulers of the early Indian state legitimized their claims to power and authority by claiming descent from a mythical ancestor. This was validated by the construction of a *vamsavali*, a genealogical record. The nature of kingship had undergone a change, as can be judged from the shifting of emphasis and centrality to the *vamsa*'.[10] The second source of legitimation came from establishing an intimate connection between the ruler and the dominant 'belief systems' of the area. The gods are believed to have bestowed 'sovereign' powers on the first amongst equals, the 'king' amongst men. The *Raja* began being viewed as being the source of all fertility in the land, a bestower of manifold bounties, and came to occupy the crucial position of being the mediator between the gods and the people.[11] The Raja and the state became the 'neutral' agents for the management of the caste-based society that had come into being. It was then that through the agency of rituals and ritualized behaviour that the elaboration, understanding and underscoring of the Raja's political authority was achieved. Rituals served to concretize royal authority and display it through simple but effective symbols like a "standardized repetitive, symbolic behaviour". The wearing and using of ceremonial regalia also enhanced royal powers, which in most cases were used with circumspection and responsibility. A shrewd understanding and awareness of these manipulative aspects of rituals and symbols may have been clearly visible in the Raja's behaviour as he effectively made use of pre-decided symbols representing power.[12]

Early state-forms in India have been categorized over the years by different scholars on the basis of the particular combinations of factors that pushed the lineage-society towards a state form. Out of the many models of state-formation seen as explaining the origins of the early medieval state in India, some seem to be of special relevance.[13] There is a model that speaks of 'segmentary states', as Burton Stein does in the context of polity in the southern region, locating alternative power centres in the peripheries along with those in the centre. This model elucidates the conception of a dual sovereignty, the ritual and the actual.[14] Hermann Kulke emphasizes a processural and integrative model, which delineates units of authority within a *mandala* of power. Marked as it is by the integration of local polities into state polities, the development and establishment of a centralized administration, this integrative model also examines other issues, like the improvement of trading networks and the penetration of the 'royal' will into local arenas of power.[15] While Tambiah speaks of a 'galactic polity' with 'centre-oriented space' rather than a 'bounded space' in the context of understanding the state,[16] Schnepel discusses 'questions concerning the nature of the Hindu king's authority, concerning the relationship between the domains of politics or concerning the relationship between the caste system and kingship'.[17] Bernard Cohn identifies, within the medieval Indian political system: the Imperial state, its successor states, states at the regional level, and the local units of 'prestige and power systems',[18] and Dirks talks with conviction about the 'little kingdoms'.[19]

Two other models of interest and relevance are the Indian feudalism model,[20] and the bureaucratic or unitary model.[21] The stress in contemporary historiographical studies is not on the discussion of the political entity of early state form, but on the *process* of state-formation as also on the *analysis* of it. Relevant to this theme, and to the present one, are cultural processes, seen as being among the major impulses that pushed the pre-state society towards the formation of a state. Also set into motion are trends of centralization and integration as opposed to the fragmentation encouraged by feudalism. The dynastic domain of the Raja was empowered by the increase of its hinterland and a subsequent absorption of it within a network of connectivity created by royally patronized religious institutions. Consequently, sacred places, as the focus of political interest, have to be studied with care for identifying the channels through which royal power operated. It is through the gifts made by kings to temples that the royal will appears to have started penetrating into local affairs.[22]

In the context of Kulu with which we are chiefly concerned here, this method of 'penetrating into local affairs' through gifts made by kings to temples, seems to be of special interest. It is following this manner perhaps that Bahadur Singh of Kulu (ca. 1532 to ca. 1559), aligned himself initially to the powerful local *deota*, Panchabir of Kotkandi, in the tehsil of Kulu, and gained a strong and essential control over matters concerning the *deota*.[23] Bahadur Singh's strong association with another powerful local *deota*, the goddess Hidimba or Hirima of Manali, is recorded in an inscription carved on the wooden doorway of her temple, and again makes a strong point, for while the king pays tribute to her in this manner and possibly makes a grant, she blesses him in turn. The inscription in Takri is not easy to read in its entirety, but it clearly begins with the words *Om ..Sri devi Hidema*. It goes on to mention *Sri Mharaja Sri Bahadar Singh ji* and ends with *Devi ra dehare*.[24] Even before Bahadur Singh, his predecessor, the famed Raja Sidh Singh (ca 1500 to ca.1532), had paid homage to Vishnu, something that is recorded in an inscription, also in the local Takri script, engraved on a silver *mohra*-mask of the *deota* at Jagatsukh. It is not unlikely that the Rajas had made a large gift or a grant to the *deota* in commemoration of which the figure is inscribed. Much of the inscription is now obscured, but clearly legible is the name of the Raja, *Sidh Pal* (the Raja changed his dynastic name from Pal lto Singh later) and a year – *"1422 (or 1433)"* in the *Saka kala*, meaning the Shaka Era.[25] In general, it would seem that with impulses of the Bhakti movement coming into the hills from the northern plains, temples started turning even more than before into major symbols of the sacred within the material space around them. In several instances, the Raja surrendered his temporal power to a divinity, whose cult was then raised to the level of becoming the central cult, the Raja acting as the agent of the divinity. It is in line with this, thus, that King Anangabhumi of Orissa surrendered his temporal powers to Lord Jagannath.[26] In Kulu, the situation was very similar when Raja Jagat Singh, surrendering his temporal powers as a king, ruled as the *Diwan* of Raghunathji.[27] The process of legitimation was therefore not simply a matter of seeking validation of this act, through the putting into place of an ideological apparatus through which temporal power reached out to its temporal domain. In the neighbouring state of Chamba, state formation was helped by, "... ritually legitimized and consecrated kingship ..., (and) consent for its rule was devised by manipulating ideological underpinnings, devising genealogy, forging bonds with the subcontinental sacred cosmos, demonstrating piety and virtuosity and finally claiming the warrior status as cultural protector and upholder of the norms and the values of caste society".[28] Factors like this determined the ongoing validation of the powers of the king, just as local cults, rituals and sacred centres sought to be integrated into a pantheistic supra-local structure. It has been noticed that in such cases the deity and sacred centre selected by the king were supra-local in significance, with the geography of the local sacred space being very often transformed into the sacred space of the deity's origins.[29] Tribal gods were then integrated into the system by the granting of special privileges along with an elevated status. Sometimes local gods were given the status of *kula-devata* or *kula-Devi*, and thus co-opted into the main belief system. The elevating of gods and temples reflected itself in a similar elevation of the status of the Raja. Though not deified in a real sense, the Raja was brought as close to the status of a divinity as possible.[30]

One realizes that all these are reachings out, in one's attempt to piece together and reconstruct a connected account of the coming into being of Kulu as a state. But in the absence of any significant literary evidence or texts, or sustained sources of information, this reliance on scrappy bits of information is inevitable. One also has to keep reminding oneself that some of the information one lands upon – numismatic or epigraphic survivals, for instance – needs to be evaluated or read into with caution for usages and descriptions of titles, terms, situations that one comes upon in these bits of evidence, might have their origins in conventions picked up from classical sources rather than grounded in local reality. Whether a janapada as mentioned in a stray record is to be understood in the same sense as a janapada in the Gangetic plains, for instance, would remain a question; likewise, whether the terms *raja* or *samanta* as used in the hills carried the same connotation as in the plains is a subject that could be debated. To be sure local centres of power must have been created in the region, authorities established, chiefships created. But a whole picture remains something like a dim outline: not without significance or interest, but still dim.

To jump a little. When one notices clear moves towards statehood in Kulu emerging, some factors of interest draw attention to themselves. When power had to be consolidated, various means were adopted by the king. Among them: the inviting and importing of Brahmins from established centres of learning like Kashmir and Benares. This must have helped considerably in lending credence and creating the desired image connected with an established and time-honoured centre of power.[31] A move of considerable significance, likewise, must have been the creation of *Samantas* or tributary chiefs, through the issuing of land-grants and important privileges. Through this measure the Raja surrounded himself by a 'circle of little kings' ensuring the protection of royal power. It is more than likely that, with the passage of time, the *Samantas* often developed personal ambitions of and took on grandiose titles. The famous Nirmand copper-plate inscription of ca. 7th century CE could be seen as a case in point. It is issued under the orders of Samudrasena, *the Mahasamanta and Maharaja, ... who was begotten on the Paramadevi, the Bhattarika, the illustrious Mihiralakshmi; who, like the spotless full-moon of autumn, causes the delight of (all) living creatures; who has uprooted all enemies; who confers upon the expectant rewards that are not (even) sought for (by them); who is tender to the poor, the helpless, and the afflicted; who is a most devout worshipper of (the god) Mahesvara....* The point of the copper-plate is the grant of an *agrahara* for the maintenance and feeding of Brahmins, but before that is stated, the ancestry of Samudrasena who descended from *the illustrious Varunasena, whose fame stretched out over the four oceans; the waterlilies of whose feet were covered over with the rays of the jewels in the bowed-down tiaras on the heads of many feudal chiefs; (and) who celebrated sacrifices*".[32] Clearly, classical models of royal grants have been followed here and surely an *agrahara* with attendant grants is the theme of the copper plate. But how much was the domain that Samudrasena had sway over, or what exactly did these titles signify remains largely unknown. To go back to other moves towards statehood, however, An important visible sign of an emerging state society is the conscious shifting of the capital from the peripheries towards the core region of the kingdom. This seems to have happened in Kulu from the 15th centuries onwards, or just a little later: we find the capital being shifted from Makarsa to Jagatsukh, to Naggar and, finally, to Sultanpur-Kulu.[33]

One is struck by the fact that as far as the models of state that we have spoken of before, Kulu – or for that matter any of the kingdoms in the neighbourhood – does not quite fall four square in any of them. Kulu, as we know it, does not seem to belong to the pattern of a segmentary state, or a 'little kingdom', or a processural integrative state.[34] The logic of the situation is different here it seems, and the forces at work are not only complex but remain to a considerable extent, hidden from view.[35] All that can be done is to gain some insights from the models cited and put some questions into sharper focus.[36]

The focus of this study, the Dussehra of Kulu, is relatively limited, and as far as the nature of the state in Kulu is concerned, what stands out as of prime importance is the relationship between state and religion. There is a need to stay close to the earth, and not to theory. Specifically, to what extent religion was used as 'an instrument of state policy', remains of deep interest.[37] The term 'state', it might be added, is being persisted here – broadly in the sense in which it figures in the discourses of western political theory – even as one is entitled to wonder if native terms like *Raj* or *Riyasat* would not be more appropriate. Peripherally, it might be mentioned that while the rulers of the states in the hills used for themselves own titles like *Raja*, *Maharaja*, even *Parambhattaraka*, during the period of Mughal dominance of the hills from the 17th century onwards, the overlords in Agra or Delhi routinely referred to the rulers of the Pahari states simply as *Zamindars*. A part of the difficulty in arriving at a 'final understanding' of things as they were – since they kept evolving – lies in the fact that the sources of history in Kulu are essentially "scanty and unreliable", as nearly everyone states. In sum, one is essentially in the area of speculation. Documents like the *vamsavalis* range from the partial and the fragmentary, to the clichè bound and the 'authorized version'-like. Oral traditions, valuable as they are, tend to remain soft at the edges, and can vary from account to account, or from locus to locus. Odd and scattered slivers of information, regarding the presence of some form of 'state' or governance, can be glimpsed in the legends on some locally issued coins. Casual references in the records of other states like Chamba or Kashmir, tradition as preserved in popular memory, do not help much in reconstructing things with any degree of certitude. There are no clearly discernible lines along which the processes of early state formation can be perceived.

All the same, constructing a narrative needs to be attempted. Early traditions and literary and inscriptional evidence, few and far between as they are, point to the presence of a system of governance and authority in Kulu among the *Kunindas* and the *Kulutas* – whom one has met before – from the time of the *Mahabharata* onwards. Both tribal kingdoms and *janapadas* (republics) appear to have been in existence. Speculations that the early *Kunindas* were none other than the *Kanets*, who were from the local aboriginal stock and now form a major agricultural caste of Kulu and the Shimla hill states, are to be seen along with the fact that the *Kuluta* king, mentioned in Vishakhadatta's famous play, the *Mudrarakshasha*, was addressed as a *mleccha*, i.e. one who is outside the pale of *Brahmanic* Aryan culture. A process of 'sanskritization' seems to have been at work in the region that of the *Kulutas*, around this time and might have been accomplished at least in part, possibly by the 2nd CE, judging from a coin of that period bearing the legend '*Rajno Kulutasya Virayasasya*'.[38] The 4th/5th CE rock inscription of Salri, at the border of Mandi and Kulu, speaks of a '*Maharaja Sri Chandesvarhastin*, son of *Maharaja Sri Ishwar hastin* of *the Vatsa Gotra*...'. The 6th/7th century Nirmand copper-plate, noticed before, found in the Placch area of Kulu, mentions a dynasty of donors whose names were prefixed by the combined title of *Mahasamanta-Maharaja*. The puzzling double-title makes one wonder if they were 'rajas' but were known to some paramount power placed outside Kulu as *Mahasamantas*. The 7th CE account of Hiuen Tsang mentions the kingdom of 'Kiu-lu-to', i.e. *Kuluta,* as a large tract of 500 miles, but makes no comment on the political status of this kingdom. A late text called the *Kulantapithamahatmya* traces the etymology of the word Kulu and describes it as being derived from *Kulanta,* 'the end of the habitable world', which may perhaps refer to the way the Imperial powers of North India saw Kulu. Paramount powers, not finding the physical conquest of Kulu feasible, may have treated the local rulers as their feudatories and allowed them to continue with the task of government independently. This may well explain the double-title *Mahasamanta-Maharaja* being prefixed to the name of Samudrasena and others of the Nirmand copper-plate. Surrounded by petty chiefs, the Ranas and Thakurs, one wonders if the *Mahasamants* were possibly 'rajas' who exercised authority as independent rulers, or if they were chiefs subject to the suzerainty of a paramount power. The rule of the Ranas and Thakurs, called the *Apathakurai,* was not to the exclusion of other rulers, as evidenced by the reference in Ferishta to five hundred petty chiefs but also to the *Rajas* of Nagarkot (Kangra) and Jammu. Titles are known to have been drawn from different sources: thus, the title Rana may, as Grierson suggested, have been connected to Sanskrit *Rajanaka,* and Thakurs were possibly feudal chiefs, lower in rank and caste than the *Ranas*.[39] There could, however, be little doubt about what the term 'Raja' meant.

The titles and the tenures of the *Ranas* may well have preceded those of the *Rajas*. These early 'states' or 'baronies', as Hutchison and Vogel call them, diminutive in size, possessed of porous borders, liable to constant change in consonance with the waxing and waning of the ruler's power, were more patriarchal than monarchical in nature. One can see their as a lineage rather than a state-based society. Tribal allegiance was of primary importance. The concept of 'territory' had not yet fully developed. Yet there were no signs of bonds of confederacy and no permanent Lords. Many of the *Ranas* and the Thakurs were known to have possessed only a single fort and a handful of men who served as their army.[40] Existence for these early nucleii of power must have been difficult in a period marked by confusion, lawlessness and uncertainty. These early centres of power must, therefore, have, necessarily, alternated between brief periods of independence and subjection, to some superior power outside the hills. A trifle primitive in form, possessed with none of the organizational capacity associated with later states, these early power centres may however have been the earliest form of government present in the hills. Whatever might be the factors conducive to the formation of a state, the entire process seems to have been extremely complex, for as Thapar observes, "no single fact can cause change though some would be more central than the others..." in this "...welding of lineage-based societies into monarchical states."[41]

The earliest manifestation of political authority in the Western Himalayas appears evolving towards monarchy seems to have been through the diffusion of Sanskritic ideas and Brahmanic culture in the region. These ideas and influences penetrated the 'porous' borders of the Western Himalayas via the agencies of trade and pilgrimage, thus bringing with them, almost as a corollary, the Sanskritic ideals of the North Indian plains. Cultural and political impulses, like those of the powerful Gupta ideal, appear to have spread almost as if through capillary action. Fragmented though these early clusters of power formations may have been, elements of classical style were absorbed as seen, for example, in the late Gupta style in early sculptures and architectural edifices of the Pahari region, with some of the more sophisticated traces being present in the Brahmour complex of temples in Chamba.[42]

Into Kulu, cultural influences were also flowing both from Chamba and Kashmir, since the region was located on trade-routes connecting these parts with the Indo-Gangetic Plain. A centre of great classical learning as it was, Kashmir must have been particularly influential for within it were movements of ideas, a merging of traditions of many different kinds.[43] Thus, despite their weakening in general during this period, Gupta cultural impulses continued to come in, as evidenced by the Gauri-Shankar and Sandhyadevi temples of Jagatsukh, the Parushuram and Ambika temples of Nirmand, and the Vishveshvara temple of Bajaura, all following the Gupta style favoured by the *shilpins*.[44]

Nirmand, especially, seems to have been a receiver of Brahmanical ideas as early as the 6th/7th CE, judging from the *agrahara* land-grants – to which we have referred before – bestowed upon an entire village of Brahmins who had been invited and settled here from North India. The very fact of classical Sanskrit being the language of the Nirmand inscription is a clear indication of the flowing in of influences and ideas that were classical in nature. Even though this was, broadly, a period of the presence of warring local chiefs and the absence of a strong, centralized monarchical state,[45] the coming in of ideas of kingship of the pan-Indian kind into this region must have begun to make an impact.

In the context of the concept of kingship, as different yet from that of the state,[46] Thapar speaks of the union of royal and priestly power, the 'Divine Right' of the king seen as being quickened by the gods through the priests. The king was no longer a king by virtue of a 'social contract' alone, but a ruler by 'Divine Right'. Above him stood of course *Dharma*.[47] The king's divinity here is not his own, but that of a principle that rules over him, and of which he is the living image, the instrument and the puppet. The king, therefore, in order to ensure his ascendancy had to perforce engage in the continuing process of rejuvenating his divinity through rituals. He had, as has been stated, to "engage in a subtle and 'precarious' balancing act between proclaiming his own writ to be *Dharma* and what his subjects tell him is his *Dharma*."[48]

In the case of Kulu, it appears that, at least initially, the hold of the *Rajas* of Kulu over their territories was not firm enough. It often turned into a battle for control between the *Raja* and the rebellious *Ranas* and *Thakurs* on the one hand, and with neighbouring states on the other, to prevent their incursions into and establishment of control over territories that were of strategic or economic importance. In this ongoing struggle for the establishment of a strong centralized state, success lay in pushing back the predatory invaders. It is against the backdrop of ecology, belief patterns, social and economic structures that the emergence of a centralized state in Kulu needs to be seen. Forces set into motion by a logic, both external and internal, pushed relentlessly towards a restructuring of the state by the 16th/17th CE. Leadership imbued with a larger awareness of North Indian polities brought the process to a successful culmination. Briefly put, society in Kulu was, it seems, polarized between self-sufficiency and interdependence. This was very much in keeping with Inden's understanding of the human world in India, being ordered into, 'mutually exclusive', 'dichotomously' defined, 'interdependent parts'.[49] Each of the narrow valleys separated by steep mountain ridges, was a micro-region, economically and culturally self-contained and yet dependent in other ways upon one another. Economic disparities, an absence of social inequality and stratification, necessarily demanded an extremely diversified economy to provide the stable economic base necessary for the emergence of a centralized state. Despite inadequate cultivable land, a profitable symbiotic relationship developed between pastoralism, transhumance and agriculture. In the Kulu region inland trade mainly in grains and woollen items flourished along the main Beas valley, even though it was the opium grown in the Kulu, Malana and Siraj valleys that was the major revenue earner. At the same time, an 'assertive' *kanet* peasantry, socially mobile artisans, and the lack of dominant Brahmanic influence, helped in the overland trade with Tibet and Ladakh, which consisted principally of wool and pashmina.[50] The geographical space for setting up an entrepot capable of developing into a hub of trade was present at Dhalpur, Kulu, which was also a time-honoured nodal point on the trade-route between Tibet and the Northern plains of India. A well thought out system designed to work was put into place, as will be seen later, by Jagat Singh, at the time of the institution of the festival of Dussehra, thus ensuring continuity in matters of trade.

By about the 14th/15th CE kings, it appears, princely cadets and even enterprising ordinary men from the northern plains, started coming into Kulu in search of territory, power and new opportunities.[51] It would seem reasonable to assume that if any of the adventurers or cadets succeeded in establishing a core of power and domain in this region, it could have been only, or at least substantially, through the use of force, or sometimes through deceit and ruse. Even when one regards the case of Behangmani, who coming from outside is believed to have founded the Pal dynasty in the Kulu region and about whom more will be seen later, the use of force for establishing authority must have been inevitable despite all the blessings that he received from the goddess Hidimba, according to legend. He must have had to assert himself over the local, often petty, chieftains generally referred to as '*Ranas* and

Thakurs'. The stories that abound in the hills, of arrogant local barons imposing oppressive rule over unwilling subjects, must surely have some basis in fact. The tradition preserved at Malana, of an uprising by the followers of the local *deota*, Jamlu, against a rapacious local chief at some early point of time, is not the only one that has survived: at other places too, one gets the sense that there was much disorder and non-cooperation. Oppression was common. In that situation, it is not difficult to imagine that a determined person with some force at his command, and some vision of founding a peaceful *raj*, which guaranteed the populace a modicum of order and security, would have been able to make progress. To go back to Behangmani, the founder of the Pal dynasty again, and to try and reconstruct his career. This Rajput cadet, who came from the northern plains and was strictly an outsider, did not come with a large army of followers perhaps but was armed with a daring spirit. As per current legend, he gained the support and the blessings of the powerful local goddess, Hidimba, but still had to conquer and gain land for establishing a kingdom. Myth and metaphor were pressed into service, as far as his legend is concerned, for creating an image. According to these, the land/state was bestowed upon him by Hidimba: Legitimacy and support was created through the skilled device of 'socially constructed memories of the past'.[52] It is likely that Behangmani Pal kept adding to his possessions incrementally, and ended up with a sizeable state ruled over by the dynasty that he founded. What he was able to offer to the people he brought under his rule in return, what made his new subjects give him the 'consent to rule', remains undocumented. But one can guess that, apart from the security his rule might have offered, as against that of the *Ranas* and *Thakurs*, and against possible raids from neighbouring states, it would have been his policy of respecting the local and old 'centres of power', the *deotas*. What accommodations were worked out, what guarantees given, or in what form were any understandings arrived at, it is not possible exactly to fathom. But some transactions must have taken place touching upon spheres that extended from the political and the religious to the economic and the social.

Whatever visissitudes of fate Behangmani and his successors went through do not concern us here but it seems certain that a dynasty had been founded and in the family the memory of the beginnings of their fortunes going back to the 'alignemnt' between Behangmani and the goddess Hidimba, survived for centuries. A marker in the history of the Pal dynasty was the accession to the throne of Raja Sidh Pal (ca. 1500 CE) whose is a name remembered with great respect. He was the one who, it appears, considerably expanded his domains, subdued the oppressive 'Piti Thakurs' – believed generally to have affiliations with Spiti – who had fortified themselves in their domains,[53] constructed a strong fort like the one at Naggar for himself, and made the town his capital. Sidh Pal's fortunes waned for a while on account of local opposition and machinations of powers opposed to him, but he succeeded in re-establishing a strong authority eventually. Most interestingly, of him is told the same story as was told of his prime ancestor, Behangmani Pal: of his helping the goddess

Hidimba who was in disguise, and receiving her blessings in return. Whatever the case, Sidh Pal recovered most of the territory he had lost, consolidated his power, and aggregated the waziris of Rupi and Saraj to his domains. What he also did was to change the title of his family – and thus that of his dynasty – to Singh from the earlier Pal. That family name has lasted to this day.

The concept of the state may have emerged more clearly under Sidh Singh's successor, Bahadur Singh (ca. 1532 to 1559 CE.). By this time may have grown an awareness of all things that would hold a state together. The rest of Kulu was conquered in a campaign mounted with the help of Raja Sahib Sen of Mandi. Kulu got all of Sainj as a part of the spoils. A very informative and early document, an inscription of Bahadur Singh of Kulu dated 1559 CE, is carved on the right side of the doorway of the Hidimba temple in Manali.[54] Other things apart, the title used in the inscription for the ruler, is of significance. In the grant, Bahadur Singh is referred to as as *Surtran*. The grant being in Sanskrit, this term has generally been understood to be a sanskritized version of the Arabic-Persian term, *Sultan*, which had come into use after the imposition of Muslim rule in northern India, and was in vogue in awareness of the powers that such Sultans, whether in Delhi or Lahore, had come to command. However, possibly there is more to the term than this alone. Breaking up the word into its two components – *sur* and *trana*, meaning, in Sanskrit, respectively, 'deity' or 'god' and 'protecting' – it is not unlikely that there is an intended pun in the use of the term *Surtran*, meaning both a Sultan, and a person 'who offers protection to deities': in this case almost certainly the *deotas*. One might possibly be reading too much into this term, but a situation in which the power of the Rajas stemmed substantially from their ability, and their willingness, to leave the *deotas* in possession of their 'domains' of power, and to offer them protection, is far from being inconceivable.

The period of Raja Jagat Singh (ca. 1637-1672 CE) in the same line as Bahadur Singh appears to have been of great significance in the history of Kulu for a number of reasons. A turning point in the history of Kulu, both from the sacral and political point of view, this period was marked by a new confidence, self-assurance, and a continuation of the policies of Bahadur Singh. Predatory neighbours were pushed back. Lost territories were first reappropriated and then aggregated under a central command. Jagat Singh, freshly converted to ardent Vaishnavism by Krishnadas Payahari, as seen before, may have intuitively been quick to perceive the enduring and irreversible connection between religion and politics. Realizing that religion through ritual could serve to conquer authority and legitimize it, he saw the necessity of creating a central religious symbol as a rallying point.[55] Symbols such as these, which become 'concrete embodiments of ideas, attitudes, judgements, longings or beliefs', he must have realized, are 'models' to 'synthesize a people's ethos' and their 'world view'. They both 'shape' and are 'shaped', as conceptual form is aligned to social reality.[56] When he instituted the festival of Dussehra, and later carefully structured it, it might have been to fulfil precisely this need. For the *deotas*, their *haryan* (body of followers), in fact for the entire populace from the remote areas, this festival became the central focus of their loyalty and devotion. For the *deotas*, supporting Raghunathji, became an expression of solidarity with his self-appointed deputy, the Raja of Kulu. Armed with this expression of spiritual solidarity, Jagat Singh may have sought to reconcile people of diverse political and religious hues, through the 'agency' of his kingship, within the still nascent state of Kulu. The manipulative aspects of 'human agency' have been greatly underestimated in terms of their impact on political and sacral events.[57] One can see them at work here, though. It is through this shrewd intervention by the *Raja* that the *deotas* were subtly converted into 'aspects of the One supported by a paramount kingship'.[58] The instituting of the Dussehra with all its attendant rituals must have been perceived as being of great value by the state, which otherwise may or may not have been supported by the populace, or might not have participated in the powerful religious system associated with Vaishnava bhakti and the cult of Raghunathji.[59] A lot of these subtle processes are visible during the Dusseshra procession. Difficult contradictions are gently absorbed, understood and adjusted. There is a general sense of ease during the festival which, despite all the noise and the spectacle, generates a feeling of balance and harmony. The only discordant notes being struck (and these are attended to and resolved fairly quickly) are when a particular *deota* registers his or her protest over issues of non-acceptance, challenging of his position in the hierarchy, or when his welcome as he comes to the festival is not commensurate with his status.[60] Behind reservations and arguments such as these, one needs to add, were very often reflections of new political realities.

Judging from the festival as it is today, one notices the harmony that is established between the various belief systems. In this easy coming together of the diverse gods who formed a part of the *Raja's* personal belief structures, there appears to be no awkward contradiction that surfaces. The *Raja's* personal devotion to Kali as his *Kuldevi* has been easily adjusted with his loyalty towards Hidimba as the bestower of his kingdom. Alongside is manifest his devotion to the *deota* Pancabir of Kot Kandi, who elicits a more visceral response from the Raja.[61] Even today, the titular *Raja* of Kulu, who has no kingdom that he rules over, emerges as an important figure in the temporal sphere, firmly in charge of both his 'kingdom' and his god. Though descended from 'outsiders', who had come into this region from elsewhere, the line to which Raja Jagat Singh belonged had established itself as *the* royal family of Kulu and had become naturalized in this new setting and struck roots culturally in this world of their choice. The writ of the Kulu royal family had come to stay. Land-grant inscriptions, copper-plate grants, and *mohras* (masks) of various *deotas* granted by royalty contributed to the impression of a dynasty at home in its surrounding. The kings of Kulu had completely merged into their new political and sacral landscape. All this is on view during Dussehra time even today. By the complete identification of the *Raja* with the presiding deity of the state, the powers of the *Raja* had been greatly enhanced. His public image, which required a patina of divinity, had received one.[62]

It is of interest to note that a parallel situation exists in neighbouring Mandi. During the famed Shivratri fair, which is structured along the lines of the Dussehra of Kulu, the *Raja* of Mandi as the vice-regent of the deity Madho Rai, emerges as the de-facto ruler of Mandi: He receives the implicit obedience of the local *deotas*. Nothing moves, nothing happens, without his permission or his participation, whether it is permission to commence the festival, or to select a new *gur* (oracle) for the *deota*, or even peripheral issues of changing the canopy of a *deota*.[63] From the close-by Shimla hill states again comes the near parallel example of *deota* Junga from the Keonthal Thakurai. The complete identification, both political and the sacral, of the Rana of Keonthal with the principal *deota* of the area has been well illustrated by Singh in his documentation of the connection between nature, religion and politics in the Western Himalayas. At Keonthal, too, permission to celebrate any festival at the shrine of a local *deota* has necessarily to be obtained from the principal *deota*, Junga. All the local *deotas* have necessarily to deposit a small token, *nazrana*, into the treasury of Junga, thereby accepting their position of subordination to him. The implication, in temporal terms, of this identification of the *Rana* with Junga, meant the establishment of absolute control by the *Rana* over the territorial gods of the peasant clans and therefore over the clans themselves. In Keonthal, legitimation of his power, however, was sought by the Rana also through his worshipping of the classical goddess Tara, at the time of *Durga Ashtami*.[64]

Although on a much larger scale than in Keonthal, much the same happens in Kulu. The *deotas* by offering homage and *nazrana* to Raghunathji, at the time of the Dussehra, also accepted the overlordship of his *diwan*, the *Raja* of Kulu. This control over the *deotas* naturally extended to the peasant clans that constituted the *haryan*. The scattered presence of the *deotas* and their *haryan*, and their segregation from one another due to the presence of narrow valleys and high mountain ridges, made it difficult to reach or control them. These autonomous isolated communities could, therefore, only be controlled through the hegemony of ideas or faith. Through the unique equation established during Dussehra time with the local *deotas*, the local faiths were not only associated but subordinated and integrated under the banner of Raghunathji.

Today, as in earlier times perhaps, many of the rituals of worship are performed by the Raja himself. From the morning *bari puja* to the bathing and adorning of the images, to standing in waiting upon Raghunathji as a common servitor, the Raja participates in everything. In this process of receiving the *nazrana* of the *deotas*, bestowing a token offering upon them in return, the Raja, in the course of the seven days of the festival, gets transformed, slowly but surely into a real leader of his men. These rituals at Kulu must at an earlier time have played a very substantial role in the articulation of rank and power.[65] The *deotas* of Kulu were gifted with *muafi* – rent-free lands – by the Raja on behalf of Raghunathji and, in return for this, a compulsory attendance at the time of Dussehra was expected of them. As a token of their subordinate position a small amount as *nazrana* was paid by the *deotas* into the coffers of Raghunathji. The *deotas* however were honored by the Raja in return.[66] Through these rituals, which bound the group together, a deep sense of community was created. The state, which is otherwise an abstract entity and is not easy to see, became a concrete reality that was easily visible. Above all, monarchy became accessible to the people, carrying with it an almost 'iconic reassurance of stability'. By being the greatest servant of the reigning deity, the king both sustained and displayed his rule over men and brought it prestige. The rituals observed at Kulu served to organize, integrate, legitimize and inculcate political beliefs alongwith a deep sense of solidarity amongst the people. Authority, which is in many ways central to ritual power was, now, not only culturally constructed but dramatically displayed too. Nothing but political stability emanated from the sacred centre of the Raghunath mandir where the *Rajas* "... tried with their traditional patrimonial power to counter balance these dangerous feudal forces by ritual measures....".[67] Political power stood legitimized. The status of the *Raja* got confirmed and elevated in the process.

The establishment of the worship of Raghunathji in Kulu was made easy, it needs to be remembered, by the assimilative nature of Vaishnavism. A processes of acculturation and of sanskritization was set into motion, the reference points for which lay within the north Indian plains. A 'consent to rule' was created through the well known devices of maintaining genealogical records of the royal house of Kulu, creating links with antiquity and thereby establishing the right and legitimation to rule.[68] Emulating North Indian practices, the sacred geography of Ayodhya was sought to be recreated in the courtyard of the Raghunath temple alongwith the transformation of the Dhalpur Maidan into the battle-field of the Ramayana. Belief patterns, modes of performing *pujas* and eulogies contained within land-grants, defined the king as the upholder of the scriptures, the refuge of the poor. All this was engineered to ensure the much-needed 'consent to rule'. As already stated, cultural symbols like the Dussehra were created to bring a sense of solidarity amongst the people, and brahmins as the preservers of classical culture were invited from well known centres of learning like Kashmir and Banaras and settled in Kulu.

This constant 'interlocking of divinity and state system' bestowed powers on the Raja that were entirely different from the powers of lineage-based rulers. It is in this integrative process that factors giving rise to conflict were sought to be controlled and settled.[69] There was no repudiation of local deities, the *deotas*, etc.; also no assimilation; it was a matter of arriving at accommodations, a sharing of sovereignty so to speak.

Of relevance to the study is also an examination of the *relationship* that obtained, or was worked out, between the Raja of Kulu, the central authority of the state, and local gods, the *deotas*, in the political and religious sense. As already stated, the *Raja*, as the representative and deputy of *Raghunath ji* or *Rama, required* the host of local *deotas* whose temples dotted the entire state and who, despite wielding great power over their *haryan* or 'subjects' within their own 'domains', to be present at the Dussehra, year after year. How the Raja saw the *deotas*, or was seen by them, could, in some manner, provide some insights into the nature of this relationship. Terms like 'paramountcy', 'hegemony', 'suzerainty', 'divided sovereignty', could hang about in the air, and could of course be considered as we seek to define the nature of these connections. It would perhaps be closer to the truth to state that there was no uniformity in this matter: no monolithic pattern that emerged. The entire belief patterns perhaps contained coded information on political and social issues. What does emerge is an extremely layered and complex relationship.

One can speak here of at least three different aspects of this relationship between the Raja and the local *deotas*. There is, thus, the relationship between the Raja and his family with the goddess Hidimba of Dhungri, near Manali. Nothing in the entire series of events that constitute the celebration of Dussehra happens without the Raja assigning primacy of importance to Hidimba. Before anything begins, she is the one who is consulted about the very holding of the event, with the Raja presenting himself before her. Sending his *chhari* through an empowered emissary, he invites her to make her way from Manali to Kulu, to participate in the Dussehra in the manner of the other *deotas*. Hidimba is, however, singled out for being formally received and honoured, again by royal functionaries carrying a *chhari* or 'royal mace', on the outskirts of the town of Kulu, at Ram Shila on the right bank of the Beas. After she enters the town with great fanfare, she heads straight for the Raja's palace which is 'vacated' by the royal family out of respect for her, so that she can come and occupy the whole of it to enable all and sundry who gather there to render her homage. At each step she is feted and honoured. Clearly, the Raja, followed by his entire family, sees himself, and is seen by everyone else, in the light of a devoted 'servant' of the goddess rather than as her master. Consistently, she is referred to as the 'Dadi', the grandmother, all of whose commands are to be obeyed. Even her *gur*, or oracle, wields great authority. It is he who, when approached with questions about what the ensuing year will turn out to be like, makes his oracular pronouncements.[70] It all goes back to remembered history: to the times of Behangmani who founded the Pal dynasty of Kulu in earlier, unchronicled, times. The story has often been told but everyone recalls it at this time. The times were disturbed, and resistance to the oppressive local chieftains – the Ranas and Thakurs – was in the air. Behangmani, having come as an outsider to these parts, had gained a foothold on power, but was still far from being a ruler of Kulu, when he went to attend a large fair, near Jagatsukh. On the way he was accosted by an old woman who asked him to take her on his back, as she was unable to walk. This he did, with great humility, promising that he would do the same on his return. When they reached Jura, opposite Basnara, according to this account, the old woman revealed herself as a goddess: she jumped down from his back and told Behangmani to climb on her back instead and look around into the distances. The goddess was Hidimba: she had been moved by the young man's kindness and wanted to reward him. 'Till as far your eyes can see, this land will be yours,' she said. Events did transpire in the same fashion. The stir against the Ranas and Thakurs succeeded, and Behangmani did become the Raja of the land. The Pal dynasty that he founded flourished, and even though some believe that the present Raja and his ancestors do not belong to the same line, the memory of the Raj having been a 'gift', a bestowal, from the goddess survives. Logically, therefore, the Raja regards himself as having descended from that *dadi* or grandmother and, quite voluntarily, stands in a relationship of subordination to her.[71]

At the opposite end is the case of the *deota*, Jamlu of Malana. A great deal has been written on Jamlu. Some accounts identify Jamlu with the sage Jamadagni of ancient times. The *janapada* of Malana, with its traditions, at odds with those of the rest of Kulu, offers a rich area for anthropological, historical, and linguistic studies, for its 'ruler', the *deota* Jamlu, does not conform to usual practices. Being a somewhat 'angry' and 'self-willed' *deota*, he does not take orders. Emphatically, therefore, he declines to accept the 'invitation' to attend the Dussehra at Kulu. From time to time, some emissaries of the *deota* come and camp on the left bank of the Beas, at some distance from Kulu town, but the *deota* does not himself enter Kulu. Whatever this assertion of independence goes back to stays unclear, but the fact remains that Jamlu does not personally attend the Dussehra that celebrates the triumphs of Raghunath ji. Traditionally, however, this act of defiance, which can to be seen as an assertion of independence and defiance of the Raja's authority, goes 'unpunished'. Jamlu remains his own person.[72]

Occupying the space between the positions of Hidimba and Jamlu – those of submission and defiance – are numerous other *deotas*, whose relationship with the Raja's authority can be seen as exemplified by Gohri *deota*.[73] Gohri is a 'friend', living in the neighourhood of the royal palace at Sultanpur-Kulu, amiable and easy to approach. He is consulted over various things; to the royal palace he comes and goes with ease; he stays close to the Raja when the procession from the Raja's palace to the *maidan* of Dhalpur starts making its way. There are no undertones in the relationship: neither defiance nor subservience comes into play. There is warmth in the air.

How, over long years, relationships of such varying kinds – so different in tone and substance from one another – were worked out is not easy to establish. In the case of the goddess Hidimba, a continuing link – after the initial blessing that she gave Behangmani Pal – is seen in an inscription dateable to the year equivalent to 1418 CE, found on her *mohra* or metal mask, which mentions the devotion of Raja Udhran Pal, a descendant of Behangmani, to her. The connection between the ruling house and the goddess is re-stated.[74] The authority she must have wielded in the region from very early times must have been very considerable, something that needed to be acknowledged. What is significant, however, also is the fact that this authority went beyond the religious or spiritual spheres alone. She was given by the rulers, as Hutchison and Vogel record, a very considerable *jagir*, land free of rent, at the upper end of the Kulu valley, and in these lands "the royal writ did not run". They add: "The *jagir* also enjoyed the right of sanctuary, and when a criminal or any one, fleeing the Raja's displeasure, succeeded in reaching the borders of the *jagir*, at Okhiragolu about two miles below Manali, he became Hidimba's refugee, and was not given up to his pursuers, who if they followed farther became blind. The place thus bore the meaning of 'freedom from hardship."[75]

There are valuable signs here of accommodation, of a mutuality of relationship, between the Raja and the goddess. The early Rajas, whether Behangmani or Udhran Pal, can be seen here receiving or seeking the blessings of the goddess, paying her homage, and she as receiving grants of land together with other privileges. In the case of Behangmani, as oral tradition records, his power, even the very foundation of his dynasty, is derived from his close association with her. It can be seen that here we are in the area of legitimization of authority, of power derived from a widely respected and ancient source. Undoubtedly, in the custom followed to this day where the goddess Hidimba is treated with the greatest of respect and referred to always as 'the grandmother', there is much meaning. Of interest also is the fact that, as Hutchison and Vogel record, privileges of this kind, although not perhaps on the same scale, were extended to other *deotas* who held *jagirs* bestowed or confirmed by royal authority. The ruler clearly bestows, and receives, at the same time. Even though the situation has now changed completely – the Raja is no longer in a position to give or take back, and the *deotas* are no longer truly obliged to offer him their respect – this mutuality of relationship continues to exist. One can see all of this in terms of symbols. Everything is beautifully choreographed. When the *deotas* start gathering for the Dussehra at Kulu, their first stop is the temple of Raghunath ji where homage must, as per traditional norms, be paid. This visit is listed in the *hazari* or attendance register.[76] But then the *deotas* also make their way to the Raja's palace, with musicians and bands of followers in tow. Here they are received with honour. The palanquins or basket-like *karadus*, in which they are carried on their shoulders by *sewaks*, come into the courtyard where the Raja and his family station themselves to welcome them. As a mark of respect to the Raja, the palanquin is made to dip and tilt towards him as if the *deota* were bending low in homage. However, acknowledging that the Raja, respectfully, makes an offering to the *deota* in turn, a token sum: not as largesse but as a devotee's tribute. This goes on throughout the day, and continues even after the Raja shifts his camp from his palace to the Dhalpur *maidan*. Each time a *deota* comes to the Raja's camp and encounters the Raja, the palanquin dips and tilts in his direction: each time the Raja stands up in respect and makes an humble offering.[77]

It is not difficult to see that these ceremonies, these ritual exchanges, must have *evolved* over a long period of time. The symbolic sights that one witnesses today, or could have witnessed till yesterday when the Rajas wielded real power, were evidently the 'mature flower' of the plant of tradition that had its roots in the past. Much must have gone into the making of the relationships between the *deotas* and the Raja, or between subjects and ruler, that is reflected in these ceremonies and exchanges. Nothing could have been laid down at the very outset. Nuanced situations expressing reluctance, opposition, negotiation, persuasion, inducement, pressure, force, and the like can be envisioned. Unfortunately, however, there is little that is documented. A true penetration of the past seems not to be possible. Several questions arise. How did the *deotas* come into the possession of the lands that 'belong' to them, and at what point of time, even when local records state that these possessions were theirs 'since times of old'. On the subject of land alone, questions would continue to persist. Were these 'old possessions' always respected and left undisturbed by the Rajas of the past, for instance? Did the relationship of the Raja with the *deotas*, or vice versa, remain constant, or did it keep changing, with some coming into favour and others falling out of it, with predictable consequences? How and when were fresh grants of land – *jagirs*, in other words – made by the Raja? Were *jagirs* or grants in cash constantly the subject of negotiation? Did any resumption or curtailment of grants go unchallenged, or unopposed? Were transfers of land – those by a devotee in favour of his *ishta deota*, for instance – permitted and acknowledged by the Raja? There are gaps in our information, which are difficult to fill and which make it difficult to arrive at a true understanding of the nature of the state and its authority, among other things.

In respect of governance, again – in the exercise of judicial or administrative powers, for instance – it remains difficult to reach any level of detail, even if the texture of the times can be felt. One knows that the land was divided into *waziris* – from the Persian word *wazir*, meaning minister or deputy – and those listed include *waziris* Parol, Rupi, Lag-Maharaja, Lag-Sari, Siraj, and Bangahal. It would have been natural for trusted people, whether from the royal family or not, to be appointed to head them. Other officials and functionaries like *Tehsildars, Negis, Palasaras, Kuthialas, Kaiths and Kardars* are also spoken of.[78] What *their* relationships with the time-honoured local centres of power – the *deotas* – were, remains difficult to establish. That, traditionally, *deotas* wielded considerable power within their 'domains' is well known. Disputes would be brought to them by their subjects or *haryan*, for instance; through their priests, they adjudicated and punished; they could ostracize individuals, even whole families; impose fines or demand offerings for the shrine. But it is not easy to say what transpired when this authority or power of theirs came into conflict with that exercised by the central authority: the Raja or his appointed functionary. The right of sanctuary alone, as enjoyed by some *deotas*, something to which reference has been made before, must have imposed some constraints. Local sentiment must again have carried serious weight in many matters. Are we then in the region of 'spheres of power' and 'spheres of influence', one wonders? Much in the manner of 'overlapping societies', could there have been 'overlapping powers', of the kind that Inden speaks of, in the context of understanding the nature of the state in south India? In the area of his inquiry, he stated that: "We do not see a polity consisting of a distant repressive state on the one hand and a ... society of isolated, inwardly oriented villages organized into auto-reproductive castes on the other."[79] To adapt from this, however – for a hill state like Kulu was not of the dimensions of some of the south Indian states, and the social dynamics here were of a different order – this might come close to describing the situation here: 'isolated, inwardly oriented villages' not excessively leaned upon by 'a distant, repressive state'. This situation could perhaps be described as one of 'shared sovereignty' in the judicial and religious field. In practical terms, the common man then had two masters, the Raja and his personal *deota*. Both these powers controlled the same man. In the case of conflict it is not clear if the Raja's writ could prevail over that of the *deota*. One recalls in this context the description of the nature of Mughal overlordship over the hill states by Hutchison and Vogel. "Mughal authority sat lightly upon the hills," they say. One knows that Imperial commands were issued from time to time. Some of the hill chiefs were commissioned into serving on hard and distant campaigns. Centrally appointed *faujdars* kept an eye upon things. Token tributes were also levied, and an acknowledgement of the suzerainty of the Mughals was expected at all times. But by and large, unless prickly issues arose, the hill chiefs were left to themselves in matters of local administration, to rule over their domains in their own manner.[80] It is not unlikely that this pattern held in the matter of the relationship that existed between the Raja of Kulu and the local centres of power – the *deotas* – also. The authority of the Raja sat lightly upon them. The nature of the geography of the region, with valleys cut off by high mountain ranges and turbulent streams, combined with other environmental factors like agriculture, trade, populations, lifestyles, belief patterns and the strength of age-old traditions, might well have resulted in the coming into being of mutually understood, and respected, spheres of power. It is possible to envisage the existence of a situation in which, in a broad range of matters, the central authority of the Raja was widely, even explicitly, acknowledged but not always rigidly exercised.

There were of course areas in which space existed for the Raja to take on different roles and exercise his powers, even in distant places, when it was required. As Chetan Singh points out, the ruler was compelled to perform a balancing act when conflicts rose between different local centres of power, for instance.[81] The "moral order" prevalent in the Himalayan kingdoms, as he says, was the complex network of hierarchically placed deities that stretched from the political capital to the remotest villages. But even within the fairly rigidly established 'system', there were situations in which this hierarchy was contested and even re-ordered because of the social transformations occurring in villages.[82] When this happened, the Raja's authority was almost invariably invoked, something that gave him the opportunity to assert, or re-assert, his "ideological supremacy". In the case of Kulu, especially after the establishment in the early 17th century there of 'ardent Vaishnavism', and the installation of Raghunathji as the state deity in Raja Jagat Singh's reign, the authority of the Raja had come to rest upon the twin pillars of political control and religious precedence. Here, as in the case of Kumharsain and Keonthal, 'political organization' and 'religious ideology' could be seen as 'critical components of a single public space' in which religion and politics were used in 'constantly shifting combinations'.[83]

The term *deota*, it is to be understood, is not gender-specific in local usage, and applies as much to male deities as to female ones. The spectrum of *deotas* is remarkably broad in Kulu. It also encompasses deities of all shades and persuasions: Shaiva and Vaishnava and Shakta, of classical origin or local extraction, Devis and Devas, Rishis and Nags, Sidhs and Birs, and the like. A point of interest to consider in this context would be whether, in his dealing with various *deotas* and their domains, administrative or religious, the Raja's own religious inclinations might have played a part: in other words, whether he favoured some over others. Interestingly, from the evidence available this does not appear to have been the case. For one thing, the Raja, even after he took on the role of the Dewan of Raghunath ji and ruled in his name, was not a Vaishnava to the exclusion of other beliefs. The *kula-devi* of the Raja's family, as has been already mentioned, is the goddess Kali whose image is installed in the royal palace, and who is offered worship before any other god on Dussehra day. She is also invoked in all personal matters. And then the Rajas have had long and intimate associations with other *deotas* who have played a significant part in the history of the family and in the coming of Raghunath ji to Kulu. Hidimba Devi of Dhungri-Manali, without whom nothing moves; Bijli Mahadeo, a Shaiva deity, who camps next to the royal palace when he comes to Kulu on the occasion of the Dussehra; the Panch Birs in whose area the image of Raghunath ji was first brought when it came from Ayodhya and whose *gur* sits on the *rath* along with the other functionaries of Raghunath ji; and Dhumal Nag, who plays such a prominent role in the Dussehra procession, clearing the field and acting as the avant-garde.[84] History and tradition, not personal religious inclination, seem to have been the guiding factors. Early Indian thought was flexible, integrative, inclusive but not exclusive. Even handedly, it seems, respect was offered to the *deotas* and received from them in turn: something that must have had its impact on the nature of authority exercised by the state.

In the end, it needs to be stated that all we have on the nature as also the formation of the state of Kulu, like that of other states in the region perhaps, is fragmented information: not enough to make any confident statements possible but enough to tempt one to speculate upon the nature of things as they might have been.

Somehow, however, the past continues to live on and symbols afford us some glimpses of it. To go back to the series of events that make up the Dussehra as it is still celebrated in Kulu is not without meaning, therefore. Among these events is the routine followed on the Dhalpur maidan after Raghunath ji's camp is set up there. Despite all power having gone out of the Raja's hands today, and despite so much time having passed, each afternoon a small procession is formed with the Raja on horseback setting out along with an entourage to visit the *deotas* in the tiny lodgings that house them on the maidan. The *Jaleb* procession stops every few minutes; the Raja pays his homage to the *deota*; the *sewaks* and priests of the *deota*, members and representatives of his *haryan*, stand out of respect, hands folded.[85] There is a semblance of pomp, at least a memory of it; some music is played; then the Raja returns to his own camp. For the round to begin the next day again. The mutuality of relationship that one spoke of at the beginning is established; the Raja plays his part and the *deotas* theirs. The scale and the distances might have been different in days of old, but this ceremony catches perhaps the tenor of things as they might have been once.

II

THE ROLE OF THE RAJA

In the 'state festival' that Dussehra is, attention needs to shift now to the event as it unfolds and to the role that the Raja plays in it.[86] In the process one will be looking at a series of rituals and ceremonies that constitute an integral part of the event. A *rich* description of the festival in some part would be needed, since detail is of the essence for understanding some of the 'statements' that are made through it and the implications that it holds. The description of some of the ritual acts will take centre stage, for rituals, as we well understand, are rich in resonances.[87] They contain religious and cultural meanings, marking off and sanctifying sacred spaces, establishing or confirming social relations, articulating issues of rank and power. Authority, including in this case the authority of the Raja of Kulu, being central to ritual power, reference will be seen as constantly being made to 'political linkages and hierarchies of privilege and status', as much as to 'structures of order and authority'.[88]

The Dussehra of Kulu is visibly different, in so many ways, from the festival of the same name that is celebrated in large parts of northern India. Rama is here, as elsewhere, the central figure, and it is his triumph and glory in all its plenitude that one is reminded of, year after year, through the celebrations. But there are no enactments here, such as the Ramalila, that precede the event; the celebrations that stretch over seven days begin here on the very day that they have ended in the plains; no great effigies of Ravana and his kinsmen are raised and then consigned to flames. The spectacle takes another form here. The entire area that constitutes the town of Kulu – the former Raghunathpur, later and now known as Sultanpur,[89] in the north, on the other side of the Sarwari stream that is a tributary of the Beas, and the sprawling *chaugan*-grounds of Dhalpur[90] towards the south – springs to life in a different manner. From all directions, the 'gods' of Kulu, village *deotas* and *devis*,[91] taking the form of *mohra*-masks, converge upon the spaces of the town, their richly decorated *ratha*-palanquins, sometimes simple *karadu*-baskets, having been carried on the shoulders of their followers over long distances on foot. There is rich colour everywhere, and the heady aroma of marigolds. Music fills the air, for no *deota* or *devi* travels without a band of dedicated musicians and essential functionaries; and at any given time scores of small 'processions' can be seen to be moving about. Rama, in the form of a small metal image designated as Raghunath ji, the 'state deity', installed in a shrine within the royal complex of buildings in Sultanpur, is whom the *deotas* come visiting, their carriages being first directed to those quarters before they settle in their assigned places in the Dhalpur plain. A series of events is set into motion from the very first day, in which the Raja occupies a central place: ritual worship of Raghunathji's image inside the shrine first; the formal journey of the image in a procession to Dhalpur where an elaborate *ratha* is already in place; the *yatra* of the image in the *ratha* pulled by devotees headed by the Raja; the transfer of the image to another temporary residence, the 'camp'; the performance of daily worship there for the next few days; the rounds that the Raja keeps making of the *chaugan*-plain visiting the *deotas*, or their coming to visit him; the climax of the celebrations in the form of a 'battle' prior to which animals are ritually sacrificed; the return of the triumphant forces back to the permanent abode of Raghunathji in Sultanpur, and the departure of the gathered *deotas* to their own homes and shrines. There is a sense of closure; 'sacredness' departs, if only to return. But, during the celebrations, in significant ways, the entire town of Kulu turns into some 'epic space' year after year; the series of events that constitute the Dussehra of Kulu become a 'performance of magnitude'.

It would be necessary to look at many of these things in close detail. Before that, however, as a reminder to oneself and for establishing a framework of related references, it might be appropriate to recall some events and practices followed elsewhere in other parts of India. There is thus the great *ratha-yatra* of Puri, the so-called 'car festival', spread over nine days in the month of Asharh (June-July), with enormous throngs of devotees converging upon the town to celebrate an 'event' in the life of the 'Lord of the World', Jagannath.[92] Going back to the 13th century, the festival has remained, despite serious vicissitudes in the fortunes of Orissa, and frequent political disruptions, so central to the life and the people of Orissa that it can be seen as a 'State Festival'. With its celebration is inextricably bound the Raja of Puri, who is the first servant of the Lord. While great religious fervour seems to run through every heart on this occasion, it is the Raja who takes on time-honoured tasks: *seba* in local parlance. Even as the three sacred effigies of Jagannath, Subhadra and Balbhadra are taken out and placed in the great chariots, with designated priests working their way through milling crowds and performing an incredible number of complex rituals, the Raja is 'summoned' by the deities. He arrives, dressed in full regalia, but then proceeds to sweep, like a menial servant, the spaces around the mobile sanctum with a broom – the famous *chera-pahaura* ritual. Then, as the *rathas* are readied to move towards the Gundicha temple, and musicians and dancers begin to perform in front of the *rathas*, which are like the Lord's court, it is the Raja who becomes the first among the chariot-pullers. Service is his, but so is the honour.

Of a different order, and certainly observed on a significantly smaller scale, is the 'state festival' of Dussehra as celebrated in the tribal region of Bastar.[93] The festivities here centre around the figure of the great tutelary deity of the royal family, Danteshwari Devi, but there are aspects of the momentous event that remind one of other places, other celebrations. Large crowds of people assemble; weapons are worshipped; animals are sacrificed; a chariot is prepared and drawn. In all this, the Raja of Bastar features with prominence: going out barefoot to receive the goddess who travels from her own shrine, 57 miles away, and bringing her to be installed, temporarily, in her new abode in the capital; his offering the sword-sceptre of the state to her; his ritual 'abdication' of the throne only to return on a big chariot of the goddess, for being re-enthroned. There is enthusiasm and fervour, participation and enactment, all in a collective invocation of racial memories.

In the Rajasthani state of Kota, cast as it is in the classical Rajput mould, Dussehra is only one of the many festivals, but the pageantry that forms part of it, and the series of time-honoured rituals that accompany the celebrations, are marked by great lustre.[94] Vast crowds assemble; fireworks are set off; cannons boom in the distance; priests and *acharyas* bustle about with sacred tasks in hand. But at the centre of every part of the celebration has always been the ruler of Kota, the Maharao: he appears seated atop the state elephant, walks in front of his troops, performs the ritual worship of weapons and steeds and vehicles of war, participates in all the prayers offered to the *kula-devis*. The evil figure of Ravana remains a challenge, but Rama has an ally, and a devout follower, in the ruler.

At Ramnagar, where the titular 'Maharajas of Benares' have ruled since 1752, the joyous celebration of Rama's life and deeds spreads over a full thirty days and takes the form of an enactment – the great Ramalila, based upon the text of Tulasi's *Ramacharitamanasa* – on a scale that has few parallels.[95] Inspired and 'presided over' in so many ways by the Maharaja in person, the event transforms the entire space of the city into a sacred space, the performance covering almost the whole town, action shifting from place to place as days pass and events unfold. There are the most elaborate of preparations: the selection of persons who will be transformed into mythical characters, the construction of sets, the worship of accessories including the sacred *pothis* from which the text would be recited, the gathering together of funds, and the like. And at each step the Maharaja is there in person: seated atop an elephant with three sets of texts in front of him, regulating the ebb and flow of the performance, becoming in turn king, god, and actor. Everything culminates eventually in the annihilation of the great effigies of Ravana and his kinsmen. But throughout all this, even though this is a festival of the people, the Maharaja remains at the very heart of things, always commanding attention: enjoying privileges as spectator and leader, performing ritual service, interacting with the massive audience and becoming one with the crowd.

It would take long to examine each phenomenon in detail, and to work out the manner in which in each are reflected structures and ideas that go well beyond what is visible on the surface. Everywhere there is mass participation and great fervour, but also linkages, those 'hierarchies of privilege and status' that one spoke of. What is outwardly only a religious celebration or event contains also at its heart elements that are at once political and social and cultural. Rituals and enactments contain pointers, roles affirm identities, participation binds. There is much that is embedded.

As can easily be seen, there are common threads that run through state festivals or celebrations, and similarities are not hard to find. But the history of each place is different, and is differently invoked; the manner in which these festivals came to be established also remains varied. Very little is recorded, unfortunately, of the early history of Kulu. But myths, and traditional accounts, about the founding of the state survive, and continue to influence the way in which matters like origins, power, relationships, issues of legitimacy *et al.* are perceived, even if not expressly so stated.[96] One of the myths that has endured here and told before is the manner in which the kingdom came to be founded.[97] No dates are mentioned. But the 'ancestor', Behangmani Pal, the founder of the dynasty – to which the present 'Raja' of Kulu belongs – is believed to have descended from a family that used to rule in the Haridwar region. With the blessings of the local goddess, Hidimba, a legitimate dynasty came to be founded. Hidimba – one recognizes a classical connection here, for the great Pandava hero, Bhima, is said to have married a 'flesh-eating demoness' by that name – came to occupy therefore a special place, as benefactor and protector, in the founder's heart and that of all his descendants from then on.

The second event of relevance, and one within reasonable reach of history, goes back to the middle of the 17th century when, under Raja Jagat Singh[98] – the family title had changed from Pal to Singh under Sidh Singh as we have seen – Vaishnavism, and the worship of Rama as Raghunath ji, came to these hills.[99] The story has been told repeatedly, but to recall it in its outline: local legend connects the event with a series of developments beginning with the suicide of a Brahmin whose daughter, or a bunch of uncommon pearls in another version, the Raja had coveted. Before killing himself in despair, however, the Brahmin placed a curse upon the ruler who, from then on, could neither eat nor drink, seeing worms and blood in everything that was placed before him. Seeking deliverance from this state, he turned to a Vaishnava saint, the Bairagi Krishnadasa Payahari, who lived not far from the Raja's capital town of Naggar then. The Bairagi told the Raja that his redemption could come only if an image of Rama were to be brought to Kulu from Ayodhya. Complicated but determined action followed: a contingent was dispatched to Ayodhya, the image was surreptitiously 'lifted' from the Treta Nath temple, some of the priests of that temple[100] travelled with the image towards Kulu, the image was personally received by the Raja at a place that was at some distance from his capital, and then, at an appropriate time, conveyed to the capital town for being formally installed there.[101] With the blessings of Rama, the ruler was cured of his affliction; great celebrations followed; Raghunath ji was declared as the state deity from then on; and the ruler took on the role of the chief *sewak*, or servitor, of the deity, assuming for himself the designation of 'Dewan' or deputy.

Other developments, having a bearing upon our understanding of the Dussehra of Kulu, followed soon after. Nothing is firmly recorded, but it would seem that Jagat Singh conceived at this time a grand design: that of instituting a great state festival that would serve several purposes at once.[102] Once every year, on the occasion of the Dussehra, all the 365 – a traditional, magical number – tribal or folk gods and godlings of the region, the *deotas* and *devis* to whom the local populace owed unquestioning allegiance, would be asked, by royal decree, to come to the capital town to pay homage to the state deity and partake of the celebrations in which the Raja, apart from the temple-priests, was a principal officiant. In this manner, the supremacy of the Vaishnava strain of classical Hinduism would be endorsed; the Raja's power would be seen as reaching far and wide; centres of local power and influence would be subordinated to central authority; integration would result; segments of population living in far-flung areas of the kingdom would be brought in contact with the mainstream; opportunities of exchanges of different kind, social and economic, would be opened up.

It is doubtful if the issue of one royal decree would have sufficed to achieve all that was intended, and, even though nothing is recorded, one can imagine that the processes through which the state festival was established, and compliance with the decree ensured, must have been complex. There must have been give and take in the negotiations leading to agreement; the power of granting rent-free tenures in exchange for services must have been used;[103] local loyalties must have come into play; social and cultural tensions must naturally have surfaced; accommodation would have been made between the Raja's own old loyalties to his family-deity or the local *deotas*, and his newly-acquired faith in the great Vaishnava deity;[104] hard-won exceptions to the rule of attendance – *deotas* like Jamlu of Malana, Bhekhli Devi, Parashar Rishi, still do not attend the festival and only send token tribute from a distance – must have had to be conceded.[105] Much of this series of processes remains obscured from our view, however, the documentation from the region being thin. But, in the final analysis, the Dussehra did come to be established as the state festival of Kulu, and more or less in the same form in which it is celebrated today. For upwards of three hundred and fifty years it has so stayed, with its core and its essence intact, except for two recorded occasions when the continuity was disrupted.[106]

III
THE EVENT

[*NOTE:* Nearly all event/s described in this section are illustrated and the illustrations from nos. 1 to 110 carry captions which are self-explanatory. Further reference, if needed, can be made to the List of Illustrations.]

The event that is the Dussehra can be described in colourful terms, like those of Peter Sutherland. "When west Himalayan drummers play, power presents itself in everyday settings," he writes. "Objects, people and places are transformed. Things become gods, gods become kings, and oracles give voice to their royal persons. As gods dance and move through the landscape, buildings, trees, persons, and rocks are reconfigured as sites of power in an otherwise unseen web of relations." But then he also asks the questions one has been asking before: "What is this dance of transformation? What does it mean, and how is the effect of empowerment produced?"[107]

What happens during the week-long Dussehra festival at Kulu and its environs, the sequence of events that make it what it is, needs to be described – this is where *rich* description comes in – before the role that the Raja plays in it can be properly understood.[108] The description that follows is based on my personal observations of the Dussehra over several seasons, and inquiries in the field in the present, but it might not be far from what things were like in the past.[109] As it is now, in and around the Dussehra, event follows well-defined event, even as seeming confusion, caused in part by milling crowds that converge upon the town during these days, reigns. In a manner of speaking, there is a clear 'narrative' that everyone who is part of it understands: it is the outsider who needs to piece it all together to be able to comprehend it.

Briefly put, as things proceed, designated priests are consulted at the outset for determining the day and time, within a known framework, for the opening of festivities. In the days gone by, it was the Raja who would seek this consultation and the determination; after independence and merger of the state, the government set up a formal committee, and the responsibility of fixing the date was vested in it. However, for pragmatic reasons, the responsibility came to rest again with the 'Raja' of Kulu through his being appointed as the Chairman of that committee.[110] The proper time determined, messages are prepared and dispatched, in the name of Raghunath ji, to all the *deotas* of the region, including the goddess Hidimba of Dungri, Manali, asking them to attend the festival. There is some difference, however: the missive sent to Hidimba is in the nature of a request, a humble invitation, she being the '*Dadi*' – grandmother – of the royal household; to all the other *deotas*, couched as the letter might be in polite and deferential language, it is in the nature of a royal order – formerly referred to, in feudal terms, as *begar hukam*, according to one informant, Pandit Chandrashekhar[111] – reminding them of their obligation. The *deotas* – the term includes, it is widely understood, *devis* and *rishis* and *nagas and birs* – enjoy different ranks, and bear a remarkably wide range of names that go back to diverse sources[112] – classical, like Adi Brahma, Shesh Naga, Tripurasundari, Bhima, Jamadagni; classical but now localized, like Bijli Mahadeo, Pancha Bir; purely local like Phungani Devi, Gauhri *Deota*, Dhumal Naga – but each one is subject to the same command. Once the information is received, the *deota* begins preparing for the journey to Kulu. At each shrine, the *mohras* or metal 'masks' representing the *deota* are taken out, cleaned and decorated with flower garlands and colourful textiles; a small *puja* comprising often of a sacrifice, is performed; and the *deota* mounted on his *ratha*-palanquin or *karadu*-basket, is ready for the journey, borne on shoulders across long and sometimes very rough terrain. A procession is formed: the group of the devotees – called the *haryan* – of the *deota* could consist of anything between 25 and 50 persons, but essential to the group is the *pujari* or ministering priest, the *gur* or the shamanic medium, the *kardar* or manager of the affairs of the *deota's* shrine, and several *bajantris*, musicians traditionally attached to the shrine, carrying and playing upon instruments like simple drums, *shehnai*-clarinets, and *narsingha*-trumpets. Coming from different directions, the *rathas* of the *deotas* start descending upon the Dhalpur plain, with the *gur* leading, carrying an iron *dharach*-ladle in his hand filled with smouldering incense, and stopping occasionally to utter prophesies on behalf of the *deota* or to answer queries or *puchh*[113] made by devotees about the future.

At this very time, in the royal complex of buildings at Sultanpur, within which is located the small, unpretentious shrine of Raghunath ji, there is ceaseless activity, involving initially the Raja and the priests of the temple. To be sure, some purely personal things have preceded this day: the *sair puja* – part of the 'big worship', celebrating the winter crop, in which walnuts and '*doob*-grass' figure – has been conducted, the *puja-paddhati* being carefully followed, and the Raja being assisted in the *shodasha-upacharas* by the priests. The family deity of the royal household, the *kula-devi*, whose black stone image – the goddess standing triumphant atop the prostrate body of Shiva – is installed in a shrine within the palace, has received homage to the accompaniment of the recitation of the *Chandi-patha*. On the very first day of the Dussehra, however, the Vijaya-dashmi, intense public activity begins. The Raja is constantly in and out of his palace and the temple – the two are connected through a door accessible only to the royal family or the priests – throughout the day. Early in the day, having performed the usual personal worship in his private chambers, he offers homage, following time-honoured Rajput usage, to his weapons and the emblems of his state. Then, for participating in all the religious ceremonies, he presents himself before Raghunath ji, the 'lord of *his* kingdom', who is bathed and clothed, and offered food in preparation for the day. At the outer gate leading to the courtyard of the temple, the Raja also receives and honours a steed, the *Narsingh-ji ki ghodi*, recalling the ancient ceremony of waving incense in front of the royal mount, but also invoking the blessings of Narasimha who, in a layering of identities, is both the classical man-lion incarnation of Vishnu and a warrior-hero locally worshipped as Narsing-Bir.[114] Soon, the *deotas* start arriving, one by one, carried in their shoulder-borne *rathas*, at the Raghunath temple, and render homage by stopping in front of

Raghunath-ji's image and gently tipping towards it as if bowing. The Raja is not present in the Raghunath temple at the time of each *deota's* visit: he, or representative members of his family, is present in the adjoining palace to receive the *deotas* who make their way towards it after having offered homage to Raghunath ji. The *rathas* or *karadus*, carried and accompanied by their respective followers, traverse the large outer courtyard, pass through the main gate and the narrow passage, which leads to the inner courtyard, and there 'present themselves' – *hazri* or attendance is the word used – before the Raja, tipping in respect to the temporal master, while the Raja offers them reverence on his own part. On the *deota's* behalf a token amount – however small the amount, it is referred to as a *nazrana* or tribute to the liege lord – is offered, and duly noted in a register by a functionary; in return, the Raja makes a small offering – a recognition of the exalted spiritual status of the *deota* – which is placed in a small cloth bag that is then tied to one of the poles of the *ratha*-palanquin. The *deota* departs soon thereafter, the *gur* leading the group of devotees, music playing, the *ratha* sometimes tipping, as if in greeting or embrace, towards that of another *deota* on his way to the royal complex.

The big event in this part of the day is the arrival of Hidimba. There is much anticipation. While the request had gone to her well ahead of time, asking her to come for the Dussehra, she is now to be formally received. This reception takes place on the outskirts of the town, at the spot called Ram Shila on the bank of the Beas, where a representative of the Raja remains personally present, with the royal staff, the silver-topped *chhari*, in hand. Having journeyed long from Dungri, Manali, and having been greeted with honour, the goddess proceeds straight to the Raghunath temple to offer the customary homage, and then makes her way through the winding streets to the royal palace, her *gur* – an awe-inspiring, big-bodied figure, with wide eyes and long tongue – walking in front carrying a *dharach*-ladle. Her arrival at the palace, however, is quite an event, for there is great commotion. As her approach is announced, all the members of the family leave their chambers, as if vacating the palace for her, and taking cover behind a carved doorway[115] out of fear and reverence. Hidimba, along with her *gur* and other *pujaris*, then goes in and occupies the main chamber of the palace, and no member of the royal household comes out of hiding till she, through the *gur*, calls out for her *potru* – 'grandchild'; so the Raja is addressed by her with affection – to come to her presence. This is seen as a token of her being pleased with the way things have gone. The Raja appears before her, seeks her blessings, and addresses queries about the future to the *gur* – his *puchh* – as if to ensure that the entire Dussehra celebrations will proceed without hindrance or impediment. This over, Hidimba leaves the palace, since the time for the moving out of Rama, as Raghunath ji, from his temple abode to the 'field of battle', approaches.

Raghunath ji, however, does not proceed all by himself. On his behalf, an order is sent to the Raja – once again, a silver-topped *chhari* or staff, is sent in token of a royal command – asking him to join the *jaleb*, which is the procession that stands for the lord's army. The Raja presents himself; the divine weapons are worshipped; the image is placed, with all ceremony, in a palanquin; and the procession sets off, large crowds of people, and many *deotas* in their *rathas*, joining. The Raja, dressed in full regalia and riding, in recognition of his own royal status, in a shoulder-borne *sukhpal*-palanquin, along with all the richly attired male members of his immediate and extended family who are on foot, follows the deity's palanquin, but at the head of the procession, as it moves through the winding lanes of Sultanpur and crosses the Sarwari stream for reaching the Dhalpur plain, are the *Narsinghji ki ghodi* and Hidimba's *ratha*. It is a rich, joyous sight, great enthusiasm writ upon faces, loud notes of music – countless drums and *shehnais* and *narsinghas* all playing – filling the air.

The immediate aim is to reach the large chariot – a proper wooden *ratha* with large wheels – that is already stationed in one part of the Dhalpur *chaugan*, completely covered with colourful textiles and topped by a *kalasha*-like member: a truly mobile shrine that, despite its comparatively smaller size, brings to mind one of the great *ratha*s of the Jagannath triad at Puri in distant Orissa. Once here, the image of Raghunath ji is to be installed inside the chariot, and it is the Raja who is called upon by the priests to do this. After performing the ritual *parikrama* or circumambulation of the chariot, sacred water in hand, the Raja does this; then comes the moment that everyone in the large crowds that have gathered is waiting for: the pulling of the *ratha* of Raghunath ji. Large ropes attached to the chariot are the means, and considerable force is needed to pull the chariot, but it is the Raja who first holds the rope in his hands standing at the head of a team of persons that includes members of the royal family, men of prominence, and, now, some government officials. As the first movement of the chariot takes place, a great shout goes up; virtual melee ensues; the *deotas* who have gathered all around also move behind the *ratha*. But, slowly, the *ratha* reaches its destination, another part of the Dhalpur *chaugan* where a tented enclosure – the *chhauni* or encampment – has been set up for Raghunath ji. He will sojourn here for the next few days. The Raja helps move the images from the chariot to inside the enclosure, working along with the priests – not everyone is allowed to touch or approach the idols from this close – and formally installs them in their new abode. As for himself, he moves to his own temporary home for the next few days: a tented enclosure set up at a slight distance from that of his deities. He will return to his palace complex only when all the celebrations are concluded for that year.

The days that follow are filled with a routine. The *deotas* have all occupied their allocated spaces on the *chaugan*, the allocation taking into account, as best as is possible, past histories, issues of rank and precedence, the size of the *ratha*-palanquin, the numbers of the *haryan*-attendants who accompany the *deota*. This is where they will stay except when, on occasions, they move out either to go and pay homage to Raghunath ji in his camp, visit one another, or to appear at the 'court' of the Raja in his camp. At Raghunath ji's camp, the customary temple ceremonies are regularly performed: the images are taken out at appropriate times from the makeshift *sanctum sanctorum* and installed on their throne for everyone to view, great tasteful ceremony accompanying each step. The idols are lustrated and clothed and adorned, the Raja assisting all the time, and performing a range of services: applying *tilak* marks and unguents on the bodies, arranging flowers, sounding or playing upon a bell when *kirtana*-chanting takes place, waving a flywhisk over the heads of the idols, standing solemnly with a staff in hand, like a common servitor in attendance. The deities are served food – offered *bhog* – at suitable times after which large groups of devotees are fed – a *dham*, in Pahari usage – from the *rasoi* or kitchen of the lord, as a token of his great favour. The Raja receives his share of the food.

But, each of these days, the Raja has other functions to perform apart from being attendant upon Raghunath ji. Each day, at an appointed hour, he mounts a *sukhpal*-palanquin, dressed in regal clothing, and, followed by several functionaries of the royal household, goes around the *chaugan* plain, negotiating the large crowds and the temporary bazaars that come up, the festival having turned also into an enormous *mandi* or trading mart.[116] But he heads essentially towards the spots where the *deotas* are camping: inquiring if all is well, receiving homage, and offering respects in return. This *jaleb* procession, as it is called, mirrors, on a small scale and as is appropriate to the occasion, the kind of tour that a ruler would have undertaken of his *riyasat* or *thakurai* in olden times. Not much is transacted, but the routine is observed with strictness. During these days, towards the evening, the Raja also receives visitors in his camp, seated regally attired as if holding a 'durbar': here dignitaries come, *deotas* put in an appearance, performers come to perform and entertain. Troupes of actors used to appear here in earlier days coming from places as distant as Mathura, informants say[117]. Members of the public also come to greet their 'Raja Sahib'. But nothing comes in the way of the Raja presenting himself before Raghunath ji every evening at *sandhya* time, when the deities are formally put to bed only to be woken up the next morning and installed on their thrones again. There, in the deities' camp, an occasional performance is also held in the night with the Raja watching along with others: a 'Chandravali' dance, an enactment of Durga riding her tiger mount, a circular *rasa* performed by men dressed up as women.[118]

Thus days go by, with no specific event attached to each. It is as if these are days spent on the gathering of energies before the final assault. Finally, it is time for Raghunath ji to spring into action. Just before that, however, on the day referred to locally as *mohalla*, the goddess is to be propitiated much as she was, in popular belief, propitiated and invoked by Rama before the attack upon Lanka. On that evening, the Raja of Kulu stations himself outside the camp of Raghunath ji, in an attitude of subservience, resting his hands upon the silver knob of a *chhari*-staff, waiting for the goddess Tripurasundari of Naggar, the *kula-devi* of the royal family, to arrive, and lend her energies to the campaign. On the day of assault, the image of Raghunath ji is placed once again in the chariot, for the *ratha* to be pulled by devotees and taken some distance towards the river-bed. On this occasion, five animals are to be sacrificed, the traditional *panchabali*,[119] in honour of divine powers. The Raja does not always participate personally in the sacrifice; however, the honour of beheading the buffalo – the largest and most difficult of the animals in the *panchabali* – is conferred by him upon a member of the royal family. The moment when the gleaming blade lands upon the neck of the designated animal is dramatic, and not for the faint-hearted. But a large and curious crowd watches the entire proceeding with eagerness. Hidimba has accompanied the *ratha* up to this site, and it is her *gur* who receives the severed head of the buffalo as *prasada*. This done, a token, perfunctory battle is fought: no great effigies are burnt, but arrows are shot in the air upon some small masks that represent the enemy, and a pile of brush is set to fire recalling the destruction of Lanka. Shouts of victory go up, and Raghunath ji, accompanied this time by Sita whose image is placed in the chariot by his side, sets off on the return journey, the *ratha* pulled by devotees and taken back to the same point in the *chaugan* from where it had originally started.

It is time for the triumphant troops to return. The images are transferred to a palanquin, and the Raja walks ahead of the procession as it forms, till the temple in Sultanpur is reached. With great reverence, the image of Raghunath ji is re-installed in the temple where the women of the royal household receive the heroes with honour, applying saffron marks on their foreheads, and showering flowers. An *utsava* or celebration is organized in the courtyard of the temple, and the *rajyabhisheka* – the ceremony of formal enthronement – of Raghunath ji takes place in the presence of the entire royal household. Meanwhile, the *deotas*, including Hidimba who sets off for Dungri, Manali, instead of accompanying the procession to the temple, begin leaving for their respective places. The Dussehra is over.

In this entire event, spread as it is over several days, and continued as it has over upwards of three centuries, there are things that seem evident, and visible. It is easy to see for example that the role of the Raja in the whole range of celebrations and ceremonies is central. Raghunath ji apart, and in some ways even more than Raghunath ji, he is pivotal to the Dussehra. He seems to be everywhere in person: moving between the palace complex and the Raghunath temple, between Sultanpur and Dhalpur, moving in front of the chariot and standing in attendance at the entrance of the deity's camp: offering worship, despatching invitations, receiving, disbursing, walking, pulling, riding, issuing commands, serving food, joining hands in prayer, plying the flywhisk. The present 'Raja' of Kulu, Maheshwar Singh,[120] has for years been playing these roles sensitively, with gravity and devotion. But one can imagine his situation, his place in the scheme of things, located as he is in today's times – with no real power as Raja, no subjects to command, and little to govern – as being materially different from that of his forebears. There are no grounds to doubt that the Rajas of old were also devout men who saw the Dussehra as a religious festival, celebrating the glory of Rama, instituted in a historical moment, and then continued. But engaged as they must have been as rulers with issues of power and authority, the everyday reality of governance, the creation and preservation of social balances, they must also have seen the Dussehra as a political and socio-economic institution that became, over time, a meaningful part of the awareness of the people of the state. In the manner in which it was organized and meant to proceed, then, there would have been seen a clear opportunity to embed messages, and make statements that mattered. This opportunity appears to have been seized with care and foresight.

A complete understanding of the entire structure of the festival, as it evolved over time – and one can imagine that it would have been thought through in stages – might elude us, especially because documentation remains thin all through the past. But one can at least begin to read meanings, taking some prominent junctures or practices that form part of the chain of events, as examples. There is, thus, the sending out of messages to the *deotas*, making known the date of the holding of the Dussehra, and asking them to assemble for participating in it in the capital town. Apart from the difference noted earlier between the humble 'invitation' to the goddess Hidimba and the virtual command to the other *deotas*, there is the fact of the missive being issued by the Raja as the Dewan of Raghunath ji. This was no simple announcement of a festival: it was a reminder. The spiritual authority rested clearly with the deity, but the temporal executor of the wishes of Raghunath ji was the Raja, and this could possibly not have been lost upon the receivers of the 'invitation'. All that went into the negotiations between the local power of the *deotas* and the central authority of the Raja, or the fact that the *deotas*, for all their spiritual sway over the local populace, were essentially tenure-holders from the state, might have been in the past. But, year after year, the *deotas* were reminded of their obligation to the Raja, their status being underscored through their being asked to 'attend'. It is in this light that one can see the practice of the *deotas* visiting first, upon their arrival in Kulu, Raghunath ji in his temple to offer homage, and then proceeding to present themselves before the Raja inside his palace complex: the required '*hazri*' which was duly noted in a register by a functionary.

The Raja's relationship with the goddess Hidimba is of another order, but holds clear meaning. The entire series of events comprising the invitation to her requesting her to come, her being received at the Ramshila on the outskirts of the town by a representative of the Raja carrying the state *chhari*, the palace being vacated by members of the royal household for being occupied by the goddess, the waiting for her commanding the Raja to come to her presence, is something that could easily have been seen as being in the private domain, expression of a personal relationship with the *Dadi* of the family. But, as things unfold, it is something that all and sundry are made witness to, everything being done in public view. Clearly, there is design behind this, for the special honour accorded to the goddess Hidimba is an emphatic, yearly reminder of the origins of the state, and the manner in which 'legitimate' power came to rest in the dynasty through its founder in these hills. That the authority which the first Raja, and therefore his descendants, came to possess had a spiritual basis, apart from that which comes through conquest or other means, must have been seen as a message with a meaning for the subjects of the state.

Again, the exchanges that take place when the *deotas* come visiting Raghunath ji and the Raja are replete with subtle meanings. The offerings that are made by the *deota* might be trivial in material terms – a few coins, a handful of corn, a bunch of greens, and the like – but they are in the nature essentially of a *nazrana*, yearly tribute in feudal terms. But, tribute having been formally paid, it is the turn of the Raja to render homage to the *deotas*, in recognition of their 'divinity' or the spiritual power they without question wield over their 'own' people, within their own respective areas. Something akin to a circular relationship can be seen to exist. The gift that the Raja makes on this occasion to each *deota* might not be of the nature of tribute, but it is an offering that betokens humility, a lack of the arrogance that comes naturally to holders of temporal power. Upon the *haryan* – body of devoted followers – of each *deota*, the gesture would clearly register, and leave an imprint. One sees this yet again in the practices followed in the camp at Dhalpur. The Raja, as sovereign, or as the embodiment of Narasimha (Narsing Bir?) moves about day after day in the *jaleb* procession, but each time he would stop, solicitously, before the temporary abodes in which the *deotas* live on the *chaugan* grounds, inquiring about their well-being, offering to be of help in case of need.

In the course of all the ceremonies and rituals conducted at the temple, or the 'camp', of Raghunath ji, the Raja appears again and again as a humble servitor of the lord, the first among his *sewaks*: offering prayers, performing menial tasks, standing guard. The roles are seen by everyone as being reversed: the ruler turning into a servant. But, personal devotion and the feelings of the Raja apart – and these elicit natural respect – there is significance even in this stance, for no one reads the message wrong. The Raja still remains, in the eyes of everyone, a Raja. In fact, he gains in prestige, and power, as he goes through this reversed role, for the spiritual authority of Raghunath ji is seen as descending upon, or being vested in, him. He remains no longer the Dewan of the lord; he turns into his *alter ego*.

It is in manners like this that, over generations of time, the Raja of Kulu seems to have been seen and perceived by the people of the state. In their eyes the Dussehra of Kulu would be unthinkable without him, and without his playing the role/s that he does.[121] There is reassurance, and meaning, in these continuities. And whenever there is a break in this continuity, a rupture, as happened in 1972 when the Raja's role or powers were questioned by 'secular' authority and violence resulted,[122] something goes seriously amiss; things go askew.

NOTES AND REFERENCES

1. *Encyclopedia Britannica,* Macropedia, Vol. 17, pp. 609-14. There is, however, no universally accepted definition of a state.
2. Ronald Inden, *Imagining India*, p. 265.
3. Henri J.M. Claessen and Peter Skalnik, *The Early State*, 1978; see, also, Henri J.M. Claessen and Jarich G. Oosten (eds.), *Ideology and the formation of early states*, 1996.
4. Inden, *op. cit.*, p. 265; see, also, Georges Balandier, *Political Anthropology*, pp. 104-07.
5. Claessen and Skalnik, *op. cit.*, p. 4, 1978.
6. Ronald Cohen, "State Origins: A Reappraisal", pp. 39, 62, in Claessen and Skalnik (eds.), *op. cit.*, 1978. See, also, Romila Thapar, "Ideology and Interpretation of Early Indian History", in Thapar, *Cultural Pasts: Essays in Early Indian History*, p. 14.
7. Claessen and Skalnik (eds.), *op. cit.*, pp. 12, 21.
8. *Ibid.*, pp. 10, 11, 12, 14.
9. *Ibid.*, p. 12.
10. Thapar, *Cultural Pasts: Essays in Early Indian History*, pp. 790-92. Also, N. Dirks, "Political Authority and Structural Change in Early South Indian History", *The Indian Economic and Social History Review*, pp. 25-58, 13.2, (1972).
11. Charles Drekmeier, *Kingship and Community in Early India*, pp. 34-35.
12. "Ritual... constitutes a tremendously important arena for the cultural construction of authority and dramatic display of the social lineaments of power. Authority is central to ritual power", See, Dirks, *The Hollow Crown: Ethno-History of an Indian Kingdom*, p. 220. Also Mahesh Sharma, "State formation and Cultural complex in Western Himalayas: Chamba Genealogy and Epigraphs – 700-1650 CE", p. 391, in *The Indian Economic and Social History Review*, 41, 4 (2004) The above article is also helpful in gaining an understanding of the use of cultural symbols in general. See also David L. Kertzer, "The Role of Ritual in State Formation", pp. 85-103, in Eric R. Wolf (ed.), *Religious Regimes and State Formation: Perspectives from European Ethnology*.
13. Hermann Kulke, "Introduction: The Study of the State in Pre-Modern India", in Kulke (ed.), *The State in India, 1000-1700*.
14. Burton Stein, "The Segmentary State in South Indian History", in R.G. Fox (ed.), *Realm and Region in Traditional India*.
15. Kulke, "The Early and Imperial Kingdom; A Processural Model of Integrative State Formation in Early Medieval India", pp. 233-62 in Kulke, *The State in India 1000-1700*.
16. Stanley J. Tambiah, *World Conqueror and World Renouncer*, Cambridge, 1976.
17. For researches on the tributary or little kings of Southern Orissa, See, B. Schnepel, *Twinned Beings: Kings and Effigies in Southern Sudan, East India and Renaissance France*. Also see, Schnepel's use of Ethno-history in his study of the jungle kings of Orissa, *Die Dschungel konige: Ethnohistorische aspekte von Politik and Ritual in Orissa*. Also Schnepel, "Kings and Rebel Kings: Rituals of Incorporation and Dissent in south Orissa" in Kulke and Schnepel, *Jagannath Revisited: Studying Society, Religion and the State in Orissa*.
18. Bernard Cohn, "Political Systems and Political Structures in Eighteenth Century India: The Benares Region", *Journal of American Oriental Society*, Vol. 82, No. 3, 1962, pp. 312-20. Also in, Cohn, *An Anthropologist among the Historians and Other Essays*, pp. 483-89.
19. Dirks, *The Hollow Crown: Ethno-history of an Indian Kingdom*, p. 220.
20. D.N. Jha (ed.), *Feudal Social Formation in Early India*.

21. Mahesh Sharma provides a precise summary of the principal models of the processes of state formation in his article, "State formation and cultural complex in western Himalaya: Chamba genealogy and epigraphs – 700-1650 CE", in *The Indian Economic and Social History Review*, Vol. 41, 4 (2004), p. 387. Also see Stephen P. Blake, "The Patrimonial–Bureaucratic Empire of the Mughals", in Kulke, *The State in India*, 1000-1700.
22. See, Hans Bakker (ed.), *Introduction*, p. vii and "Throne and Temple: Political Power and Religions Prestige in Vidarbha", pp. 83-100 in Bakker, *The Sacred Centre as the Focus of Political Interest*.
23. Interview with Kardar of *deota* Pancavir of Kot Kandi, Dussehra 2000.
24. For a reproduction of the inscription, see M. Postel, A. Neven and K. Mankodi, *Antiquities of Himachal*, p. 255.
25. For a reproduction, see Postel, Neven and Mankodi, *op. cit.*, p. 255.
26. Kulke, *Kings and Cults: State Formation and Legitimation in India and South East Asia*, pp. 17-32.
27. J. Hutchison and J. Ph. Vogel, *History of the Panjab Hill States*, Vol. II, p. 459.
28. Mahesh Sharma, 2004, p. 431.
29. It is interesting that a space within the inner courtyard of the Raghunath Temple of Kulu, where the family of the Ayodhyabasis – those whose ancestors came with the Raghunath image to Kulu in the first instance - stand during the Dussehra celebration, was deemed to be transformed into the sacred space of Ayodhya. This was clearly the case as I observed it in the course of fieldwork during Dussehra, 2000.
30. This process has long roots in the past. For the nature of the authority of the king, see, Drekmeier, *op. cit.*, pp. 245-62.
31. The custom of importing brahmins, scholars from well known centres of learning in North India seem to have been prevalent over a long period of time. See Mahesh Sharma, 2004, *op. cit.*, pp. 390-91, 401.
32. The text of the inscription is reproduced in J. Fleet, *Corpus Inscriptionum Indicarum*, Vol. III, No. 80, Plate XLIV, p. 286. See also V.C. Ohri, *The Sculpture of Western Himalayas*, pp. 13-19.
33. Mahesh Sharma, 2004; Also, Hutchison and Vogel, *op. cit.*, Vol. II, p. 460.
34. Speaking of Chamba in the context of processes of state formation, Sharma 'extends the debate' by contemplating an 'inter-transposability' between the state system and cultural complex in Chamba. See his article on 'State formation and cultural complex in western Himalaya: ....", cited above. See note 21.
35. Similar conclusions are arrived at during the transformation of society from a lineage to state system, in Thapar, *From Lineage to State*, p. 173.
36. Speaking essentially with reference to what happens in the neighbouring area of Bashahr, especially on the occasion of the Dussehra at Sarahan, Peter Sutherland has the following interesting observation: "Pahari ritual memory", he says, "presents an alternative history of divine kingship as viewed from below, in which the creation of translocal forms of sovereignty was not limited to the top-down creation of networks of clientage by kings, but also involved the ritual construction of translocal political formations from below." See his article, "T(r)opologies of Rule (*Raj*): Ritual Sovereignty and Theistic Subjection", in the *European Bulletin of Himalayan Research*, Vol. 29-30, p. 112.
37. M. Lambeck, *A Reader in the Anthropology of Religion*, and Eric Wolf (ed.), *Religious Regimes and State Formation*, speak of the theme in general, but in considerable detail.
38. See P.L. Gupta, *Numismatic History of Himachal Pradesh*, for a discussion; also Devendra Handa, *Tribal Coins of Ancient India*, pp. 42-43.

39. Hutchison and Vogel, *op. cit.*, pp. 415-21.
40. *Ibid.*, Vol. I, pp. 12-38.
41. Thapar, *From Lineage to State*, pp. 155-73.
42. Ohri, *op. cit.*, pp. 76-88.
43. Karuna Goswamy, *Kashmiri Painting*, pp. 1-9.
44. See S.L. Nagar, *The Temples of Himachal Pradesh*, pp. 153-84, for an analysis.
45. Hutchison and Vogel, *op. cit.*, pp. 413-73.
46. Thapar, *From Lineage to State*, p. 116.
47. A.K. Coomaraswamy, *Spiritual Authority and Temporal Power in the Indian Theory of Government*, pp. 2, 9.
48. *Ibid.*, p. 84; J.C. Heesterman, "The Conundrum of the King's Authority", in J.F. Richards (ed.), *Kingship and Authority in South Asia*, pp. 21-22.
49. Inden, *op. cit.*, p. 263.
50. Chetan Singh, *Natural Premises: Ecology and Peasant Life in the Western Himalaya 1800-1950*, pp. 6-32; 207-235.
51. A fairly good connected account of this period is to be found in Hutchison and Vogel, *op. cit.*, pp. 429-62.
52. Chetan Singh, "Nature, Religion and Politics in the Himachal (Western) Himalaya: Case Studies of Keonthal and Kumharsain", p. 1 (unpublished till then but seen in mimeographed form through the courtesy of the author.).
53. N.F. Howard has studied these places and written an article on them in two parts, "The Fortified Places of Upper Kulu, India" in *South Asian Studies*, 11 and 12, 1995-96.
54. Reproduced in Postel, Neven and Mankodi, *Antiquities of Himachal*, p. 255.
55. David T. Kertzer, "The Role of Ritual in State Formation" pp. 88-89, in Eric R. Wolf (ed.), *Religious Regimes and State Formation*, provides very useful insights and parallels.
56. Clifford Geertz, "Religion as a Cultural System" in R. Bocock and K. Thompson (eds.), *Religion and Ideology*, pp. 66-75.
57. Inden, *op. cit.*, pp. 22-33, 263-70.
58. *Ibid.*, p. 266.
59. The Political and the religious aspects of life are seen as two sides of the same coin by the Indian theorist whose sense of theological realism could create moments of political unity by factoring in the dominant religious discourse but presenting it as the result of a 'conjoint will', created by a *Chakravartin* and the interaction between his court with the gods. This was often brought into being in the consciousness of what was transpiring in other courts. See, Inden, *op. cit.*, p. 269.
60. It has been observed during field work that Hidimba sometimes registers her protest if she is not given a welcome in accordance with the strict protocol laid down in advance by the Raja of Kulu. In recent years, on the issue of the *Dhur*, Shringa Rishi, supposed to be Rama's spiritual Guru and Balu Nag who is none other than Lakshmana, have both fought out a wordy battle over their right to stand on the right hand side of Raghunathji ratha in the Dussehra. Very often these disputes reflect the clash of opposing political leanings on the part of their followers. Chetan Singh, "The place of Myth, Legend and Folklore in Western Himalayan History" paper read at Seminar in Department of History, Panjab University, Chandigarh, 2004.
61. Interview with Raja Maheswar Singh of Kulu, 2000.

62. For the span of the ten days of the Dussehra festival one forgets that there are no longer any kingdoms or kingships in the India of today: such is the transformation observed during the Dussehra.
63. Sudarshan Vashistha, *Mandi Dev Milan* (in Hindi) Also, Chetan Singh, *Natural Premises: Ecology and Peasant Life in the Western Himalaya* 1800-1910.
64. Chetan Singh, "Nature, Religion and Politics in the Himachal (Western) Himalaya: Case Studies of Keonthal and Kumharsain", 2005, (Seen in mimeo form through the courtesy of the author).
65. Participant-observation, Dussehra, 2000.
66. *Gazetteer of Kangra District*, Part II, Kulu and Saraj, 1947, pp. 63, 153. Also, R.M. Harcourt, *Assessment Report of Waziri Rupi of the Kulu Tehsil of the Kulu Sub-division*, p. 1; J. Coldstream, *Final Report of the Pard, Lag Maharaja, and Lag Sari, Sub-Tabsil Saraj, Rupi, Lahoul and Spiti Waziri of the Kulu subdivision of Kangra*, 1913, p. 17, Letter No. 58, 264-2; *Register* of Muafis, Tehsil Kulu, District Kangra, Bandobast, 1868-1948, pp. 386, 376-90.
67. Kertzer, "the Role of Ritual in State Formation, pp. 86-100, in Wolf (ed.), *Religious Regimes and State Formation Perspectives from Eurpoean Ethnology*. Also see, Bakker, *The Sacred Centre as the focus of Political Interest*, pp. ix, 96-100.
68. For instructive parallels, see Kulke, "Royal Temple Policy and the Structure of Medieval Hindu Kingdoms", p. 132, in Eschmann, Kulke and Tripathi, *The Cult of Jagarnnath and the Regional Tradition of Orissa*. D.N. Jha, "State Formation in Early Medieval Chamba" pp. 129-30 in, Jha (ed.), *Society and Ideology in India: Essays in honour of Professor R.S. Sharma*, Also, Thapar, "The Mouse in the Ancestry", pp. 803-804, in Thapar, *Cultural Pasts: Essays in Early Indian History*.
69. Thapar, *From Lineage to State*, p. 119. Also, Thapar, *Cultural Pasts*, p. 385.
70. This description of events is based on participant observations at the time of the field trip conducted during different seasons of the Dussehra festival.
71. Hutchison and Vogel, *op. cit.*, Vol. I, pp. 429-31.
72. Narendra Kumar Sharma, *Malana: Puratan Sanskriti ka Prateek*, (in Hindi).
73. For further information, see, Vashishtha, *Kulu: Dev Samagam*, (in Hindi).
74. The other inscription ascribed to Udhran Pal is on a stone in the wall of the Sandhya Devi temple at Jagat Sukh. The text reads: "Sri Maharaja Udhran Pal Sandhya Devi Kali Muraihai, S. 4. ba, ta, 1"= AD 1428. See, Hutchison and Vogel, Vol. II, pp. 441-42.
75. *Ibid.*, p. 427.
76. This register exists to the present day and entries are made in it as each *deota* comes in to the Raghunath temple at Dussehra.
77. The account is based on participant observation at the time of the Dussehra of 2000.
78. *Panjab District Gazetteers, Kangra District, Part II- Kulu and Saraj*, 1917, pp. 5, 156.
79. Inden, *op. cit.*, p. 224.
80. Hutchison and Vogel, *op. cit.*, Vol. II, p. 461.
81. Chetan Singh, "Nature, Religion and Politics in the Himachal (Western) Himalaya: Case Studies of Keonthal and Kumharsain", p. 13, 2005, (seen in mimeograph form through the courtesy of the author).
82. *Ibid.*, p. 4.
83. *Ibid.*, p. 1.
84. This information was collected from personal interviews with priests, *gurs*, Kardars and knowledgeable citizens of Kulu as also from participant observations.

85. Participant observation during field work conducted during repeated seasons of the Dussehra.
86. The institution of the Dussehra as a state festival is credited to Jagat Singh (AD 1637-1672). For a detailed discussion of the coming of Vaishnavism to Kulu and the strategies employed by Raja Jagat Singh to ensure its establishment on a firm footing, see, chapter 4 above, and Karuna Goswamy, *Vaishnavism in the Panjab Hills and Pahari Painting*, Ph.D. dissertation, Panjab University, 1968, pp. 69-70.
87. Performative in nature, rituals introduce, as has been said, meaning, energy, persuasion and encouragement into the functioning of society as a collective. Dramatizing myths, rituals, display and stabilise existing social relations as well as inculcate values. The resonances thus are many. See Roy Rappaport, *Ritual and Religion in the making of Humanity*, pp. 104-38; Maurice Bloch, "The disconnection between Power and Rank as a Process: An Outline of the Development of Kingdoms", in, *Ritual, History and Power: Selected Papers in Anthropology*, London, 1989, pp. 46-88.
88. Yaaminey Mubayi, *Altar of Power: The Temple and the State in the Land of Jagannatha: sixteenth to nineteenth Centuries*, pp. 16-17. Also see, Murray Milner Jr., *Status and Sacredness: A General Theory of Status Relations and an Analysis of Indian Culture*, 1994.
89. The older name of the town of Kulu seems to have been Raghunathpur. This is the form in which the town is referred to in the *bahis* of the Pandas of Kulu at Haridwar. My attention was drawn to this by Professor B.N. Goswamy who in the course of his own researches had seen the *bahis* of Pt. Som Nath Chaklan at Haridwar. All entries made by the Rajas of Kulu mention Raghunathpur. Some of these entries go back to the 80's of the 18th century in the time of Raja Pritam Singh of Kulu. The time from which it came to be called Sultanpur is not clear.
90. The old name of the segment of the town now called Dhalpur, where all the administrative offices are located, appears to have been '*Rani ke ropey*'. The reference obviously is to this area having been gifted by the queen and these were once rice fields. The habitation here is relatively new. Interview with Raja Maheshwar Singh of Kulu, October, 2000.
91. A great deal has been written about the Kulu *Deotas*. The treatment varies from being cursory to being very detailed. See, thus, J.B. Lyall, *Report of the Land Revenue Settlement of the Kangra District*, Punjab, 1865-72, Lahore, 1874; *Gazetteer of the Kangra District, Kulu, Lahul and Spiti, Parts II to IV*, 1897, pp. 40-56; H.A. Rose, *A Glossary of the Tribes and Castes in Punjab and North-West Frontier Provinces*, 1911; M.R. Thakur, *Himachal mein Pujit Devi-Devta*, Delhi, 1981; B.R. Sharma, "The Institution of the Village Gods in the Western Himalayas", in Rustomji, N.K. and Charles Ramble (eds.), *Himalyan Environment and Culture*, Indian Institute of Advanced Study, Shimla, 1990; C.P. Pandey, *Dev Bhumi-Kulu-ke-Parmukh Dev Sthal*, Shimla, 1990; Sudarshan Vashishta, *Dev-Samagam*, Shimla, n.d.; Dilaram Shabab, Kullu; *Himalayan Abode of the Divine*; Gautam Dayanand (ed.), '*Bebas' Sahitya Sadhna, Visheshank* [8-23] *Shrikhand*, Shimla, n.d.
92. The Puri temple and the *yatra* of Jagannath has been the subject of innumerable and frequently dense studies. See, thus, K.C. Mishra, *The Cult of Jagannatha*, 1971; Gopinath Mahapatra, *Jagannatha in History and Religious Traditions of Orissa*, 1982; Nityananda Patnaik, *Cultural Tradition in Puri: Structure and Organisation of a Pilgrim Centre*, 1977; Bijayananda Kar, *Major trends in Orissan Philosophy*, 1989, pp. 57-88. Kulke, *Kings and Cults: State Formation and Legitimation in India and South East Asia*, 1993; Ishita Bannerjee Dube, *Divine Affairs: Religion, Pilgrimage, and the State in Colonial and Post Colonial India*, 2001; Mubayi, *op. cit.*, pp. 21, 115.

93. For a detailed account, see, Nandini Sundar, *Subalterns and Sovereigns: An Anthropological History of Bastar, 1854-1996*, 1997, pp. 47-76.
94. See the interesting and recent study, H. Metzger, H., Maharao Brij Raj Singh of Kotah, *Festivals and Ceremonies observed by the Royal Family of Kotah*, Zurich, n.d.
95. Studies of the Ram Lila of Ramnagar have been made from different perspectives. Thus, Sandra Freitag, *Culture and Power in Benaras: Community, Performance and Environment*, 1800-1980, 1989; Anuradha Kapur, *Actors, Pilgrims, Kings and Gods*, 1990; Richard Schechner, *The Future of Ritual: Writings on Culture and Performance*, 1993.
96. For a succinct delineation of myths legends and folklore, see, Chetan Singh, "The Place of Myth, Legend and Folklore in Western Himalayan History", Paper read at seminar on Folklore at the Department of History, Punjab University in 2005. Also see, Bronislaw Malinowski, *Magic, Science and Religion and other Essays*, 1954, pp. 100-26.
97. This myth has been listed in a large number of texts, *Gazetteers* and *Settlement Reports* of the Colonial period and publications of the Department of Language, Culture and Art, Himachal Government, Shimla. Most of these have already been listed above.
98. The date AD 1637-1672 ascribed to Jagat Singh by Hutchison and Vogel, *op. cit.*, Vol. II, p. 458. is tentative. Most of the dates given by them are in their very nature approximate, and need to be reworked.
99. For a study of Vaishnavism in Himachal Pradesh [the erstwhile Punjab Hill States] see, Karuna Goswamy, *op. cit.*, pp. 41-93.
100. To be seen present but standing at a distance at all major functions centering around Raghunathaji, is a family of priests, popularly referred to as *'Ayodhya-Basis'*. These priests had accompanied the image from Ayodhya and were given land-grants at Bhuntar. No function relating to Raghunathji is considered complete without their presence. Interestingly they are never left alone with the image for fear they might steal it and take it back to Ayodhya.
101. The Raja of Kulu must necessarily have experienced difficulties while trying to gain acceptance for the new faith. This is evident from the quick change in the place of *sthapana* of the image of Raghunath, which 'travelled' from Makarsa, Kot Kandi, Jagatsukh, Thawa, and, finally, to Sultanpur, to its present temple.
102. Even though this is a conjecture, the fact of Jagat Singh's conversion to Vaishnavism is strongly supported by the evidence of painting. See, Karuna Goswamy, *op. cit.*, pp. 94-166.
103. For information on *muafis* (rent-free tenures of land) in exchange for services, see Lyall, *op. cit.*, pp. 124-29; *Kangra District-Gazetteers* of 1897 and 1917; A.H. Diack, *Final Report of the Revised Settlement of the Kulu Subdivision of the Kangra District*, 1898. Also see, Milner, *op. cit.*, p. 50.
104. From interviews with Pt. Chandra Sekhar 'Bebas', from the family of the Raj-Purohits of the Raja of Kulu and *Kardars* of several *Deota* temples, it appears that the Pancaviras of Kot Kandi occupied a place of pre-eminence in terms of being the *deotas* whom the Kulu Raja paid personal homage. This is prior to the coming of Raghunathji and the Raja's conversion to Vaishnavism.
105. The question of certain *deotas* not attending the Kulu Dussehra masks conflicts arising out of social, political and religious issues. Independence, rebellion and non-conformance gets reflected in their attitude.
106. The two known occasions on which the Dussehra was discontinued – in 1947 and 1972 – created a tremendous imbalance in society. Again in 1986 the attendance of the *deotas* at the Dussehra went down. The need for the Dussehra is evident from the fact that a joint effort by

government officials, public figures and religious Mahants was made to restart the festival at that time.

107. Peter Sutherland, "T (r)opologies of Rule (*Raj*):) Ritual Sovereignty and Theistic Subjection", in *European Bulletin of Himalayan Research*, Vol. 29-30, pp. 82-119.

108. Daniela Berti has examined the role of the Raja in today's circumstances as far as the Kulu Dussehra is concerned in an interesting article: "Ritual Kingship, Divine Bureaucracy and Electoral Politics in Kullu". See *European Bulletin of Himalayan Research*, Vol. 29-30, pp. 39-61.

109. During the course of my extended stay in Kulu at Dusshera time in 1996, 1998 and 2000, I noticed that no significant changes had taken place in the general format of the festival. My personal observation apart, interviews in the field were conducted with officials from the D.C.'s office and local heads of the regional branch of the Language, Culture and Arts Akademi of Himachal Pradesh at Kulu. Dr. Sita Ram Shastri, Dr. Vidya Chand Thakur and Dr. Vidya Sharma, were interviewed as was the Dussehra clerk from the D.C's office.

110. The Raja of Kulu along with another representative of the Raghunath Temple, is an important member of the *Devta Sub-committee* of the Kulu administration. There are many occasions on which he chairs and is the convenor of the Devta committee. In deference to the Raja sahib being the central figure of the Dussehra festival, the administration asks him to decide and give the dates and days on which the festival would be held. This information was collected from the Dussehra and the *Deota* sub-committee files of the Kulu administration.

111. A simple classification of the *deotas* is given in J.B. Lyall, *op. cit.*, p. 83. Detailed information was shared with me by Pt. Chandrakant, formerly a priest of the Raghunath Temple.

112. For a fairly comprehensive list of the important *deotas* of Kulu, see, Vashishtha, *op. cit.*, pp. 37-140; Vidya Sharma, *Kulanta Darpana*, 2001, pp. 1-7.

113. It is quite customary for the people to ask the *deotas* to make a prophecy in response to their *puchch* [query]. The *puchch* made from the *gur* of Hidimba is considered to be the most important.

114. Classical and tribal strands appear to have coalesced in the persona of Narsingh ji who is worshipped along with Raghunathji, as has been discussed at length in chapter 4 above. In brief, Kulu is referred to as a *Narsingh gaddi*. *Deota Narsingh Bir*, one of the *Pancaviras*, somehow gets mixed up with the classical *Narsingh avatar*. This reflects itself in the worship patterns and the *bhog* of *Narsinghji* as also in the worship of *Narsingh-ji-ki-ghodi*.

115. The doorway is known as *Atharah kardu ka parol*. This probably has a reference to a legend involving the spread of the *deota* cult in Kulu. Specifically, it may well signify that these were the first eighteen *deotas* to pay homage to Raghunathji. Also see, Dayanand Gautam, *op. cit.*, pp. 21-22; Laxman Thakur, *op. cit.*, pp. 323-24.

116. I have not yet explored the economic dimensions of the Kulu Dussehra. Combining business with a religious festival appears to be a well known concept. Pilgrims going to Jwalamukhi, Kangra district, often say, "*Nale Devi de darsan, nale munj da vyapara*". This refers to the combining of pilgrimage with trading in hemp. Trade appears to have flourished between Ladakh, Tibet, Yarkand and the Northern Plains of India, according to Pt. Chandra Shekhar. For detailed information see, *Gazetteer of the Kangra District*, Parts II, III and IV pp. 129-30; Poonam Minhas, *Traditional Trade and Trading Centres in Himachal Pradesh*, 1998.

117. Troupes performing the *Raslila* of Krishna and also the *Ramlila* were known to travel throughout the country to present their "miracle" plays to audiences located in different parts of the Northern Plains. Paintings of Maharana Sangram Singh of Mewar watching the

plays of the *Rgsdharis* of Mathura are in the Binney Collection, San Diego Museum, San Diego U.S.

118. For useful information on *Chandravali* and other local dramatic forms, see, Kamal Kishore Sharma, *Kuluvi Lok Natya Parampara: ek Adhyayan*, M. Phil. Dissertation, 1984-85, H.P. University, Shimla. (mimeograph) pp. 17-18, 56. Also see, Norvin Hein, *The Miracle Plays of Mathura*, Delhi, 1972.
119. The *pancabali* consists of the sacrifice of a buffalo, a lamb, a crab, a fish, and a cock.
120. The title of 'Raja' was no longer 'applicable' after the abolition of the princely states. But in memory of the past and as a matter of courtesy these titles continue to be used by everyone. Technically also 'The Raja of Rupi' was just a formal title because the state had spilt up into two different states: those of Rupi and Shangri. I would like to acknowledge with immense gratitude the help received by me from Raja Maheshwar Singhji during my fieldwork.
121. Cf. Galey's statement about the situation in the western Himalayan regions. "In short, kingship has survived the eviction of the king and the disappearance of the dynasty. In spite of the fact that it has officially remove and its palatial headquarters abandoned, its importance as an operating agency has remained almost unaffected." Cited by William Sax in "Introduction: Divine Kingship in the Western Himalayas", *European Bulletin of Himalayan Research*, Vol. 29-30, p. 10.
122. Lal Chand Prarthi, at one time an MLA and a minister, had attempted to impinge upon the Raja's territory in matters concerning the *jaleb*. This had resulted in a firing. The matter went to court and the jurisdiction of the Raja was restored. For details of this case, see chapter 6 below.

Chapter SIX

Recent Developments and the Dussehra Today

Festivals and celebrations have always been a part of the lives of the people of Kulu. Long before the Dussehra was instituted as a 'festival' in the 17th century – according to one account, the image of Raghunath ji reached the Kulu region in 1653 when a temple to Rama was constructed at Manikaran; in 1660, the image was installed at Kulu; and the first Dussehra was held in 1661 – there existed, almost everywhere, local fairs and festivals at which nearly everyone in the village gathered: the *kahika*, the *phagli*, the *birshu*, and the like. These festivals, celebrated with great music and mirth and dancing, figure in countless folk songs and legends – including that surrounding Behangmani, who came from outside and founded a new ruling dynasty, for it was on his way to seeing a festival that he encountered the goddess Hidimba who was then in the guise of a helpless old woman[1] and continue to be held to this day. However, the Dussehra went on, with time, to become *the* great festival of Kulu: an event which came to form a part of everyone's awareness in the hills. The attendance at this festival by hundreds of *deotas*, who came to the festival accompanied by their *gurs* and *pujaris* and *bajantris* and prominent members of the *haryan*, ensured the fact that everyone, even in far-flung villages, knew that something great and festive was happening in the capital town.

No figures are available, but it is possible that when it began, the number of *deotas* and their followers who came to attend the Dussehra in Kulu, was relatively small. But as time went on, and resistance to the idea of being *required* to attend a festival in honour of a classical Vaishnava god weakened, the Dussehra grew in terms of numbers and stature. Traditionally, it is said that the number of *deotas* who used to come to the Dussehra was 365, but this seems to be a notional number embedded in popular memory, like other magical numbers: "84" siddhas, "9" nagas, and the like.[2] For one thing, the number of *deotas* in Kulu has never been constant, for they have kept proliferating over the centuries; for another, no exact count was kept, for it must not have been needed, or deemed necessary. Local legends repeatedly speak of the original number of *deotas* in Kulu having been only 18: those whose existence, and names, are celebrated in different stories and locations, remembered as they are as the *athara karadus* who got scattered by a wind that blew at an unrecorded time, or the *athara karaduon ki parol*, which exists in the palace of the Rajas of Kulu at Sultanpur. An 'official' list prepared some fifty years ago contained, in contrast, 401 names, complete with the names of places where the shrines of the *deotas* are, and the land they own, etc.[3] In more recent years, if more than a hundred *deotas* arrive at Kulu for the Dussehra, in their *rathas* or *karadus*, it is generally regarded as a good number. Today, as they arrive, and pay their homage at the Raghunath mandir, their 'having come' is noted down in what is called a "*haziri* register', a kind of roll-call record. But, related as these appearances must have been to the *muafis* or rent-free lands that the *deotas* enjoyed, access to old registers of this kind, kept presumably either in the temple of Raghunath ji, or in the records in the Raja's palace, is not now possible. One can only guess that the numbers of the *deotas* in the region of Kulu kept growing, and the numbers of those who made their annual journey to Kulu for the Dussehra was always inconstant. There were some without whom the Dussehra celebrations would have been deemed to be incomplete – Hidimba Devi, Bijli Mahadeva, Gauhri *deota*, Dhumal nag, for instance – but not everyone came each year.

On the other hand, the Dussehra has continued to be held each year for the last 350 years or so. It is generally believed that from the time it came to be founded in 1660, or thereabouts – there is a short time-lag between the arrival of the Rama image from Ayodhya and the beginnings of the Dussehra at Kulu[4] – there has never been a break in the holding of the event. Except for two years, to both of which are connected unhappy events and memories. The first break that stands out in popular memory came in the year 1841. That was when there was real trouble between the Raja of Kulu and the Sikh governor of the hills[5]: there was turmoil and conflict and the Dussehra had to be put off on grounds of fear for safety, alike of the *deotas* who come and of Raghunath ji. Things soon took a turn for the better, however, and the very next year, 1842, the Dussehra was held as always. The other break that took place is within recent, and painful, memory. In 1971, the event was marred, even as it was being held, by an altercation between the Raja of Kulu and his followers, and the state police. The police, acting upon orders, fired on the crowd, leading to one death and several injuries.[6] For the two years following, there was fear and unease, and the Dussehra could not be held. This unfortunate incident had a political angle to it, however, something to which one would have to turn later. However, the Dussehra celebrations were resumed within a couple of years.

Between these two dates, there was a period of uncertainty and concern as to the future of the Dussehra as a festival. A great part of this was linked to the momentous political changes that were taking place. Following the attainment of independence by India in 1947, the future of the erstwhile rulers of 'Indian states' came into question. Within a short span of time, virtually all the erstwhile states got merged in the Indian Union; hereditary rulerships came to an end; and the powers that former rulers used to wield were reduced to a memory. The state of Himachal Pradesh was formed in 1948. The impact of these developments upon the personal finances of the former rulers was serious, and especially deep as far as events, in which money spent upon celebrations traditionally came from sources that were part personal and part state-owned, were concerned. The Dussehra of Kulu, being an event of the last-mentioned kind, was also naturally affected. What is more, here much had always hinged upon the power and the prestige of the Raja whose conduct of and participation in the Dussehra was crucial. Evidently, new equations had to come into being, or being worked out.

For the first few years after independence, the Dussehra appeared to be on the point of losing its sheen and lustre. The centuries-old tradition of holding it was continued, but the depressing fall in the number of *deotas* who came to Sultanpur for attending the festival in Raghunath ji's honour was noticeable. It was reported at one time that, in the years following 1950, the number of *deotas* who came to Kulu hovered in the neighbourhood only of fifty. This began to cause concern not only to the populace of the entire erstwhile state of Kulu, but also to the government which had in all other respects taken upon itself the role and the responsibilities of the erstwhile states. Kulu was still a sub-division of the District of Kangra, which was part of the Punjab, and, in 1961, a senior civil servant, Dayanand Dhir, Sub-Divisional Officer, Civil, Kulu, wrote to the revenue officers of the sub-division, the Tehsildar and the Naib-Tehsildars, on the subject of conducting a 'Census of Devtas in Kulu Sub-Division'.[7] "With a view to envisage a scheme for the future of the *Devtas* in the Sub Division, that provide nucleus for community, social and religious life, certain proposals are under consideration with the Government," the note said. A pre-requisite for deciding upon the scheme that was being contemplated, it was necessary to "obtain correct data regarding these institutions"; accordingly, the order said, patwaris were to be instructed to collect details in a given proforma, and it was trusted that that job "could be efficiently done during the ensuing *Girdawari* for Rabbi 1961, commencing from the 15th of April, 1961". The consolidated report was to be submitted within a month "without fail". The proforma asked for information in 12 columns, which read, respectively: 1. "Serial no."; 2. "Name of Devta"; 3. "Name of Kardar/Mukhtar, if any"; 4. "Names of the Members, if the management committee exists"; 5. "Place of the temple of Devta"; 6. "Place or places (by *phatis*) where the worshippers of the Devta reside"; 7. "Amount of the land revenue, payable *phati*-wise annually"; 8. "Rough estimate of the movable property of the Devta in the shape of gold, jewellery, etc. etc."; 9. "Details of the land now existing with the Devta, which is under self cultivation or is cultivated by the tenants-at-will"; 10. "Approximate annual income of the Devta from the offerings"; 11. "Annual income of the Devta from the land, in cash (kind should be converted into cash)"; and 12. "Total income now obtainable (annual)".

It was evident that a thorough survey was intended, and it appears that it was conducted with diligence. A great deal of data was collected, as can be seen from the appendix attached.[8] As many as 401 *deota* temples were listed, as has been stated. Most of the information about the *deotas* – like the name, place, numbers of followers, land-revenue payable were verifiable – and was possibly entirely accurate, but the value of the property and land owned by the *deotas*, as declared by the functionaries of the temples, seems to be considerably understated, possibly on account of apprehensions about the intentions of the government. To take some examples: the total value of movable property in the shape of gold, jewellery, etc. as owned by Devi Phungani of Bisar is given as Rs. 35 only in this list; of *deota* Sat Narain of Karain as "nil"; of *deota* Danu Nag of Rougi as Rs. 50, and so on.[9] Likewise, the approximate annual income of *deotas* from offerings is given as "nil" in a number of cases, like the *deotas* Gonu of Gordor, Madho Rai of Haripur, Nar Singh of Karjan; it goes up to Rs. two or three in some cases; and in rare cases crosses the sum of a hundred rupees. Clearly, some variation in these figures is to be expected, for the size of the *deota's* following, the antiquity of the temple, must all have mattered. And one can be certain that, in general, the *deotas* were not really affluent. But it is difficult to escape the feeling that there are serious inaccuracies here, the underplaying of incomes and values being the rule rather than the exception.

Much of this, one surmises, must have stemmed from a basic distrust of the *sarkari* machinery that was now swinging into action. It is not that nothing might have been known, or recorded, in the earlier, or "Raja's", times as the people keep on saying, even though such information might have been informal, and is now inaccessible. But getting on to the records of the *sarkar* was another matter. A different age was perceived as having set in by the people in general, and the *deota* temples in particular.

From the government's point of view – following a reorganization of states in 1966, it might be added here, Kulu became a part of Himachal Pradesh, and got the status of a district – continuing the old tradition of holding the Dussehra at Kulu, in a form as close to the 'earlier' one, was important on several counts: it made political sense; at the social level, it ensured that there was minimal disturbance in the fabric, or mindset, of the community; on the economic plane, again, it meant some revenue, for to the Dussehra had always been attached the holding for seven days or more of a large *mandi* or bazaar, to which large crowds of people were drawn. Since it was evident that the coming of the *deotas* to the Dussehra was critical to the event, both on account of its continuity and its spectacular nature, steps were now taken to ensure their attendance. Realizing that the will of the *deotas* to travel to Kulu along very difficult terrains, often across long distances, having weakened – the Raja's rule having ended thus affecting old loyalties – one of the steps thought of was the defraying of expenses incurred by the *deotas* and their followers on travelling to Kulu. The payment to the *deotas* on this count was described as a *nazrana* – old-world term, signifying humble gift given in tribute – and the amounts were fixed keeping in mind different considerations: the distance travelled; the number of persons in the party; and the mode of their transportation. This amount was meant to serve as an inducement to the *deotas* to continue coming to the Dussehra. From a register relating to the year 1996, which was available for consultation,[10] it was noted that in that year 134 *deotas* came to Kulu for the Dussehra festival, and were paid *nazranas*, the amounts varying from Rs. 15,286 paid to Raghunath ji (the great deity was not kept out of the net), to as little as Rs. 600 to *deota* Gada of Kothi Shikari in the Banjar tehsil. The amount of *nazranas* was gradually increased, sometimes by 10% in the year; regular *haziri* registers, like those kept at the Raghunath temple,[11] were now being maintained.

Whether arising from steps such as these, or from the fact that the *deotas'* initial misgivings about the attitude of the government had started to go down, the attendance at the Kulu Dussehra began steadily to pick up. From the fifty or so *deotas* who came to the Dussehra in the years immediately following India's independence, the numbers climbed up, on an average, to close to one hundred and fifty or so. However, the *deotas* had now to deal with the bureaucratic set-up at nearly all levels: a relationship which had an altogether different air from that belonging to their traditional links with, and affiliation to, the Raja in earlier times. In 1972, with the passing of the Himachal Pradesh Tenancy Act, the *deotas* – never in truly affluent circumstances – started getting further impoverished, for, in terms of the act, they lost nearly all their lands to the cultivators who were formerly their tenants. One still hears in the field stories about how difficult their circumstances had now become.

The Dussehra of Kulu was given the formal status of a 'State Festival' in 1972 by the Government of Himachal Pradesh. This resulted in a further increase in bureaucratic involvement in, and control of, the event, and when to it was attached an "International Folk Dance Festival", a host of sub-committees started being formed "to conduct various affairs of the Dussera Festival". The local administration had the overall charge of the holding of the festival but with the sub-committees were associated prominent local persons, *kardars* of some of the *deotas*, businessmen who made donations for the event, and the like. Each year a souvenir volume began being printed with 'messages' from the Governor of the State downwards, short articles on different aspects and history of the Dussehra by knowledgeable people, and advertisements. The annual souvenirs, looked after by a 'Board of Editors', also listed the names of the various sub-committees and their members.[12] In the 1997 souvenir, thus, the committees listed were: 1. the Mela Sub-committee; 2. the Devta sub-committee; 3. the Cultural Affairs sub-committee; 4. the Sanitation sub-committee;

5. the Exhibition sub-committee; 6. the Transportation sub-committee; 7. the Decoration and Beautification sub-committee; 8. The Souvenir sub-committee; 9. the Accommodation sub-committee; 10. the Sports sub-committee; 11. the Allotment sub-committee; and 12. the Resource sub-committee. With the Committees is associated a representative of the Raghunath temple. For many years, Shri Maheshwar Singh, former Raja of Kulu, has also been associated with this kind of work in his personal capacity, evidently in acknowledgement of the role that the Rajas of Kulu had always played in the holding of the Dussehra.

Along with the official machinery of the state has steadily expanded the involvement of politicians of the state in the Dussehra. In a sense, this was inevitable perhaps, for every politician is able to see in the event a great opportunity for projecting himself, his party, and, to an extent, the cause of the event itself. But this development has not been without its consequences. The infamous firing incident that took place during the Dussehra of 1971 – something that caused one of those extremely rare breaks in the holding of the more than three centuries old festival – is widely believed to have had its source in political rivalries. A single-member Commission of Enquiry had to be appointed by the state government with Justice D.B. Lal as the Commissioner. The Commission went into the whole incident with thoroughness and the report of the enquiry submitted by Justice Lal in August 1973[13] contains some revealing details. The Commission, Justice Lal wrote in his preliminary remarks, was appointed because "Kulu, the valley of Gods, has been a scene of [an] unfortunate firing incident", the valley having been "disturbed by the booming of guns". The incident took place, as per the report, on "the occasion of Dussehra festival which is stated to be the premier festival of Kulu valley". The duration of the festival was from 30th Septemeber, 1971 to 6th October, 1971. Raja Mohinder Singh (then the 'Raja') of Kulu was taking out a procession inside Kala Kendra which is a stadium earmarked by the Government for cultural programmes, on 'lanka dahan' day, which is the last day of the festival. The procession was interrupted by the police, and due to assault committed by the Raja and his men, firing was resorted to outside the Kala Kendra." The whole matter is far too complicated, and the report, which runs into 48 closely typed pages, far too detailed to go into here. But at the heart of the incident lay the fact that the customary daily procession of the Raja in the course of the Dussehra after the idol has been installed in its camp at the Dhalpur *maidan* – the *jaleb* as it is called, and has been referred to before – tried to pass through the Kala Kendra, claiming rights as of old and believing that the Kala Kendra was a public place. The police tried to stop the procession; an altercation ensued; there was much confusion; the police perceived a major threat; the Raja's party kept insisting on its rights; and eventually the police opened fire. Further disturbances followed, for trouble spread beyond the Kala Kendra. While examining all the witnesses that were summoned, the Commissioner also went into the question of whether the political rivalry that obtained between the Raja of Kulu and one of his prominent supporters, the advocate Thakur Beli Ram, who belonged to a political party in opposition, and

Shri Lal Chand Prarthi, a Minister then in the Congress Government, had been the cause of, or contributed to, the incident. Shri Lal Chand Prarthi is credited by many people with having helped revive the Dussehra festival when it was losing its old prestige and form, and with encouraging increased cultural activity on the occasion – the Kala Kendra is called the Lal Chand Prarthi Kala Kendra after him – and it is not unlikely that he took more than usual interest in the festival. What is more, he was personally present on the day of the firing in Kulu. In the course of the enquiry, three witnesses alleged that they had seen the minister standing in the rest house with some officers of the district, and that they heard him say that "the Raja should not be allowed to enter Kala Kendra and should be arrested and humiliated". The Raja was indeed arrested – in fact, handcuffed and taken on foot to the police station, to the horror of the local population – but the Commission gave no credence to the suggestion that this was done at the instance of the Minister on that occasion.[14]

Whatever the facts of the case, what is apparent is that the Dussehra festival now attracts politicians of all hue who see in it rich ground for their activities. In fact, politics seem gradually to have entered other levels, and other events connected with the Dussehra festival, bringing old rivalries to the fore, and creating new situations. News of the holding of the Dussehra of the year 2007 were at that time filled with reports[15] about a serious confrontation between two *deotas* – Shringa Rishi and Balu Nath – (which in effect means between their followers), over the question of who has precedence, or the place of pride, in the procession of Raghunath ji when it is formed following the movement of the idol from the temple to the Dhalpur *maidan*. Rivalries between *deotas* over matters of precedence, and of assertion of rights, have always existed perhaps, but what is different now is the involvement of political parties in these. The present incident is generally believed to stem from differences of opinion, on political grounds, between the *hariyan* or followers of the two *deotas*. One hears other voices too. Why, for instance – one group protests – should the 'Raja' be carried in a palanquin in this democratic age? Why, another asks, are the *bajantris* – musicians traditionally associated with and playing for the *deotas'* temples – paid so low? The Kardars of the *deota* temples have formed a Union of their own, and frequently raise questions or make demands upon the administration. Different elements are increasingly becoming emphasized, it would seem. Increased tourism, and the gains to be made from it, are within the sights of the powers that be, as is entertainment of a kind different from that provided by folk dances of a purely local kind: hence the International Folk Dance Festival for which fancy souvenirs are published year after year.

Is, then, the Dussehra of Kulu, or at least some part of it, beginning to move into a different orbit, one wonders? Is it in the process of changing from an essentially religious event with spectacle built into it, to essentially a spectacle with some religious feeling attached to it? On the other hand, superficially viewed, the Dussehra remains the same: a performance of magnitude, a great and colourful event that has been part of the imagination of the people of Kulu, even perhaps of the whole of Himachal

Pradesh, for upwards of three centuries and a half. As the *rathas* or *karadus* of the *deotas*, brilliantly decorated and laden with marigolds, start converging upon the town of Kulu, as Raghunath ji receives their homage and offers them reverence in return, as the great procession of Rama with his *rath* pulled by the Raja and so many others, starts moving towards the Dhalpur *maidan*, and as the air fills up with the music of the *bajantris*, one gets the feeling that the more the festival has changed over the years, the more it remains the same, as the saying goes. And perhaps, for expressing his real devotion, the common man of Kulu still turns to his local *deota*, always there for him in his inconspicuous little temple located close to where he lives in his village.

NOTES AND REFERENCES

1. The story has been told several times, and has been referred to earlier in the present work also.
2. As noted before in the present study, there is a whole range of 'magical numbers' which keep appearing in Indian myths and legends with significance or hidden references attaching to them. 3, for instance, which relates to *gunas* or the eyes of Shiva; 4 recalling the four *yugas* or *purusharthas*; 7 is the number of *rishis*, or days of the week; and several multiples yielding 'sacred numbers': 84 being the product of seven multiplied by twelve; 108 being the product of nine multiplied by twelve, and so on.
3. See Appendix E for the full list.
4. One is inclined to think that the years between 1653 and 1660 or 1661 were spent planning out a strategy that would achieve two ends at the same time: that of establishing the supremacy of Rama in the area, and of binding the peripheries to the centre.
5. The supremacy established by Maharaja Ranjit Singh over the hill chiefs was never fully accepted by them, and there were constant issues even if the Rajas were too weak to challenge this supremacy in any meaningful manner.
6. See *infra*, notes 13 and 14.
7. The note sent out by Shri Dayanand Dhir was addressed to the Tehsildar of Kulu and the Tehsildars of Kulu, Banjar and Nirmand by name. It was issued on the 6th of April, 1961 and bore the nos. 1353-1356.
8. See Appendix E below.
9. One is tempted to contrast these figures with those cited by reporters writing in local newspapers (see, thus, the front page report dated October 4, 2003 in the *Amar Ujala*, published from Chandigarh) about the wealth of the *deotas* running into "hundreds of crores of rupees". Neither of them, one guesses, comes anywhere close to the truth.
10. This register was seen in the office of the Deputy Commissioner, Kulu.
11. A *haziri* register kept at the Raghunath temple relating to the year 1996 was submitted by Shri Rewat Ram of village Mohal to the Raja of Kulu. Shri Rewat Ram also maintained a trihara register in which the token offerings – between rupees 15 and 25 generally – made by the *deotas* to Raghunath ji upon arrival in Kulu as 'tribute', were duly noted down.
12. Every year now a Souvenir is brought out with more or less the same kind of 'messages' from politicians and civil servants, wishing the event great success. Officers of the district are always involved. The 1997 Souvenir of the 'International Folk Dance Festival', for instance, was published by the Deputy Commissioner of Kulu, Shri. R.D. Dhiman. Shri B.R. Jamwal,

Additional Deputy Commissioner was the chief editor; on the editorial board also was Shri Sita Ram Thakur, District Languages Officer of Kulu.

13. The Report of the Enquiry Commission was published on Tuesday, the 28th of August, 1973 from Shimla in the *Gazette Extraordinary of the Himachal Pradesh Government, bearing no. 14-21/71-Home*. I am grateful to Shri Deepak Sanan, IAS, for securing for me a copy of the Gazette.
14. *Ibid.*, p. 1392. Justice Lal stated in his report that "despite this political rivalry, there is no evidence for a finding that Shri Lal Chand Prarthi, Minister, was in any way directly connected with the firing incident either in the Kala Kendra or in the Court compound."
15. These reports appeared not only in vernacular newspapers of local circulation, but also in regionally important national newspapers. See, thus, the reports in the *Divya Himachal* of October, 2007; the *Dainik Jagaran* of Oct. 22, 2007; the *Tribune* of October 8, 2007.

Appendix A

LIST OF THE RAJAS OF KULU

Reproduced from:
Hiranand Shastri, "Historical Documents of Kulu",
Annual Report of the Archaeological Survey of India, 1907-08, pp. 260-76.

No.	Name as Given by Captain Harcourt	Corrected Name[1]	Dates	Reference
1.	Behungamunnee	Bihangamani Pal		
2.	Puch Pal	Pachch (ksa) Pal		
3.	Baheg Pal	Bihang Pal		
4.	Doorheen Pal	Hin Pal		
5.	Soorg Pal	Svarg Pal		
6.	Sooktee Pal	Sakti Pal		
7.	Mahida Pal	Mahisvar (or Mahindar ?) Pal		
8.	Oom Pal	Om Pal		
9.	Rajinda Pal	Rajendar Pal		
10.	Busud Pal	Visad Pal		
11.	Busuda Pal	Visunddh Pal		
12.	Ootum Pal	Uttam Pal		
13.	Doja Pal	Dvij Pal		

No.	Name as Given by Captain Harcourt	Corrected Name[1]	Dates	Reference
14.	Chnkkur Pal	Chakar Pal		
15.	Kurun Pal	Karn Pal		
16.	Sooruj Pal	Suraj Pal		
17.	Ruxsh Pal	Raksh Pal		
18.	Roodur Pal	Rudar Pal		
19.	Haemur Pal	Hamir Pal		
20.	Pursidh Pal	Parsidh Pal		
21.	Hurree Chund Pal	Harichand Pal		
22.	Soobut Pal	Subhat Pal		
23.	Saom Pal	Som Pal		
24.	Sunsar Pal	Sansar Pal		
25.	Bagh Pal	Bhog Pal		
26.	Bubyah Pal	Vibhay Pal		
27.	Brahmo Pal	Brahm Pal		
28.	Gunaesh Pal	Ganes Pal		
29.	Gumbheer Pal	Gambhir Pal		
30.	Bhoomee Pal	Bhumi Pal		
31.	Shureedut Taeshur Pal	Sriddattesvar Pal		
32.	Umr Pal	Amar Pal		
33.	Seetul Pal	Sital Pal		
34.	Shirree Jerashur Pal	Sri Jaresvar Pal		
35.	Purkash Pal	Parkas Pal		
36.	Ajumbạ Pal	Ajambar (?) Pal (perhaps Achamba)		
37.	Tupanaeshur Pal	Tapanesvar Pal		
38.	Purum Pal	Param Pal		
39.	Najindur Pal	Nagendra Pal		
40.	Nard Pal	Rarad Pal		
41.	Norotum Pal	Narottam Pal		
42.	Shaesh pal	Sesh Pal		

No.	Name as Given by Captain Harcourt	Corrected Name[1]	Dates	Reference
43.	Bhoob Pal	Bhu (or Bhup) Pal		
44.	Janeerood Pal	Aniruddh Pal		
45.	Hust Pal	Hast Pal		
46.	Soortee Pal	Sur (or Surat Pal)		
47.	Suntokh Pal	Santokh Pal		
48.	Taegya Pal	Tegh Pal		
49.	Oocht, or Kuchet Pal	Uchit Pal		
50.	Sichundur Pal	Sikandar Pal		
51.	Surus Pal	Saras Pal		
52.	Saedaeb Pal	Sahdev Pal		
53.	Siri Mahadaeb Pal	Sri Mahadev Pal		
54.	Nirtee Pal	Nirati Pal		
55.	Baen Pal	Bain Pal		
56.	Hust Pal	Hast Pal		
57.	Saesee Pal	Sasi Pal		
58.	Gumbheer Pal	Gambhir Pal		
59.	Nisodhun Pal	Nishudan Pal		
60.	Narinda Pal	Narendar Pal		
61.	Suntokh Pal	Santokh Pal		
62.	Nundh Pal	Nand Pal		
63.	Dhurtee Pal	Dharti Pal		
64.	Indur Pal	Indar Pal		
65.	Mahee Chukur Pal	Mahi-chakar Pal		
66.	Yeodhur Pal	Jaya (or Yaso) dhar Pal		
67.	Keral pal	Keral Pal		
68.	Hans Pal	Hans Pal		
69.	Augusth Pal	Agast Pal		
70.	Muddum Pal	Madan Pal		
71.	Muddho Pal	Madhu Pal		

No.	Name as Given by Captain Harcourt	Corrected Name[1]	Dates	Reference
72.	Oodhun Pal	Udhran Pal	1418-28	Hirma mask and Sandhya Devi temple inscription.
73.	Kelas Pal	Kailas Pal		
74.	Sidh Pal	Siddh Pal	1500	Vishnu mask inscription Sajla, Kothi Barsaiya.
75.	Bhadur Sing	Bahadur Singh	1553-9	Hirma Temple and copperplate inscriptions. Also Tinan chronicles.
76.	Pertab Sing	Pratap Singh		Tibetan document from Barbog.
77.	Purbut Sing	Parbat Singh	1575	Devi Sidh-Bhaga mask inscription at Pini, Kothi Kayas.
78.	Prithi Sing	Prithi Singh	1608-35	Tibetan documents, Barbog, and mask inscriptions of Deo Dhumval in Syal, Kothi Chong and Deo Chirmal at Nagain Kothis Kot Kandi.
79.	Kalian Sing	Kalyan Singh		
80.	Juggut Sing	Jagat Singh	1651-7	Cooperplate inscriptions and farmans.
81.	Boodh Singh	Bidhi Singh	1688	Narayan Deo Mask inscriptions at Chamahan, Kothi Kayas.
82.	Maun Sing	Man Singh	1712-19	Mahadeo mask inscription at Jvani, Kothi Rayasan and Kapilamuni mask inscription at Basauna, Kothi Kot Kandi.

No.	Name as Given by Captain Harcourt	Corrected Name[1]	Dates	Reference
83.	Raj Sing	Raj Singh	1729	Devi Kotali mask inscription at Chanahan, Kothi Kayas.
84.	Tedhi Sing	Tedhi Singh	1753	Adi-Brahma inscription at Silha in Khokhan.
85.	Prithum Sing	Pritam Singh	1780	Cooper-plate inscription.
86.	Bikhama Sing	Bikram Singh	1802-7	Hardasa mask at Manikarn.
87.	Jeet Sing	Jit Singh	—	—

1. The corrected names in the list, as far as the Pal dynasty is concerned, are necessarily conjectural; the dates are those of the inscriptions referred to in the last column. The names Hamir (Arabic amir), Surat, Tegh and Sikandar can, of course, never have been borne by rulers of the pre-Muhammadan period. [J.Ph. V.]

   [Postscript. – To the document above discussed may be added certain papers in the Archives of Chamba State, which have lately become available and are now being exmined by Dr. Hutchison. A list of them will shortly appear in an Appendix to the Chamba State Gazetteer and in the Catalogue of the Bhuri Singh Museum. J.Ph. V.]

Appendix B

THE NIRMAND COPPERPLATE OF SAMUDRASENA

From: J. Fleet, *Corpus Inscriptionum Indicarum,* Vol. III, p. 286.

TEXT[1]

1 [2].............. bhikhyata - narapati - vansa - jas = sama[3]bhavach = chatur-udadhisamatikkranta-kirttir=aneka-samant-ottamang-avanata-mukuta - mani- mayukha-vichchhurita-charanaravinda-[4]

2 vugala[5]h = kratu-yaji mahasamanta-maharaja-sri-Varunasenas=Tasya putras=tat-pad-anudhyatah= paramadevyap(m) = Prava (ba)lika-bhat[t*]arikayam=utpannah= pitr= aiva tulyo gunair = mma-

3 hasamanta-maharaj-sri-Sanjayasenas=Tasya putras=tat-pad-anudhyatah= parama-devyam Sikharasvamini- bhat [t*] arikayam = uptannas = samara-sata-lavdha (bdha)- jayas=tyagi ma-

4 hasamanta-maharaja-sri-Ravishenas = tasya putras = tat-p[a*]d-anudhyatah=parama-devyam sri-Mihiralakshmi-bhat[t*]arikayam= utpannas=sarad-amala-sakala-rajanikara iva prani-

5 nam samahladana-karas=samutkhat-asesha-ripur=asavatam=aprartthita-phala-prado din-anath-atura-dayaluh=paramamahesvaro= ti-vra(bra)hmanyah=parartthy (rtth)- aika-rato mahasamanta-

6 maharaja-sri-Samudraseno janani-sri-Mihiralakshmya dharmm-arttham bhagavatas= Tripurantakasya lok-aloka-karasya pranat- anukampinar= sarvva- duhkha- kshaya-karo[6] Kapale-

7 svare janani-pratishthitasya sri-Mihiresvarasya Kapalesvara-vva(ba)li- charu-sat[t*]ra-srag-dhupa-dipi(pa)-danaya satatam sirnna-khanda-sphutita-sadhanaya cha Ni-

8 rmmand-agrahar-Atharvvana-vra(bra)hmana-stomaya Sulisagrama-navavaidila-karmm-anta-Vakkhalika-kutumvi(mbi)na dvesa-bhumi-paryanta paribhuta- namna Phakkas= cha Talapura-

9 ka-kutumvi(mbi)na dvesa-bhumi s-odranga sa-sim-anta-paryanta Sulabhaka-kutumva(mba)-Dinna-kutumva(mba)s=cha I Kapalesvara-devasya purvva-pratishthayam maharaja-Sarvvavarmmena7 bhumi data I Sulisagramasya Sri-Mihi-

10 ralakshmya dattasya sam-audaka-jangala-bhumi-sametam=asesham sa-prativasi-jana-sametam s-odranga[m*] sva-sima-trina-kashtha-prasravana-yuti(ti)-paryantam devagraharatven=a-cha-

11 ndr-arkka-tara-samakalinam pratipadayati sma[II*] Viditv=aitad=rajabhis=tad-asri(sri)tajanen=adhikrit-anadhikritena hitam=ichchhata pratipalaniya [I*] yo=nyatha kuryat=paripanthanam= apaha-

12 rana-pid-opadravam vas a panchabhir=mmahapatakair=upapatakais=cha samyuktas= syat II Uktan=cha [I*] Va (ba)hubir8=vvasudha bhukta rajabhis=Sagar-adibhi[h*] yasya yasya yada bhumis=tasya tasya tada

13 phalam [II*] Shashtim varsha-sahasrani svargge modati bhumi-dah achchhetta ch= anumanta cha tany=eva narake vaset [II*] Sva-dattam para-dattam=va yo hareta vasundharam shashti-varsha-

14 sahasrani vishthayam jayate krimir=iti II Duto=tra Nihilapati Kusalaprakasas=cha I lekhako=tra Udyota-arkkas9= cha gana-srostha10 [II*] Samvat 6 Khe11 su di io I [II*]

15 Rashtra-sametasy=a(e)yam datti[h*] paripalya II Ai(?)ngi(?)k=attar udya(?)na(?)-sthavara-vadittra-ka(?)visva-sa(?) hadra upalava12

16 kagalalancha(?) tika dva13ya (?) Mihi(hi)ralakshmi (kshmi)-pratipad[i*]ta iti [II*]

1. From the original plate.
2. Four letters, or perhaps five, are broken away and lost here. A small part of the last of them, immediately preceding the first legible syllable, *bhi*, is visible; but it is impossible to say what the entire letter may have been.
3. The mark over this *ma* is a fault in the copper, making a hole right through it.
4. The mark between the *vi* and the *nda* is a fault in the copper, making a hole right through it.
5. The upper parts of these three letters are broken away and lost; but enough remains to show distinctly what they were.
6. Read *Karasya.*
7. Read *sarvvavarmmand.*
8. Metre, Sloka (Anushtubh); and in the following two verses.

9. Read *udyotarkkas.*
10. This seems to be intended for *gana-sreshthah.*
11. This is what is engraved. But of course it is a mistake for *vai,* i.e. *vaisakha;* and it is easy to see how the engraver made the mistake in copying from the draft before him.
12. The mark that follows this *va* is a fault in the copper, making a hole right through it.
13. The mark before this *dva* is a fault in the copper, making a hole right through it.

TRANSLATION

Born in the lineage of the famous kings..................... there was the *Mahasamanta* and *Maharaja,* the illustrious **Varunasena**, whose fame stretched out over the four oceans; the waterlilies of whose feet were covered over with the rays of the jewels in the bowed-down tiaras on the heads of many feudal chiefs; (and) who celebrated sacrifices.

(Line 2.)—His son, who meditated on his feet, *(and)* who was verily equal to (*his*) father in virtuous qualities, (*was*) the *Mahasamanta* and *Maharaja*, the illustrious **Samjayasena**, begotten on the *Paramadevi*,[1] the *Bhattarika* Prabalika.

(L. 3.)—His son, who meditated on his feet, *(and)* who attained victory in a hundred battles, (*and*) who was full of liberality, (*was*) the *Mahasamanta* and *Maharaja*, the illustrious **Ravishena**, begotten on the *Paramadevi* Sikharasvamini.

(L. 4.)—His son, who meditates on his feet, the *Mahasamanta* and *Maharaja*, the illustrious Samudrasena,—who was begotten on the *Paramadevi*, the *Bhattarika*, the illustrious Mihiralakshmi; who, like the spotless full-moon of autumn, causes the delight of (all) living creatures; who has uprooted all enemies; who confers upon the expectant rewards that are not (even) sought for (by them); who is tender to the poor, the helpless, and the afflicted; who is a most devout worshipper of (the god) Mahesvara; who is extremely friendly to Brahmans; (and) who is entirely intent upon the supreme good,— for the sake of the religious purposes of (his) mother, the illustrious Mihiralakshmi, has allotted, as an *agrahara* of the god, to endure for the same time with the moon and the sun and the stars, to the body of *Brahmans* who study the *Atharva-Veda* at the *agrahara* of **Nirmanda**,—for the purpose of giving, at (*the temple of the god*) *Kapalesvara*, the *bali, charu, sattra*, garlands, incense, and lights) of the holy (god) Mihiresvara, who is the divine Tiipurantaka, the maker of the visible and invisible world, compassionate to those who worship (him), the destroyer of all sorrows, (and) who was established by (his) mother at (the temple of the god) Kapalesvara; and for the purpose of always repairing whatever may become worn out and broken and torn,—the whole of the village of **Sulisagrama**, that was granted by the illustrious Mihiralakshmi, together with the level and marsh and forest lands; together with the inhabitants; with the *udranga*; (and) including all its boundaries, grass, timber, and springs,—(viz.) (the land) including the dvesa-land[2] (that had been given) by the cultivator Vakkhalika, (whose holding was) on the edge of the newly constructed vaidila[3] of the village of **Sulisagrama**; and the *duesa*-land, with the *udranga* (and) including the edges of (*its*) boundaries, *(that had been given)* by a cultivator of the town of Talapura,[4] who under a nick-name (was called) Phakka,[5] and the holding of

Sulabhaka and the holding of Dinna; (and) the land that had been given by the *Maharaja* Sarvavarman at the former installation of the god Kapalesvara.

(L. ii.)—(This grant) should be preserved by (future) kings, becoming aware of it; (and) by the people, whether holding office or not holding office, dependent on them, who are desirous of welfare! Whosoever (acting) otherwise may cause obstruction or the annoyance of the pain caused by confiscation,—he shall become invested with (the guilt of) the five great sins and the minor sins!

(L. 12.)—And it has been said:—"The earth has been enjoyed by many kings, commencing with Sagara; whosoever at any time possesses the earth, to him belongs at that time the reward (of this grant that is now made, if he continue it)! The giver of land enjoys happiness in heaven for sixty thousand years; (but) the confiscator (of a grant), and he who assents (to an act of confiscation), shall dwell for the same number of years in hell! He who confiscates land that has been given, whether by himself or by another, is born as a worm in ordure for the duration of sixty thousand years.

(L. 14.)- And the Duta[6] in this matter (is) the *Nihilapati*[7] Kusalaprakasa and the writer in this matter (is) Udyotarka, the leader of the assemblage (?)[8] The year 6; (the month) Vaisakha; the bright fortnight; the day 10 (and) 1.

(L. 15.)—This grant, which is one of the whole assembly of (the people of) the country, should be preserved! ....[9]

1. Paramadevi, lit. 'supreme goddess,' was a technical title of the wives of *Maharajas*. The more usual title, however, was *Mahadevi* (see page 16 above, note 2).
2. Dvesa.—I have not been able to obtain any explanation of this word, which is probably a local term. Dr. R. Mitra translated it by 'grazing-ground,' but quoted no authority for this.—The purport of the passage from *Sulisagrama-nava*, line 8, down to *bhumi dattd*, line 9, is not quite clear. But it seems to specify certain previous grants which make up the *asesham* or 'entirety' of Sulisagrama, as now bestowed by Samudrasena.
3. *vaidila*.—This is another word of which I have not been able to obtain any explanation.
4. Or perhaps Talapura, with the short vowel *a* in the first syllable.
5. *lit*. the cripple.
6. *Duta*; see page 100 above, note 3.—An Ujjain grant of Vikrama-Samvat 1192 (Colebrooke's Essays, Vol. II. p. 273; and Indian Inscriptions, No. 51, line 13) gives an instance of more than one original *Duta* or *Dutaka* being employed for one and the same grant,—viz. "the *Purohita*, the *Thakkura*, the illustrious *Vamanasvamin*; the *Thakkura*, the illustrious *Purushottama*; the *Maha pradhana*, the *Rajaputra*, the illustrious *Devadhara*; and others,"—without any such circumstances as those indicated in No. 30 above, page 134, which necessitated the despatch of a second *Dutaka* lo authorise the insertion of additional privileges in the charter.
7. *Nihilapati*.—I have not been able to obtain any explanation of the first component of this official title.
8. *gana-sreshtha* (?).—If this is the proper intended reading, the word must have some technical meaning; but its exact purport is not apparent.
9. The passage commencing with *ai*(?) *ngi*(?) *k=atra*, in line 15, is too corrupt to be capable of translation. But it appears to record two other grants made by Mihiralakshmi; and it mentions a park, some immovable property, and some musical instruments.

Appendix C

AN ACCOUNT OF RAJA JAGAT SINGH

This account is taken from: J. Hutchison and J.Ph. Vogel, *History of the Panjab Hill States*, Vol. II, pp. 458-62.

The Rajas who followed Bahadur Singh continued to reside at Makaraha, though Nagar seems to have been regarded as the capital of the state.

Jagat Singh (AD 1637—1672): Jagat Singh was one of the most notable of the Kulu Chiefs, and during his reign the kingdom was further enlarged and consolidated. For some time after his accession, he continued to reside at Makaraha, and from there he directed his conquest of Outer Saraj and the territory on the right bank of the Beas, still under the rule of Lag.

In the beginning of Jagat Singh's reign an incident occurred which had important political consequences. A Brahman residing at Tippari between Chaman and Jhari was said to have a *patha* (i.e. about three pounds) of pearls. The Raja sent to demand the pearls and met with a refusal. He was on his way to Manikarn, and at Sarsari he again sent to the Brahman for the pearls. Losing his temper, the latter replied that he would produce them on the Raja's return from Manikarn, but on the approach of the royal party he set fire to his house, and perished with all his family. The ruins are still shown. The Raja then went on to Makaraha, and on food being set before him, it all turned to worms.[1] This caused much alarm, and a Brahman of reputed piety was sent for from Suket, who came unwillingly. On the matter being laid before him, he told the Raja that it had been revealed to him in a dream that the sin of Brahman murder could be expiated only by bringing the image of Raghunathji from Oudh,[2] and making a surrender of the kingdom to that deity. On hearing this, Jagat Singh ordered the Brahman, named Damodar, to bring the image. Now Damodar had a *gutka-sidh*, or ball used by devotees, which, on being put in the mouth, made the bearer invisible. He went to Oudh—probably the city of Ajudhya—and lived a long time in the temple waiting for an opportunity to carry off the image. Having at last secured it, he put the *gutka-sidh* in his mouth and at once reached Hardwar. On the theft being discovered, one of the temple attendants, who also had a *gutka-sidh*, started in pursuit, and arrived at Hardwar, where he found Damodar worshipping the image. Being challenged with the theft, he replied that he had not stolen the god, as it was at the latter's own request that he was being taken to Raja Jagat Singh of Kulu. "If I do not speak the truth," said Damodar, "take the god back if you can." The Oudh Brahman then tried to lift the image, but in vain, while Damodar raised it with one hand. Being satisfied, the Oudh Brahman returned empty-handed, and Damodar brought the image to Makaraha. There Jagat Singh formally conveyed his realm to the god, by placing the image on the *gaddi*, and henceforth the Rajas of Kulu regarded themselves as only the vice-regents of Raghunath (Rama), and as ruling only in his name. A great feast or *yagya*[1] was also held on the occasion. A similar transfer of the kingdom to a god took place in Mandi about the same time, in the reign of Suraj-Sen, AD 1637–64. In this way the curse was removed, and in gratitude Damodar was granted 84 coolie loads of goods and also a temple at Bhuin village with all its rights. Jagat-sukh Kothi was also made dharmarth, that is, made over as a religious gift in the name of the god. Jagat Singh also ordered one rupee and two copper coins to be placed daily before the god, and gave orders that this money was to be put aside and sent every year to Ajudhya.

As we have already seen, the first invasion of Lag probably took place in the reign of Partap Singh. But although much of the territory was then lost, the Rajas of Lag continued to hold the rest of the State down to the reign of Jagat Singh. It included the whole of Lag proper; Kodh-Sawar of Chhota-Bangahal; and all the slopes to the Uhl River from the outer Himalaya, the upper part of which is now known as Chuhar—originally a part of Bangahal state.

Jagat Singh invaded Lag in conjunction with the Raja of Mandi, probably Suraj Sen. After the conquest Mandi took Chuhar, and all the rest seems to have gone to Kulu. The Lag state was then ruled by two brothers, one of whom, Jai Chand or Jog Chand, resided at Dughi-Lag, and the other, Sultan Chand, at Sultanpur, which, according to tradition, was founded by and named after him. Jagat Singh invaded Lag, and his advance was made by way of Dhalpur, near Sultanpur, where he attacked Sultan Chand. The latter was a renowned warrior, and a large cave is still shown on a mountain near Sultanpur, as the favourite hiding place of the two brothers, when carrying on a guerilla war against Jagat Singh. At last Sultan Chand is said to have had his head severed from his body in battle, but it remained in place, and he went on fighting till he reached the Padhka—a kind of pillar in Sultanpur—

where the head fell off and he died. Traditionally, however, Jai or Jog Chand is said to have been the hero of this incident. However this may be, the second brother was also soon afterwards killed, and the whole territory of Lag was then annexed to Mandi and Kulu as already related, probably about AD 1650–55.

Jagat Singh's attack upon the Lag state is fully corroborated by one of the farmans already referred to, addressed to him by Dara Shikoh in the year AH 1067 = AD 1657. In this document, it is stated that Jagat Singh had taken possession of the state of Jog Chand after the latter's demise, and carried captive some of his relatives, knowing them to be under the protection of the emperor. He is enjoined to surrender the tract seized, and "if from obstinacy and imprudence he defers releasing Jog Chand's grandson and giving up the district, an order will be issued to Raja Rajrup. ....Jahangir Quli Beg and the Faujdar of Jammu, that they should go up to the districts of his Zamindari and annihilate him." Raja Rajrup was the Raja of Nurpur and son of Raja Jagat Singh of that state, and not an uncle of Jaswant Singh of Jodhpur as is stated in the Kirmur State Gazetteer. Jahangir Quli Beg may have been the Kiladar of Kangra, who resided in the Kangra Fort.

Jagat Singh did not comply with the royal command. He had probably heard rumours of the impending conflict between Dara Shikoh and his three brothers, and felt himself safe in disregarding the order.

Having thus subdued the whole of the Upper Kulu Valley, Jagat Singh transferred the capital from Nagar to Sultanpur, probably about AD 1660, and built a palace for himself and a temple for Raghunathji. Thereafter he resided alternately at Sultanpur, Nagar and Thawa—the last named place being above Nagar. It is now a heap of ruins, and tradition says that Nagar Castle was built with the stones from Thawa.

Makaraha was then abandoned, and probably soon fell into decay. It had enjoyed great prosperity during the reign of Jagat Singh, who erected a temple there to Rama and deposited in it a *Murli* (flute), which he had obtained from Ayadhya. The following couplet is also interesting as it shows the prosperous condition of the place:

Makarahar Ajodyapuri manohem Braj ki rit
Jagat-Singh Maharaj ki Sri Ragho-ji sen prit.

Makarahar is another Ayodhva and is the counterpart of Braj (tract round Mathura).
Maharaja Jagat-Singh is devoted to the illustrious Raghuji (i.e. Rama Chandra).

Of the thirteen farmans referred to, twelve are addressed to Jagat Singh between AD 1650 and 1658. In them he is called 'Zamindar of Kulu', and is only once styled Raja. One of the farmans is from Aurangzeb, in which Jagat Singh is spoken of as "well-established in his royal ways." He sent presents of hawks and falcons to Delhi, and deputed his son as a hostage at the Imperial Court. In the farman referred to, Jagat Singh was asked to join hands with Dhan Chand Kahiuria of Bilaspur, in order to close the roads through the hills against Sulaiman Shikoh, son of Dara Shikoh, who sought to rejoin his father. The latter had fled to the Panjab, after his defeat by Aurangzeb and Murad Bakhsh at the battle of Samugarh in AD 1658.—Vide Bernier's Voyages, Volume I, pages 84 ff; also Manucci, Volume I, page 271.

An amusing tradition has come down about Jagat Singh and a Brahman sadhu, who lived in a small forest, called Nagar-Jhir forest, near Nagar and Thawa. The Raja went to visit the saint, who changed himself into a tiger; but not being in the least afraid, Jagat Singh lifted the tiger off the ground. At this the tiger was pleased, and, patting the Raja, again changed himself into a sadhu. He made Jagat Singh his disciple, and put a garland round his neck, at the same time giving him the god Narsingh to worship. He then added, "You are of the Kshatri caste, so you should have one bird shot every day and cooked and then offered to the god; after which half is to be given to my disciple, and the other part you should eat yourself." He also said, "Eight of your descendants will reign at Makaraha and the ninth at Pandori; after that whoever obeys Raghunath the most will be king."

It appears that most of Outer Saraj was still in the possession of Suket and Bashahr, so Jagat Singh went there with his army and captured the forts of Naraingarh, Sirigarh and Himri, and annexed them to the state. He died soon afterwards, having reigned about 35 years.

Appendix D

THE DEOTAS OF KULU

This list of different categories of deities was compiled from the Census Reports of 1883 and 1892 by Denzil Ibbetson and Edward Maclagan, as compiled by H.A. Rose in *A Glossary of the Tribes and Castes of the Punjab and North-West Frontier Province* (reprinted, 1970).

Nag Deotas of Saraj

Name of Deotas/Devi	**Site of Temple**	**Dates of fairs**
Chhamanu Nag	Bhunga (Saraj) Kali wan *deota*	Annual fairs are held in Chet, during the naurdiras in Baisakh on the biaspuja in Har, on nag panchmi in Bhadon, and in Magh and Phagan. The practice is to choose auspicious days for the fairs.
Badi Nagan		A fair is held annually on 7th Baisakh and 15th Jeth.
Balu Nag	Balugohar	The fairs are held on 20th Baisakh and on the puranmashi in Bhadon every year.
Kirtha nag	Shinli	One fair lasts from 15th Poh or 2nd Magh; another

Name of Deotas/Devi	Site of Temple	Dates of fairs
		is held on 1st Phagan and the third on 20th Sawan. These fairs are held annually.
Sharshai Nag	Shassha	The annual fairs are held on 2nd and 3rd Asauj and at the Dewali.
Paneo Nag (Also called Panun and Kungash)		The annual fairs are held on 2nd and 12th Asauj and on 10th Maghar.
Kui Kandha Nag		The fairs are held annually on Sankrants of Jeth and Bhadon at Diwali.
Shankhu Nag	Keoli Bau Rahwali Rupa	The two fairs are held, one on 1st Bhadon and the other on 1st Phagan.
Takrasi Nag	Takrasi	The annual fairs are held on 1st Jeth, 10th and 12th Sawan and on 1st Poh.
Jaru, The deaf Nag	Phali Tunar	
Danwi Nag	Danw, Kothi Naraingarh	

Nag Deotas of Kulu

Name of Deotas/Devi	Site of Temple	Dates of fairs
Basu Nag	Batahar Village, Kothi Nagar	Nine days on the ikadshi of Phagun, one day on the 1st Chet, four days on the new year's Baisakh, and one day in Asauj.
Pahal Nag at Bharka Dera	Phal Nala	10th of the lunar month of Baisakh.
Kali Nag at Dera Kal Nag	Raison Kothi	1st to 14th Asauj and Maghar, and on the 3rd, 5th, and 7th of the light half of Sawan and Bhadon.
Kali Nag at Matiora in K. Har Khandi		4th Baisakh, besides a yag on 5th Bhadon.

Name of Deotas/Devi	Site of Temple	Dates of fairs
Kali Nag Shirar at Kat Kali Nag		(1) 1st of naurata in the light half of Chet., (2) light half of Jeth, (3) a yag (Narmedh) is performed every third year in the light half of Sawan (4th) 1st of Magh, (5) 1st of Phagun, (6) 1st of Chet.
Piuli Nag at Batahar Dera in K.Nagar	V. Batahar	1st of Phagun, 1st day of Phagun and 1st of Chet, four days in the light half of Chet at the beginning of the new year.
Sargun Nag	Jagalsildi	31st Bhadon to 2nd Asauj.
Ramnun Nag at Kehli Aga		1st to 3rd Chet, 31st Sawan to 3rd Bhadon and 1st to 3rd Asauj.
Shukli Nag at Naudla Dera		1st to 3rd Asauj and for two days from full moon day of Maghar.
Goshali Nag	Goshal	
Dhunbal Nag	Halan	
Kiani Nag	Kiani	
Bhalogu Nag	Dera Bhalogi	
Jalsu Nag	Jalse	

Temples of Mahadev in Kulu

Deota Mahadeo	Chohki Dera	9th of the light half of Maghar.
Deota Bijli Mahadeo or Bijlishar Mahadeo	Malthan Dera	1st of Chet and 1st of Har, 1st to 7th Asuj, five fairs from 1st to 5th Baisakh. Pipal Jatra for 12 days at Sultanpur. 18th Baisakh and 19th Baisakh.
Deota Gauri Shankar Mahadeo	Dawala Washal Waugar	Shivratri in the dark half of the month of Phagan for 2 days.

Deota Jawanu Mahadeo	Dera Jawanu Mahadeo	1st and 2nd Chet, during the same month in the light half of Parwa and Dutia, 1st to 3rd Baisakh, 1st and 2nd Sawan and 1st to 3rd Bhadon.
Deota Lurain Mahadeo	Laran Dera	In Phagan, 2nd Chet, new year's day 1st baisakh, 1st Jeth, 1st Bhadon, Janam-ashtmi and 1st Asuj.
Deota Manglishar Mahadeo	Chhanwar Dera	6th Baisakh and a yag every 2nd year from 1st to 4th Sawan.
Nilkanth Mahadeoji	Known by the name of its deity	On Shivratri, the 4th of the dark half of Phagan and Kali Puja from 1st to 4th of Jeth.
Sangam Mahadeo	—	No fair, but two festivals called Tara Ratri and Shiv Ratri.
Deota Siali Mahadeo	Dera Siali Mahadeo	26th of Phagan on the Shivratri, 12th and 13th of Chet.
Deota Shibrharach	Dera	1st of Phagan

Devi Temples in Kulu

Name of Devi	Site of Temple	Dates of fairs
Bhaga Siddh[1]	Named after the goddess	12th and 13th Baisakh and in Sawan.
Bhaga Siddh	Dera	7th Jeth
Bhaga Siddh	Dera Dughi Lag	1st of Chet, 3rd of the light halves of Phagan and Chet, 1st of Baisakh, Jeth, Bhadon and Asauj, and on the full moon day of Maghar.
The goddess Hirma	Dhungri Dera	Dhungri jatra on the 1st Jeth for three days, on the Phagali on the 4th Magh, 1st of Sawan and Baisakh.

Name of Devi	Site of Temple	Dates of fairs
Devi Harman	—	7th and 15th Magh, 1st Baisakh and 1st Asauj.
Devi Kali Auri	Devi in Kotli Mangarh	1st Baisakh, 1st Bhadon and 3rd Jeth.
Kali Auri	Archhandi Dera	1st and 2nd of Chet, 1st to 3rd of Baisakh, 1st of Bhadon and 1st of Asauj.
Kali Mahi Khasuri, Kali Auri or Phungni	Dera Devi in Kothi Raisan	1st Baisakh and Bhadon.
Devi Phungni	Dera Phungani in K Mandalgarh	5th and 7th of the lunar months of Baisakh and Phagan and on Wednesday and Thursday in the light halves of Sawan and Maghar.
Devi Phungni	Dera Devi Phungani in Biasar	1st of Chet, 3rd and 5th of the light halves.
Devi Phungni[2]	Tiun Dera in Kothi Mangarh	In addition to fairs in Sawan, Asauj, Maghar and Phagan, a fair is held on the 3rd, 5th and 7th in the dark half of Baisakh.
Devi Bhotanti[3]	Parai Dera in Kothi Chung	1st to 3rd Assuj.

1. The temples of the goddess Chamunda, of Narain, Doli Nag, the goddess Indarol and Dharat Pal are connected with this.
2. South of the temple is a *bhandar* (storehouse) of the goddess and to the west are two rooms for cooking food. At 100 paces in the latter direction is a *marah* where a fair is held in her honour.
3. Two temples are connected with this, those at Bhati Dera and Garan Dera. The goddess visits these temples on the occasion of the fair.

Name of Devi	Site of Temple	Dates of fairs
The Goddess Bhanthali	Banthali Dera	7th of Jeth and 1st of Asauj.
Devi Bharari	Mel	3rd Asauj.
Devi Chamunda[1]	Dabogi Dera at Nashala	On the dwadshi (12th) in the light half of Phagan, 1st Chet, new year's day, 1st to 4th Baisakh, 1st Jeth, 1st Bhadon and 1st Asauj.
Devi Chamunda[2]	Nalar Dera	1st Sawan.

Name of Devi	Site of Temple	Dates of fairs
Shri Devi Dasmi Barda	Kalar Dera	1st to 3rd Chet, 31st Chet to 3rd Baisakh, 6th to 3rd Har, 31st Sawan to 5th Bhadon and a yag every 12 years.
The goddess Ducha and Mucha	Gajjan and Karjan Deras	The gajjan on the 4th Jeth and the chachopali on the full moon day of Chet, lasting four days.
Devi Garan Puri	Narainin Garan Dera, Upar Rela Dera and Ringu Dera	1st Phagan, 1st Baisakh, 8th Baisakh, Ganesh chaudas in Sawan in Har, 1st of Poh and 21st Baisakh.
The goddess Jaggannathi	Jaggannathi Dera	8th to 11th of the light half of Baisakh, 7th to 10th of the light half of Har, and 7th to 10th of the light of Asauj.
Devi Jaggannathi ji	—	Baisakh shudi ashtami 3 days, Har shudi ashtami 3 days, Asauj shudi ashtami 3 days, besides 15th Phagan, 1st Chet, 1st of new year, 1st Baisakh.
Jaishari or Mahi Kashur[3]	Hat in Bajaura Kothi	9th of Baisakh and 8th of Bhadon.
Jawalamukhi	Dera Pali Sari in Kothi Hurang	1st of Baisakh, Jeth and Har, and on the 2nd of the light half of Sawan. A grand yag is performed 12 years.
Jawalamukhi	Shamshi Dera in Kothi Khokhan	1st of Baisakh, Sawan and Asauj, and on the full moon day of Maghar. Each lasts one day.

1. Another temple called Dera Nishala is connected with this. It contains an image said to be that of the goddess Bhaga Sidh and it is worshipped in the same room as the other goddess.
2. The temple at Dhara Dera and Sungal Dera are connected with this. The god's chariot is taken to these at a festival.
3. The temple also contains an image of Bhole Nath. It is of stone, and is one cubit high. It is worshipped along with the goddess.

Name of Devi	Site of Temple	Dates of fairs
Devi Khaudasan	Naumi Dera	The Japari jatra in the beginning of the new year in the light half of the month of Chet for four days, and Sawan jatra on the 31st of Sawan for four days.
Devi Kodaula[1]	Gohi Dera	2nd, 12th, 13th and 14th Baisakh, and 2nd Asauj.
Kowanal	Dera Soil	The shivratri on the 4th of the dark half of Phagan, Phagli on the ikadshi of Phagan, chachopali on the full moon day, on the bir shiv on the 1st Baisakh, the kapo on the 1st of Jeth, the shevno on the 1st of Sawan and the sari on the 1st of Asauj.
Devi Maha Maya	Maha Maya	Tuesday of the light half of Phagan.
Maha Mai Jagui	Choppar	
Nainan	Bhulang Dera in Kothi Khokhan	1st of Baisakh, Sawan and Bhadon, each lasting one day.
Phungni Bari Shahi	Dera Phungani	3rd, 5th & 7th of the light half of Baisakh.
Phungni	Dera Phungani Gauuani in Hauani	1st of Chet and 7th of the light half of Asanj.
Sri Rani Neoli	Rani	
Devi Sandhia	Dera Devi Sandhia	4th to 7th of the dark half of the month.
Sarwari	Shuru Dera	Naumi (9th) of Baisakh.
Deota Singhasau	Singhasan Devi Dera	1st of Baisakh and illuminations on the tij (3rd) of Poh.

Name of Devi	Site of Temple	Dates of fairs
Tripura Sundari	Nagar	5th to 10th Jeth, 1st of Asauj, Durga ashtami in Asauj, 3rd of the light half of Poh, one day in the light half of Chet, 2nd and 3rd Baisakh.
Devi Rupashna	Sharani Berh in Kothi Harkandi	1st Baisakh and yag ever 3rd year on 2nd Bhadon.

1. No temple is connected with this, but fairs are held on the 21st Maghar and 21st Sawan when the gods and goddesses visit the fair and return in the evening.

Vishnu Temples in Kulu[1]

Name of Devis/Deotas	Site of Temple	Dates of fairs
Deota Narain	Garauge Dera	Either on Sunday, Monday, Wednesday or Saturday in the light halves of Phagan and Sawan. A large fair is held every 12th year.
Ditto	Dera Narain	On the 3rd, 5th or 7th of the light half of Sawan and Phagan.
Ditto (a)	Dera	1st, 3rd and 8th Baisakh, and 1st to 7th Magh.
Ditto	Dera Bishkola in Bishkola	
Ditto (b)	No special name, in Dumchiv	Full moon day of Maghar, 9th, 15th and 16th of Bhadon and 2nd, 15th and 16th of Phagan.
Deota Lachhmi Narain	Narain Sari	1st Phagan, in Chet, 1st to 11th and 21st Baisakh, 1st Jeth, 7th Har, in Sawan, during the Anant Chaudas, 1st Asauj, in Har, 1st Maghar, and 1st Poh.
Thakur Lachhmi Narain (d)	Lachchmi Narain	

Name of Devis/Deotas	Site of Temple	Dates of fairs
Thakur Lachhmi Narain	Mandir Shailru	Third of the lunar month of Poh.
Thakur Lachhmi Narain	Lachhmi Narain and Narshingh Ji temples in Chogan	Ram Naumi, Janam Ashtami, Dasehra, Jal Buhar, Ban Beehar, Diwali, Ankut, Narsingh, Chaudhas Phag, Panj Bhikhami and Utran.
Ditto	No particular name	No fair.
Deota Lachhmi Narain	Kharasui and Batadhi	9th Baisakh and 6th Bhadon
Bhaltu Narain	Dera Bhalta	On Sunday, Monday, Wednesday, and Thursday in Phagan, Sawan and Asauj.
Deota Chagard Narain	Chagari dera	1st of Chet and full moon day of Chet.
Thakur Chhamaini Narain	Dera Chhamaini Narain	31st Chet, 1st Baisakh and 32nd Har to 2nd Sawan.
Harangu Narain	Dera Gadyara	Sunday, Monday, Wednesday, and Thursday in the light halves of Phagan and Sawan, on the 2nd of Baisakh, the 3rd and 4th of Har (Asarh), the 3rd of Asauj and on the full moon day of Maghar.
Deota Habab Narain	Naraindi Dera	Ikadshi of the light half of Phagan for 6th days, 1st and 2nd Baisakh, 1st of Jeth, 2nd and 3rd Bhadon, 1st Asauj, Uchhab Atrain Sankrant for one day, first Thursday in Poh, and a yag after 12 years.
Deota Karchali Narain (e)	Kalun Dera	On the 3rd, 5th, 7th, 8th and 10th of the dark halves of Sawan, Maghar, Phagan and Baisakh.

Name of Devis/Deotas	Site of Temple	Dates of fairs
Karosi Narain (f)	Naraindi Dera in K. Tarapur	Yearly from Sunday to Thursday in the dark half of Phagan and on the same days in Sawan. But in Baisakh the fairs are only held on Wednesday and Thursday. Another is held for one day in Maghar. Every third year a large gathering takes place during five days in Sawan.
Deota Kasoli Narain	Kasoli Narain in K. Kanawar	1st of Chet and Shivaratri.
Deota Kesho Narain	Dhara	1st Baisakh, 1st Chet and 1st Asauj.
Deota Khalari Narain	Dera Khalari Narain	No fairs, but two festivals during light halves of Phagan and Sawan.
Phalaini Narain	Dera Phallan	Sundays, Mondays, Wednesdays and Thursdays in the light halves of Sawan and Phagan.
Deota Sammon Narain	Dhedai	1st Phagan.
Deota Sapurra Narain or Sapat Rikhi (g)	Dera	5th Baisakh and 30th Chet.
Deota Sarashti Narain	Basti Katon	First Sunday in Phagan, at the beginning of the new year and on the Dhongari.
Siam Narain	Dera Siam Narain	On the dwadashi of the dark half of Phagan. Another on the 1st half of Asauj lasts for three days.
Deota Sikho Narain (h)	Nagi Dera	1st of Baisakh, 7th of Sawan
Thakur Tarjogi Narain (i)	Tarjogi Narain	13th Har, Ram Naumi in Baisakh, Janam Ashtami in Bhadon, Holi in Phagan, Ankut and Dewali in Katak. Also, a yag every 2nd year on 18th Har.

Name of Devis/Deotas	Site of Temple	Dates of fairs
Deota Narain Lapas	*Deota* Narain	9th & 10th Sawan.
Deota Narain Maha	Ditto	Phagan.
Deota Narain Pulga	Dera	1st of Jeth.
Thakur Chatar Bhoj in Kothi Dugi Lag	Thakur Dawala Dugi Lag	On the full moon days of Phagan and Chet.
Thakur Gopal	Thakur Dawala Sarsai	Japari fair for half a day, 3rd light half of the month of Chet, Uchhab Ram Naumi one day in the month of Chet, Uchhab Janam Ashtami one day in the month of Bhadon, Ankut Dip Mala for two days on the Amawas of the light half of Katak, Uchhab Phag one day in Phagan.
Sri Gopal Ji	Kastar Dera	One festival in the month of Chet.
Deota Hari Narain (j)	Dera Narain	Full moon day in Maghar, on the 9th, 10th, 16th of Bhadon and on the 9th, 15th and 16th of Phagan.
Thakur Jagan Nath	Jagar Nath ra Dawala	Naumi of Chet, on the Janam Ashtami.
Thakur Madho Rai (k)	Thakur Dawala Haripur	Desehra for 6 days, Basant Panchami for 1 day, birthday of Rama, 1 day, Dev Saini on ikadshi, Janam Ashtami for two days, Holi for 8 days, Dip Mala of ikadshi, Ankut for 1 day.
Thakur Murlidhar and Chatar Chug (l)	Two temples which bear the names of the deities to whom they are dedicated	Ninth of Asauj and lasts till full moon light half of Magh for one day, one day in the light half of Phagan, and one in Jeth.
Thakur Murlidhar ji	Name of the god	
Thakur Murlidhar attached to Ram Chandra Ji	Murlidhar	Dassehra.

Name of Devis/Deotas	Site of Temple	Dates of fairs
Thakur Murlidhar	Thakur Dowara	No fair.
Thakur Har Sinhk Ji (m)	Thakur Dawala Lohar in K. Khokhan	Ninth of the light half of Chet. On the Janam Ashtami, i.e. the 8th of the dark half of Bhadon and on the day of the full moon of Phagan.
Thakur Narsingh Ji	Thakurdowara Narsingh Ji	
Ditto	Dawala Karjan	1st Magh, Sawan and Phagan.
Ditto	Harma Nainan Ji	Ram Naumi in Chet, on Janamashtami in Bhadon, on Ankut in Katak, on Holi in Phagan and on the Dewali in Katak.
Ditto	Thakur Dawala Washal	Ram Naumi, which may fall either in Baisakh or in the light half of Chet and Janamashtami in the light half of Bhadon for one day.
Deota Naro Mani (n)	Dera in K.Kothi Kandhi	1st Baisakh, 1st Jeth, 15th Har, 3rd Bhadon and any day in Bhadon.
Thakur Narsingh ji	In Jharin known by the name of the place.	One day in the month of Bhadon, 1 day in Katak, 3 days during the dark half of Katak, 1 in the light half of Phagan, one in the light half of Baisakh, and one in the light half of Sawan.
Sri Thakur Raghu Nath Ji	Called after the god in K.Shari	10th to 16th of light half Asauj, 5th of light half of Magh, full moon day in Phagan, 12th of light half of Baisakh, and ikadshi of light half of Jeth.
Thakur Ram Chandra ji	Thakurdawara Ram Chandra ji in Dorab.	
Deota Ram Chander	Known by the name of the god	Full moon day of Asauj or Katak.

Name of Devis/Deotas	Site of Temple	Dates of fairs
Thakur Ram Chander Ji (o), Raghu Nath ji, Chatar Bhuj and Narsingh Ji	Thakurdawara	Dassehra on Dashmi.
Thakur Ram Chander ji	Ram Chandar ji	Ram Naumi in Baisakh, Janamashtami in Bhadon, Holi in Phagan Ankut and Diwali in Katak.
Ditto	Thakurdawara	No fair.
Thakur Saligram ji	Thakur Saligram Ji	
Thakur Sita Ram	Sita Ram Ji	Ninth of the light half of each month.
Ditto	Sita Ram Ji, Kothi Maharaja	Ram Naumi in Chet, on the Janamashtami of Bhadon, on Ankut and Holi in Phagan and on the Dip Malka (Diwali) in Katak.
Ditto	——	Dip Mala, Ram Janam, Baisakh Ichhia Tirpana, Bin Beher, Jal Bihar, Narsingh Chaudas, Janam Ashtami, Dasami, Basant, Ankut.
Ditto	Gujar Dawal	Asauj, Ankut, Phag, Ram Naumi, Dev Sati ikadshi, Jal Bahar, Panj Bhesham, Dip Mala.
Deota Bishnu	Dera Bishnuwala	
Thakur Bishnu Bhagwan (p)	Called after the name of the god	Ram Naumi and on Janamashtami.
Deota Bishnu (q)	Dera Sajla in K. Barsai	The Jeth Bir Shiv on 1st of Chet, the Chachopali for 5 days on the full moon day of Chet, the Kanhiya Bir Shiv on 1st Baisakh, the Devkhel for three days on 6th Baisakh. Also the Kapu fair on 1st Jeth, the Sharhnu on 1st Har, the Deori Parabh on the 1st of Bhadon, the Janamashtami in the dark half of Bhadon, the Sutari on 1st Asauj.

1. For further notes on Narain, etc. in Kulu, see under Hinduism in the Himalayas inform.
    (a) Three small temples are connected with this.
    (b) Another temple of this god in Dumchin is connected with this temple.
    (c) The temple of Shesh Nag is connected with this; it is called Sara Aga.
    (d) These two temples are connected with that of Ram Chander.
    (e) Two temples and a *bhandar* are connected with this. The *bhandar* and one temple are in Garaling village and the other temple in Rajang.
    (f) The temples of the goddesses Nanti Hothi Mahajani and Phungani are connected with this. The expenses of their worship are borne by the god himself.
    (g) Beside this there is another temple belonging to this god in Barogi Narain. The ceremonies performed at these places are the same.
    (h) A temple of the god Manun Rikhi is connected with this and is situated in Bhati village. Manun Rishi came to Manali in the guise of a *faqir*. He saw a woman named Gauri Mani and the rishi asked her for milk. She replied "my cow has gone to graze in the jungle; I cannot get you milk at present." The rishi bade her, "Milk these calves." She did so and from them drew milk, which the rishi drank. He displayed another miracle by killing a demon who lived in the village. Seeing this the people began to believe in him and built him a temple. The pujari is a Kanet of the Kashab qot.
    (i) Close to the big temple there is a smaller one.
    (j) Another temple of this god in Kokari village is connected with this.
    (k) A temple of the goddess Bhalamasan is connected with this.
    (l) The temple Chatar Bhuj is connected with this. It is worshipped in the same way as Thakur Murlidhars.
    (m) Inside the temple are images of Thakur Murlidhar and Sita Ji. They resemble a human being in appearance. Each of them is of stone and 1 ˊcubits high. It is said that in the time of Raja Kans who troubled Parichhat and oppressed the people, Sri Bhagwan appeared as an incarnation of Krishan and killed Kans. In the time of the hill chiefs, these images were in Bir Kotgarh whence they were removed by the *kardar* of Adi Brahma and made over to a Bairagi for worship when this territory passed into the hands of the Sikhs. When the Bairagi died, they were brought to this temple. No *muafi* is attached to these temples and the god Brahmma gives them some money as *dharma arth* to meet the expenses of worship.
    (n) Including the big temple there are six temples in all and at each, fairs are held and ceremonies performed.
    (o) The temples connected with this are those of Raghu Nath, Char Bhuj, Narsingh, Murlidhar and Lachhmi Narain.
    (p) No other temple is connected with this except a *dharmsala* where *faqirs* put up.
    (q) No temple save that of Nag Dnumal is connected with this. It contains an image of stone about a foot high. Its worship is performed by the *pujari* of Bishnu *Deota*.

Rishi Temples in Kulu

Name of Rishi	Site of Temple	Dates of fairs
Kartak Swami	Dera at Sheonsar	5th of Baisakh.
Do	Dera or Deri	6th of the light half of Baisakh, 1st of Chet, commencement of the new year in Chet, and 1st of Bhadon.
Do	Dera at Shaushar	5th of lunar part of Baisakh, 20th Bhadon and 20th Magh.
Kapai Mnui	Dera at Kalath	On the Ram Naumi, the 16th of Chet, and the janamashtami, the 21st of Bhadon.
Do	Dera at Bashona	25th Baisakh and a yag every year on 1st & 2nd Sawan.
Bashist Rikhi	Bashist Dera	1st of Baisakh and 12th of Katak.
Gautam Rishi[1]	Dera Gautam Rishi	12th of Phagan and 1st Baisakh
Gautam Rikhi or Ghumal Rikhi[2]	Dera in K.Kot Khandi	1st Phagan.
Gamal Rikhi[3]	Pone Dera	Ikadshi of the light half of Phaugan.
Parasar Rishi Ji[4]	Kamandu Haru	In Magh, Chet, Baisakh and Sawan.
Chiman Rikhi or Chirmal[5]	Dera	7th Phagan, 11th Baisakh, and 5th Jeth.
Do	Chiman Rikhi	1st of Phagan.
Sandal Rikhi	Dera Kahim in K.Manali	8th of Phagan, 2nd of Baisakh, and the janamashtami, the 26th of Sawan.
Markanda[6]	Mukrah temple	1st Phagan, 1st Baisakh, and 20th Sawan.

1. The temple of Beas Rishi is connected with this. The *Puranas* say that the place where he practiced penance was the source of the river Beas. Anyone visiting Beas Kund is fed here. The *pujaris* are Gaurs, Kanets and Bairagis.

2. At another temple the chariot of the god is kept. It is decorated with fine clothes. Besides ornaments of silver and gold, the images of gods are arranged init. The chariot is also worshipped at the fair.
3. A temple called Guran Dera is connected with this. When the chariot is elsewhere, the god is kept in the temple.
4. This rishi also has a temple in Sanor in Mandi (*Gazetteer*, p. 40).
5. Two other temples are connected with this.
6. Markanda fair is held annually on the 1st Baisakh in Kangra. Markanda was an ascetic, but his name is now applied to any water which flows eastward. On the Saukrant of each month, people bathe in this water and give alms. In Kulu proper Markanda's image seems to have been placed on bridges and as guardian of bridges he would appear to have been known as Mangleshar – unless that was the name of his spouse. The god Mangleshar Deo is alluded to in the triplet.

   Mangli Rani, Mangleshar Deo
   Dhauns phuti, Saund seo,
   Markanda Makral neo.

   "When Mangli was queen, Maugleshar's drum was burst; the bridge of Saund carried the god Markanda to Makral."

   And the legend goes that when queen Mangli ruled at Jia, at the junction of the Beas and Parbati rivers, the latter used to be spanned by a bridge at Saund. Just above the confluence, when the drum used in the worship of Mangleshar burst, the bridge fell but the idol of Markanda, which was on the bridge when it fell, was carried on the timbers of the fallen structure down the river to Makral where Markanda's temple now stands: Diack, Kuluhi Dialect, p. 39.

Jamlu Temples in Kulu.

Name of God	Site of Temple	Date of fairs
Deota Jamlu	Kharon Mandir in Kothi Malana	10th of Maghar, full moon day of Maghar, one day in the dark half of Poh, one Thursday in Magh, one day in the light half of Magh, one in the light half of Phagan, 8 days in Phagan, 2 in Chet, 10 in the light half of chet, 1st and 2nd of Baisakh, one in the light half of Baisakh, 1st of Jeth, 1st of Har, 3 days in the light half of Sawan, 31st of Sawan to 5th of Bhadon, Sheori Shankrant for 2 days, 5 in the light half of Asauj, and 1st of Katak.

Name of God	Site of Temple	Date of fairs
Deota Jamlu	Dera Jamlu Saman in Saman	Ikdam of Phagan sudi lasting 4 days, 1st of Chet, 1st of Bhadon, lasting 4 days, and full moon of Maghar for 2 days.
	Dera Jamdaggan Rishi in Sati	One lasting 4 days from the ikadshi of the light half of the month, another one 1st of Chet, a third lasting 4 days in Bhadon, and a fourth 2 days on the full moon day of Maghar.
	Dera Daifri in Daifri.	4 days in the light half of Phagan, 2 from 1st Chet and Baisakh, 4 days from 1st Bhadon, in Sawan, and 2 days on the full moon day of Maghar.
	Dera Shangchar in Shangchar	7 days on the ikadshi of the light half of Phagan, 2 days beginning on 1st of Chet, 1st of Baisakh, and 1st of Bhadon, lasting 4 days.
Deota Jamlu	Dera Shegli Jamlu in Shaigli	4 days on the ikadshi of the light half of Phagan, 2 days on the 1st of Chet & Baisakh, and 4 days on 1st of Bhadon, and in Sawan.
	—	Phagli from 7th to 10th Phagan, Khauni Phagli on 1st of Chet, and Sawan Jatra on 1st Bhadon.
	Dera Sakho Sah in Parain	Baisakh and Phagan.
	Dera Jamdaggan Rishi	1st of Bhadon, full moon days of Maghar, 9th of the light half of Phagan, and 1st of Chet.

Name of God	Site of Temple	Date of fairs
	Dhari Narol in Jagat Sukh	Phagan and Chet, a Sawan jatra in Sawan and Bhadon, and a fair on the full moon day of Maghar.
	Dera in mausa Shiah	1st Baisakh and 24th Sawan.
	Dera in Jamdaggan Rikhi Ursu Village	7th Baisakh.
	Pashi Dera or Khalangoha Dera in Pashi.	7th Phagan and 1st to 7th Baisakh also Rakhri Punian.
	Jamdaggan Rishi's temple in Neri	On the ikadshi and dwadshi of Phagan, 1st of Chet and Bhadon, and on the full moon day of Maghar.
	Dera in village Sisa	12th Bhadon, 3rd Phadan and 1st and 3rd Baisakh.
Deota Jamlu Badagaran	Dera *Deota* Jamlu	8 days from the ikadshi of the light half of Phagan, 1st of Chet for 2 days. 1st of Baisakh for 2 days, 1st of Bhadon for 5 days, in Sawan, and on the full moon day of Maghar for 2 days.
Deota Jamlu Baharka	Naroli re Deri	5 days in the light half of Phagan, 2 in the light part of Chet, 3 days on the 1st of Bhadon, and uchhab bir puja for one day.
Deota Jamlu Gajjan Wala	Gajjan Dera	1st of Chet.
Deota Jamlu Karjan Wala	Dera Karjan	Phagli in Magh on the ikadshi of the lunar month for 2 days, phagli on the full moon day of Chet, Sawan, jatra from 1st to 4th of Bhadon, and in Maghar on the full moon day.

Name of God	Site of Temple	Date of fairs
Deota Jamlu Kasheri	Dera Jamlu Kasheri	On the ikadshi of the light half of Phagan for 3 days, 1st of Baisakh for 2 days, 1st of Chet for 2 days, 1st of Bhadon for 4 days, and 1st of Asauj for 2 days.
Deota Jamlu Kulang	Dera Jamlu	7th of Phagan till 10th and Sawan jatra on 1st Bhado.
Deota Jamlu Majachh	Do	Phagli kauni, phagli and Sawan jatra on 7th Phagan, 1st Chet, and 1st Bhadon, respectively.
Shakohri Jamlu	Mehr Bari	On the holi in Sawan and on the naumi of Maghar. A large gathering also takes place every third year in Sawan.
Deota Jamlu Soil Wala	Dheri Narol	5 days in Bhadon, phagli in Phagan and Chet, dhara pujani in Asauj and pone for 2 days in Maghar.
Deota Jamlu Tapri	Dera Jamlu	Ikadshi and dwadshi of the light half of Chet, 1st Friday of Bhadon, and 1st of Bhadon.
Deota Jamlu Tos	*Deota* Jamlu	Tuesday of the light half of Bhadon.

List of Unclassified Deotas in Kulu

Name of God	Site of Temple	Date of fairs
Baradhi Bir	Nandi Dera	1st Baisakh, in Bhadon, 1st Asauj, during nauratras, 1st Poh, 1st Phagan, and in Phagan.
Berruthan	Berraithan in K. Maharaja	From end of Phagan to 1st Baisakh, from end of Chet to beginning of Baisakh, from end of Sawan to beginning of Bhadon.

Name of God	Site of Temple	Date of fairs
Panj Bir	Dera	In Sawan and Baisakh.
Bir Nath	Dera Bir Nath Mandrol in K. Pashan	Full moon in Maghar and on janamashtami.
Gauhri	Dera *Deota* Gauhri	1st Chet, 1st Baisakh, 1st and 2nd Asauj, and festivals during light half of Sawan and on 15th Phagan.
Bir Nath	Dera Bir Nath Dachani in Dorah	12th of Baisakh and full moon of Maghar.
Gauhri	Lakri Shiva	1st of Baisakh, Chet and Asauj.
Bir Nath or Gahri	Dera *Deota* Guahri in Biasar	1st of Jeth.
Deota Bir Nath	Dera Bir Nath	
Gauhri	Dera Gauhri in Karain.	
Gauhri	Dera	5th Phagan and 3rd Baisakh.
Gauhri	Dheri Bhosh Jeth Bir Shiv in Bhosh	2nd of Chet and one day on the new year.
Bir Nath or Gauhri	Gauhri Dera in K. Maharaja	1st of Chet and Baisakh, and on the 16th Baisakh.
Bir Nath	Dera Sargati Padhar in Paugan	1st of Chet, 1st of Jeth, light half of Sawan, 1st of Asauj, 5th of light half of Asauj, 10th (Dasehra) of the light half of Asauj, light half of Maghar, 12th of Phagan, and light half of Jeth.
Gauhri or Bir Nath	—	4th of Bhadon, 1st of Baisakh, Bhadon and Asauj and on the day of the full moon of Maghar.
Gauhri or Bir Nath	Hatai Dera	1st of Asauj and 3rd, 5th and 7th of dark half of Phagan.
Basheshar Nath	Hatai Dera	No fair.

Name of God	Site of Temple	Date of fairs
Ajmal	Ajmal Naraindi	1st to 7th Phagan, 31st Baisakh and 1st Jeth. Every 12 years a yag from 1st to 3rd Bhadon.
Amal	Naraindi Dera	Seven days in the light part of Phagan, 3rd of Baisakh, 1st of Har, and in Bhadon.
Arjan Gophar	Arjan Gopha	——
Bania Masho	Lain Dera	From Sunday to Thursday in the dark half of Sawan and Phagan and on 1st of Magh.
Chunga Shin	Chkuhan Dera	1st to 3rd Jeth.
Damohal	Maror	1st Asauj.
Bhonbal	Dera *Deota* Dhonbal in K. Hawang	Friday to Monday in Phagan.
Dhonbal	Dera Dhonbal in K.Badagara	11th to 20th of Phagan and on Tuesday.
Durbha Sharshi	Pagli Dera, Dhara, dera, Gahra Dera, Rawara Dera and Mohani Dera	1st Baisakh, 11th Baisakh, 26th Baisakh, 9th Jeth, on dev saini ikadshi in Asauj or Bhadon, 5th Poh.
Donkhru	Mewa	Amawas in Bhadon.
Gauhri Mahu Khat	Gahri Mahu Khat	Shivratri.
Jagitam	Narain-di Dera in K Badagar	For three days from 1st of Baisakh.
Jagti pat	—	—
Jagmata	Dhara Dera	Amawas in Bhadon.
Karardan	—	In Phagan, on the 1st of Asauj and on the full moon of Maghar.
Mandasan	Dera	29th Chet, 8th Baisakh, 25th Baisakh, and 5th Asauj.
Nawani	Kasanti Dera	3rd, 5th, 7th and 8th of the dark half of Baisakh, Phagan and Maghar.

Name of God	Site of Temple	Date of fairs
Pith	Shakai	7th Baisakh and 1st Asauj.
Raimal	Dera Narol in K. Bhalat, Narain Nabi.	Bhog on 11th Baisakh, 9th or 11th Maghar, beth on 9th or 11th Baisakh, nagni panchmi in Bhadon, and parchain on 1st Phagan.
Raupal	Lohal Dera in K. Khokhan	1st of Chet and Baisakh on the 23rd and 24th of Baisakh and on the 1st of Sawan and Bhadon.
Resha	Talarah Dera or Rarah Dera, Dhemol *Deota*, Gausari Dera, Chamala Dera, Pabhiari Kot, Pabhiari Koti, Pabhiari Parol, Ghat Kot, Kaniargi Dera, Kaniargi Mara, Kaniargi Kot, and Rupiali Dera in Bhai Rot.	9th and 10th Baisakh, 9th and 10th Bhadon, 11th Baisakh, 11th Bhadon, dwadshi of Sawan, 1st Phagan, 3rd to 5th Phagan, 1st of Chet and first Sunday of Sawan.
Gurg Resna	Dhara in K Dera	12th Baisakh and 9th Har.
Reshi Chashbui	Gara Dera	Rakhri punian, birthday, shawan jotra, after 6th and 11th days of the birthday, janamashtami in Bhadon, Kosheri jatra on 1st Asauj, Mehta jatra on Panu Bhikha ashtami, parchhani jatra on 1st Phagan, and bir shiv jatra on 1st Baisakh.
Resha	Mahashui Dera	7th Jeth.
Surajpal	Dera	1st of Har.
Than	Bahuthi dera in K. Tarapur	1st of Chet, Baisakh, Sawan, Bhadon, and Asauj.
Than	Than	1st of Chet, 7th of Baisakh, and 1st of Asauj.
Than Balarga	Dera *Deota* Than	1st of Phagan, 7th Magh, and 1st Bhadon.

Name of God	Site of Temple	Date of fairs
Thir Mal	Narlan-di Dera	1st to 9th Phagan and 1st to 5th Bhadon.
Shargan	Dera *Deota* Shargan	1st & 2nd or 3rd of Chet.
Shubh	Narain-di Dera	9th of Phagan, 1st of Har, and 1st of Baisakh.
Rawal	Dera in Garahan	2nd and 3rd of Bhadon.
Do	Rawal in Uch	9th and 10th of Baisakh.

Appendix E

The document that follows is a copy made in hand from a register of the holdings of the *deota* temples that was prepared soon after Indian independence between the years 1947 and 1949. The original is in the office of the Deputy Commissioner of Kulu.

Mauza	File No.	Ser. No.	area + revenue	Orders re garding Muafi	Name	Location
Jagatsukh	40	1	[illegible]	Initial grant 26th Nov 1847; amendment in 1869; further amendments 1890 and 1912. In each settlement minor changes and adjustments in area; cultivable and non cultivable. confirmed 22nd June 1951 on grounds that the temple is intact; people hold the Devta in reverence. Muafi maintained on condition of good character of the Kardar and during the pleasure of the State and till the temple is intact; ~~and~~ the Muafi is not transferable. This Devta offers a Nazrana of 8 annas per year to Thakur Raghunathji as per previous practice	Devta Arjun Gupha under the control of Purkhu son of Prakash Brahmin Kardar age 60.	Mandir Gupha, village Shiran, Kothi Jagatsukh
Jagatsukh	42	2	[illegible]	-do- Nazrana to Raghunathji per annum [illegible]	Devta Bisht Rikhi Kardar ~~village Bisht (Vashist~~ Mani son of Thakur (Rajput) age 50.	village Vashisht Kothi Jagatsukh
Jagatsukh	43	3	[illegible]	-do- Nazrana to Raghunathji per annum (amount not mentioned)	Devta Phakal Kardar Chetram son of Chaini Ram, age 36.	village Paraini Kothi Jagatsukh
Jagatsukh	44	4	[illegible]	-do- Nazrana to Raghunathji per annum [illegible]	Thakur Jagannath Kardar Gobardhan son of Jaglu Brahmin age 45	In Jagatsukh Roper.

Jagatsukh	45	No 5	[illegible]	-do- No Nazrana mentioned	Deota Jamlu Paraini wala Kardar Kushal Chand son of Khub Ram Brahmin, 35 yrs	village Paraini Kothi Jagatsukh
Jagatsukh	46	6	[illegible]	-do- No mention of Nazrana	Deota Jamlu Jagat Sukhwala Kardar Amin Chand son of Khub Ram Brahmin 40 yrs	village Jagatsukh Proper.
Jagatsukh	47	7	[illegible]	-do- Nazrana Raghunathji [illegible]	Thakur Ramchandra Ji of Vashasht Kardar Sachan son of Puran Das Bairagi, 96 yrs	village, Vashast Kothi Jagatsukh
Jagatsukh	48	8	[illegible]	-do- No Nazrana mentioned	Thakur Ramchandraji of Manikaran Kardar Ladde Mani son of Prem Das Brahmin, 56 yrs	village Manikaran Proper

Mauza	Khasra no.	No. of	area + revenue				
Jagatsukh	49	9	[illegible]	Nazrana to Raghunathji	[illegible]	Thakur Sita Ram of Gojra, Kardar, Geru s/o Kushro Brahmin, 72 yrs	Village Gojra Kothi Jagatsukh
Jagatsukh	50	10	[illegible]	Nazrana to Raghunathji	[illegible]	Deota Shatrughan Kardar Devi Ram son of Daya Ram Rajput age 50	Village Banara or Teara, Kothi Jagatsukh
Jagatsukh	51	11	[illegible]	Nazrana to Raghunathji annually	[illegible]	Devi Sarvali of Shoru, Kardar Ramdas s/o Bhagtu, Rajput, 50	Village Shoru Kothi Jagatsukh
Jagatsukh	52	12	[illegible]	Nazrana to Raghunathji PA	[illegible]	Deota Shirdi Narain, Kardar Nathu s/o Ballu Rajput 5[illegible]	Village Ishu Kothi Jagatsukh
Jagatsukh	53	13	[illegible]	Nazrana PA to Raghunathji	[illegible]	Deota Kartika swami Kardar Hukum Ram s/o Hari Das Rajput, 35	Village Khaganal or Khalenal Kothi Jagatsukh

Jagatsukh	54	14	[illegible]	Nazrana -do- P.A. to Raghunathji	Devi Sandhya, Kardar Raghunath Das, s/o Khub Ram, Brahmin 38	village Jagatsukh mohal
Jagatsukh	55	15	[illegible]	Nazrana P.A. -do- to Raghunathji	Devi Mahamayi Jogini, Kardar Rautu s/o Prakash Rajput 60 yrs	village No temple worshipped where the water of Chornal falls.
Jagatsukh	56	16	[illegible]	Nazrana ~~to~~ P.A. -do- to Raghunathji. A summary of orders is available under Kothi Manali	Deota Kapal Muni Kardar Pyare Ram s/o Dille Ram Banagi, age 43	village Kalath in Kothi Manali
Jagatsukh	57	17	[illegible]	Nazrana ~~to~~ P.A. to Raghunathji. ~~Order~~ Available under Kothi Kayas 106	Thakur Sita Ram, Kardar Dyal Das s/o Tiloo, goldsmith 50 yrs	village Sewabagh Kothi Kayas
Jagatsukh	58	18	[illegible]	Entered under Kothi Manali No. 46.	Deota Gautam Rikhi Kardar Dolu s/o Khindu, Rajput 48	village Goshal Kothi Manali
Jagatsukh	59	19	[illegible]	Entered under Kothi Naggar, No. 84	Devi Tripura Sundari, Kardar Cheepu s/o Gehru Brahmin, 57, ~~wd~~	village Naggar mohal.

Mauza	Khewat No.	Ser. No.	area & revenue	Orders regarding	Name Thakur Narsingh	Location village
Jagatsukh	60	20	[illegible]	Detail under Kothi Maharaja No. 147	of Dhalpur, Damodar Das s/o Dyal Das Bairagi, 28 yrs	Dhalpur, Kothi Maharaja
Jagatsukh	61	21	[illegible]	Entered under No. 35, Kothi Manali	Devta Jamlu of Bordh (or Barwah) Kardar Lachhi Ram s/o Neken age 50	village Bordh, Kothi Manali
Jagatsukh	62	22	[illegible]	Entered under No. 36, Kothi Manali	Devta Jamlu of Majhach, Kardar Tallu s/o Harbans, Rajput, 55	village Majhach Kothi Manali
Jagatsukh	63	23	[illegible]	Entered under No. 25, Kothi Manali	Devta Byas Rikhi, Kardar Dolu s/o Khandu, Rajput 48	village Ghoshal Kothi Manali
Jagatsukh	65	24	[illegible]	— do — Nazrana to Raghunathji PA [illegible]	Devi Hidimba, Kardar Khub Ram, s/o Tula Ram, Brahmin, 50 yrs JT Kardar Buddhu, son of Doglu, Rajput, 50 yrs	village Dhungri Kothi Manali

Mauza	File No	Ser No	Area + revenue	Orders re: Muafi	Name	Location
Baragarh	34	44	[illegible]	—do— Gives Nazrana to Raghunathji	Deota Nilakantha alias Barani Mahadev K. Nathu s/o Bolu, 39, Rathore	Village Baran, Baragarh
Manali	66	25	[illegible]	—do— Nazrana to Raghunathji PA [illegible]	Deota Byas Rikhi Kardar Dolu s/o Khandu age 48 (Rajput)	Village Ghoshal Kothi Manali
Manali	67	26	[illegible]	—do— Nazrana paid to Deota Jamlu ~~but discretion left to Kardar to pay or not to pay. (No mention of Raghunathji)~~ Nazrana paid to Raghunathji, ~~PA~~ [illegible]	Deota Gautam Rikhi, Kardar Dolu s/o Khandu Rajput age 45	village Ghoshal Kothi Manali
Manali	1	27	[illegible]	Nazrana paid to Deota Jamlu of Malana [illegible] — It is however at the discretion of the Kardar. No mention of Raghunathji	Deota Jamlu Kothiwali Kardar Tulsi Ram s/o Tehlu Rajput, 35	village Kothig Kothi Manali
Manali	68	28	[illegible]	—do— Nazrana paid to Raghunathji [illegible]	Deota Kartik Swami, Kardar Bhalu s/o Chainu Rajput 31 (Real Kardar Khub Ram s/o Mani Ram Rajput	Village Seonsa, Kothi Manali

Mauza	Khet N°	Khasra N°	Area + revenue	Brief reg. Nazrana	Deota Name & Karadar	Location
Manali	69	29	[illegible] 19 [illegible]	-do- Pays Nazrana p.a to Raghunathji	Deota Sandal Rishi Kardar, Tethu s/o Nuanjar, Rajput 48.	village Shanani
Manali	70	30	[illegible] 14 [illegible]	-do- Pays Nazrana to Raghunathji	Deota Shankhan Narain, Kardar Talle Ram s/o Jagtu Rajput. 44	village Basogi Kothi Manali
Manali	71	31	[illegible]	-do- Pays Nazrana p.a to Raghunathji.	Deota Siyali Mahadeo Kardar Tholu s/o Dodu, Rajput, 46,	village Siyal Kothi Manali
Manali	72	32	[illegible] 14 [illegible]	-do- No mention of Nazrana to Raghunathji	Thakar Narsingh, Kardar, Raibat Ram s/o Damodar Das Bairagi 32	village Baroh Kothi Manali
Manali	73	33	[illegible]	-do- No mention of Nazrana Raghunathji	Deota Tilok Nath Kardar Luddhu s/o Doglu, Rajput, 47	Temple of Tilok Nath in Chamba State
Manali	56	34	[illegible]	-do- No mention of Nazrana Raghunathji	Deota Kapil Muni, Kardar Pyare Ram, s/o Dilla Ram Bairagi age 45	village Kalath Kothi Manali

Manali	75	35	[illegible]	No mention of Nazrana to Raghunathji	Devta Jamlu Boroh wala, Kardar Sacchi Ram S/o Neku Rajput, 50	village Boroh, Kothi Manali
Manali	76	36	[illegible]	No mention of Nazrana to Raghunathji — do —	Devta Jamlu Majhach wala, Kardar Tallu S/o Harbans Rajput 55	village Majhach, Kothi Manali
Manali	78	37	[illegible]	Nazrana paid to Raghunathji Rs to — do —	Devta Vishnu Pinjas Kardar Lalu S/o Dharam das Baragr 54	V. Boroh K. Manali
Baragarh	3	38	[illegible]	Gives Nazrana to Devta Jamlu of Malana — do —	Devta Jamlu of Baragram Kardar Sidhu S/o Kesho Ram, 75	V. Baragram K. Baragarh
Baragarh	10	39	[illegible]	Gives Nazrana to Devta Jamlu of Malana — do —	Devta Jamlu, Dafriwala Kardar, Topu S/o Damodar, Rajput. 70 yrs	V. Dafri or Dalfri K. Baragarh

Mauza	Plot No	Sl No	Area + Revenue	Remarks re. Nazrana	Name	Locality
Baragarh	8	40	[illegible]	No mention of Nazrana	Devta Jamlu Shegriwala, Kardar Ramdas s/o Biwan, Rajput 53	V. Shegri K. Baragarh
Baragarh	11	41	[illegible]	Pays Nazrana to Jamlu Malana	Devta Jamlu Shangcharwala Kardar Tulle Ram s/o Bhikku Rajput 65	V. Shangchar K. Baragarh
Baragarh	33	42	[illegible]	No mention	Devta Jamlu, Kasiriwala Kardar, Sobhu s/o Lehru, Rajput 61	V. Kaseri K. Baragarh
Baragarh	35	43	[illegible]	-do- Pays Nazrana to Raghunath ji	Devta Dhumal Kardar Bhimi Ram s/o Ganga, Rajput 30 yrs	V. Halana K. Baragarh
Baragarh	34	44	[illegible]	-do- Gives Nazrana to Raghunathji	Devta Nilakantha Baraniwala Kardar K. Mastu s/o Balu 39, Rajput	Village Baran K. Baragarh

Mauza	Khata No	Kh. No	Area + Revenue	Orders re Nazrana	Name	Location
Baragarh	9	45	[illegible] 12 [illegible]	Pays Nazrana to Raghunathji	Devta Jagatam, Kardar Uttam s/o Kat[illegible], Rajput, 65	V. Pangan K. Baragarh
Baragarh	13	46	[illegible] 19 [illegible] 11	Pays Nazrana to Thakur Raghunathji	Devi Sunghasini, Kardar Nanak Chand s/o Devi Singh Khati, 60 yrs	V. Baragran K. Dardogh
Baragarh	5	47	[illegible] 9 [illegible] 11	No mention of Nazrana to any Devta	Devta Jamlu, Chani wala, Kardar Jai Nand Lala s/o Mohanlal, B. 45	V. Chani K. Baragarh
Baragarh	12	48	[illegible]	No mention of Nazrana	Devta Jamlu, Sahan wala, Kardar Ishri Das s/o Khohru Khati, 55 yrs	V. Sahan, K. Baragarh
Baragarh	4	49	[illegible]	Pay Nazrana to Raghunathji	Devta Bishna, Kardar Jai Nand Lal s/o Mohanlal 45 Brahmin	V. Darasdh K. Darasd

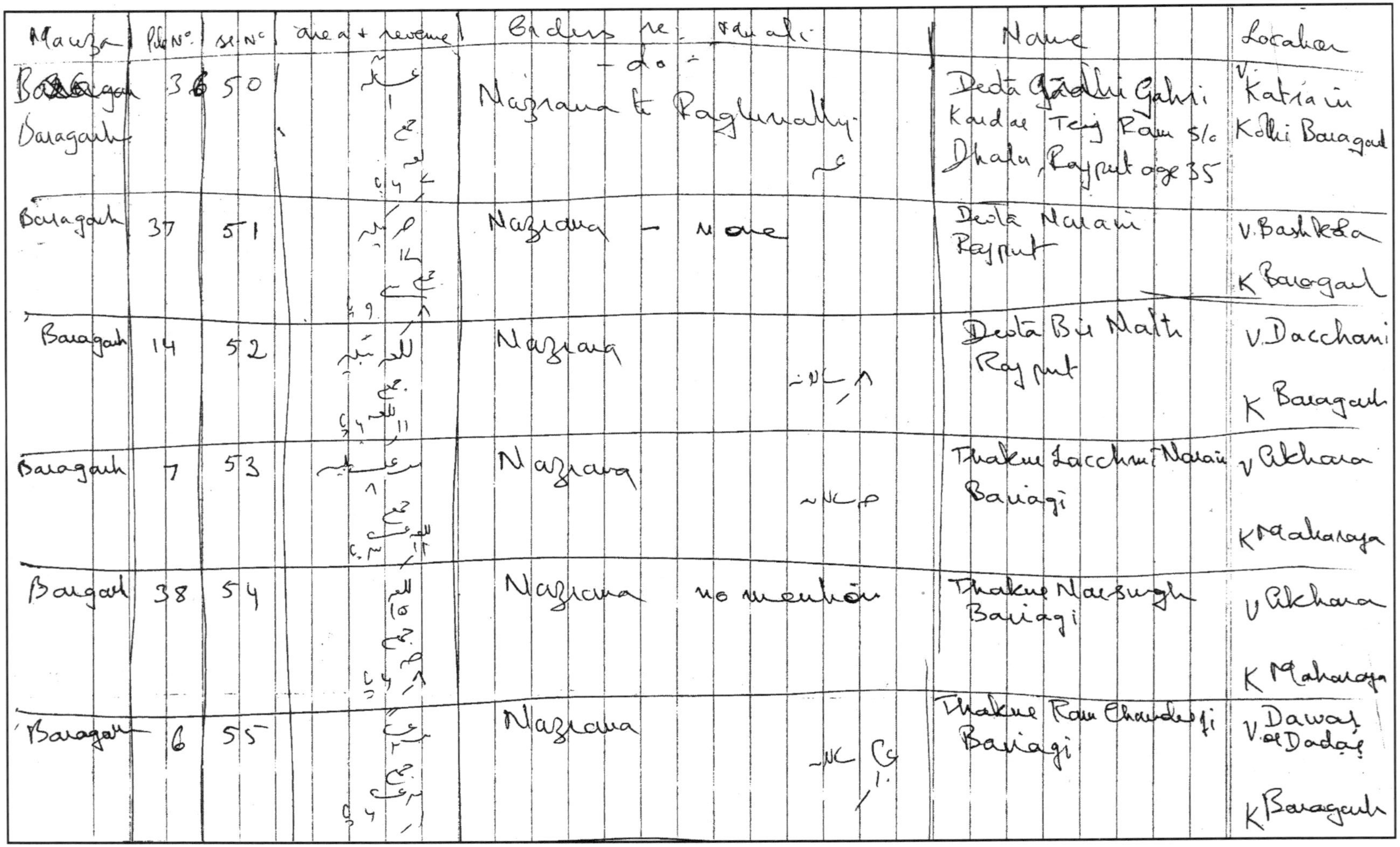

Mauza	Plot No.	Sl. No.	Area + revenue	Orders re: Nazrana	Name	Location
Baragarh Baragarh	36	50	[illegible]	Nazrana to Raghunathji [illegible]	Deota Gādhi Gahri Kardar Tej Ram s/o Dhalu, Rajput age 35	V. Katra in Kothi Baragarh
Baragarh	37	51	[illegible]	Nazrana – None	Deota Narain Rajput	V. Bashkola K. Baragarh
Baragarh	14	52	[illegible]	Nazrana [illegible]	Deota Bir Nath Rajput	V. Dacchani K. Baragarh
Baragarh	7	53	[illegible]	Nazrana [illegible]	Thakur Lacchmi Narain Bairagi	V. Akhara K. Maharaja
Baragarh	38	54	[illegible]	Nazrana no mention	Thakur Narsingh Bairagi	V. Akhara K. Maharaja
Baragarh	6	55	[illegible]	Nazrana [illegible]	Thakur Ram Chanderji Bairagi	V. Dawar of Dadaç K. Baragarh

Baragah	39	56	[illegible]	Nazrana – no mention		Devta Jamlu – Soyal or Shoyalwala Rajput	V. Soyal K Barsai
~~Baragah~~ Barsai	23	57	[illegible]	Nazrana –	[illegible]	Devta Bishanu Rajput (2 household)	V Sajjla K Barsai
Barsai	20	58	[illegible]	Nazrana	[illegible]	Thakur Madho Rai Brahmin	V Haripur K Barsai
Barsai	19	59	[illegible]	Nazrana	[illegible]	~~Deota~~ Devi Doccha-Moccha Rajput	V Kaijan K Barsai
Barsai	35	60	[illegible]	Nazrana – no mention		Deota Jamlu Kaijan wala Rajput	V. Kaijan K Barsai
Barsai	18	61	[illegible]	Nazrana [illegible] Earlier gave Nazrana to the Govt. ~~This was cancelled~~ + N to be paid to Raghunathji.		Thakur Narsing Brahmin	V. Kaijan K Barsai

Mauza	Khewat No.	Kh. No.	area + Revenue	Orders re: Muafi	Name	Location
Barsai	17	62	[illegible]	Nazrana ... K.C.	Deoi Kotki Rajput	V. ~~Soyal~~ Sloyal K Barsai
Barsai	~~13~~ 21	63	[illegible]	Nazrana — ~~no mention~~ Entry is under Kothi Baragarh 56	Deota Jamlu Soyal wala Rajput	V. Sloyal K Barsai
Barsai	15	64	[illegible] (no [illegible])	Nazrana ~~no mention~~ Orders under Koti Baragarh 41	Deota Jamlu Sangchar wala Rajput	V. Sangchar K Baragarh
Barsai	24	65	[illegible]	Nazrana no mention	Deota Jamlu Gunjan wala Rajput	V. Gunjan K Barsai
Barsai	23	66	[illegible]	Nazrana no mention	Deota Dhumal Nag Rajput	V. Sajjla K Barsai
Naggar	81	67	[illegible]	Nazrana : This Deota does not offer any to Raghunathji ; ~~Elaka~~ Elakawar Detail down to Phatis where land is Longest entry	Deota Jamlu Malana wala Rajput	V. Malana K Naggar

Mauza	File No.	Sr. No.	Area + Revenue	Orders re: Muafi		Name	Location
Naggar	82	68	[illegible]	Nazrana	NC [illegible]	Devta Rain Mahadeo Rajput	V. Rān K Naggar
Naggar	83	69	[illegible]	Nazrana	NC [illegible]	Devta Jiw Narain Rajput	V. Royana (of Jamal?) K. Naggar
Naggar	84	70	[illegible]	Nazrana	[illegible]	Devi Chamunda Brahmin	V Mashala K Naggar
Naggar	85	71	[illegible]	Nazrana	NC [illegible]	Devta Gauri Shankar Rajput	V Dashala K Naggar
Naggar	86	72	[illegible]	Nazrana	NC [illegible]	Devta Ambal (or Anambal) Rajput	V Chajogi K Naggar
Naggar	87	73	[illegible]	Nazrana	NC [illegible]	Devta Kartika Swami Rajput	V Hantān K Naggar
Naggar	[illegible]	74	[illegible]	Nazrana	NC [illegible]	Devta Gauri Shankar Brahmin	V Naggar. K
Naggar	89	75	[illegible]	Nazrana — no mention		Devta Jamlu Bhaukarwala Brahmin	V Bhauka K Naggar.
Naggar	90	76	[illegible]	Nazrana	NC [illegible]	Devta Basu Nag Rajput (2 households)	V Khamarti Balta Chaki K Naggar.

Mauza	File No	Sr. No	Area + Revenue	Oe dues re Manali		Name	Location
Naggar	91	77	[illegible]	Nazrana	[illegible]	Devi Khandasni Goldsmith	V. Bhaqka K Naggar.
Naggar	92	78	[illegible]	Nazrana	[illegible]	Devtā Peoli ae Phuli Nag Rajput	V. Battahar K Naggar.
Naggar	93	79	[illegible]	Nazrana	[illegible]	Devtā Gāhri Rajput	V. Bahoosh K Naggar
Naggar	94	80	[illegible]	Nazrana	No mention.	Thakur Lacchi Narain Brahmin	V. Naggar. No nee K
Naggar	95	81	[illegible]	Nazrana	[illegible]	Devi Kali Odhni Brahmin Kali Odhni	V. Archhandi K Naggar.
Naggar	96	82	[illegible]	Nazrana	[illegible]	Thakur Narsingh Bairagi	V. Jhiri K Naggar.
Naggar	97	83	[illegible]	Nazrana wari entry wdue 56	Kothi Barsaguh	Devtā Jamdu Soyalwala Rajput	V. Soyal K Barsai

Naggar	98	84	[illegible]	Nazrana	NL	Devi Tripura Sundari Brahmin	V. Naggar none. K
Naggar	99	85	[illegible]	Nazrana Detailed very long entry (Have Pattad Manali)	NL	Thakur Murlidhar Chaturbhuj Brahmin	V. Naggar none. K
Naggar	100	86	[illegible]	Nazrana no mention.		Devta Jagti Patta Brahmin	V. K. Kachehri Naggar
Naggar	101	87	[illegible]	Nazrana Entry Under No. 32. Kothi Bansar		Devi Kotli Rajput	V. Soyal K Bansai
Naggar	102	88	[illegible]	Nazrana	[illegible]	Thakur Gopal ji Goldsmith	V. Sarsai K Naggar
Naggar	103	89	[illegible]	Nazrana — no mention		Thakur Narsing of Dashal Bairagi	V. Dashal K Naggar [illegible]

Mauza	Khe No	Sr. No	area + revenue	Declns Re: Muafi		Name	Location
Kayas	158	90	[illegible]	Nazrana Long Entry	[illegible]	Devta Bijli Mahadev Rajput	V. Phati Kashawari K. Kayas
Kayas	159	91	[illegible]	Nazrana	[illegible]	Thakur Salig Ram + Rani Neoli Rajput	V. Neoli K Kayas
Kayas	16	92	[illegible]	Nazrana	[illegible]	Devi Bhaga Siddh Rajput	V Bhati Paini K Kayas
Kayas	161	93	[illegible]	Nazrana	[illegible]	Devi Dasmi Barda Rajput	V, Kayas K Kayas
Kayas	162	94	[illegible]	Nazrana	[illegible]	Devta Chhamani Narain Rajput	V. Chhamahan K Kayas.
Kayas	163	95	[illegible]	Nazrana	[illegible]	Devi Jaggarnathi Rajput	V. Pawaid K Kayas
Kayas	164	96	[illegible]	Nazrana	[illegible]	Devta Ajmal Rajput	V. Soyal K Kayas

Mauza	Pile No	Sr No	Area + revenue	Cedus Ke Muafi		Name	Locale
Kayas	165	97	[illegible]	Nazrana	-NL-	Deota Bir Nath Rajput	V Bari K Kayas
Kayas	166	98	[illegible]	Nazrana	-NL-	Deota Bhalogu Nag Rajput	V Bhalogi K Kayas
Kayas	167	99	[illegible]	Nazrana	-NL-	Deota Ramanu Nag Rajput	V Raogi K Kayas
Kayas	168	100	[illegible]	Nazrana See under No 85	Kolhi Naggar	Thakur Murli Dhar Chatur Bhuj Brahman	V Naggar [illegible] K
Kayas	169	101	[illegible]	Nazrana	-NL-	Deota Takali or Pagli Nag Rajput Shegli Nag	V Tandla K Kayas
Kayas	170	102	[illegible]	Nazrana No mention of	Nazrana	Deota Jamlu of Tipri Brahman	V Tipri K Kayas

Mauza	Khewat No.	Sr. No.	Area + Revenue	Orders Re: Muafi	Name	Location
Kayas	171	103	[illegible]	Nazrana Mau Enly Kothi Naggar '67	Deota Jamlu of Malana Rajput	V. Malana K. Naggar
Kayas	183	104	[illegible]	Nazrana No mention	Thakur Murli Dhar of Jia Brahmin	V. Jia K Kayas
Kayas	184	105	[illegible]	Nazrana See under No. 8 Kothi Jagatsukh Muafis are in Jagatsukh / Kayas / Kanwar / Harkandi Chong + Kothkandi	Thakur Ram Chander of Mani Karan Brahmins	V. Manikaran K
Kayas	185	106	[illegible]	Nazrana	Thakur Sita Ram Bairagis	V. SenBagh K Kayas
Kayas	186	107	[illegible]	Nazrana Is already entered under Bairagarh ..	Thakur Lachmi Narain Bairagi.	V. Akhara K Maharaja
Kayas	172	108	[illegible]	Nazrana Mau Enly under Kothi Sari 113	Thakur Lachmi Narain Bairagi.	V Tarn Sultanpur Raghunathpur K Bhoru

Kayas	non checked	109	[illegible] 14	Nazrana to Ajodhya Basis Mahant Rupi Sahai/ Brahmin Ajudhya Basi — are entitled to produce. After death resumed by permission of Govt. Nazrana is received from Devtas [illegible] Nazrana Long Entry Pramuedeola [illegible] (from Jogi Rupi [illegible]) Raja who is also the living Nazrana [illegible] Sultanpur offers great Rev. treasury spiritual concern. Barnes increased the impl. temple. Declared that in place of Nazrana offered by Deolia [illegible] Muafi should be given. Rent was waived by [illegible] commission in 1873. Rai of Rupi has represented that the expenses have gone up & Muafi is not enough. The file was badly treated (comment by [illegible]) Nazrana	Thakur Raghu Nath Pd. Brahmin Eid-Gaon	V. Taun of Raghunathpur Sultanpur K. Maharaja
		~~1120~~				V. K
		~~2411~~	Nazrana			V. K
Kayas	174	110	[illegible]	Nazrana Nazrana [illegible]	Deota Jawani Mahadeo Bavagi	V. Jawani K. Kayas
Kayas	178 (?)	111	[illegible]	Nazrana [illegible]	Thakur Shaligram Brahmin	V. Kalaisu K. Kayas
				Nazrana		V. K.

Mauza	File No.	Kh No.	Area + Revenue	Details re: Muafi	Name	Location
Sari	121	112	[illegible]	Rs 8/– p.a	Devi Jaggarnathi alias Shekli Sood (Lala Ram Das)	V. Shekli K Sari
Sari	122	113	[illegible]	Rs 6/12/– p.a	Thakur Lachmi Narain Bairagi	V. Raghunath Mela... K
Sari	123	114	[illegible]	Rs 2/– p.a	Deota Sangam Mahadeo Brahmin	V. Confluence of Beas + Sarvari K Sari
Raison	113	115	[illegible]	Rs 2/– p.a.	Devi Phungani Rajput	V. Shalh K Raison
Raison	134 131-32	116	[illegible]	Rs 10/8/– p.a	Deota Kali Nag Rajput	V. Sharyh K Raison

Mauza	File No.	Sr. No.	area + Revenue	Details re: Muafi	Name	Location
Rason	114	117	[illegible]	There Nazrana is merged with Devi Dhungani	Deota Narain Rajput	V. Shalh K Rason
Rason	116	118	[illegible]	Rs 2/- p.a.	Deota Bij Nath Rajput	V. Panci Balçi of Manci K Rason
Rason	115	119	[illegible]	Detail under Kothi Sari 114	Deota Sargan Mahadev Brahman	V. Confluence of Beas and Sarvai K Sari
Rason	117	120	[illegible]	See under Kothi Baragarh No. 38	Deota Jamlu of Baragran Rajput	V. Baragran K Baragarh
Mandalgarh	125	121	[illegible]	Rs 10/8/- p.a.	Deota Kali Nag Rajput	V. Sharah K Rason
Mandalgarh	126	122	[illegible]	Details under Kothi Naggar No. 85	Thakur Murlidhar Chaturbhuj Brahman	V. Naggar Nomp K Tehsil Kulu
[illegible]			[illegible]		Devi Dhungani	V. Parmai

Mandalgarh	127	123	[illegible]	Rs 6/- p.a	Rajput	K. Mandalgarh
Mandalgarh	128	124	[illegible]	8 aims p.a	Deota Tham Rajput	V. Shamha K. Mandalgarh
Mandalgarh	130	125	[illegible]	Rs 1/8/- p.a	Devi Kali Bodhi alias Dodni Rajput	V. Shamha K. Mandalgarh
Hurang	131	126	[illegible]	Rs 1/8/- p.a	Devi Jwala Mukhi Rajput	V. Phogal K. Hurang
Hurang	129	127	[illegible]	Rs 1/8/- p.a	Deota Marachi Rajput	V. Bagani K. Hurang
Hurang	132	128	[illegible]	See under Kothi Baragarh No. 43	Deota Dhumal Rajput	V. Halana K. Baragarh

Mauza	Pilo No.	Sr. No.	area + Revenue	Details re: Muafi	Name	Location
Hurang	123	129	[illegible]	8 annas p.a	Devta Hari Narain Rajput	V. Kathi K Hurang
Dooghidag	107	130	[illegible]	Rs1/- p.a	Devta Phalani Narain Rajput	V. Phalan K Doogidag
Dooghidag	108	131	[illegible]	Rs1/8/-	Devi Bhaga Siddh Goldsmith	V. ~~Dooghi~~ Dooghidag K
Dooghidag	109	132	[illegible]	Rs1/8/- p.a	Thakur Chatur Bhuj Goldsmith	V. Dooghidag Mopep K.
Dooghilag	110	133	[illegible]	Rs2/ p.a	Devta Narain Rajput	V. Gramang K Dooghilag
Dooghilag	121	134	[illegible]	8 annas p.a	Devta Hurangu Narain Rajput	V. Tandari K. Dooghilag
				X———X		V K

Mauza	File No.	Sr. No.	area + revenue	Details re: Muafi	Name	Location
Mangarh	143	135	[illegible]	Rs 41/- p.a	Devi Phungani Rajput	V. Téun K Mangarh
Mangarh	142	136	[illegible]	Rs 41/- p-a	Devi Naoni Rajput	V. Thach K Mangarh
Chaupassa	136	137	[illegible]	Rs 5/- p-a	Devta Narain Rajput	V. Gramang K Chaupassa
Chaupassa	137	138	[illegible]	Under Kolhi Mangarh 135	Devi Phungani Rajput	V. Tewan of Téun K Mangarh
Tarapur	135	139	[illegible]	Nazrana -NLC	Devta Kathoosi Narain Rajput	V. Phati Balh K Tarapur

Mauza	File No.	S. No.	area + Revenue	Details re: [illegible]	Name	Location
Maharaja	148	140	[illegible]	~ K G	Devta Jamlu Shakhohri Rajput	V. Peej K. Maharaja
Maharaja	147	141	[illegible]	Rs1/- p a Mazrana	Devta Parasar Pehdi Rajput	V. Phati Khaira K Maharaja
Maharaja	146	142	[illegible]	8 annas p. a Mazrana	Devt Parasar Than Brahman	V. Paraji K Maharaja
Maharaja	145	143	[illegible]	8 annas p. a Mazrana	Devta Sri Pal Rajput	V. Phati Kharihar K Maharaja
Maharaja	153	144	[illegible]	Rs1/- p. a.	Devta Gahri Rajput	V. Dhalpur K Maharaja.
Maharaja	152	145	[illegible]	Details under Kothi Sari No 113	~~Thakur~~ Lachhmi Narain Banaras	V Tan of Raghunathpur K (Sultanpur)

Kothi						K
Maharaja	151	146	[illegible]	See under Kothi Kayas 110	Deota Jawani Mahadeo Bairagi	V. Jawani K Kais
Maharaja	150	147	[illegible]	Rs 12/1/- p.a	Thakur Narsingh Bairagi under the control of a goldsmith	V. Dhalpur K Maharaja
Maharaja	149	148	[illegible]	Rs 1/8/- p.a.	Thakur Sila Ram Bairagi	V. Dhalpur K Maharaja
Khokhan	27	149	[illegible]	Main Entry under Kothi Bajaura 154	Deota Ad-Brahma Rajput	V. Khokhan K Khokhan
Khokhan	319	150	[illegible]	Rs 1/- p.a	Devi Jwala Mukhi Rajput	V. Shamsi K Khokhan
Khokhan	29	151	[illegible]	Rs 2/- p.a	Deota Narsingh Bairagi	V. Mohal K Khokhan

Mauza	File No.	Sr. No.	area + revenue	Details re: Muafi	Name	location
Khokhan	140	152	[illegible]	8 annas p.a.	Deota Anpal Bairagi	V. Mohal K. Khokhan
Khokhan	26	153	[illegible]	Details under Kothi Maharaja 142	Deota Pashu Thaun Brahmin	V. Parsi K. Maharaja
Bajaura	28	154	[illegible]	Rs 20/- p.a.	Deota Ghat-Brahma Rajput	V. Khokhan proper K
~~Mohal~~				X———X		V. K
						V. K
						V. K

Kot Kandi | 1 | 155 | See details under Kothi Kanawar 194 | Thakur Ram Chander Brahmin | Manikaran ... K. Kanwar

Mauza	Khewat No	Serial No	area	revenue	Orders regarding Muafi	Name	Location
Kot Kandi	237	156	[illegible]	[illegible]	Settlement, 1st entry relates to settlement of March 1877. This seems to be reviewed by various officers. Later three orders relating to year 1891 and 1912. This settlement relates to 1948-49. Final orders issued in June 1951. It appears that the settlement of this wazir is late because this area passed into British hands on account of resumption of some jagirs of the royal family. This however needs to be checked. Nazrana to Raghunath Rs 1/8 annas.	Thakur Ram Chandra Ji Brahmin	V. Tarayan K. Kot Khandi.
Kot Kandi	238	157	[illegible]	[illegible]	Nazrana no mention. The land is granted during the regime of the Jagirdar but the Jagirdar cannot resume the muafi except with the permission of the Govt. Condition of the muafi remain the same as in the muafis of Wazir Pandit (this applies to Suma also)	Ram Chandra Ji Bairagi	V. Bhat Gran K Kot Kandi
Kot Kandi	239	158	[illegible]	[illegible]	Nazrana to Raghunath; List of several locations of muafi	Thakur Murli Dhar Brahmin	V Bhawan K Kot Kandi
Kot Kandi	240	159	[illegible]	[illegible]	Nazrana to Raghunath ji.	Thakur Sita Ram Bairagi	V Dhalpur K Maharaja…
Kot Kandi	241	160	[illegible]	[illegible]	No mention of Nazrana but details given under Kothi Bhalan No 220	Thakur Trijugi Narain Brahmin	V Dayar K Kot Kandi

Mauza	File No.	Sr. No.	Area / Revenue	Conditions regarding Muafi	Name	Location
Kot Kandi	242	161	[illegible]	No mention of Nazrana	Thakur Lachhi Narain Bairagi	V. Hurla K Kot Kandi
Kot Kandi	243	162	[illegible]	Nazrana p.a. Rs 11/-	Devta Narad Muni Rajput	V Nainun K Kot Kandi
Kot Kandi	244	163	[illegible]	Nazrana p.a. Rs 5/-	Devta Kapil Muni Brahman	V Bashoona K Kot Kandi
Kot Kandi	245	164	[illegible]	Nazrana p.a. Rs 4/-	Devta Mangleshar Mahadeo Rajput	V Chanaun K Kot Kandi
Kot Kandi	246	165	[illegible]	Nazrana p.a. Rs 2/-	Devta Narain Rajput	V Jeshta or Jashita K Kot Kandi
Kot Kandi	247	166	[illegible]	Nazrana p.a. Rs 2/-	Devta Suraj Pal Rajput	V — K Kot Kandi
Kot Kandi	248	167	[illegible]	Nazrana P.A. Rs 4/-	Devta Gahri Rajput	V Hurla K Kot Kandi
Kot Kandi	249	168	[illegible]	Na[illegible]	Devi Bhaga Siddh	V Naroggi

Village	No.	No.	Date	Particulars	Deota / Caste	Residence
Kandi	247	168	[illegible]	Nazrana p.a. Rs 2/-	Rajput	K. Kot Kandi
Kot Kandi	250	169	[illegible]	Not Mention of Nazrana	Deotā Bijli Mahadev Rajput	V. Phāti Kashāwari K. Kais
Kot Kandi	251	170	[illegible]	Nazrana p.a. 8 annas	Deotā Jamlu Odasu wala Rajput	V. Odasu K. Kot Kandi
Kot Kandi	252	171	[illegible]	Nazrana p.a. 8 annas	Deotā Gaulān Rikhi Rajput	V. Manhias K. Kot Kandi
Kot Kandi	253	172	[illegible]	Nazrana p.a. 8 annas	Deotā Panj V.V. Rajput	V. Masu K. Kot Kandi
Kot Kandi	254	173	[illegible]	Nazrana p.a. Rs 1/-	Deotā Jamlu Rajput	V. Sis K. Kot Kandi
Kot Kandi	255	174	[illegible]	Nazrana Pa Rs 1/4/- as allegations against Kardars. Charges of embezzlement of Deotā's property. New Kardar appointed on condition of restoring Deotā's property	Deota Reesa Rajput	V. Lāhasani K. Kot Kandi

Mauza	Plan No	Kh No	area + revenue	Details re Muafi	Name	Locality
Kot Kandi	256	175	[illegible]	Nazrana p.a Rs 1/-	Devta Chaiman of Chirman Rajput	V. Najan K Kot Kand.
Kot Kandi	257	176	[illegible]	Nazrana p.a Rs 2/-	Devta Satnarsha Narani Rajput	V. Roshini K Kot Kandi
Kot Kandi	258	177	[illegible]	Details under Kothi Bhalan No 218.	Devta Trimukanda Rajput	V. Tharas K Bhalan
Kot Kandi	259	178	[illegible]	No mention of Nazrana	Thakur Sita Ram. Under the management of Raja Ram s/o Ganesh Dutt of Ajodhya / Babu Ram s/o Ganesh Dutt of Raghunath pur	V. Raghunathpur K Maharaja
Chong	206 (N) 206 (?)	179	[illegible]	In Kothi Kandi Details under 164	Mangleshwar Mahadev Rajput	V. Chanane K Kot Kandi
Chong	207	180	[illegible]	Kothi Kanawar Details 194	Thakur Ram Chander, Brahmans	V. Manikaran K Kanawar
Chang	210	181	[illegible]	Nazrana Rs 7/- p.a	Devi Chamunda Rajput	V. Dhara K Chong

Mauza	File No.	S. No.	Area & Rivaje	Details &c. of Muafi	Name	Locality
Chong	208	182	[illegible]	Rs 6/12/- pa Nazrana to Raghunathji	Thakur Lachhmi Narain, Bairagis	V. Raghunathpur Tawn K. Maharaja
Chong	209	183	[illegible]	Details under Kothi Kotkandi 158	Thakur Murli Dhar Brahmin	V. Bhaon K. Kotkandi
Chong	211	184	[illegible]	Nazrana to Raghunathji Rs 8/ p.a.	Devi Bhotanti Khatris	V. Pareyi or Patreya K. Chong
Chong	212	185	[illegible]	Nazrana to Raghunathji Rs 7/ p.a.	Devi Chongasini Rajput	V. Chong Proper K.
Chong	213	186	[illegible]	Nazrana Rs 4/- p.a.	Devta Gonmal Rajput	V. Shat K. Chong.
Harkandi	270	187	[illegible]	See under Kothi Kanawar No. 194	Thakur Ramchandarji Brahmins	V. Manikarn K. Kanawar
Harkandi	265	188	[illegible]	Rs 5/- p.a. Nazrana	Thakur Murli Dhar Bairagi	V. Manikaran K. Kanawar

Mauza	File No.	Sl. No.	Area revenue	Details reg. Muafi	Name	Locale
Harkandi	266	189	[illegible]	Nazrana – N.C. G	Thakur Lacchmi Narain Brahmin	V. Batahdi K Harkandi
Harkandi	271	190	[illegible]	No mention of Nazrana	Deota Solong Narain Rajput	V. Dhadhi K Harkandi
Harkandi	267	191	[illegible]	Nazrana Rs 7/- pa	Deota Kali Nag Goldsmiths	V. Matyana K Harkandi
Harkandi	268	192	[illegible]	Nazrana Rs 3/8/- pan	Devi Rupasini Rajputs	V. Sarani Bir K Harkandi
Harkandi	269	193	[illegible]	Details under Kot Kandi under 169	Deota Bijli Mahadeo Rajputs	V. Rhati Kashawari K Kais
Kanawar	221	194	[illegible]	Nazrana – N.C. G; from this temple the expenses of Bhog Prasad of other temples viz Mandi Narsingh Chaube Bhog, Chaube Bhog II and Raghunathji, Thakur Murli Dhar; Thakur Lacchmi Narain are borne.	Deota Ram Chanderji Brahmins	V. Manikaran K Kanawar
			[illegible]		Thakur Lacchmi	[illegible]

Kanawar	222	195	[illegible]	No mention of Nazrana	Naradu Banagi	V. Taulpara K Kanawar
Kanawar	223	196	[illegible]	Details under Kothi Halkadi 188	Thakur Murli Dhar Banagi	V. Manipara K Kanawar
Kanawar	224	197	[illegible]	Rs 7/- p.a. to Raghunathji	Devi Nama Rajput	V. Manikaran K Kanawar
Kanawar	225	198	[illegible]	No mention of Nazrana	Devta Jamlu Rajput	V. Malang K Naggar
Kanawar	226	199	[illegible]	No mention of Nazrana. Some land jointly by Jamlu of Malana and Maharai – but the Kardars are separate – also buildings are separate.	Devi Maharai Rajput	V. Tos K Kanawar
Kanawar	227	200	[illegible]	No mention of Nazrana land jointly held with Maharai	Devta Jamlu Toswala Rajput	V. Tos K Kanawar
Kanawar	228	201	[illegible]	Rs 4/ p.a. to Raghunathji	Devta Jagthamb Rajput	V. Barsaini or Harsaini K Kanawar

Mauza	[illegible]	x No.	area + revenue	Detail re: Nazrana / ~~Name~~	Name ~~Location~~	Location
Kanawar	229	202	[illegible]	Nazrana Rs. 2 p.a. to Raghunathji	Devta Narain Rajput	V. Pulga K. Kanawar
Kanawar	230	203	[illegible]	Rs 1/4/- p.a. to Raghunathji	Devta Aapraj Rajput	V. Nakthan K. Kanawar
Kanawar	231	204	[illegible]	Rs 2/ p.a. to Raghunathji	Devta Rawal Rajput	V. Garayan K. Kanawar
Sanesar	215	205	[illegible]	Rs 1/8 anna p.a. Raghunathji	Devta Reesa Rajput	V. Dhara beed K. Sanesar
Sanesar	216	206	[illegible]	Rs 3/- p.a. to Raghunathji	Devta Kashu Narain Rajput	V. Banadgi K. Sanesar
Sanesar	217	207	[illegible]	No mention of Nazrana	Devi Bharathi Rajput	V. Mayal K. Sanesar
Sanesar	218	208	[illegible]	8 annas p.a. to Raghunathji	Devi Aapreti Rajput	V. Manjgran, Phati Rela K. Bhalayan

Mauza	Khewat No.	Sl. No.	area + Revenue Details	Details re: Muafi	Name	Location
Sanesar	219	209	[illegible]	See under Kothi Bhalan No. 210	Thakur Lacchmi Narain Rajput	V. Rala K. Bhalan
Bhalan	188	210	[illegible]	Nazrana ~~Rs~~ [illegible] p.a.	Thakur Lacchmi Narain	V. Rala K. Bhalan
Bhalan	187	211	[illegible]	Nazrana Rs 1/- p.a.	Devi Kolaji Rajput	V. Gohi K. Bhalan
Bhalan	193	210	[illegible]	Nazrana Rs 11/- p.a.	Deota Durbasa Rikhi Rajput	V. Palgi K. Bhalan
Bhalan	191	213	[illegible]	See under Kothi Kot Kandi 165	Deota Narain Rajput	V. Jesla K. Kotkandi
Bhalan	192	214	[illegible]	Nazrana Rs 11/- p.a.	Deota Lacchmi Narain Rajput	V. Bhalan Mopee K. -

Mauza	Pile No.	Kh. No.	Area + revenue	Details reg: Muafi	Name	Location
Bhalan	194	215	[illegible]	No mention of Nazrana	Deota ~~Rambat~~ Aymal Rajput	V. Narf K. Bhalan
Bhalan	195	216	[illegible]	Rs 8 annas p.a	Bir Kandi alias Baradhi Rajput	V. Kot Tandi K. Bhalana
Bhalan	196	217	[illegible]	See under Kothi Kot Kandi 162.	Deota Narad Muni Rajput	V. Narin K. Kot Kandi
Bhalan	197	218	[illegible]	Rs 1/- p.a Nazrana	Deota Haukanda Brahmin	V. Tharas K. Bhalan
Bhalan	199	219	[illegible]	No mention of Nazrana	Deota Reesha Brahmin	V. Dhani K. Bhalan
Bhalan	198	220	[illegible]	Rs 8/- p.a. Nazrana.	Deota Jogi Narain Brahmin	V. Dyar K. Kot Kandi

Bhalan	201	221	[illegible]	Nazrana 8 annas p.a	Devi Shyama Kali Rajput	V. Dalasani K. Bhalan.
Bhalan	200	222	[illegible]	Rs 2/10/- p a	Devta Reesha Brahmin	V. Kandha K. Bhalan.
Bhalan	204	223	[illegible]	See under Kothi Kot Kandi 158	Thakur Munshi Dhar Brahmin	V. Bhaun K. Kot Kandi.
Bhalan	203	224	[illegible]	No muafi/Nazrana	Thakur Ram Chander Brahman	V. Horya alias Haecha K. Bhalan.
				X———X		

Appendix F

'CENSUS OF DEOTAS' CARRIED OUT IN 1961

In this table are reproduced, exactly as they were entered, photocopied pages from the Register of *Deotas* that was compiled as per a decision taken by the government in 1961. The original records, prepared essentially at the Patwari level, were in Urdu, using Persian numerals wherever relevant. When the information was collated to form a complete census of *deotas* based on information available at that time, the records were translated into English. The list, filled with the most useful information, runs into 401 *deotas*, a number larger even than the traditional number cited of the *deotas* of Kulu (365); however, one has to presume that the records at the village/ patwari level were accurate.

This record is now in the office of the Deputy Commissioner, Kulu. Originally, Kulu being a sub-division of the Kangra District in 1961, when it was prepared, it belonged to the office of the Sub-Divisional Officer, Civil, at Kulu.

Name of patwari halqa	Names of kothis in the patwari halqa	Names of phatis in each kothi	S.No.	Name of devta	Name of kardar/ mukhtar if any	Names of members if the manage ment committee exists	Place of temple of Devta	Place or places (by phatis) where the worshippers of the Devta reside	Amount of land revenue, payable phati wise annually	Rough estimate of moveable property of devta in shape of gold jewellery etc	Details of land now existing with the devta which is under self cultivation or is cultivated by the tenants at will. Self cultivation	cultivated by tenants at will	Approximate annual income of devta from offerings	Annual income of devta from the land, in cash (kind should be converted into cash)	Total income now obtainable annually.
			1	2	3	4	5	6	7	8	9		10	11	12
Raison	Raison	Biasar Mandrol Benchi Manjlihar Shirahr Shilihar	1	Kardan	Talu	Nil	Biasar	Biasar	Nil	65-00	1-0 (U.C.)	7-7	2-00	20-00	22-00
			2	Devi Phugni	-do-	Nil	-do-	-do-	Nil	35-00	5-12(U.N.)	Nil	1-00	Nil	1-00
			3.	Devi Phugni	-do-	Nil	-do-	-do-	0-18	30-00	Nil	7-4	1-00	50-00	51-00
			4.	Bir Nath	Tikam Ram	Nil	Mandrol	Mendrol	0-39	300-00	1-4	0-17	10-00	4-00	14-00
			5.	Bir Nath	Tek Ram	Nil	Benchi	Benchi	1-10	400-00	2-9	2-13	20-00	2-00	22-00
			6.	Kali Nag	Chetar Das	Nil	Shirahr	Shirahr & Shilihar	30-81 0-00	1000-00	36-10	5-8	5-00	200-00	205-00
			7.	Devi Phugni	Sunder Singh	Nil	-do-	Shirahr	1-39	650-00	Nil	3-7	10-00	60-00	70-00
			8.	Narain	Fatu	Nil	Barishil	Shilihar	Deleted from Bachh	Nil	0-3	Nil	Nil	Nil	Nil
			9.	Devi Phugni	Fatu	Nil	Badishil	-do-	-18	300-00	Nil	1-17	10-00	20-00	30-00
Jana Nathan	Naggar	Nathan Jana	10.	Lafan MahaDev	Hetam Ram	Bhimsan BhagatRam Galu Duglu Teku oglu Harijan	Laran	Nathan Naggar	16-19	20,000-00	17-7	31-16	20-00	45-00	65-00
			11	Devi Kali	Dila Ram	Bholu, Manu Kisan Chand	Archhandi	Jana	3-56	500-00	7-7	0-18	15-00	40-00	55-00
			12	Jeeb Narain	Bali Ram	Nil	Jana	Jana	33-97	1,000-00	21-5	72-18	20-00	180-64	200-64
							Nathan	Nathan	7-45		Nil	8-15			
			13	Chamonda (Devi)	Abhey Ram	Nil	Nashala	Nathan	41-28	18,000-00	6-2	45-6	30-00	745-00	775-00
			14	Kartik Sawami	Revat Ram	Nil	Nathan	Nathan	4-61	1,000-00	18-10	13-8	10-00	52-00	62-00
			15	Gonu	Bhagat Ram	Nil	Gordor	Naggar & Nathan	Nil	300-00	Nil	Nil	nil	nil	nil
			16	Sat Narain	Smt Heti	Nil	Katrain	Katrain	5-38	Nil	8-18	nil	nil	nil	nil
			17	Gohri	Jeebu	nil	Shad	Jana	0-37	nil	4-1	nil	nil	nil	nil
			18	Jogni	Uttam	nil	Shansher	Nathan	0-20	nil	2-4	nil	nil	nil	nil
			19	Gori Shankar	Chaman Lal	nil	Naggar	Naggar	7-87		nil	6-7			
			20	Nar Singh	Karmu	nil	do	do	32-77		nil	16-14			
			21	Murli Dhar	Mehar Chand	Lal Chand Prarthi Fateh Chand Jindu ram Abhey ram Kishan chand	do	Haljan, Naggar, Jana, Nathan	32-33		nil	44-8			

			21 MurliDhar	Mehar Chand	same	Naggar	same phatis	119-20		nil	155-12-1			
Barshai	Barshai	Sajla Karjan Soil	22 MadhoRai	Jalpu Ram	Chandi Ram Akadashiram Ram Nath Shukreo Tek Ram HuKum Raj	Hari pur	Soil	30-95	4300-00	3-4(U.C)	117-17-6	nil	560-00	560-00
			23 Jamlu	Jit Ram	Dile Ram Jalpu Ram, Nathu.	Soil	Soil, Hallan Kothi Naggar	2-98 0-78	3520-00	10-17(U.C.)	13-1	nil	16-00	16-00
			24 Chakladu Narain	BhupRam	-		Soil	5-37	40-00	nil	7-15	nil	4-25	4-25
			25 Devi Keili	Bhup Ram	-	Soil	Soil	2-05	400-00	0-4 (U.C.)	10-7	2-00	0-83	2-83
			26 Devi Rup Docha	Ugarsain	Prabhu Sonamram Kabal ram Mehar Chand	Karjan	Karjan Soil	8-76 3-57	2,000-00	0-?(U.K)	9-2 11-3	3-00	70-00	73-00
			27 Ram Raghunath	Akadashi	-	Karjan	Karjan	1-08(Soil) 4-92(Karjan 4-46(Sajla	-	1-13 10-7 2-0	- - 0-18	nil	1500-00	1500-00
			28 Jamlu(Karjan)	Chet Ram	-	Karja	Karjan	0-78(Soil) 5-84(Karjan)	800-00	-	1-6 9-16	1-00	83-00	84-00
			29 Jamlu(Gajan)	Gehru	-	Kajan	Soil Karjan	0-57	500-00	-	0-17-11	nil	12-00	12-00
			30 Bishnu	Hari Dass	-	Saja	Sajla	0-70(K) 4-55(SJ)	2500-00	7-17(U.C.)	8-12 1-14	nil	52	52-00
			31 Nar Singh	Dhalu	-	Karji	Karjan	0-61	-	0-10	0-5	nil	1-84	1-84
			32 Kamlu (Malana)		-	Malana	Malana	0-09(KRJan)		-	0-7			
Dughilag	Dughilag	Phallan Donkri Gahar Bhumter T	33 Dhemal 34 Narain	Hari Dass Rattan	6?	Sajla Gramg	Sajla Donkri Gahar	nil 1.75	nil [illegible]	nil 2.[illegible]	nil 2.16	nil 10.00	3-58 60.00	3-58 70.00
			35 Phallani Narain	Kanshi Ram	-	Phalla	Phallan Donkri Gahar	8.15	500.00	12.12	36.18	15.00	40.00	55.00
			36 Hurango Narain	Abhey Ram	-	Tanda (Bhumtr)	Bhumter Khadiha-r Peej	3.37	1000.00	Nil	17-2	15.00	128.00	143
			37. DeviBhaga Sidh	Tot Ram	-	Dugili	Dugilug	6.22	3000.00	Nil	16.17.9	50.00	30	80.00
			38. Thakar Charta-r	Bugh Bhiru alias ParsRam		Dugili	Dugilug	-	100.00	Nil	0-13	30.00	-	30.00
Kais	Ka-is	phati Kais Pini	39. Devi Tashmi Wadha	ude Ram	-	Kais	Kais	8.97	300.00	0.3	13.18	15.00	34.77	49.77
			40 Thakar Sita Ram	Damdor Dass	-	Seonig	Kais	43.82.	-	-	18.15	1.00	406.46	407.46
			41. Bhalgu Nag	Ved Ram	-	Bha.	Kais	-	1500.00	-	-	1.00	4.06	5.16
			42. Thakar Saligram	Tek Ram	-	Karu	Kais	12.75	40.00	-	84.02	1.00	527.31	528.31
			43. Deva-ta Danu Nag	Sukru	-	Rou	Kais	5.26	50.00	-	23.10	4.00	45.12	49.12
			44. Devta Natkli Nag	Chanu	-	Tun	Kais	8.50	25.00	-	26.15	3.00	125.02	128.02
			45. Devta Tarmal	AmtamaRam	-	Dhi	Kais	5.00	200.00	-	14.00	10.00	72.00	82.00

i	ii	iii	1	2	3	4	5	6	7	8	(i)	9	(ii)	10	11	12
			46	Devta Ajmal	Shri Jhabe Ram	-	Soil	Kais	Rs. 8.00	Rs 20.00	-	18-15-00		16.00	200.00	216.00
			47	Devta Surgan Nag	Sh: Reytu	-	Sar	Kais	Rs. 5.00	Rs 16.00	-	3-0-0		2.00	-	2.00
			48	Devi Bhaga Bidh	Sh: Ghotu	-	Pini	Kais	Rs.61.00	Rs. 6000.00		10-18		10.00	61.80	75.80
Naggar N.Gr: Hallan			49	Peuli Nag	Sh: Chet Ram	-	Bhosh	Naggar	Rs.6.00	Rs.300.00		10-17		10.00	100.00	110.00
			50	Basu Nag	Sh: Mehar Chand	-	Kamahrti	Naggar	Rs 5.73	Rs.200.00		36-6		5.00	150.00	155.00
			51	Devta Jamlu	sh: Hari Ram	-	Bharka	do	Rs.15.00	Rs.50.00		17-2		5.00	200.00	205.00
			52	Devi Khandasani	Sh: Teerth Ram	-	Sarsai	do	Rs.7.67	Rs.200.00		15-0		10.00	100.00	110.00
			53	Devta Ghahri	Sh: Thakar Dass	-	Bhosh	do	Rs.9.87	Rs.250.00		9-9		5.00	50.00	55.00
			54	Thakar Narsingh	Sh: Damodar Dass	-	Parsai	do	Rs. 9.02	-		10-2		5.00	50.00	50.00
			55	Devta Gorishankar	Ludaru	-	Dashal	do	Rs. [illegible]	[illegible]		x84-16		200.00	200.00	x210.00
			56	Thakar Gopal Ji	Damodar Dass	-	Sarasai	do	Rs. 64-70	Rs 100.00		84 -16		10.00	200.00	210.00
			57	Tripura Sunadar	Tikka Mohindar Singh	-	Naggar	do Nagar Halan	Rs.44-00 Rs.116-56	Rs.600.00	-	80-4		10.00	200.00	210.00
			58	Jagtipat	Kolu	-	do	do	Rs 3.75	Rs.600.00	-	2-8		1.00	20.00	21.00
			59	GoriShankar	Kolu	-	do	do	Rs 15.19	do		10-12		5.00	100.00	105.00
			60	Lakshminarain	Kolu	-	do	do	Rs 5.00	do		5-3		5.00	50.00	55.00
			61	Murlidhar Chaturbuj	Mehar Chand	-Lalchand Fateh Chand Kishan chand Chhape Ram Ram Chand	do	do Nagar	Rs 25.00 Rs 12.36	Rs 200.00		69-17		50.00	200.00	250.00
			61	Narsing	Karmu	-	do	do	Rs 28.00	Rs 50.00		36.12		5.00	100.00	105.00
			62	Devi Bhatnati	Ram chand	-	do	do	Rs 4.98	Rs200.00		20-13		5.00	100.00	105.00
			63	Shubh	Bholu	-	do	do	Rs 1.96	-		4-12		-	50.00	50.00
			64	Satnarain situated in Baragarh	Smti. Heti		-	-	-	[illegible]	1			1 -	-	-
			65	Amal	Khem Das	-	Chachogi	do	Rs 6-22	Rs 100.00		9-2		5.00	100.00	105.00
		Malana	66	Jamlu	Jhada Ram	-	Malana	Nagar Halan Malana	Rs20.12	Rs 5,000-00		60.12		200.00	400.00	600.00
Sari	Sari Jindor Banogi Sari Bastori		67	Devi JagarNathi	Chainsukh	Sohan Lal Shivram Ramdas Belisingh Tek Ram	Bhakli	Sari Bastori Banogi Jindor	Rs 30.72	Rs 7700.00	4-14	112-11		600.00	4.00	604.00
			68	Sari narain	Tandu	-	Sari	Sari Bastori	Rs 1.1?	Rs 885.00	0-9	4-0		10.00	62.00	72.00
			69	Narain	Loharu	-	Palachh	Palachh Machhang								

70			70 Gohri	Purnu	-	Kashamti	Babeli Sharan Kanal-Berh Lakhez Kashamti		-	Rs.221.00	-	0-1	10.00	0.25	10.25
			71 KashoNarain	Jhabu	-	Banegi	Banogi Kangti Bashang		-	Rs.1154.00	-	-	10-00	-	10-00
			72 Devi Kali Oori	Kunju	-	Babeli	Sharan BabeliOri Babeli-Pori		0.22	Rs 70.50	-	0-7	3.00	6.00	9.00
			73Devi Hadma	Gangu	-	Jindor	Jindor		-	Rs 517.00	0-12	-	6.00	-	6.00
			74 JeuNarain	Shiv	-	Nathan	Nathan		2.20	Rs 670.00	-	8-13	4.00	42.00	46.00
			75Gohri	Dhaniram	-	Katahar	Katahar Dhanmot Halohi		0.87	Rs 1195.00	-	4.18	6.00	132.00	138.00
Kharal			76 Devi Jagarnathi	Rudhram	-	Puid	Kharal		- 2.25	Rs 710.00	4-15	4-2	10.00	20.00	30.00
			77Thakur SaligRam & RaniSahiba (Neoli)	Hari Chand		~~Chand~~ Neoli Sesram-Tiratram Shibu Chhapu Harichand	Kais Kharal		9.84	Rs 800.00	-	17.10	10.00	209.67	219.67
			78Jawalaji Mahadev	Rewatram		Bedu,Tulu Ganguram	Neoli	Kharal Mohal Behl Jana	18.05	Rs910.00	-	49.4 1.0	2.00	30.00	32.00
			79BirNath	Motiram		-	Bari	Kharal	5.36	Rs 40.00	-	14.9	-	3.00	3.00
			80Thakur Lakshmi Narain				Raghu-nathpur	Kharal	70-86		86-1	51.16	-	250.00	250.00
			81Thakur Raghu-nath Ji	DurgaSingh			do	Kharal	41.36		12-2	119-13	-	1200-00	1200-00
			82SamuNarain	Hukmoo			Dobhi	Kharal	6.06		-	15.14	-	-	-
			83 Bijli Maha-Dev	DuniChand			Mathan	Kharal Kashawari	30.94 50.83 81.77	Rs.10000/-	0.1	220-1	40.00	800.00	840.00
			84DevtaMathan	Tirthu			Tharman	Kharal	1.06		0-1	2.6	-	-	
			85Jamlu	JinatRam			Tapri	Kashawari	.74	Rs.430.00	-2	1-4	7.00	5.00	12.00
			86JamaniNarain	Duglu		Surtu Deviram Nandram Dotram Bedu	Chhman	Kashawari	21.47.7	Rs735.00	-	45.11	10-00	25.00	35.00
Baragarh	Baragarh	Buran Riyada Shagle Halan Miyan Dawada Katrain Bari Baragarh Rangan	87Jamlu	Hukam Chand		FatehChand Dugluram Nupram Dile Ram Dhaleram BholuRam Dole Ram	Baragran	Baragran Bari Shagli	59.69 2.67 4.78 67.14	Rs 5000.00	5-13	275-5	10.00	1200.00	1210.00

			88. Dhumal	BhimiRam	-	Pihį	Hallan	53.990-00	20-6	158-14	10.00	800.00	810.00
			89.NeelKant	Nirat Ram	-	Buran	Buran	-16.1000-00	2-12	38-3	5.00	100.00	105.00
			90. Jamlu	Keshav Ram	-	Shangcher	do	15.400.00	13-3	18-18	10.00	166.00	176.00
			91.Jangham	Ishru Ram	-	Pangan	Pangan.	3.100.00	3-13	6-19	2.00	5.00	7.00
			92Jamlu	Nopu	-	Defri	Riyada	0-400.00	-	4-2	3.00	20.00	23.00
			93 Jamlu	Dle Ram (Dilu)	-	Keshri	Shagli	2-C200.00	-	11-18	5.00	50.00	55.00
			94 Jamlu	Dile Ram	-	Shagli	do	12-400.00	-	43-18	3.00	120.00	123.00
			95Bir Nath	Rup Singh	-	Katrain	Katrain	2000.00	-	12-13	5.00	200.00	205.00
			96 Devi Singhasni	Nankchand	-	Baragran	bragran	1600.00	-	48-15	2.00	210.00	212.00
			97 Jamlu	Kehar chand	-	Dawara	Dawara	500.00	0-18	24-15	20.00	100.00	120.00
			98Bishnu	Jainand Lal	-	do	do	1000.00	3-6	43-4	15.00	250.00	265.00
			99 Jamlu	do	-	Chhani	Katrain	1000.00	72-8	114-5	25.00	400.00	425.00
			100 Narain	Bhagtu	-	Bashkola	do	500.00	-	6-5	2-00	100.00	102.00
			101 Gohri	Rup Singh	-	Katrain	do	500.00	0-7	14-0	2.00	48.00	50.00
			102RamChander Ji	KaramDas	-	Dawara		40.00	-	79-2	2.00	60.00	62.00
Mandal Garh	M.Grh	Dobhi Mandal gach. Fojal Phichhli-har .	103 Devi Kali Oodi	Denu Ram	-	Shim	Dobhi shim	800.00	-	5-11	-	120.00	120.00
			104 Mathan	BhopRam	-	do	do	1200-00	-	6-6	5.00	113.00	118.00
			105 KaliNag	Ishru		Karal	Mandal-garh	700.00		1-12	18.00	22.00	40.00
			106Devi Phungni	ChandheRam		Perbhi	Perbhi	250.00	1-13	-	5-00	31-00	36-00
			107 Gohri	Chunju		Fojal	Fojal	140-00		1-13	1-00	1-00	2-00
			108Bir Nath	Rohlu		Dhara	Dhara Dhalogi	125.00	-	-	15.00	-	15.00
			109 JawalaMukhi	Nupu		Fojal	Fojal	1600.00		9-11	10-00	130-00	140.00
			110 Jamlu	Laju		Dhara	Dhara	1500.00		9-15	5-00	70-00	75.00
			111 Hari Narain	Sohnu		Kathi	Pichhli	2000.00		26-1	20.00	100.00	120.00

Jagat Sukh	Jagat Sukh	112 Narain	Jiaru	-	Daral	Daral, Neri, Pradi, Dimchin	14-75	1800.00	-	25-14	5.00	185.00	190.00
		113 Bir Nath	Chandu	-	Damchin	Damchin	-	200.00	-	-	2.00	-	2.00
		114 Jamlu	Jomtu	-	Neri	Neri, Bagani	0-72	120-00		2-10	2-00	40-00	42.00
		115 Kartik Swami	Hukam Ram	GupatRam Lot Ram	Khakhnal	Gojra	20.97	1200.00	20-14	10-11	3.00	8.00	11.00
		116 SitaRam	JaiDev	-	Gojra	do	115-50	50.00		13-5	-	60.00	60.00
		117 Shargan	Lachhmi Ram	-	Bhatara	JagatSukh	3-19 42-39 0-62	2000.00	9-10	0-19 13-7 1-19	5.00	79.02	84-02
		118 Tripura Sundri (Devi)	Chhapu	-	Naggar	Naggar	Gojral-88	-	-	-	-	-	-
		119 Ram Chander	LuderMani	-	ManiKaran	Manikaran	Gojra 5.37 Jagat sukh 33-02	-	-	3-12	-	74.00	74.00
		120 NarSingh	Damodar Das	-	Dhalpur	Dhalpur	Gojra 5-65 Jagat sukh 60-25	-	-	-	-	-	-
		121 Bashisht Rikhi	Hukam Ram	-	Bashisht	Bashisht	Gojra 4-92 Jagat sukh 20-50 Bashisht 10-39	1800.00		3.00	50.00	0.15	50.15
		122 Jagan Nath	Gobind	-	Jagatsukh	Jagatsukh	Gojra 18-25 Jagat sukh 12-51 Seri 2.50	100.00	-	- 5-10 2-12	-	60.22	60.22
		123 Jamlu	Abhir Chand		do	do	Jsukh 33.36 Seri 14-92	100.00	2-8	3-17 2-12	1.00	17.07	18.07
		124 Sandhia (Devi)	Raghunath das		do	do	25.79	1500.00	-	10.10	4.00	3.34	7.34
		125 KapalMuni	Piare Ram	-	Kalath	Shaleen	Jagat sukh 8.15	100.00	4-08	21-12	-	200.00	200.00
		126 RamChander	Dolu	-	Bashisht	Bashisht	do 93-39 Seri 4-73 Bash-isht 78-48	100.00	- - -	2-16 - 25-11	20.00	45.68	65-68
		127 PhabliNag	Nokhu	-	Prini	Prini	24-23	1600.00	-	8-2	3.00	1.97	4.97
		128 Jamlu	Kushalchand	-	do	do	99-70	1000.00	15-2	25-2	10.00	207-19	217-19
		129 ArjunGupha	Brij Lal	-	do	do	2-31	50.00		16.0	-	1.03	1.03
		130 Jamlu	Lachhmi Ram	-	Rurwa	Rurwa	[illegible]			-		-	-
		131 Sarwari	Jagat Ram	-	Prini	Prini	49.61	2000.00	37.7	12-6	3.00	24.40	27.40
		132 Gotam Rikhi	Dolu	-	Goshal	Rurwa	Prini 10.87 Bashisht 9.77	-	-	2-16	-		-

			133 Bias Rikhi	Dolu	-	Goshal	Goshal	Prini 20.19 Bashisht 4.47	-	-	2-15	-	1.17	1.17
			134Sarsai Narain	GangaRam	-	Alu	Bashisht	18-97	1600.00	6-8	3-6	10.00	11.34	21.34
			135Devi MahaMai	Utoo	-	Bashisht	do	9-29	50.00	-	-	-		-
			136 Jamlu	Twarsu	-	Majhachh	Burwa	Bashisht 5-94	-			-		-
Manali	Manali	Shaleen Nasogi Manali Burwa Palchan	137KapalMuni	Piare Ram	-	Kalath	Shaleen	Shaleen 11.58	-	.	40-3	-	47-31	47-31
			138Shandal Rikhi	Dinu	-	Parsha	do	Nasogi 3-84	500.00	4-18	9-10	5-00	35.24	40.24
			139Devi Hidama	Udhey Ram& Khub Ram	Lalu ManDas Khubu Udhey Ram	Dungri	Manali	8.52	2500.00	4.17	126-14	10.00	397.80	407.80
			140Kartik Swami	BhagChand	-	Sunsa	Nasogi	6.65	200.00	2-8	12-9	5.00	46-38	51-38
			141Sayali Mahadev	Jindu	-	Sial	do	0-61	200.00	0-12	1-10	3-00	16.70	19.70
			142 ShankuNarain	Tule Ram	-	Nasogi	do	1.22	195.00	1-18	3-11	3.00	17.67	20.67
			143Shoji	Balak Ram	-	Katrain	Katrain	Nasogi 0-75 Manali24.27	-	-	29-4	-	-	-
			144TilokNath	Udhey Ram	-	Lahaul	Manali	Manali 0.67	-	-	2-14	-	27-33	-
			145Jamlu	LachhiRam	Tikku Kisan Moti	Burwa	Burwa	1.22	150.00	0-7	2-19	2.00	9.45	11.45
			146 Bias Rikhi	Dolu	-	Goshal	do	0-23	100.00	0-8	1-9	2.00	12.27	14.27
			147Gotam Rikhi	do	-	do	do	2-15	100.00	3-2	5-4	2.50	17.59	20.09
			148Jamlu	Twarsu	-	Machhach	do	0-72	100.00	0-3	2-8	2.00	5.86	7.86
			149NarSingh	Rewat Ram	-	Burwa	do	1-59	-	0-4	11-0	-	21.97	21.97
			150 Bishnu	Piare Ram	-	do	do	-	-	-	-	-	21.47	21.47
			151 Jamlu	Tuli Ram	-	Koland	Palchan	2.97	125.00	-	10-7	3.00	24.25	27.25
Khokhan	Khokhan	Rajgiri Khokhan Shamshi Mohal Neol Bholang Shilihar	152 AdBrahma	Manglu	Chuhru Murluram Gopatram Gomtu Uttamram Chuhru	Khokhan Dohgli	Shilihar Rajgiri Mohal Bholang Shamshi Khkhan Neol	8.90 4.49 3.78 37.83 1.24 6.18 [illegible] 63.24	9000.00	-	247.2	50.00	357.00	407.00
	Bajaura	Bajaura Hat					Bajaura	45.72	600.00		104-1-9	20.00	86.00	106.00
			153 Jawalamukhi	BedRam	Chuhruram Deviram Dharamchand Khub Ram	Shamshi	Shashi							

Deity											
154. Dhanpaul	Dola Dass	-	Mohal	Mohal	4.88	150.00	-	19.10	10.00	26.00	36.00
155. PadauNathan	HukamRam	-	Padai (Maharaja)	Mohal Behl	2.73			3.12	-	6.00	6.00
156 NarSingh	Dola Dass	-	Mohal	Mohal	18.36	30.00		54-16	3.00	300.00	303.00
Maharaja Maharaja Peej Dhalpur Behl Barahar Kharihar 157 SariPaul	Bahadru	-	Kastar	Kharihar	4.25	340.00	0-10	29-9	9.00	70.00	79.00
158 Parasar Rikhi	Bali Ram	Negi Harisingh KaramDass Hetu,Todru Shukru,Budhu Bhodu,BedRam Man Dass	Kalon	do Behl,Peej Barahar	4.34	2096.00	25-16	25-8	30.00	31.89	61.89
159 Jamlu	DeviSingh	BedRam, Chhobe Ram Buta,Hetu Parsu.	ModaBadi	Peej	6.87	1100.00	53-16	39-17	20.00	50.00	70.00
160 PadaoNathan	KamleRam	Ram Chand Moti Ram Pattu	Pardi	Behl	3.50	390.00	0-14	9-3	5.00	9.34	14.34
161 Gohri	Ram Dass	Pritam Dass BahadurSingh Tej Ram	Dhalpur	Dhalpur	2.06	560.00	1-2	4-18	50.00	254.00	304.00
162 RaghuNathJee	DurgaSingh	Tej Ram Paras Ram Tek Ram Gulabo Uttam Ram	Raghunath pur	Kharal	-	15185.00	-				950.00
163 Narain	Chamaru	-	Buai	Barahar	2-10	150.00	2-3	12-18	1.00	80.00	81.00
164 Lachhmi Narain	Damodar Dass	-	RaghuNath Pur	(Private)	2-39	60.00	2-11	7-1	-	900.00	900.00
165 Sita Ram	Kahan Dass	-	Dhal Pur	Dhalpur	26.65	56.00	15-17	77-18	-	940.00	940.00
166 Nar Singh	Damodar Dass	-	do	(Private)	21.06	674.00		62-3	-	1500.00	1500.00
167 Lachhmi Narain	Dila Ram	-	Akhara	-	2-14	25.00		6.13		74.32	74.32
168 Ram Chander Bir Nathi	Shrimati Janki	-	do	-	-	4.00					
169 Ram Chander	Devi Dass	-	Bade Akhara	-	2-4	25.00		5-3		27.40	27.40
170 Murli Manohar	Sunder Mal	-	Akhara	Dhalpur	1.05	20.00	4-9	0-1		125.00	125.00
171 Ram Chander	Sant Paul	-	do	-	-	12.00					
172 Gopal	Keshav Ram	-	do	-	0-06	8.00		0-12		20.00	20.00
173 Lachhman Jee	Moti Ram	-	do	-	0-02	20.00		0-1		0.02	0.02
174 Murli Dhar	Rikhi Ram	-	do	-	0-79	20.00	0-2	1-17		2.00	2.00
175 Nar Singh	Chhetan Dass	-	do		1.19	20.00		3-13		30.19	30.19
176 Sangam Mahadev	Bhagat Ram	Molak Ram NarbdaNand FaqirChand Thakur Dass Paras Ram Maha Bir	RaghunathPur	Dhalpur	1.50	900.00	4-11	1-15	Area lying un-cultivated,no income)		
177 Lachhmi Narain	Mohan Lal	-	UpperLal Shehar		0-06			0-3			

			178 Nar Singh	Todar Dass	-	Raghu Nath pur	-	1.42	20.00	0-1	3-6	-	1-46	1-46
			179 Baba Balak Rupi	Haru	-	do					0-2			
			180 Shiv Jee	Kuljas Rai	-	Akhara				0-2				
			181 Kaili Bir	Isri Ram	-	Kharihar				0-10				
			182Kailo Bir	Dilu	-	Prakshi	Barahar			0-2				
			183 HurangoNarain	Abhey Ram	-	Jonga	do			0-6				
			184 Kailo Bir	Uttam Ram	-	Khalyani	do			0-2				
			185 Bravhi Bir	Oupat Ram	-	Karari	Kharihar			0-7				
			186 Kailo Bir	Chet Ram		Khalyani	Barahar			0-3				
			187 Devi Phungni	Bahadru		Lot	do			0-14				
			188 Narain	do		do	do	0-52		1-5	2-00	-	12.00	12.00
			189Neona	do		do	do			0-10				
Tarapur	Tarapur	Brahmin Behl Balyani Bhumteer	190 Katrosi Narain	KhiyaliRam	-	Jaitani Ropdi Balyani	Behl Brahmin Bhumter Balyani		893.00	30-19	31-5	80.00	487.65	567.65
			191 Devi Noni	do		Brahmin	Brahmin		150.00	0-1	3-18	20.00	3.60	23.60
			192 Mathan	Dine Ram		Bhutti	Behl Balyani Brahmin		412.00	2-9	8-13	10.00	10.12	20.12
			193Wamsho	Kali Dass		Bhumteer	Bhumteer		210.00	1-7	3-3	8.00	5.00	13.00
			194 Shila Dev	Sita Ra		Satreem	do Behl		312.00	0-11	1-15	10.00	5.00	15.00
			195 Hurange Narain	Bodha		Bhumteer	Bhumteer		450.00	1-12	2-18	14.00	12.00	26.00
			196 Devi Noni	Gangu		do	do		5.00	0-1		2.00		2.00
			197Bradha Bir	Kunju		do	do		2.00	0-3		1.00		1.00
			198 Qohri	Gulabo		do	do		5.00	0-14		2.00		2.00
			199 do	Anglu		Brahmin	Brahmin		450.00	0-4		15.00		15.00
Y Garh Chparsa	Mangarh Choparsa	Graming Mashna Phichhli Gahar	200 Narain	Gupat Ram		Graming	Graming Gahar Mashna	1.5	12.00	[illegible]	6-17	30.00	60.00	90.00
			201Devi Noni	Sibu		Thachh	Mashna Pichhli					0.25		0.25
			202 Gohri	Bodh Ram		do	do	4.57	8.00		14-25	[illegible] 8.00	15.00	23.00
			203 Devi Phungni	Sesu		Tayon	Pichhli	0-5	6.00		3-9	10.00	50.00	60.00
Shilihar	Kotkandi	Shilihar	204 Kapal Muni	Bed Ram		Pashkona	Shilihar	49.1	500.00		240-4	5.00	250.00	255.00
			205 Isha	Narotam Ram		Prashni	do	4-8	1700.00		32-7	3.00	147.00	150.00
			206 Suraj Paul	Bahadru	Mohar Singh Roshan Lal Durga Singh Lotu	Bhuin	do	10.6	600.00		41-5	5.00	50.00	55.00

			207 Mangeshar	Jogi Ram	Chhanor	Shilihar	6.65	550.00	-	43-9	7.00	53.00	60.00
			208 Bhaga sidh	Rhla	Narogi	do	3.40	700.00		12-0	7.00	23.00	30.00
Kotkandi	Dayar Parli Manjhli		209 Tarjogi Narain	Chone Ram	Dyar	Dyar	34.26	500.00	4-8	88-3	50.00	218.00	268.00
			210 Ramchander	Dati Ram	Bhatgran	do	8.62	25.00	0-1	17-12			
			211 Lachhmi Narain	Moti Ram	Hurla	do	-	10.00	0-1				
			212 Sita Ram	Raja Ram				50.00	0-7				
			213 Raghunath Jee	Devi Singh			10.50			12-4		396.00	396.00
			214 Gohri	Mohar Singh	Hurla	Dyar	2.31	500.00		2-17	4.00	117.00	121.00
			215 Nard Muni	Bhimi Ram	Tabnu	Parli Manjhli	12.59	600.00	1-00	45-9	10.00	200.0	210.00
			216 HarKanda	Jit Ram	Makrad	Dyar	3.69	-	6-19	12-9	-	0-25	0.25
			217 Kapal Muni	Bed Ram	Bashona		2.19			5-2	-	184.00	184.00
			218 ~~[struck]~~ Panchbir	Saranpat	Kotkandi	Manjhli	1.5	10.00		0-10	60.00		60.00
			219 Jamlu		Manjhli	do	19.72	1000.00	0-18	48-9	60.00	32.08	92.08
			220 ~~[struck]~~ Mandasan	Thenu	Kumand	do		300.00	0-15		40.00	40.00	80.00
			221 Shapreda Narain	Jagat Ram	Ashni	Parli	0-08	400.00	~~[struck]~~ 10-8	8-10	30.00	14.42	44.42
			222 Jamlu	Gianu	Adsu	do	0-02	300.00	0-15	0-1	16.00	16.00	32.00
			223 Puna Narain	Tej Ram	Jaishta	do	3.72	1500.00		12-8	20.00	88.25	108.25
			224 Jamlu	Gehru	Ses	do	3.28	700.00	12-8	17-42	47.42	30.00	77.42
			225 Gotam Rikhi	Khubu	Parli	do	0-02		0-02				
			226 Machan Rikhi	Keshav Ram	do	do	1.17	500.00	5-15	1-7	25.00	1.66	26.66
Chong	Chong	Chong, Ratocha Shat, Jalu.	227 Chuni Gasan (Devi)	Roli Ram	Chong	Chong	2.17	4000.00		18-0	60.00	70.00	130.00
			228 Devi Chamonda	Chene Ram	Tladi	Shat Ratocha	3.00	2000.00		14.0	10.00	40.00	50.00
			229 Devi Bhatanti	Bhop Ram	Padai	Jalu	19.75	3500.00		80.08	80.00	60.00	140.00
			230 Gonmbal	Nank Chand	Gulab Chand Shat Kishan Chand Tikkam Ram Uttam	Shat	27.49	3000.00		128.0	10.00	54.00	64.00
Harkandi	Harkandi	Jari Bradha	231 Lachhmi Narain	Moti Lal	Patavli	Bradha Jari	14.55	1000.00	1-4	54-13	7.00	140.27	147.27
			232 do	Sudhi Gar	Manikaran	Bradha	0.95		0.5	3-5		3.00	3.00
			233 Murli Dhar	Dile Ram	do	do Jari	2.09			4.16		12.00	12.00
			234 Simo Narain	Lebhu	Dedai	Jari	4.73	1500.00	4.4	18.1	12.00	115.00	127.00
			235 Devi Upasana	Dile Ram	ShraniBerh	do Bradha	7.44	1000.00	57-3	30-8	5.00	24.56	29.56
			236 Jamlu	Padha	Malana	Bradha	0-23		0-12	3-15		2.00	2.00
			237 Kali Nag	Giahru	[illegible]	Jari Bhardha	28.91	1000.00	21-14	107-15	20.00	135.00	155.00

			238	Ram Chander Jee	Luder Mani	Jari, Bradha	16.97	-	0-10	48-15		-	96.03	96.03
			239	Bijli Mahadev	Devi Singh	Bradha			0-3					
Kanawar	Kanawar	Manikaran Sosan	240	Ram chander ji	Luder Mani	Manikaran	19.74	3000.00		90-6			600.00	600.00
			241	Lachhmi Narain	SadhiSagar	do	11.33			44-2			150.00	150.00
			242	Mirli Dhar	Dila Ram	do	0.94			2.08			60.00	60.00
			243	Naina	Nobbi Ram	do Sosan	8.31	800.00		78-6		8.00	32.00	40.00
			244	Jamlu	Jahadha	Malana	15.48				42-0-8			
			245	Jamlu	Chana Ram	Tos	6.23	200.00			33-1	3.00	12.00	15.00
			246	Jhangam	Atru	Brashni	7.74	300.00			43.00	5.00	13.00	18.00
			247	Devi MahaMaya	Ram Singh	Tos	7.46	50.00			34-10	2.00	5.00	7.00
			248	Shiv Daharoh	Bahadru	Nakhthan	0-61	60.00			3-8	5.00	5.00	10.00
			249	Rawal	Daya Ram	Grahan	0-39	200.00			4-10	4.00	6.00	10.00
			250	Narain	Hotam Ram	Pulga	0-92	150.00			1-9	2.00	5.00	7.00
Sansar	Sansar	Sansar GadaParli	251	Kesho Narain	Rati Ram	Gara Parli	2.25	40.00		20-14	20-14	6.00	4.00	10.00
			252	Besha	Rati Ram	Sansar	3.11	74.00		24-14		10.00	10.00	20.00
Bhalan	Bhalan	Bhalan Rot Raila	253	Durbasha Rishi	Ganga Singh	Bhallan	16.92	1000.00			52-7	20.00	100.00	120.00
			254	Bradhai Bir	Jagta	do	1.99	100.00			7-1	30.00	80.00	110.00
			255	Aamal Keshav Ram		do	7.23	800.00			18-2	20.00	150.00	170.00
			256	Lachhmi Narain(Saran pat)		do Rot	25.57	1500.00			81-3	15.00	300.00	315.00
			257	Devi Asha Puri	Bhakru	Upper Raila	2.58	400.00			6-6	5.00	80.00	85.00
			258	Lachhmi Narain	Dolu	Raila	22.45	8000.00		97-15	35-10	10.00	500.00	510.00
			259	Devi Kola Jee	Hari Chand	do	0-28	400.00			1-16	5.00	20.00	25.00
			260	Jamlu	Dolu	do	4.86	80.00		4.12	14-18	5.00	100.00	105.00
			261	Markanda	Jit Ram	Rot	9.37	500.00			17.10	10.00	150.00	160.00
			262	Sayama Kali(DevI)	Dola Ram	do	6.46	500.00		3-5	8-5	5.00	200.00	205.00
			263	Isha	Mehat Chand	do	1.81	300.00		7-0	6-10	5.00	100.00	105.00
			264	Isha	Lachhmi Ram	do	15.76	9000.00		3-2	67-0	15.00	500.00	515.00

			1	2	3	4	5	6	7	8	9		10	11	12
								SUB TEHSIL B ANJAR.							
Bunga.	Bunga.	Kotla Chakur-tha Kanon Dhaugi.	265	Devta Brahma.	Jagat Ram.	-Nil-	Kanon.	Kanon.	31.65	5780.00	14-9	134-8	250-00	48.00	298-00
			266	Lachhmi Nara-in.	Dina Nath.		Dhaugi.	Dhaugi.	11.19	4635.00	2-10	57-13	150-00	2-00	152-00
			267	Chhamaun Nag.	Mohan Singh.	=	Dhaman.	Kotla.	32.86	2790.00	-	-	50-00	-	50-00
			268	-do-	Bhole Ram.	-	Cha kurtha.	Chakur-tha.	25.28	7370.00	9-16	443-08	300-00	132.00	432.00
Banogi.	Ba nogi.	Dasahar Maniashi Sachen Sha nghar Miah.	269	Jamlu.	Ala m Singh.	-	Uprli Sainja.	Da sahar	-	38.00	-	-	2-00	-	2-00
			270	Devta Panj Panir.	Alam Singh.	-	Dagehri.	Dasahar Maniashi.	-	14.00	-	-	2.00	-	2-00
			271	Devi Durga.	Lachhmi Ram.	-	Deohri.	Maniashi Dasahar Sachen.	0-27	5216.00	-	0-11	3-00	-	3-00
			272	Pander.	Harfi Ram.	-	Khiogi.	Sachen Maniashi Dasaha r.	69.99	36901.50	0.18	513-18	40-00	56-00	96-60
			273	Shri Nag.	Me har Chand.	-	Sachen.	Sachen.	4.10	7588-37	-	21-98	5-00	7-50	12-50
			274	Bhang-jol.	Sobhe Ra m.	-	Batahara.	Miah Shangar	55.26	14248-00	12.12	261-8	15-00	431-88	446-88
Mang-laur.	Mang-laur Gopal-pur.	Targali Ratoh Deotha Thanicher Chanon Bhatibir Jori Sihuli.	275	Markanda.	Gopal Dass.	-	Manglaur.	Targali Ratwah.	39.85	8505-00	129.3	129.3	15.00	100-00	125-00
			276	Chhamahun Nag.	Kisha n Singh.	-	Jori.	Jori Sihuli Thatibir.	5.44 1.75	8615-00	26.14	92.11	35-00	50-00	85-00
			277	Jamblu.	Ram Singh Teja Singh. equal s hare.	-	Galon.	Thanicher.	1.90	-	-	19-9	30-00	-	30-00
			278.	Devi Zalpa.	=do=	-	Galon.	Thanicher. Deotha. Chanon.		-	-	[illegible]	25-00	-	25-00

			279. Lachhmi Nara-in.	-do-	- [illegible]	Chera	Thaniche.r.	-	8492-00	-	4-3	20-00	-	20-00
			280. Devta Bongru.	Teja Singh Bed Ram equal share Naju. ⅓.	[illegible]	Gos hala.	Chanon Deotha Targali Thanicher.	0-55	16615-00	0-9	3-2	30-00	-	30-00
			281. Devi Hirma.	-do.	-	Goshala.	Chanon Deotha Targali Thanicher.	-	1030-00	-	-	50-00	.	50-00
Shikari.	Shikari Fatehpur Tilokpur.	Chethar Balagar Khabal Hoti Barah. Tandi Bahu.	282. Markanda.	Devi Ram	-	Bala.	Balagar	.05	16240-00	2-1	-	200-00	9-00	209-00
			283. Balla Durga.	-do-	-	Bala.	Balagar.	26.24	5250-00	2.2	97-0	50-00	14-84	64-84
			284. Devta Bhuhni.	Premu.	-	Bala.	Bala	-	191-00	-	-	-	-	-
			285. Devta B ir.	Sa ngtu. Ratnu.	-	Bala	Loha nda.	-	131-00	-	-	-	-	-
			286. Devta Bhira.	Gehru.	-	Dhar	Bhora Dhar Balun.	-	191-00	-	-	-	-	-
			287. De vta Chhoti.	Baru.	-	Belah	Balun Bela.	-	179-00	-	-	-	-	-
			288. Narain.	Ledu Babe Ram.	-	Belah	Be lah Balun.	-	1580-00	1-11	-	20-00	-	20-00
			289. Nag.	Pari.	-	Baloo n.	Baloon.	-	59-00	0-7	-	2-00	-	2-00
			290. Chalani-Bal.	Chandu.	-	Shil	Balagar Chhaner Salam.	-	640-00	0-17	-	50-00	-	50-00
			291. Thaka r Murlidhar.	Teja Singh.	-	Gadhiar.	Balagarh	-	-	5-10	-	10-00	-	10-00
			292. Balu Nag.	Lot Ram. Birbal.	1. Brikam. 2. Minoo 3. Birbal. 4. Dola Singh. 5. Parma nand 6. Dolu 7. Sangat-Ram 8. Shar Chand 9. Be li Ram 10. Chhaju Ram.	Balah.	Chhaner Khabal Balagar Bahu Sharogi.	-	30690-00	-	-	150-00	31-00	181-00

			293. Shangjol	Moti Ram Man Dass	6	Ba chhot	Toel Kamrah Jhamach Bh rmal	- -	3844.00	-	-	5.00	-	5.0 0
			294. B homasi	Dhohlu	-	Bhumasi Deora	Nachhot Chhaunr. A lora Patan	-	3610.00	-	-	50.00	-	50.00
			295. Mageshri	Bale R am	1. Bale Ram 2. Gagi 3. Dinu 4.	Magsher.	C a sheni Daluan Keradhar Jawali Jaan Buhli Dharseri.	-	8240.00	-	-	60.00	-	60.00
			296. Markanda	Dhanu	-	Sarandi	Sa randi Shara un Seobag Makerh Batan	-	5985.00	-	-	50.00	=	50.00
			296. Dialu Nag.	Tule R am	-	Borgi	Mohni Bharanda Borgi Puri Sandh Taghar G araun.	-	5418.00	-	-	50.00	-	50.00
			297. Lajari.	Teju.	-	Bhumian	Bahu	-	9040	=	=	50-00	-	50.00
			298. Jhabi Nag.	Moti R am	-	Jhabi	Mandi	-	8200 .00	-	-	50.00	-	50-00
			299. Devi Panjali.	Kuram Datt. Udhu	-	Punjali	Dhara Punjabi	-	3 889.00	0.3	8X3	30.00	-	30.00
Chehni.	Palach. Chehni. Khara-garh.	Shirikot Shapnil. B hiar. Bini. Sajwar. Giagi. Rashala Kalwari Plach.	300. Sandev.	Lal Chand.	-	Kanon.	Shrikot.	-	3034.00	0.4	-	20-00	-	20-00
			3 01. Saryoli.	B ali Ram.	-	Shapnil.	Shapnil.	-	2370-00	-	-	20-00	-	20-00
			302. Lakshmi Nar-a-in.	Atma Ram.	-	Kalwari.	Kalwari.	78.16	6665-00	0-1	358.13	30-00	352.77	382.77
			303. Ka ndha Nag.	Shanu.	-	Ha nun.	Hanun.	-	320-00	-	-	10-00	-	10-00
			304. Ja-mlu.	Gokal Ram.	-	Chhagraut	Kalwa ri. Palach.	-	-	2-16	-	10-00	-	10-00
			305. Dasher Mahadev.	Copali.	1. Padam Singh. 2. Jhali. 3. Bhagwan Dass. 4. Ruli.	Kalyuni.	Palach.	50-47	2990-00	0-14	292-19	10-00	102-00	112-00
			306. Bhandari.	Dile Ram.	-	Shoja.	Shoja.	-	1675-00	-	-	20-00	-	20-00
			307. Sharinga Rikhi.	Moti Ram.	1. Chuna Ram. 2. Ranpat.									

		3. Puranchand 4. Ke wal Ram. 5. Khub Ram. 6. Ses Ram.		Bagi	Bini. Bihar.	59-00	11413.00	3-9	272-11	200-00	350-00	550-00
	308.Devi Renka.	Sita Ram.	-	Banjar.	Banjar.	-	-	-	4-0	20-00	-	20-00
	309.Devta Narain.	Balakram.	-	Harb.	Harb.	-	1008-00	-	-	10-00	-	10-00
	310.Devta Kansri.	Dheba Ram.	-	Sajwar.	Sajwar-	-	2675-00	9-17	-	20-00	-	20-00
	311.Devi Buhri Nagan.	Shukru Ram.	-	Giagi.	Giagi.	10-12	660-00	0-10	59-4	15-00	14-69	29-69
	312.Jembi Nag.	Brij Lal.	-	Jembi.	Rashala. Tandi.	0-05	2705-00	2-11	-	20-00	-	20-00
Nohanda.Tung. Chipni. Sharchi.Mas hiar. Nohanda. Pekhri. Tandar. Sharchi. Shili.	313 Laxmi Narain.	Rama Nand.	-	Pharbari.	Chipni.	-	1900-00	-	-	15-00	-	15-00
	314.Bishnu Nara-in.	Mani Ra m.	-	Ghiar.	Mas hiar.	1-34	1460-00	-	7-0	10-00	10-00	20-00
	315.Jamlu.	Moti R am.	.	Majhali.	Mashiar.	0-75	216-50	10-5	-	-	15.00	15-00
	316.She-sh Nag.	Budh Ram.	-	Kamera.	Misnar.	-	1690-00	-	-	15-00	-	15-00
	317.Laxmi Narain.	Mani Ram.	-	Chipni.	Chipni.	3.73	2930-00	-	32-9	100-00	20.00	120-00
	31 8.-do-	Gobind Ram.	-	Tandar.	Tandar.	-	229-00	-	-	10-00	-	10-00
	319.Bhimu Nag.	Sangat Ram.	-	Baringcha.	Tandar.	-	220-00	-	-	10-00	-	10-00
	320.Kali Nag.	Kari.	-	Dingcha.	-do-	-	460-00	-	-	10-00	-	10-00
	321.Sanker.	Laje Ram.	-	Dhar.	Pekhri.	-	146-50			[illegible]	.	5-00
	322.Chorasi Sidh.	Ganga Ram.	-	Ghat.	-do-	7-32	1616-00	41-60	64-6	20-00	10-00	30-00
	323.Lageshri Mahadev.	Tej Ram.	-	Pekri.	Pekhri Charchi.	-	2068-00	-	-	20-00	-	20-00

			324.	Chohal Nag.	Saranpat.	-	Dharwal.	Shili.	-	1579-00	-	-	20-00	-	20-00
			325.	Shesh Nag.	Dile Ram.	-	J hotli.	Sha rchi.	-	124-50	-	-	50-00	-	50-00
			326.	Sha ngcholi.	Alam.	-	Yasher.	Bharchi.	-	252-00	-	-	10-00	-	10-00
			327.	Devi Gara Durga.	Dina Nath. Khem Dev.	-	Bandal.	Sharchi.	48.86	6612-00	8-3	529-9	25-00	60-00	85-00
Jalori.	Jalori.	Koila. Lajeri. Khani.	328.	Devta Bajhari.	Adam Ram.	1.Keblu. 2.Sehb Ram. 3.HaruRam.	Kot.	Lajheri.	6-71	4660-00	23-2	12-0	125-00	200-00	325-00
			329.	Devta Darshni.	Alam Chand.(.)		Deem.	Lajheri.	(.)	1865-00	-	-	50-00	-	50-00
			330.	Thakar Murli Dhar.	Uttam Ram.	1.Khub Ram. 2.Siam Chand.	Batala.	Kha ni.	0-03	3750-00	0-9	0-3	80-00	-	80-00
			331.	Gadomi Nag.	Piare Ram.	1.Tula Ram. 2.Siam Dass. 3.Luhar u. 4.Sangat Ram.	Shagag.	Khani.	-	851.00	-	-	25-00	-	25-00
			332.	-do-	Parsu.	-	Katwaa.	Koila.	-	1112-00	-	-	50-00	-	50-00
Janja.	Janja.	Karana Kungash Shili.	333.	Pa to. Nag.	Jawala Dass.	-	Pe neuu.	Shili Kungash Karana.	0-22	963-00	1-6	0-8	30-00	56-00	85-00
			334.	Banti Maha-Dev.	Jagat Ram.	-	He n.	Kungash.	2-42	825-00	8-11	5-0	40-00	32-00	72-00
			335.	Jagtamba Rishi.	Kanshi Ram.	-	Zehra.	Shili.	0-19	35-00	6-12.	-	5-00	-	5-00
Raghopur.	Reghopur.	Kars hai Gar. Bishla dhar. Karad.	336	Chotri Nag.	Dile Ram.	1.Twaru. 2.Dodhi. 3.Shobha-ram. 4.Kolu.	Mishodha.	Karad.	-	11337-00	0-6	10-87	10-87	3-13	14-00
			337.	Khodi Jal.	Balak Ram.	1.Shukru. 2.Dhani. 3.Manglu.	Deohri.	Karshai G ar. Bishla Dhar. Karad.	12-62	14432-00	105-12	-	118-00	2082-00	2200-00
			33 8.	Takrasi Nag.	Ganga Ra m.	1.Khem Dass 2.Dalpat. 3.DhaniRam.	Tharwi.	Bishla-Dhar. Karshai-Gar.	2-39	692-00	7-3	5-8	100-07	54-93	155-00
			339.	Devta Kuthethri.	Lachhmi Dass.	1.Sangat Ram. 2.Dile Ram. 3.Mangal Chand. 4.Khem Dass. 5.Dalpat. 6.Twa ru. 7.Sangat Ram.	Kotehar.	Karad. Bishla-dhar. Janja.	-	14319-00	-	-	220-69	52.31	273-00
						SUB TEHSIL NIRMAND									
Br amgarh.	Braugarh. Kot.	Chail. Sarahan. Jhabhlertha. Koi. Shili. Dethwi.	340.	Jhalahndi.	Teki.	-	Sarahan.	Sarhan.	4.99	8000-00	30-8	1-12	150-00	100-00	250-00

-	-	-	341. Devi Chalasan.	Nenu-	Jaun.	Chail.	0-34	6000-00	-	5-6	100-00	2-50	102-50
-	-	-	342. Rayasi Nag.	Bhagat Singh.	Dhaler.	Jhaler.	0-64	6000-00	6-13	1-4	50-00	100-00	150.00
-	-	-	343. Markanda.	Mani Ram.	Shilat.	N oor.	0-33	1000-00	4-9	0-11	50-00	50-00	100-00
			344. Markanda.	Jagat Ram.	Noor.	Noor.	5-14	1000-00	9-11	-	30-00	100-00	130-00
			345. Bharalu.	Indru.	Kot.	Dethwa.	7-06	5500-00	11-1	20.6	30-00	250-00	280-00
			346. Rai Nag.	Sangat Ram.	Dethwa.	Kot.	2-69	4500-00	1-4	4.5	200-00	50-00	250-00
Pandrabis.	Pandrabis.	Sarga. Kashwa. Tuha n. Thachwa.	347. Jhakru Nag.	Gopal.	Ukludhar.	Sarga.	-	1340-00	-	-	50-00	-	50-00
			348. Devi Dalasan.	Ramanand.	Kashwa.	Kashwa.	-	1730-00	-	-	40-00	-	40-00
-			349. Jahru Nag.	Jitu. KhemiRam. Ga nga Ram.	G hagga. Tuhan.	Tuhan.	24.31	2680-00	20.6	19-19	100-00	200-00	300-00
			350. Devi Bel.	Ganga Ram.	Bel.	Tuhan.	-	700-00	-	-	40-00	-	40-00
Dhol.	Dhol. Ka ndhi.	Kashol. Bari. Arso. Shohch. Posha. Kasani. Tawar.	351. Devi Bari.	Kardar former died, new not appointed.	Bari. Chortha. Shathal.	Shohch. Bari. Arsu.	2-65	5120.00	1-6	20-19	20.00	48.00	68.00
			352. Dararu.	P halli Ram	Panko	Bari	-	-	0-2	-	-	-	-
			353. Bir.	Bija Ram	Dhol	Dhol Shoh Tawar.	0.32	60.00	3.16	1-1	-	-	-
			354. Natli Nag	Het R am	-	Tawar Nishani.	6.43	-	3-10	-	-	-	-
			355. Devi Pujari	Knub Ram	Pujari	Nishan Tawar.	14.00	1 7?0.00	6-17	87.?0	-	70.00	70.00
			356. Devi A-mbla	Kardar has been died now not appointed	-	Poshana	6-15	-	-	41-2	-	200.00	200.00
			357. -do-	-do- 1. Harinder Singh 2. Gopala Ram 3. Rima Datt 4. Jagu.	Nirmand.	Nirmand.	6.6839	10000.00	1 89=17	110-12	140.00	1300.00	1440.00
			358. S iri Negala.	Bij Ram	Domohli	Bari	4.69	-	2=9	25-0	60.00	25.00	85.00
			359. Chambhu.	Chran Dass.	Kasholi	Kosholi Potna.	42.48	3340.00	3-8	342-12	50.00	370.00	420.00
			360. -do-	Coli Chand	R andal	Kosholi Poshna	3.13	6040.00	4-13	43-18	-	30.00	30.00
			361. Devi Durga.	Karam Datt.	Tikri	A rsu Shohch	0.40	500.00	5-19	35-19	-	90.00	90.00
			362. Narsing.	Gopa Dass.	Suma.	A rsu	0.36	200.00	-	4.18	5.00	10.00	15.00
			363. Saat Narain.	Dharam Pal	-	A r su.	0.	-	-	0-19	-	10.00	20.00
Nir mand.	Nimri.	Nirmand. Tall.	364. Devta Hatli Nag.	Het R am.	Ramgarh.	Nirmand Bail.	26.91	100-00	30-2	-	15-00	150-00	265-00
			365. Chandi Devi.	Dola Ra m.	Nirmand.	Nirmand.	100-31	115-00	-	-	-	60-00	60-00
			366. Thakar lachhmi Narain.	Kardar has been died, New not appointed	Nirmand.	Nirmand.	3-05	-	1-18	3.4	-	3-00	3-00

		367.	Bashesha r Mahadev.	Dhaler Dev.	-	Nirmand.	Nirmand.	41-72	120-00	1-15	-	10-00	30-00	40-00
		368.	Bakshni Mahadev.	Bega Nand.	-	Nirmand.	Nirmand.	44-62	90-00	3-10	3-9	-	33-00	33-00
		369.	Sat Nara in.	Dharmpal.	-	Rampur - Bashehar (H.P).	Dail.	10-86	-	0-7	21-16	-	-	-
Gade ja.	Nirmri. Gadeja. Shili. Lot.	370.	Devi Ambka.	Khardar die d.	-	Nirmand.	Gadeja. Shili. Lot.	15-57	-	101-14	-	-	-	-
		371-	Koila Devi.	Sadhu Ram.	-	Koil.	Gade ja.	6-71	200-00	7-19	-	-	25-00	25-00
		372.	Darbha Devi.	Sangat Ram.	-	Daroha.	Lot.	3-98	400-00	24-2	-	-	50-00	50-00
		373.	Chebri Devi. Dagei Devi.	Khut Ram.	-	-	Shili.	-	-	-	-	-	-	-
		374.	Devta Shars hai Nag.	Surat Ram.	-	-	Shili.	-	-	-	-	-	-	-
Nether. Nirmri.	Nether. Palai.	375.	Bada Mahadev.	Baresi	-	Nether.	Nether.	172-35	2000-00	1-17	0-7	10-00	-	10-00
		376.	Cheri Devi. Degaini Devi.	Khub Ram.	-	Cheri - Degaini.	Shili. Nether.	86-24	300-00	1-1	6-0	5-00	80-00	85-00
		377.	Dha nya Devi.	Ram Nath.	-	Dhanah.	Nether.	56-39	300-00	0-16	4-12	4-00	60-00	64-00
		378.	Koikandha Nag. Zaildari-Shath Devi.	Keshab Ram.	-	Tandi.	Plai.	0-34	-	5-8	C-5	-	20-00	20-00
Kandha.	Siri-garh. Jaban Beuingal. Soidhar.	379.	Pichhla Devi.	Dola Ram.	-	De ohri.	Jaban.	108-03	2000-00	14-4	471-18	20-00	100-00	120-00
		380.	Koikandha Nag.	Teji. Chura R am.	-	Shagogi.	Beuingal	46-48	200-00	-	197-6	10-00	80-00	90-00
		381.	Devta Jager Ma hadev.	Gokli.	-	Dalash.	Soidhar.	81-22	3000-00	-	204-12-6	40-00	200 -00	240-00
		382.	Ka mbaha Devi.	Kesha b Ram.	-	Khegu.	-do-	6-06	100-00	8-13	29-19	5.00	20-00	25-00
Pharanali. Siri-garh.	Pharanali. Dingidhar.	383.	Banha Mahadev.	Narain Dass.	-	Benha.	Dingidh	14-81	1000-00	-	134-14	20-00	40-00	60-00
		384.	Thakar Raghunath.	Rai Raghbir S ingh.	-	-do-	-do-	1-1 2	200-00	-	18-14	5-00	10-00	15-00
		385.	Kulchetha r Mahadev.	Durga Nand.	-	Olda.	Pharana	6-91	350-00	-	93-16	5-00	20-00	35-00
		386.	Bari Devi.	Jai.	-	Ba ri.	-do-	2-95	200-00	-	27-6	10-00	12-00	22-00
		387.	Pichhla Devi.	Dola Ram.	-	Deohri.	Jaban.	17-03	2000-00	-	100-15	20-00	60-00	80-00
Manjhadesh. Narain-garh.	Bachher. Manjha-desh.	388.	Devta Shamshri Mahadev.	B hagwan Dass.	-	Shamshar.	Manjha Bachher Koideol Janja.	376-03	3000-00	20.00	1064-16	50-00	300-00	350-00
		389.	Thakar Lachhmi Narain.	Balu.	-	Dohba.	Manjhad	23-04	-	-	13-13	5-00	10-00	15-00
		390.	Dohba Nag.	Dolu.	-	-do-	-do-	-	-	-	-	10-00	-	10-00
		391.	Khadoi Nag.	Mansa Ram.	-	Khadoi.	Bachher	-	-	-	-	10-00	-	10-00
		392.	Serajpal.	Dile Ra m.	-	Jaun.	-do-					6-00	-	6-00
		393.	Narain.	Jaga t Ram	-	Nias.	-d-	-	-	-	-	4-00	-	4-00
		394.	Kali Nag.	Laje Ram	-	Tarala.	-do-	-	100-00	-	-	15-00	-	15-00

	395.	Kali Nag.	Tula Ram.	-	Ladhagi.	Bachher.	-	200-00	-	-	20-00	-	20-00
hnu.Naraingarh.Chatu. Rahnu.	396.	Devi Ambka.	Kardar has been died.		Nirmand.	Ghatu.	97-08	-	7-9	23-8	-	-	-
	397.	Sharshathi Nag.	Surat Ram.	-	Barashar-s hah.	-do-	15-65	-	8-10	2.8	4-00	2.00	6-00
	398.	Satnarain.	Dharmpal.	-	Rampur-Bushaher. (H.P).	-do-	5-52	-	-	4-6	-	-	-
	399.	Katamri Nag.	Chet Ram.	-	Kamadar.	Rahun.	-	500-00	-	-	3-00	-	3-00
	400.	Devta Chambhu.	Dodhu. Piare Ram.	-	Deogi.	Rahnu. Ghatu.	81-97	1200-00	11-14	1 41-16	20-00	40-00	60-00
	401.	Shagath Rikhi.	Chet Ram.	-	Thanthal.	Rahnu.	-	250-00	-	-	4-00	-	4-00

Appendix G

Copies of Different Registers

This Appendix consists of three sections:

(a) Register of the *Hazari* of *Deotas* of Kullu.
(b) Register of the *Nazrana* Paid the *Deotas*.
(c) Sample Page of the *Tirhara* Register Recording a 1/3 Share of the Offerings Received by the *Deotas* that has to be Sent to the Treta Nath Temple at Ayodhya, Together with the Announcement of the Holding of the Dussehra Festival.

(a) Register of the *Hazari* of *Deotas* of Kullu

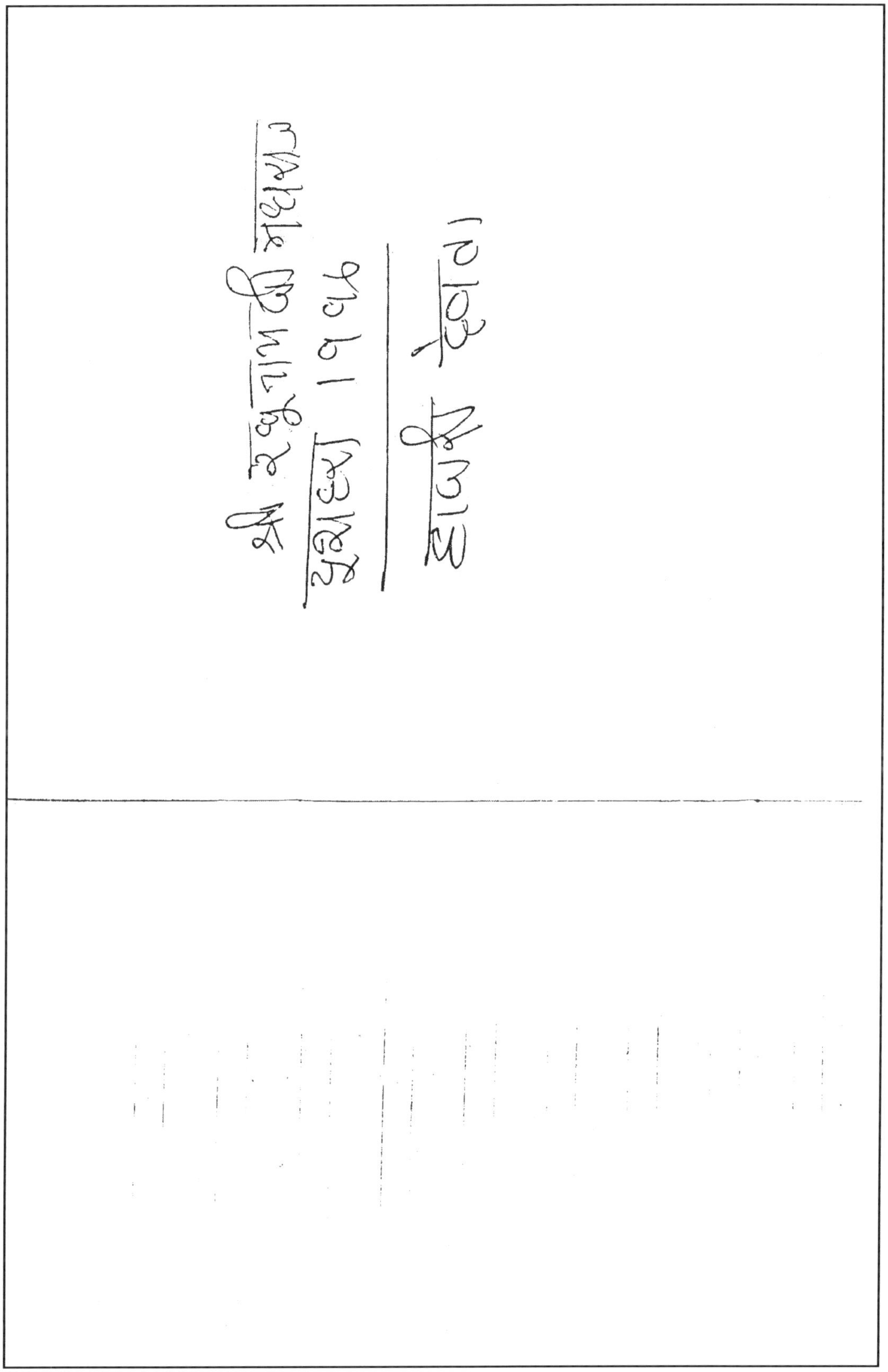

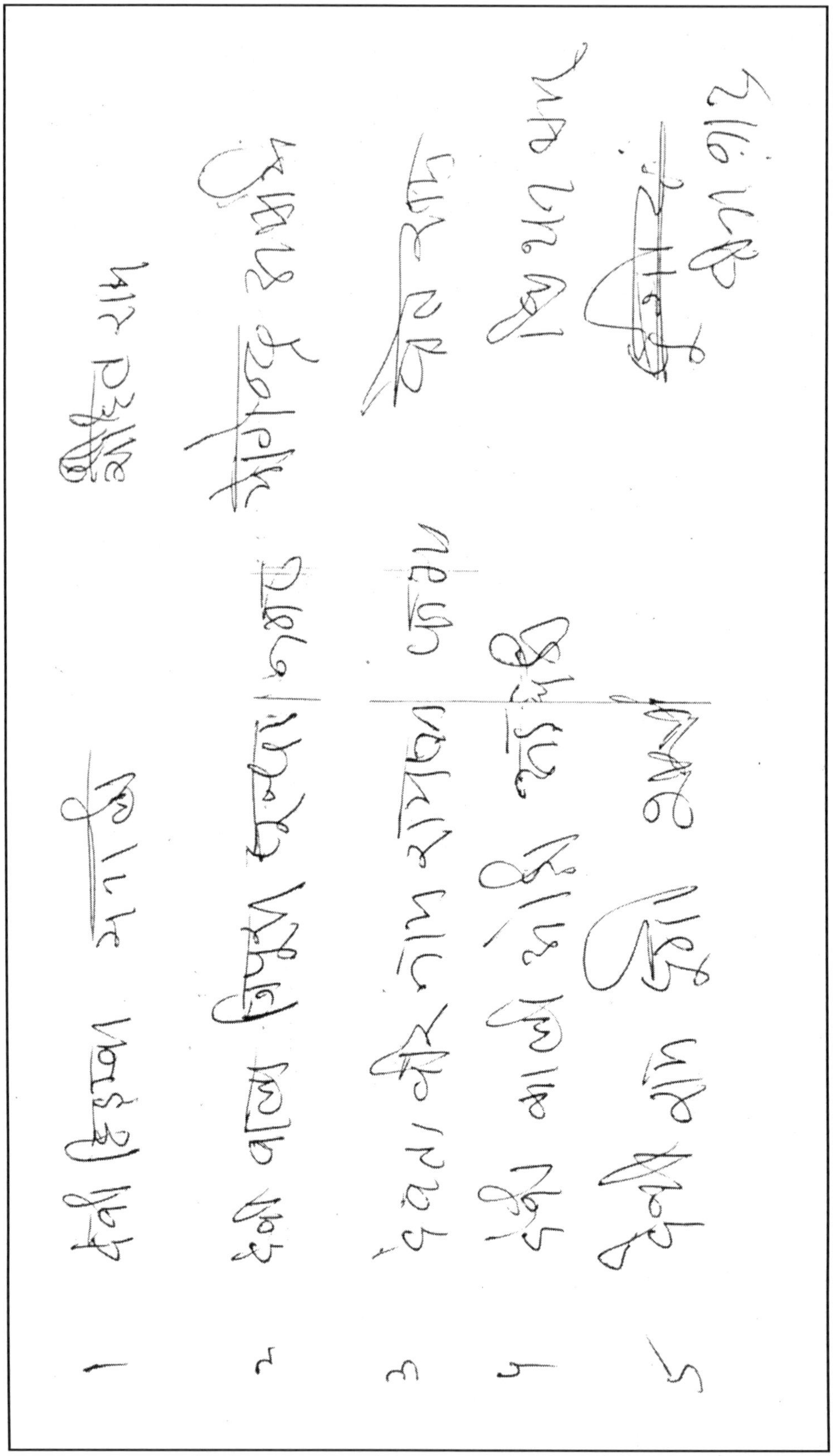

1 देवी हिडम्बा मनाली — [illegible] राम
2 देवी बाला त्रिपुर सुन्दरी नग्गर — योगेन्द्र शर्मा
3 देवता बीर नाथ [illegible] [illegible] — [illegible] राम
4 देवी काली ओझी [illegible] — [illegible]
5 देवी [illegible] दुर्गा [illegible] — [illegible]

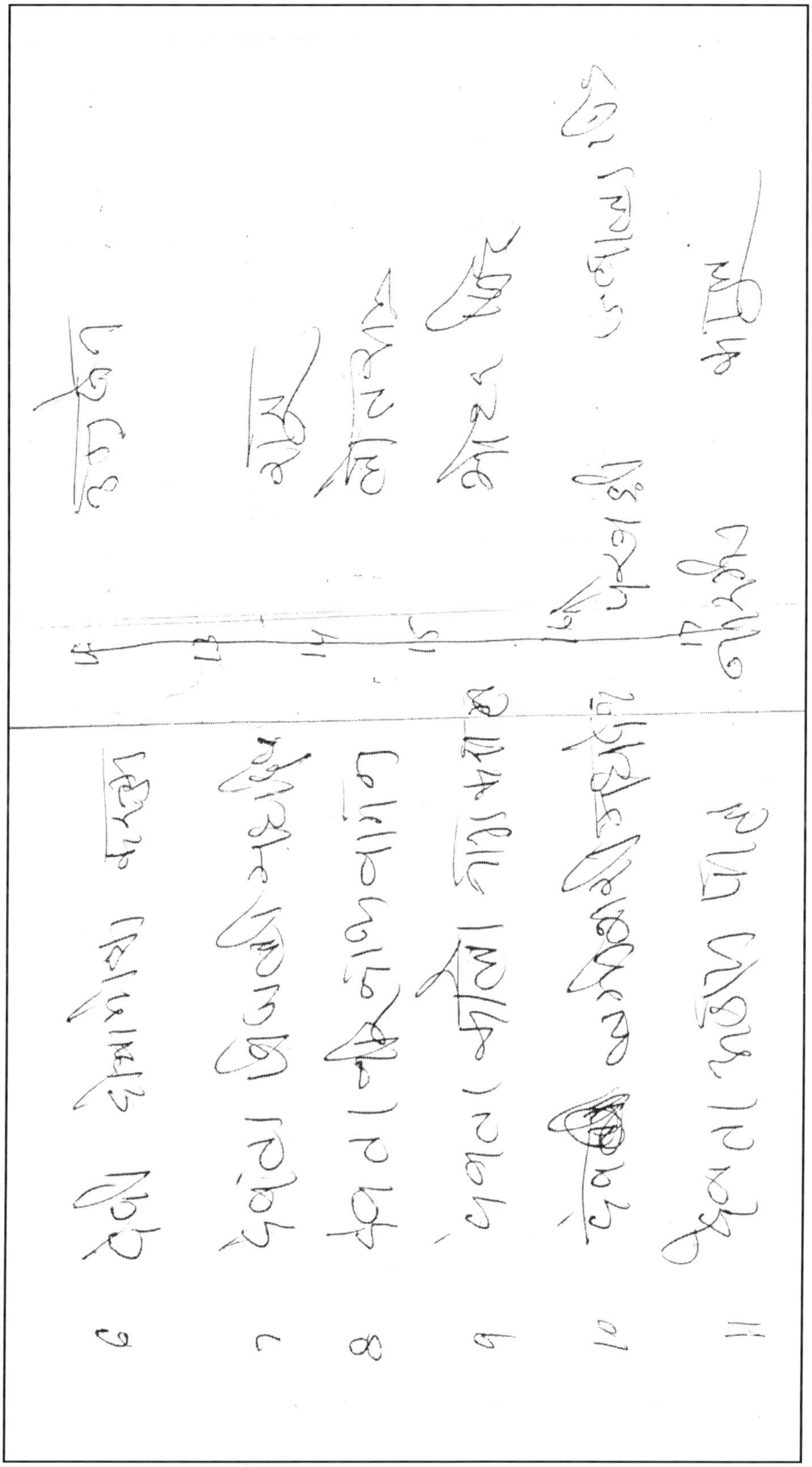

(b) Register of the *Nazrana* Paid the *Deotas*.

कुल्लू दशहरा 1996 में उपस्थित देवतागण को नजराना वितरण सूचि

क्रम संख्या	नाम देवता	नाम कारदार	पुहचने की तारीख	दूरी कि मी.	बाजे वाले की संख्या जो देवता के साथ आए हैं	अन्य हारियान	कु.	देवता रथ या पालकी	देवता के साथ नाटी पार्टी है या नहीं	नजराना जो गत वर्ष दिया गया	बढ़ोतरी	कुल नजराना जो इस वर्ष दिया गया	हस्ताक्षर वसूल कर्ता नजराना
1.	2.	3.	4	5	6	7	8	9	10	11	12	13	14
1.	ठाकुर रघुनाथ जी वाक्या सुलतानपुर कुल्लू।	श्री दानविन्द्र सिंह	21-10-96	3 किमी	130	410	540	रथ	नहीं	13897/-	1389	15286	
2.	देवता बिजली महादेव वाक्या मथाण [illegible]	श्री राजेश कुमार	21-10-96	20	90	310	400	रथ	नहीं	4308/-	430	4708	[signature]
3.	देवी हिडिम्बा वाक्या डुंगरी फाटी व कोठी मनाली	श्री तिर्थ राम	21-10-96	50	18	70	88	रथ	नहीं	5309/-	530	5839	[signature]
4.	देवता जमलू वाक्या चकाणी फाटी पीज	श्री देवी सिंह	21-10-96	6	50	350	400	रथ	नहीं	4980/-	498	5478	[thumb impression]
5.	देवता आदि ब्रह्मा वाक्या खोखण फाटीव कोठी खोखण	श्री राम सिंह	20-10-96	20	60	180	240	रथ	नहीं	3167/-	316	3483	[signature]
6.	देवता जुआणी महादेव वाक्या जुआणी फाटी हारहल कोठी कायस	श्री ओम प्रकाश	21-10-96	5	16	60	75	रथ	नहीं	1975/-	197	2172	[signature]
7.	देवता गाहड़ा पारली वाक्या कुल्णी फाटी व [illegible] कोठी शिकारी तहसील बन्जार	श्री [illegible]	20-10-96	55	7	35	[illegible]	रथ	हराफ़िर	500/-	100	600	[signature]

8.	देवता जान्थू वाक्या वरणु तन्दारी फाटी नरोणा कोठी गोपाल-पुर	श्री लोभा राम	20-10-96	60	9	45	54	रहा	हां	500	100	600
9.	देवता बझारी कोट वाक्या कोट फाटी क्वौरी कोठी बलोड़ी	श्री आत्मा राम	21-10-96	80	15	70	85	रहा	नहीं	2815	281	3096
10.	देवी चोगासन वाक्या चोग फाटी व कोठी चोग	श्री श्यामचन्द	21-10-96	25	9	65	74	रहा	नहीं	2455	245	2700
11.	देवी सरवरी वाक्या शुक्र फाटी प्रोणी	कमेटी प्रधान श्री पुन राम	20-10-96	36	21	100	121	रहा	नहीं	1866/-	186	2052
12.	देवता पजंवीर वाक्या करेरी फाटीलाड़ीहार कोठी महाराजा	श्री लालचन्द	21-10-96	12	12	85	97	रहा	नहीं	3211	321	3532
13.	देवता चौरासी सिद्ध वाक्या घाट फाटी पैलाड़ी कोठी नोहण्डा	श्री दिले राम	21-10-96	60	12	70	82	रहा	नहीं	1867	186	2053
14.	देवता ईश्वर महादेव वाक्या फाटीव कोठी पलाच तह, बन्जार	श्री कुर्म दत	21-10-96	60	16	150	166	रहा	नहीं	2494	249	2743
15.	देवी बूढी नागनी छ्यागी फाटी छ्यागी कोठी लाड़ागाड़	श्री ज्ञान चन्द	20.10.96	68	15	150	165	रप	नहीं	2750/-	275	3025
16.	देवता काली नारायण वाक्या जगी फाटी वाराहार कोठी महाराजा	श्री टेक चन्द	21.10.96	15	15	100	115	रप	नहीं	1724/-	172	1896
17.	देवता वेद व्यास वाक्या गशाल फाटी कुरुआ	श्री खेम राज	21.10.96	47	12	30	42	रप	नहीं	1834/-	183	2017
18.	देवता पुंवीर वाक्या तरमाल फाटी तान्दी कोठी तुंगीपुर	श्री लाल चन्द	20.10.96	70	18	162	162	रप	नहीं	3939/-	393	4332

19.	देवता गौडल ऋषि साकुन शलीण कोठी मनाली	श्री [illegible] राम	21.10.96	33	12	70	82	रथ	नहीं	1962	196	2158 [illegible]
20.	देवी चामुण्डा वाक्या धारा पाटी शाट कोठी चोंग	श्री बीरबल	21.10.96	30	10	70	80	रथ	नहीं	2001	200	2201 [illegible]
21.	देवता नाग धुम्बल वाक्या हलाण-2 कोठी कराहगढ़	श्री जीत राम	21.10.96	32	10	80	90	रथ	नहीं	2991/=	299	3290
22.	देवता [illegible] महादेव वाक्या [illegible] पाटी कोठी रघुपुर तह. आनी	श्री जवाहर लाल किशनधारी	21-10-96	120	6	25	31	रथ	नहीं	3163/-	316	3479 [illegible]
23.	देवता वीर कैलु वाक्या क्मान्द पाटी लाहीहार कोठी महाराजा	श्री हरी सिंह	21-10-96	11	12	70	62	रथ	नहीं	1548	154	1702 [illegible]
24.	देवता रियालु नाग वाक्या मौहिणी पाटी मौहिणी तह० बन्जार	श्री किशन चन्द	21-10-96	72	15	300	315	रथ	नहीं	2250	250	2500 किशनचन्द

...2...

	देवता वीर नाथ वारी फाटी हारहल कोठी काफ्स	श्री हरी चन्द	21-10-96	15	17	40	57	एक	नहीं	961/-	96/-	1057/-
26.	देवता देव नाग वाफा राजपुर फाटी करांड कोठी राजपुर तह. आनी	श्रीचन्द सिंह	20-10-96	120	6	100	106	एक	नहीं	2750/-	275/-	3025/-
27.	देवता पराशर कोट वाफा रैली फाटी खण्डाहू	श्री रूप चन्द	21-10-96	30	8	75	83	एक	नहीं	1841/-	184/-	2025/-
28.	देवता जय पाल वाफा बल्ही फाटी पलेस कोठी हुरंग	श्री पिहू	21-10-96	30	6	55	61	एक	नहीं	1900/-	190/-	2090/-
29.	देवी गढ़ा दुरगा वाफा रारमी फाटी व कोठी हारिबो तह. बन्जार	श्री चिन्तामणि	21-10-96	80	50	250	[illegible]	एक	नहीं	3000/-	3[illegible]0/-	33[illegible]0/-
30.	देवता नील कण्ठ फाटी वरशी कोठी खड़ागढ़	श्री गोरत राम कारिदार प्रीतम चन्द पुत्र रूमीकी	20-10-96	28	22	65	[illegible]	एक	नहीं	2674/-	267/-	2941/-
31.	देवता [illegible] वाफा वर्गांगा फाटी चकुंगा कोठी	श्री रामलाल खड़ागढ़	21-10-96	32	13	100	[illegible]	एक	नहीं	2377/-	237/-	2614/-
32.	देवता चटोलिया वाफा शिरशिर फाटी तरगाली तहसील बन्जार	श्री देवी चन्द	21-10-96	55	25	95	120	एक	नहीं	1522/-	152/-	1674/-
33.	देवता वीर नाथ वाफा कमीणा फाटी शिकारीसर कोठी हुरंग	श्री लाल चन्द	21-10-96	35	11	65	70	एक	नहीं	1806/-	180/-	1986/-
34.	देवता नाग वाफा कण्ठी फाटी सेउली कोठी गोपालपुर तह० बन्जार	श्री सुरत राम	21-10-96	75	6	200	206	एक	नहीं	3563 /-	356/-	3919/-
35.	देवी ज्वाला मुखी वाफा व फाटी कोलेस	उत्तम सिंह	21-10-96	25	10	140	150	एक	नहीं	1640/-	164/-	1804/-

36.	देवता लक्ष्मी नारायण वाजा फाटी [illegible] कोठी तलोकपुर तह० बन्जार	श्री टेक राम [illegible] मन्दिर कमेटी	21-10-96	70	10	250	260	रुट	नहीं	2616/-	261/-	3099/-
37.	देवता महर्षि नारायणी वाजा बालागाड़ फाटी बालागाड़ तह० बन्जार	श्री चेतन दास	21-10-96	55	15	350	365	रुट	नहीं	3000/-	300/-	3300/-
38.	देवता [illegible] वाजा बरकोला फाटी [illegible]	श्री अमर सिंह प्रधान कमेटी	21-10-96	23	6	50	56	रुट	नहीं	1349/-	134/-	1483/-
39.	देवता [illegible] वाजा [illegible] फाटी [illegible]	श्री [illegible]	21-10-96	23	4	25	29	[illegible]	नहीं	550/-	155/-	600/-
40.	देवता बीर नाथ वाजा [illegible] फाटी [illegible] कोठी [illegible]	श्री [illegible] राम	20-10-96	12	12	80	92	रुट	नहीं	1616/-	161/-	1770/-
41.	देवता बीर नाथ वाजा [illegible] कोठी [illegible]	श्री केहर सिंह	21-10-96	15	12	250	262	रुट	नहीं	1525/-	152/-	1677/-
42.	देवता श्री नारायण वाजा [illegible] फाटी [illegible]	श्री रूप दास	21-10-96	25	4	60	64	रुट	नहीं	2113/-	211/-	2324/-
43.	देवता श्री नाग वाजा [illegible] फाटी [illegible] कोठी [illegible]	श्री मेहर चन्द	21-10-96	65	8	50	58	रुट	नहीं	3161/-	316/-	3477/-
44.	देवी त्रिपुरा सुन्दरी वाजा नगर	श्री [illegible]	21-10-96	25	16	250	266	रुट	नहीं	4245/-	424/-	4669/-
45.	देवी [illegible] वाजा [illegible]	श्री [illegible] सिंह	21-10-96	18	7	120	127	रुट	नहीं	1454/-	145/-	1599/-

46.	देवी [illegible] नगर	श्री [illegible] चन्द	21-10-96	25	10	180	190	[illegible]	नहीं	2259/-	225/-	2477/-
47.	देवता [illegible] महादेव [illegible]	श्री [illegible] राम	21-10-96	38	15	125	140	[illegible]	नहीं	1550/-	155/-	1705/-
48.	देवता [illegible] कोठी [illegible]	श्री पूरन चन्द	21-10-96	45	11	150	161	[illegible]	नहीं	2552/-	255/-	2807/-
49.	देवता कार्तिक स्वामी [illegible] कोठी [illegible]	श्री [illegible] राम	20-10-96	50	10	30	40	[illegible]	नहीं	1375/-	625/-	2000/-
50.	देवता [illegible] कोठी [illegible]	श्री [illegible] राम	35 21-10-96/x	10 35	70 10	80 70	80	[illegible]	नहीं	3164/-	316/-	3480/-
51.	देवता नारायण [illegible] कोठी [illegible]	श्री [illegible] चन्द	21-10-96	15	6	40	46	[illegible]	नहीं	2273/-	227/-	2500/-
~~52.~~	~~देवी [illegible] मुनी [illegible] कोठी [illegible]~~											

...3....

52. [दे]वता नारद मुनि वाक्या नोण्डू फाटी पारली कोठी कोटकण्डी	श्री [illegible] राम	20-10-96	34	10	80	90	रटा	नहीं	2701/-	270/-	2971/-	[illegible]
53. देवता पीरहू [illegible] वाक्या मिरही फाटी बरल कोठी महाराजा	श्री बलदेव राम	21-10-96	6	20	80	100	रटा	नहीं	1652/-	165/-	1817/-	[illegible]
54. देवता लक्ष्मी नारायण वाक्या रैला फाटी रैला कोठी [illegible]लाण	श्री तामे राम	21-10-96	45	20	340	360	रटा	हां	4267/-	426/-	4693/-	[illegible]
55. देवी महामाई [illegible]पुरी वाक्या [illegible] फाटी रैला कोठी [illegible]लाणा-I	श्री हरी राम	21-10-96	50	12	150	162	रटा	नहीं	2684/-	268/-	2952/-	[illegible]
56. देवता [illegible] वाक्या देउगी फाटी [illegible] कोठी [illegible] तह निरमण्ड	श्री [illegible] राम दास	21-10-96	300	15	105	120	रटा	नहीं	3302/-	330/-	3632/-	[illegible]
57. देवी कोला की वाक्या गोई फाटी रैला कोठी [illegible]	श्री तुलसी राम	21-10-96	62	15	100	115	रटा	नहीं	2651/-	265/-	2916/-	तुलसी राम
58. देवता वीर नाथ [illegible] फाटी [illegible] कोठी हुरंग	श्री प्रीतम चन्द	21-10-96	26	10	60	70	रटा	नहीं	1876/-	187/	206[illegible]	
59. देवता [illegible] कोर फाटी रोट कोठी [illegible]	श्री भाग राम	20-10-96	27	10	150	160	रटा	नहीं	873/-	87/-	960/-	भागराम
60. देवता [illegible] वाक्या सोल फाटी पारली कोठी कोटकण्डी	श्री मोती राम	21-10-96	30	3	35	38	रटा	नहीं	2905/-	290/-	3195/-	
61. देवता हुरंग नारायण वाक्या फाटी पिछड़ीहार कोठी हुरंग	श्री परस राम	21-10-96	30	8	50	58	रटा	नहीं	1745/-	174/-	1919/-	[illegible]
62. देवता [illegible] नारायण वाक्या [illegible] फाटी पारली कोठी कोटकण्डी	श्री [illegible] राम	21-10-96	45	25	125	150	रटा	नहीं	2683/-	268/-	2951/-	[illegible]

धारली कोठी कोटखण्डी												
63. देवता वासुकी नाग बारवा घाटीवीड़ कोठी गोपालपुर तह०	श्री तुलसी राम	21-10-96	45	25	125	150	रटT	नहो	1700/-	170/-	1870/-	
64. कुन्हार देवता शीरा नाग बालम कुठार कोठी गोपालपुर तह० कन्हार	श्री किशन सिंह	21-10-96	49	30	200	230	रटT	नहो	4048/-	404/-	4452/-	
65. देवी चन्द्रालीका बाबा फतेहपुर फाटी खावल कोठी फतेहपुर	श्री [illegible] राम	21-10-96	145	13	300	313	रटT	नहो	3720/-	372/-	4092/-	
66. देवता [illegible] ऋषि बाहवा [illegible] फाटी [illegible] कोठी कोटखण्डी	श्री दौत राम	21-10-96	40	15	100	115	रटT	नही	3566/-	356/-	3922/-	Dal Ram
67. देवी [illegible] बाबा कोर्कत गाड़भार फाटी गाड़ापार कोठी [illegible]	श्री सरदे राम-चन्द	21-10-96	100	12	50	62	रटT	नही	2492/-	249/-	2741/-	
68. देवी [illegible] बाबा [illegible] भुलैंग कोठी [illegible]	श्री [illegible]	21-10-96	20	10	60	70	रटT	नही	500/-	100/-	600/-	
69. देवता [illegible] पाल बाबा तारी [illegible] फाटी भुलैंग	श्री [illegible] राम	21-10-96	30	14		74	रटT	नही	793/-	69/-	872/-	
70. देवता ब्रह्मा क्लोणा बाबा क्लोणा फाटी क्लोणा कोठी बुर्गा	भीमो राम	21-10-96	45	16	150	166	रटT	हा	3538/-	353/-	389/-	
71. देवी महामाई बाबा [illegible] फाटी क्लोणा कोठी बुर्गा	श्री सुरत राम	21-10-96	45	15	150	166	रटT	हा	1238/-	123/-	1361/-	
72. देवी [illegible] बाबा बड़ागां फाटी बड़ागा	श्री [illegible] सिंह	21-10-96	32	15	60	175	रटT	नही	2640/-	264/-	2904/-	
73. देवता [illegible] ऋषि बाबा [illegible] फाटी [illegible] कोठी [illegible] तह० बन्जार	श्री [illegible] चन्द	21-10-96	50	15	100	115	रटT	नही	2543/-	254/-	2797/-	

74.	देवता कली नाग बाका क्वाल पनटी कोठी म्हल्लग्ड	श्री मोहर सिंह	21-10-96	14	14	60	174	र५T	नही	1595/-	159/-	1754/-	मोहर सिंह
75.	देवता बनासर बाका रैहद गटी मनियारिता कोठी बन गी	दगादि स	21-10-96	58	70	~~X~~	80	र५T	नही	1650/-	165/-	1815/-	[illegible]
76.	देवता छमाणी कनारायण बाजया छमाणा पुनटो कारावरी कोठी कमस	श्री गोपी चन्द प्रधान कमेटी	21-10-96	~~88~~ 30	~~XX~~ 10	~~XX~~ 70	~~XX~~ 80	र५T	नही	1464/-	146/-	1610/-	Gopi Chand
77.	देवता नारायण बाका बड़ोरिशल पनटी शिरा लोहार	दौलत राम	21-10-96~~XX~~	35	20	140	160	र५T	नही	1580/-	158/-	1738/-	दौलत राम
78.	देवता बीर नाथ बाका पनेल कोठी हुरंग	श्री राम चन्द	21-10-96	20	15	120	135	र५T	नही	1770/-	177/-	1947/-	[illegible]
79.	देवता रणपाल पनटी मोहल कोठी हालिणा	श्री झोला राम	21-10-96	11	6	35	41	र५T	नही	1962/-	196/-	2158/-	[illegible]
80.	देवता अजय पाल बाका नारगी पनझो पोज कोठी महाराजा	श्री कालू	21-10-96	6	12	120	132	र५T	नही	500/-	100/-	600/-	कालू

...4..

81. माता [illegible]मा काली वाक्या रोट फाटी रोट कोठी भलाणा	श्री जय चन्द	21-10-96	60	10	120	130	रहा	नहीं	1689	168	1857	[illegible]
82. देवता वरीन्द्र फाटी व कोठी कायस	श्री हुकम चन्द	21-10-96	22	20	100	120	रहा	नहीं	500	50 100	600	[illegible]
83. देवता पजवीर व ाक्या फाटी मलैली कोठी कोटकण्डी	श्री दुनी चन्द	20-10-96	40	10	70	80	XXX वमी कम म	नहीं	1267	126	1393	[illegible]
84. देवता कार्तिक स्वामी वाक्या नरगाणा फाटी नरगाणा कोठी नगर	श्री कुन्दन लाल	21-10-96	25	-	25	25	राणटी राहा	नहीं	1008	100	1108	सिंगी [illegible]
85 देवता वमन ऋषि फाटी पारली कोठी कोटकण्डी	श्री विष्णु राम	21-10-96	35	12	70	82	रहा	हाँ	3164	316	3480	ईश्वरराम
86. देवता छमाऊनाग फाटी कोटला कोठी बूंगा	श्री मोहन सिंह	21-10-96	75	16	450	466	रहा	हाँ	3614	361	3975	[illegible]
87. XXX माता भागासिद्ध वाक्या पीणी कोठी कायस	श्री नूप राम	21-10-96	40	18	80	98	रहा	नहीं	1573	157	1730	नूपराम
88. देवता कम्फू नाग फाटी व कोठी कायस	श्री भागो	21-10-96	80x 2.5	8 12	80x 30	x88 42	रहा	नहीं	500	100	600	भागो
89. देवता वनशीरा फाटी कणौरा कोठी बूंगा	श्री निमत राम	21-10-96	60	6	80	86	रहा	नहीं	963	96	1059	नौमतराम
90. देवता वीरनाथ वाक्या वागन कोठी महाराजा	श्री लौत राम	21-10-96	8	8	50	58	रहा	नहीं	730	73	803	लौतराम
91. देवी भागासिद्ध नरोगी कोठी कोटकण्डी	श्री सालगो राम	21-10-96	18	9	70	79	रहा	नहीं	1276	127	1403	सालगोराम

92.	देवता लाहडु महादेव अन्तरेणा फाटी शिलीहार कोठी कोटकण्डी	श्री निमत राम	21-10-96	15	7	50	57	रथ	नहीं	500	105	600
93.	श्री महादेव तगीशारी पेखड़ी बन्जार कोठी तुहाण्डा	श्री ज्वाला सिंह	21-10-96	70	10	150	160	रथ	नहीं	2873	287	2160
94.	देवता जेहर ... कोठी कोटकण्डी	श्री ... राम	21-10-96	50	6	55	61	रथ	नहीं	500	100	600
95.	देवता पटूरणू नाग बाक्या पनयाणा फाटी चुकरठा कोठी बुगां	श्री तुले राम	21-10-96	60	10	50	60	रथ	नहीं	865	86	951
96.	देवता दरवासा ऋषि गांव पुलिगी फाटी भलाणा	श्री ऋषि पाल	21-10-96	36	15	55	60	रथ	नहीं	2455	245	2700
97.	देवता श्रृंग ऋषि सचाणी फाटी रोट -1	श्री जगर नाथ	21-10-96	30	5	60	65	रथ	नहीं	2552	255	2807
98.	देवी मैना भूलिंग फाटी भूलिंग कोठी हरीहाणा	श्री कुले राम	21-10-96	11	7	60	67	रथ	नहीं	2371/- ~~500~~	237/- ~~100~~	2608/- ~~600~~
99.	देवता आहिड़ू नाग देऊरी फाटी कान कोठी बुगां	श्री गोकल	21-10-96	60	6	100	160	रथ	नहीं	1077	107	1184
100.	देवता रूपणा पाल गांव पाल्फाटी हाडीहार	श्री राम दास	21-10-96	16	8	60	68	रथ	नहीं	721	72	793
101.	देवता प.. बीर ... फाटी शिलीहार कोठी ...	श्री वोधू राम	21-10-96	14	8	60	68	रथ	नहीं	1027	102	1129 Disputed
102	देवता महावीर गांव ... सेरी फाटी शिलीहार कोठी ...	श्री परस राम	21-10-96	16	8	60	68	रथ	नहीं	500	100	600
103	देवता ... गांव गढूले फाटी शिली कोठी शारची	श्री सोभा राम	21-10-96	80	5	22	27	रथ	नहीं	634	63	697

104 देवी भारथा ~~देवी~~ गाँव मलेठ पाटी तीटी मण्डलगढ़	श्री भीमो राम	21-10-96	20	12	38	50	रदा	नहीं	[illegible]	112	1258	[illegible]
105. देवता जीवनारायण गाँव जम्पाटी जाणा कोठी नगर	जगत राम	21-10-96	22	6	24	30	रान्डी राछा	नहीं	775	77	852	[illegible]
106. देवी० भाग सिंह वाक्या हुलीलग पाटी व कोठी हुलीलग	विनाद वर्मा	21-10-96	8	80	50	10	रदा	नहीं	1372	137	1509	[illegible]
107. देवता शपर ढ़ा नारायण वाक्या बढ़ोगी पाटी शिलीहार कोठी कोटकण्डी	श्री गिरो धार	21-10-96	25	8	92	100	रदा	नहीं	2615	261	2876	गिरिधार
108. देवता पण्डीर वाक्या ~~[illegible]~~ पाटी सवेलण कोठी बनौगी	श्री तौतम राम	21-10-96	60	25	150	175	रदा	नहीं	4160	416	4576	लोहत राम
109. देवता श्री पाल वाक्या वान्सु पाटी लाडीहार कोठी महाराजा	श्री उतम राम	21-10-96	18	7	70	77	रदा	नहीं	2686	268	2954	
110. देवता आढ़ू महावीर वाकर पाटी ~~कलनौरा~~ कोठी बुंगा	श्री देत राम	21-10-96	70	6	100	106	रदा	नहीं	970	97	1067→	
111. देवता धान साकनभुठो कोठी तारापुर	श्री राम सिंह	21-10-96	9	9	61	70	रदा	नहीं	1040	104	1144 [illegible]	

~~112. देवी महाकाली चामुण्डा~~

..5..

112. देवी म[illegible] काली वाक्या वामुण्डा ग[illegible] छतर डा. [illegible] पा मुन्दरनगर	परम [illegible]	21-10-96	100	2	11	13	रथ	नहीं	500	100/-	600/-	[illegible]
113. देवता लक्ष्मीनारायण वाक्या जेष्ठा प[illegible]टी पारली कोठी कोटकण्डी	श्री हरदे राम	21-10-96	20		60	60	रथ	नहीं	3164	316	3480	[illegible]
114. देवता जमलू वाक्या [illegible]	श्री [illegible]	21-10-96	42	–	30	30	हान्डी ढाक्का	नहीं	1674	167	1841	
115. देवता [illegible] नाग वाक्या [illegible] वाक्या बनोगी तह० [illegible]	श्री मान दास	21-10-96	60	8	30	38	रथ	नहीं	500	100	600	मानदास
116. देवी काली ओढ़ी वाक्या अरछण्डी [illegible]	श्री किशन चन्द	21-10-96	18	70	70	77	रथ	नहीं	1593	159	1752	[illegible]
117. देवता गाहरी वाक्या [illegible]	श्री मंगल चन्द	21-10-96	–	+2	40	-52	रथ	नहीं	1258	125	1383	[illegible]
118. देवता महावीर मनोहर	श्री जेठू राम	21-10-96	60	12	88	100	रथ	नहीं	865	86	951	[illegible]
119. देवता [illegible] वाक्या देवटार फाटी टालपुर	श्री दौलत राम	21-10-96	2	7	35	40	रथ	नहीं	500	100	600	[illegible]
120. देवता वीर [illegible] वाक्या [illegible] फाटी दुवाड़ा	श्री जवाहर लाल	21-10-96	19	4	20	24	रथ	नहीं	1336	133	1469	[illegible]
121. देवी चामुण्डा वाक्या [illegible] फाटी [illegible]	श्री हरी प्रकाश सरबराह कारदार	21-10-96	20	14	70	84	रथ	नहीं	1691	169	1860	[illegible]
122. देवता [illegible]वीर वाक्या [illegible] गोपालपुर तह० बन्जार	श्री सेस राम	21-10-96	45	9	100	105	रथ	नहीं	500	100	600	[illegible]
123. देवी ज्वाला [illegible] वाक्या [illegible]	श्री [illegible] कमेटी सदस्य	21-10-96	8	10	50	60	रथ	नहीं	1465	146	1611	
124. देवता [illegible] महादेव वाक्या [illegible] तह० आनी	श्री [illegible] कुमार	21-10-96	174	18	120	138	रथ	नहीं	3100	310	3410	[illegible]

125. देवता लक्ष्मी नारायण वाक्या कमीवहड़ कोठी महाराज	श्री हेत राम	21-10-96	7	7	30	37	रटा	नही	500	100	600	[illegible]
126. देवता गाहरी वाक्या दालपुर	श्री राज कुमार	21-10-96	–	10	40	50	रटा	नही	1255	125	1383	[illegible]
127. देवता महावीर वाक्या कोठी बाराहार	श्री नागेन्द चन्द	21-10-96	15	15	100	115	रटा	नही	1712	171	1883	[illegible]
128. देवता जम्लू वाक्या कोठार फाटी कापस	श्री कुंज लाल	22-10-96	12	–	8	8	चान्दी टाइप	नही	500	100	600	[illegible]
129. देवता त्रिशूली महादेव वाक्या देहरा नाला फाटी लाहीहार	श्री चिरु राम	21-10-96	10	2	13	15	मोहरा और त्रिशूल	नही	500	100	600	[illegible]
130. देवी दोधा माता वाक्या करज कोठी वरशाई	श्री अमर सैन	22-10-96	30	12	120	135	रटा	नही	1866	186	2052	[illegible]
131. देवता बराही वीर वाक्या लौट फाटी वाराहार	श्री हेत राम	21-10-96	12	5	40	45	रटा	नही	847	84	931	[illegible]
132. देवता गर्ग ऋषि वाक्या लाहरानी फाटी लिहार कोठी कोटकण्डी	श्री कांशीराम	21-10-96	20	9	61	70	रटा	नही	1702	170	1872	[illegible]
133. देवता जल वाक्या बहुमाग फाटी व कोठी पलाच तह० बन्जार	श्री लगन चन्द	21-10-96	55	7	25	32	रटा	नही	500	100	600	
134. देवता हरि नारायण वाक्या कोठी दुव्वीलग	श्री अनन्त राम	21-10-96	9	15	87	102	रटा	नही	1272	127	1399	

(c) Sample Page of the Tirhara Register

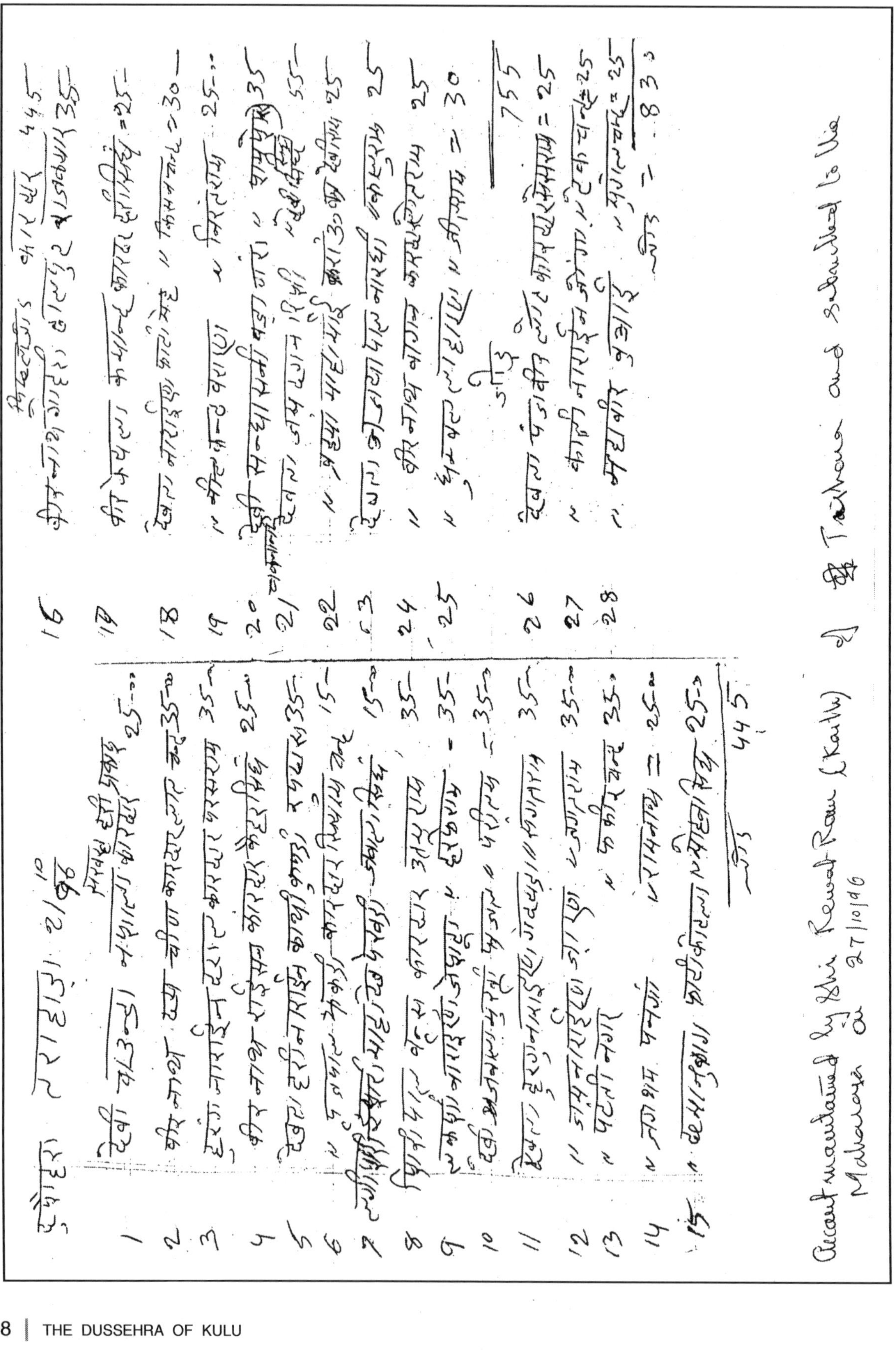

Appendix H

(a) Copy of Standard Invitation by the Dussehra Committee to the Deotas.
(b) Copy of Brochure of International Dussehra Festival, 1996.
(c) Copy of Brochure of International Dussehra Festival, 2003.

(a) Copy of Standard Invitation by the Dussehra Committee to the Deotas.

अध्यक्ष एवं कुल्लू दशहरा समिति के सदस्यगण

अन्तर्राष्ट्रीय लोकनृत्य समारोह कुल्लू दशहरा

के पावन अबसर पर

कारदार, देवता, देवी ....

गांव ....डाकघर ....

तहसील ....जिला कुल्लू (हि० प्र०)

को

सादर आमन्त्रित करते हैं।

—: आमन्त्रक :—

श्री भगवान रघुनाथ जी	**जिलाधीश एवं उपाध्यक्ष**
के प्रतिनिधि की ओर से	दशहरा उत्सव समिति कुल्लू।

महोदय,

विगत वर्षों की भान्ति इस वर्ष भी कुल्लू का सुप्रसिद्ध धार्मिक, सांस्कृतिक एवं विजय दशमी (दशहरा) 21 अक्तूबर 1996 से आरम्भ होकर 27 अक्तूबर 1996 को सम्पन हो रहा है। दशहरा समिति आपको इस महान् पर्व में सम्मिलित होने के लिए सादर आमन्त्रित करती है।

दशहरा समिति यह आशा करती है कि आप कुल्लू दशहरा की मान्यताओं को शाश्वत बनाए रखने के लिए इस वर्ष भी मेले में धूमधाम से सम्मिलित होगे।

दशहरा समिति ने देवताओं को भेंट की 'जाने वाली राशि बाँटने के लिए जो आधार माने हैं वे इस प्रकार हैं :—

1. देवी-देवता की पुरातन कीर्ति और शोभा।
2. अपने स्थान से कुल्लू एवं वापसी सहित दूरी।
3. देवता के साथ आने वाले (कर्मचारी, नाटी व हारी)

दशहरा समिति ने यह भी निर्णय किया है कि जो देवी-देवता केवल शाँगल या मोहरा लेकर दशहरा में शामिल होंगे वे भेंट के भागीदार नहीं माने जायेंगे। इस प्रकार वे ही देवता नजराना प्राप्त करने के वास्तविक अधिकारी होंगे जो रथ यात्रा में शामिल होंगे और दशहरा आरम्भ होने के पहले दिन से लेकर लंका दहन तक कुल्लू दशहरा में उपस्थित रहेंगे।

अतः आपसे प्रार्थना है कि आप अपने देवी-देवता सहित 21 अक्तूबर को यानि जिस दिन रथ यात्रा होगी, कुल्लू पहुंचने की कोशिश करें।

यदि आप 21 अक्तूबर को प्रातः 10 बजे यहाँ पहुंच जाएं तो अपने पहुंचने की सूचना श्री रघुनाथ जी के मन्दिर में या तहसीलदार/उप-तहसीलदार कुल्लू अथवा उनके किसी भी प्रतिनिधि जो भी वहाँ उपस्थित को दे दें। जो देवी-देवता किसी भी कारणवश 21 अक्तूबर को मन्दिर में जाकर हाजरी न दे सके वे ढालपुर के कैम्प मन्दिर में हाजरी दे सकते हैं। अपने आने की सूचना 31 अगस्त तक देने की कृपा करें। जिससे प्रबन्ध करने में आसानी हो।

सभी देवी-देवताओं को लंका दहन के समय उपस्थित होना चाहिए और रघुनाथ जी के साथ आरम्भ से गंतव्य स्थान तक साथ चलना चाहिए जिससे रथ यात्रा भी अच्छी लगेगी, और नजराना की राशि में कटौती भी न करनी पड़े। देवता उपसमिती द्वारा निश्चित भेंट को राशि दशहरे के अन्तिम दिन में भेंट की जाएगी। नजराने के भागीदार वही देवतागण होंगे जो कि दशहरा समिति द्वारा आमन्त्रित हैं।

(b) Copy of Brochure of International Dussehra Festival, 1996.

कुल्लू दशहरा - 1996

21 अक्तूबर से 27 अक्तूबर 1996

ऋषि वशिष्ठ जी

सांस्कृतिक कार्यक्रम

कुल्लू दशहरा - 1996

आपको सूचित किया जाता है कि इस वर्ष पारम्परिक कुल्लू दशहरा एवं अन्तर्राष्ट्रीय लोक नृत्य उत्सव ***21*** अक्तूबर ***1996*** से ***27*** अक्तूबर ***1996*** तक मनाया जा रहा है। इस उत्सव की शोभा को बढ़ाने तथा परम्परा की निरन्तरता को चरितार्थ करते हुए इस वर्ष भी ग्राम्य देवता इस उत्सव में सम्मिलित होने हेतु आ रहे हैं। इस के अतिरिक्त इस वर्ष अन्तर्राष्ट्रीय ख्याति प्राप्त प्रसिद्ध नायिका हेमा मालिनी, पार्श्व गायक हरिहरण तथा गायिका वन्दना वाजपेयी आदि दशहरा उत्सव में अपना कार्यक्रम प्रस्तुत करेंगे।

21 अक्तूबर 96

1. रा० महाविद्यालय कुल्लू के छात्रो द्वारा कुल्वी नाटी
2. मिजोरम पार्टी द्वारा रंगारंग कार्यक्रम
3. हमीरपुर के कलाकारों द्वारा कार्यक्रम
4. राजस्थान पार्टी का कार्यक्रम
5. प्रसिद्ध अभिनेत्री हेमा मालिनी द्वारा लक्ष्मी स्वयंवर नृत्य

22 अक्तूबर 96

1. कुल्लू लोक नृत्य।
2. मध्य प्रदेश पार्टी द्वारा कार्यक्रम
3. आन्ध्र प्रदेश के कलाकारों द्वारा कार्यक्रम
4. लाहौल पार्टी द्वारा रंगारंग कार्यक्रम
5. साउण्ड-एन-साउण्ड द्वारा कार्यक्रम
6. उत्तर क्षेत्रीय सांस्कृतिक केन्द्र पटियाला द्वारा कार्यक्रम

23 अक्तूबर 96

1. कुल्लू के कलाकारों द्वारा लोक नृत्य
2. पश्चिम बंगाल के कलाकारों द्वारा कार्यक्रम
3. कांगड़ा पार्टी द्वारा कार्यक्रम
4. गुजरात राज्य के कलाकारों द्वारा कार्यक्रम
5. न्यू एज क्रियेटिव थियेटर कुल्लू द्वारा कार्यक्रम
6. आकाशवाणी शिमला द्वारा कार्यक्रम

24 अक्तूबर 96

1. कुल्लू लोक नृत्य
2. पंजाब पार्टी द्वारा कार्यक्रम
3. सूत्रधार कला संगम द्वारा रंगारंग कार्यक्रम
4. रूस देश के कलाकारों द्वारा कार्यक्रम
5. सिरमौर पार्टी द्वारा कार्यक्रम
6. उत्तर क्षेत्रीय सांस्कृतिक केन्द्र पटियाला द्वारा कार्यक्रम

विशेष आकर्षण

21 अक्तूबर 1996 को प्रसिद्ध अभिनेत्री हेमा मालिनी द्वारा लक्ष्मी स्वयंवर नृत्य, 24 अक्तूबर को रूस के कलाकारों द्वारा कार्यक्रम की प्रस्तुति एवं 26 अक्तूबर को प्रसिद्ध पार्श्व गायिका वन्दना वाजपेयी द्वारा कार्यक्रम, इसके अतिरिक्त 25 अक्तूबर 1996 को सिनेमा जगत् के प्रसिद्ध पार्श्व गायक हरिहरण अपना कार्यक्रम प्रस्तुत करेंगे जो टिकटों पर दिखाया जायेगा। इस कार्यक्रम के लिए टिकटों की दरें 100/-रु० 50/-रु० 30/-रु० तथा 10/-रु० होंगी। यह टिकटें आप सहायक आयुक्त व जिलाधीश कुल्लू के कार्यालय से प्राप्त कर सकते हैं।

दिनांक 22-10-96 से 25-10-96 तक

प्रतिदिन अपराहण 2 बजे तथा दिनांक *26-10-96* को *11* बजे प्रातः कुल्लू नाटी प्रतियोगिता तथा स्कूली बच्चों के विविध रंगारंग कार्यक्रम प्रातः *11* बजे से *2* बजे तक प्रतिदिन आयोजित होंगे।

25 अक्तूबर 96

1. कुल्लू लोक नृत्य
2. प्रसिद्ध पार्श्व गायक हरिहरण द्वारा रंगारंग कार्यक्रम
3. हरियाणा पार्टी द्वारा कार्यक्रम
4. उत्तर क्षेत्रीय सांस्कृतिक केन्द्र पटियाला द्वारा कार्यक्रम

26 अक्तूबर 96

1. कुल्लू लोक नृत्य
2. निरमण्ड पार्टी द्वारा कार्यक्रम
3. सिनेमा जगत् की प्रसिद्ध पार्श्व गायिका वन्दना वाजपेयी द्वारा कार्यक्रम
4. किन्नौर पार्टी द्वारा कार्यक्रम
5. दक्षिण क्षेत्रिय सांस्कृतिक केन्द्र तंजावर (मद्रास) द्वारा कार्यक्रम
5. उत्तर क्षेत्रीय सांस्कृतिक केन्द्र पटियाला द्वारा कार्यक्रम

27 अक्तूबर 96

1. कुल्लू लोक नृत्य
2. युवक भारत सेवा मण्डल (महाराष्ट्र) द्वारा कार्यक्रम
3. सृजन मंच शिमला द्वारा कार्यक्रम
4. रा० व० मा० वि० शक्ति नगर दिल्ली की छात्राओ द्वारा कार्यक्रम
5. उत्तर क्षेत्रीय सांस्कृतिक केन्द्र पटियाला द्वारा कार्यक्रम
6. बन्जार पार्टी द्वारा मनोरंजक कार्यक्रम

अनिल खाची
(भा० प्र० से०)
उपायुक्त एवं उपाध्यक्ष
कुल्लू दशहरा समिति

बबलू प्रिंटर्ज शमशी फोन : 65108

अध्यक्ष एवं कुल्लू दशहरा उत्सव समिति के सदस्यगण

अन्तर्राष्ट्रीय लोकनृत्य समारोह कुल्लू दशहरा

के पावन अवसर पर

आपको सपरिवार सादर आमन्त्रित करते हैं।

समारोह का उद्घाटन

श्री महावीर प्रसाद

महामहिम राज्यपाल हिमाचल प्रदेश

के द्वारा

दिनांक 21 अक्तूबर, 1996 को सायं 7-30 बजे किया जायेगा।

समारोह का समापन

माननीय मुख्य मन्त्री श्री वीरभद्र सिंह

द्वारा

दिनांक 27 अक्तूबर, 1996 को किया जायेगा।

सम्पर्क
दूरभाष : 22486

निवेदक :
उपायुक्त एवं उपाध्यक्ष
दशहरा उत्सव समिति कुल्लू।

सांस्कृतिक कार्यक्रम

दिनांक	कार्यक्रम
21-10-96	3-00 से 5-00 बजे रथ यात्रा। 6-30 से 7-30 बजे प्रदर्शनी का उद्घाटन। 7-30 से 8-00 बजे कुल्लू दशहरा उत्सव का उद्घाटन। 8-00 से 11-00 बजे महाविद्यालय कुल्लू के छात्रों, मिजोरम, हमीरपुर, राजस्थान पार्टी एवं प्रसिद्ध अभिनेत्री हेमा मालिनी द्वारा स्वयंवर नृत्य की प्रस्तुति।
22-10-96	कुल्लू लोक नृत्य, मध्यप्रदेश, आन्ध्र प्रदेश, लाहौल पार्टी, साउण्ड-एन-साउण्ड तथा उत्तर क्षेत्रीय सांस्कृतिक केन्द्र के कलाकारों द्वारा कार्यक्रम।
23-10-96	कुल्लू लोक नृत्य, पश्चिम बंगाल, रूस देश, कांगड़ा, गुजरात पार्टी, आकाशवाणी शिमला तथा न्यु एज क्रियेटिव थियेटर के कलाकारों द्वारा कार्यक्रम।
24-10-96	कुल्लू लोक नृत्य, पंजाब, सूत्रधार कला संगम कुल्लू, सिरमौर पार्टी, तथा उत्तर क्षेत्रीय सांस्कृतिक केन्द्र पटियाला के कलाकारों द्वारा कार्यक्रम।
25-10-96	प्रसिद्ध पार्श्व गायक हरिहरण, हरियाणा पार्टी, उत्तर क्षेत्रीय सांस्कृतिक केन्द्र पटियाला के कलाकारों द्वारा कार्यक्रम।
26-10-96	कुल्लू लोक नृत्य, निरमण्ड पार्टी, प्रसिद्ध पार्श्व गायिका वन्दना वाजपेयी, किन्नौर पार्टी, दक्षिण क्षेत्रीय सांस्कृतिक केन्द्र तन्जावर (मद्रास), तथा उत्तर क्षेत्रीय साँस्कृतिक केन्द्र पटियाला के कलाकारों द्वारा कार्यक्रम।
27-10-96	महाराष्ट्र पार्टी, सृजन मंच शिमला, रा० कन्या मा० विद्यालय शक्ति नगर दिल्ली की छात्राओं, बन्जार पार्टी तथा उत्तर क्षेत्रीय साँस्कृतिक केन्द्र पटियाला के कलाकारों द्वारा कार्यक्रम।

★ समय : सभी कार्यक्रम सायं 7-30 से रात्री 11-30 बजे तक ★

(c) Copy of Brochure of International Dussehra Festival, 2003.

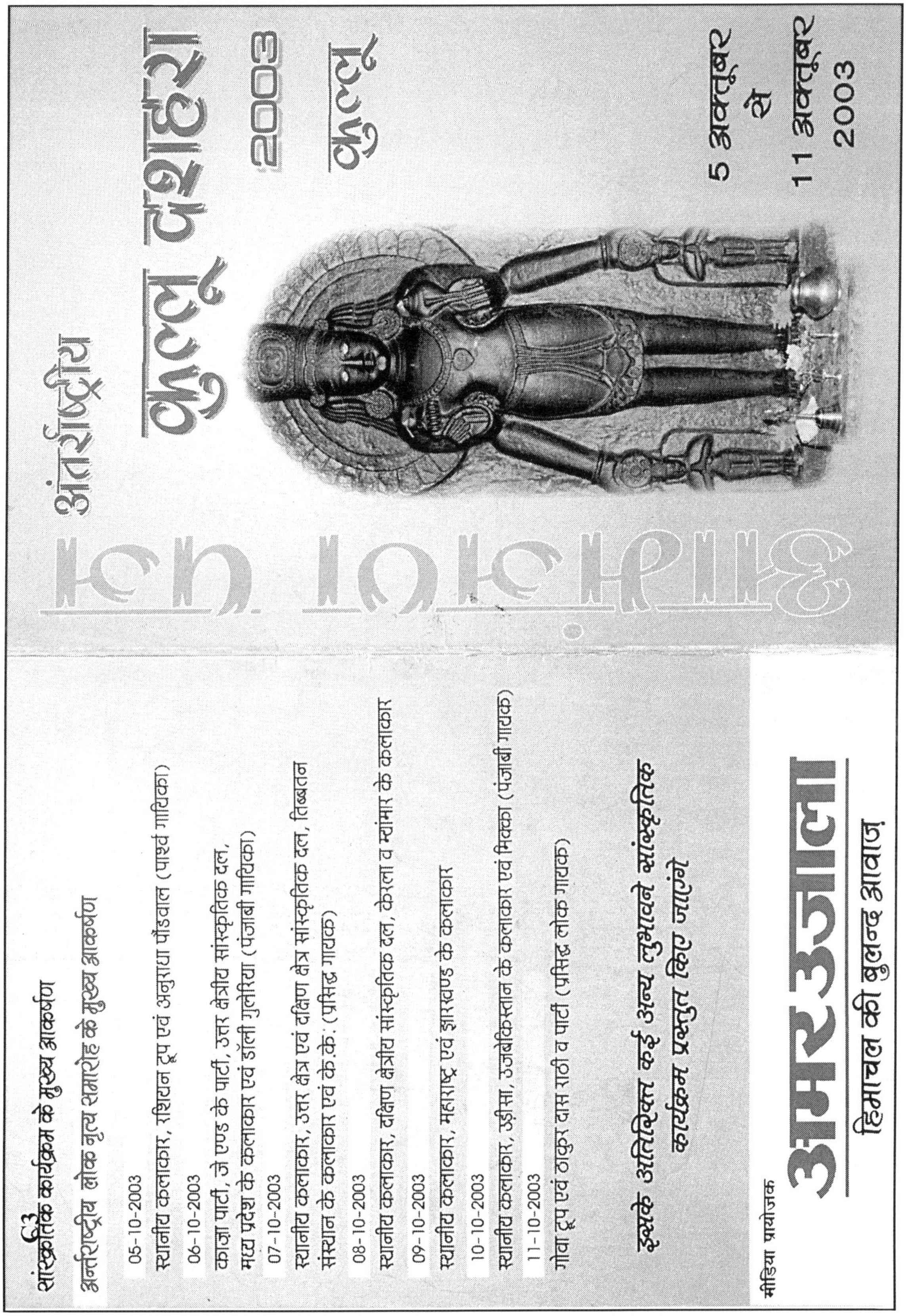

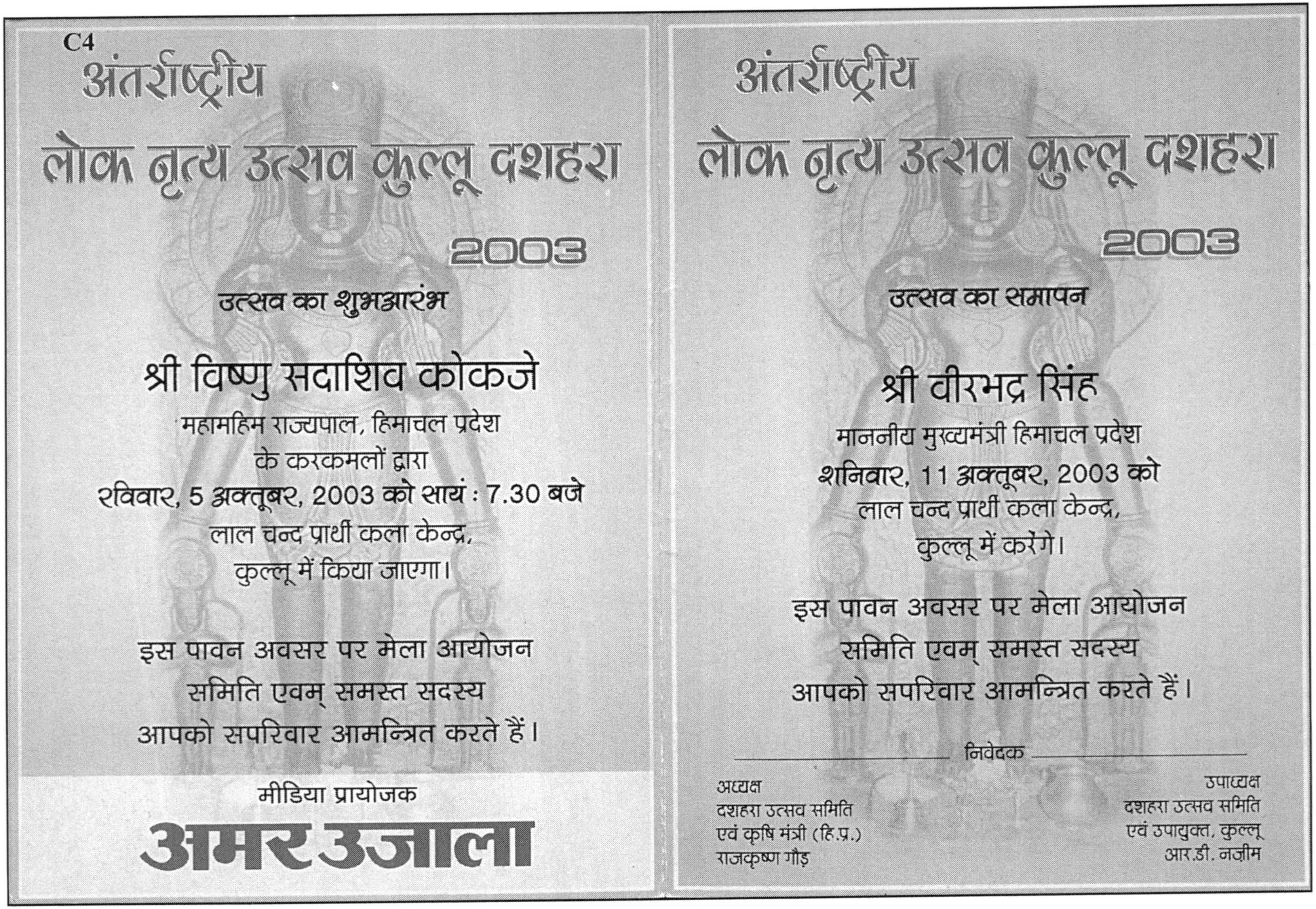

C4

अंतर्राष्ट्रीय

लोक नृत्य उत्सव कुल्लू दशहरा

2003

उत्सव का शुभआरंभ

श्री विष्णु सदाशिव कोकजे

महामहिम राज्यपाल, हिमाचल प्रदेश

के करकमलों द्वारा

रविवार, 5 अक्तूबर, 2003 को सायं : 7.30 बजे

लाल चन्द प्रार्थी कला केन्द्र,

कुल्लू में किया जाएगा।

इस पावन अवसर पर मेला आयोजन

समिति एवम् समस्त सदस्य

आपको सपरिवार आमन्त्रित करते हैं।

मीडिया प्रायोजक

अमर उजाला

अंतर्राष्ट्रीय

लोक नृत्य उत्सव कुल्लू दशहरा

2003

उत्सव का समापन

श्री वीरभद्र सिंह

माननीय मुख्यमंत्री हिमाचल प्रदेश

शनिवार, 11 अक्तूबर, 2003 को

लाल चन्द प्रार्थी कला केन्द्र,

कुल्लू में करेंगे।

इस पावन अवसर पर मेला आयोजन

समिति एवम् समस्त सदस्य

आपको सपरिवार आमन्त्रित करते हैं।

निवेदक

अध्यक्ष
दशहरा उत्सव समिति
एवं कृषि मंत्री (हि.प्र.)
राजकृष्ण गौड़

उपाध्यक्ष
दशहरा उत्सव समिति
एवं उपायुक्त, कुल्लू
आर.डी. नज़ीम

Bibliography

Ajit K. Singh. *Tribal Festivals of Bihar: A Functional Analysis.* Concept Publishers, New Delhi, 1980.

Anderson, Benedict. *Imagined Communities: Reflections on the Origin and Spread of Nationalism.* Verso, London, 1991.

Appadurai, Arjun. *Worship and Conflict under Colonial Rule: A South Indian Case.* Orient Longman, 1981.

Appadurai, Arjun. "Kings, Sects and Temples in South India, 1350-1700 AD", *The Indian Economic and Social History Review,* Jan-March, 1977, Vol. XIV, No. 1.

Bachittar Singh. *Rewaj-i-am: [Kulu, Lahaul, Spiti] Settlement 1945-51.* Rpt. Shimla, 2003.

Bakker, Hans. *The Sacred Centre as the Focus of Political Interest.* Egbert Forsten, 1992.

Balandier, Georges. *Political Anthropology.* Allan Lane, The Penguin Press, 1967.

Balhari, Sardaru. "The Worship of Narsingh in Kangra", *Indian Antiquary,* XXIV, 1905.

Bannerjee Dube, Ishita. *Divine Affairs: Religion, Pilgrimage, and the State in Colonial and Post Colonial India.* 2001.

Barnes, George C. *Report on the Kangra Settlement,* 1889.

Bebas, Chandra Shekhar. *Bebas Sahitya Sadhana, Visheshank,* 8-23, *Shrikhand, Journal of Culture and Literature.*

Beetham, David. *The Legitimation of Power: Issues in Political Theory.* Macmillan, 1991.

Berreman, Gerald D. *Hindus of the Himalayas.* Oxford University Press, Bombay, 1963.

Berti, Daniela. "Ritual Kingship, Divine Bureaucracy and Electoral Politics in Kullu", *European Bulletin of Himalayan Research,* Vol. 29-30.

Bharadwaj, S.M. *Hindu Places of Pilgrimage in India.* University of California Press, Berkeley, 1973.

Bhattacharyya, N.N. *Ancient Indian Rituals and Their Social Contents.* Manohar, New Delhi, 1996.

Biardeau, Madeleine. *Hinduism: The Anthropology of a Civilisation.* Oxford University Press, New Delhi, 1989.

Blake, Stephen P. "The Patrimonial–Bureaucratic Empire of the Mughals", in Kulke, *The State in India,* 1000-1700.

Bloch, Maurice."The Disconnection between Power and Rank as a Process: An Outline of the Development of Kingdoms", in *Ritual, History and Power: Selected Papers in Anthropology.* London, 1989.

Bocock, Robert and Kenneth Thompson (eds.). *Religion and Ideology: A Reader.* Manchester University Press, Manchester, 1985.

Braudel, Fernand. *The Identity of France,* 2 vols. Harper Collins, 1990.

Burke, Peter. *What is Cultural History?* Polity Press, U.K., 2004.

——. *Varieties of Cultural History.* Polity Press, U.K., 1997.

Census of India 1961: *Himachal Pradesh, Fairs and Festivals,* XX, Part VII, B 1961.

Chakrabarti, Kunal. *Religious Process: The Puranas and the Makings of a Regional Tradition.* Oxford University Press, Delhi, 2001.

Charak, Sukhdev Singh. *History and Culture of Himalayan States,* Vol. II, Part II. Light and Life Publishers, New Delhi, 1979.

Chattopadhyaya, Brajdulal. *The Making of Early Medieval India.* Oxford University Press, New Delhi, 1994.

Chetan Singh. "The Place of Myth, Legend and Folklore in Western Himalayan History". Paper Read at a Seminar of Department of History, Panjab University, 2004.

——. *Natural Premises: Ecology and Peasant Life in Western Himalaya,* 1800-1950. Indian Institute of Advanced Study and Oxford University Press, New Delhi, 1998.

——. "Nature, Religion and Politics in the Himachal (Western) Himalaya: Case Studies of Keonthal and Kumharsain", 2005. (Article consulted in mimeo form).

Chetwode, Penelope. *Kulu: The End of the Habitable World.* John Murray, London, 1972; Indian reprint, Allied Publishers, Delhi 1980.

Choudhury, Sujit. *Folklore and History: A Study of the Hindu Folk Cults of the Barak Valley of North East India.* K.K. Publishers, New Delhi.

Claessen, Henri J.M. and Peter Skalnik (eds.). *The Early State.* Mouton Publishers, The Hague, 1978.

Claessen, Henri J.M. *Ideology and the Formation of Early States.* Brill, Leiden, 1996.

Cohn, Bernard, S. *An Anthropologist Among the Historians and Other Essays,* Oxford University Press, New Delhi, 1990.

Cohn, Bernard S. "Political Systems and Political Structures in Eighteenth Century India: The Benares Region", *Journal of American Oriental Society,* Vol. 82, No. 3, 1962.

Coldstream, J. *Final Report of the Third Revised Settlement of the Kulu Sub-division of the Kangra District.* Lahore, 1913.

Comaroff, John and Jean. *Ethnography and the Historical Imagination.* Westview Press, Oxford, 1992.

Coomaraswamy, A.K. *Spiritual Authority and Temporal Power in the Indian Theory of Government.* American Oriental Society, New Haven, Connecticut, 1942.

Dehejia, Harsha. *Gods Beyond Temples.* Motilal Banarsidass, Delhi, 2006.

Diack, A.H. *Final Report of the Revised Settlement of the Kulu Sub-Division of the Kangra District.* Lahore, 1898.

Dirks, Nicholas B. *The Hollow Crown: Ethno-history of an Indian Kingdom.* Cambridge University Press, 1987

Drekmeier, Charles. *Kingship and Community in Early India.* Oxford University Press, Bombay, 1962.

Dube, Ishita Banerjee. *Divine Affairs: Religion, Pilgrimage and the State in Colonial and Post Colonial India.* Shimla, 2001.
Dundes, Alan (ed.). *Sacred Narrative: Readings in the Theory of Myth.* University of California Press, 1984.
Eliade, Mircea. *Shamanism: Archaic Techniques of Ecstasy.* Routledge and Kegan Paul, U.K., 1951.
Eschmann, Anncharlott, Hermann Kulke and Gaya Charan Tripathi. *The Cult of Jagannath and the Regional Tradition of Orissa.* Manohar, Delhi, 1978.
Fleet, J.F. *Corpus Inscriptionum Indicarum,* Vol. III. Reprint, Varanasi, 1970.
Freitag, Sandra. *Culture and Power in Benares: Community, Performance and Environment.* University of California Press, Berkeley, 1989.
Gazetteer of the Kangra District, Part I. 1883-84.
Gazetteer of the Kangra District, Parts II to IV, *Kulu, Lahul and Spiti.* 1897.
Gazetteer of the Simla District, 1888-89 Indian reprint, Hillman Publishers, 1992.
Goetz, Hermann. *Studies in History and Art of Kashmir and the Indian Himalaya.* Otto Harrassowitz, Wiesbaden, 1969.
——. *Studies in History, Religion and Art of Classical and Medieval India.* Franz Steiner, Wiesbaden, 1973.
Goswamy, B.N. *The Social Background of Kangra Valley Painting.* Ph.D. dissertation, 1961, Panjab University Library.
Goswamy, Karuna. *Kashmiri Painting: Assimilation and Diffusion, Production and Patronage.* Indian Institute of Advanced Study, Shimla & Aryan Books International, New Delhi, 1998.
——. *Vaishnavism in the Panjab Hills and Pahari Painting.* Ph.D. dissertation, 1968, Panjab University, Chandigarh.
Goverdhan Singh, Mian. *Himachal Pradesh ka Itihas* (in Hindi). Delhi, 1996.
——. *Descriptive Bibliography of Himachal Pradesh.* Himachal Academy of Arts, Culture & Languages, Shimla, 1985.
Gupta, P.L. *Numismatic History of Himachal Pradesh.* B.R. Publications, Delhi, 1988.
Gurevich, Aron. *Categories of Medieval Culture.* Routledge and Kegan Paul, London, 1985.
——. *Medieval Popular Culture: Problems of Belief and Perception.* Cambridge University Press, U.K., 1988.
Handa, Devendra. *Tribal Coins of Ancient India.* Aryan Books International, New Delhi, 2010.
Harcourt, A.F.P., *The Himalayan Districts of Kooloo, Lahoul and Spiti.* Allen & Co. 1871; Indian reprint, Delhi, 1972
Hardayal Singh. *Tawarikh-i Majmua-i Riyasat-hai Kohistan-i Punjab* (in Urdu). Moradabad, 1886.
Harnot, S.R. *Himachal ke Mandir aur Unse Judi Lok-Kathayen (in Hindi).* Shimla, 1991.
Harper, Edward B. *Religion in South Asia.* University of Washington Press, Seattle, 1964.
Hein, Norwin. *The Miracle Plays of Mathura.* Oxford University Press, New Delhi, 1972.
Heitzman, James. *Gifts of Power: Lordship in an Early Indian State.* Oxford University Press, New Delhi, 1997.
Henning, Charles L., "On the Origin of Religion", *The American Anthropologist,* Vol. XI, Dec., 1898.
Henri, Lefebvre. *The Production of Space.* Blackwell, U.K., 1991.
Himachal Pradesh Census Atlas, Vol. XX, Part IX to Part XII.
Horton, Robin. "A Definition of Religion, and Its Uses", *Journal of the Royal Anthropological Institute,* 90, Part 2. London, 1960.

Howard, N.F. "The Fortified Places of Upper Kulu, India", *South Asian Studies*, 11 and 12, 1995-96.

Hutchison, J. and J. Ph. Vogel. *History of the Panjab Hill States*, Vols. I & II. Lahore, 1933.

Ibbetson, Denzil. *Panjab Castes*. Lahore, 1916.

Inden, Ronald. *Imagining India*. Basil Blackwell, U.K., 1990.

Jha, D.N. (ed.). *Society and Ideology in India*. Munshiram Manoharlal, Delhi, 1996.

Kahan Singh Balauria, Thakur. *Tawarikh-i Rajputan-i Mulk-i Punjab* (in Urdu). Jammu, 1912.

Kapur, Anuradha. *Actors, Pilgrims, Kings and Gods: The Ramalila at Ram Nagar*. Seagull, Calcutta. 1990.

Kaur, Raminder. *Performative Politics and the Cultures of Hinduism: Public Uses of Religion in Western India*. Permanent Black, 2003.

Kaushik, Kamal Kishore, *Shri Raghunath Mandir ka Itihas* (in Hindi), Kulu, n.d.

Kertzer, David T. "The Role of Ritual in State Formation" pp. 88-89, in Eric R. Wolf (ed.), *Religious Regimes and State Formation*.

Kulke, Hermann and B. Schnepel. *Jagannath Revisited: Studying Society, Religion and the State in Orissa*. Manohar, Delhi, 2001.

Kulke, Hermann. *The State in India, 1000-1700 AD*. Oxford University Press. New Delhi, 1995.

——. *Kings and Cults: State Formation and Legitimation in India and South East Asia*. Manohar, Delhi, 1993.

Kulu and Saraj: Kangra District Gazetteers, 1917. Reprint, Himachal Academy of Arts, Culture and Languages, Shimla.

Kulu Dussehra Souvenirs: from the year 1971 to 2007. Department of Languages and Culture, Govt. of Himachal Pradesh.

Lambeck, Michael. *A Reader in the Anthropology of Religion*. Blackwell, 2002.

Levi-Strauss, Claude. *Anthropology and Myth: Lectures*, 1951-1982. Blackwell, U.K., 1984.

——. *Myth and Meaning*. Routledge and Kegan Paul, London, 1977.

Levy, Robert I. *Mesocosm: Hinduism and the Organization of a Traditional Newar City in Nepal*. Motilal Banarsidass, Delhi, 1992.

Lorenzen, David. *Kabir Legends and Anant-dasa's Kabir Parichay*. State University of New York Press, 1991.

Lyall, J.B. *Kangra Settlement Report*, 1872.

Mahapatra, Sitakant. *Realm of the Sacred*. Oxford University Press, New Delhi, 1992.

Majumdar, R.C. *British Paramountcy and Indian Renaissance*, Part I. Bharatiya Vidya Bhavan, Bombay, 1963.

Man Mohan. *A History of the Mandi State*. Lahore, 1930.

Mandiron ki Suchi (in Hindi). Department of Languages Art and Culture, Shimla, n.d.

Marriott, Mckim. *Village India: Studies in the Little Community*. University of Chicago Press, Chicago, 1955.

Meister, Michael. "Mountain Temples and Temple-Mountains: Masrur", *Journal of the Society of Architectural Historians*, Vol. 65, No. 1, 2006.

Metzger, H. and Maharao Brij Raj Singh of Kotah. *Festivals and Ceremonies Observed by the Royal Family of Kotah*. Museum Rietberg, Zurich, n.d.

Milner Jr., Murray. *Status and Sacredness: A General Theory of Status Relations and an Analysis of Indian Culture*. Oxford University Press, New York, 1994.

Minhas, Poonam. *Traditional Trade and Trading Centres in Himachal Pradesh*. Indus, Delhi, 1998.

Morris, Brian. *Anthropological Studies of Religion: An Introductory Text.* Cambridge University Press, New York, 1987.

Mubayi, Yaaminey. *Altars of Power: The Temple and the State in the Land of Jagannatha.* Manohar, Delhi, 2005.

Nagar, S.L. *The Temples of Himachal Pradesh.* Aditya Prakashan, New Delhi, 1990.

Noble, Christina. *At Home in the Himalayas.* London, 1991.

O'Flaherty, Wendy Doniger. *Hindu Myths.* Penguin, 1975.

Ohri, V.C. *The Sculpture of Western Himalayas.* Agam Kala Prakashan, Delhi, 1991.

Ostor, Akos. *Culture and Power: Legend, Ritual, Bazaar and Rebellion in a Bengali Society.* Sage Publications, Delhi, 1984.

——. *The Play of the Gods: Locality, Ideology, Structure and Time in the Festivals of a Bengali Town,* University of Chicago, London.

Panjab States Gazetteers: Mandi and Suket States with Maps, 1904. Lahore, 1908.

Parry, Jonathan P. *Caste and Kinship in Kangra.* Routledge and Kegan Paul, London, 1979.

Patnaik, Nityananda. *Cultural Traditions in Puri: Structure and Organization of a Pilgrim Centre.* Indian Institute of Advanced Study, Shimla, 1977.

Pfaff-Czarnecka, J. "The Nepalese Durga Puja Festival or Displaying Political Supremacy on Ritual Occasions", in Charles Ramble & Martin Brauen (eds.), *Anthropology of Tibet and the Himalaya.* Zurich, 1998.

Pickering, Michael. *History Experience and Cultural Studies.* Macmillan Press, London, 1997.

Pinney, Christopher. *Photos of the Gods: The Printed Image and Political Struggle in India.* Oxford University Press, New Delhi, 2004

Postel, M., A. Neven and K. Mankodi. *Antiquities of Himachal.* Bombay, 1985.

Prarthi, Lalchand. *Kulut Desh ki Kahani* (in Hindi). Neel Kamal Prakashan, Kulu, 2000.

Raghunath Singh, Mian. *Tarikah-Rajgan Pathania* (in Urdu).

Ranchan, Som P. and H.R. Justa. *Folk Tales of Himachal Pradesh.* Bombay, 1981.

Ranzor Singh, Kunwar. *Tarikh-i Riyasat Sirmur* (in Urdu). Allahabad, 1912.

Rappaport, Roy A. *Ritual and Religion in the Making of Humanity.* Cambridge University Press, U.K., 1999.

——. "The Sacred in Human Evolution", *Annual Review of Ecology and Systematics,* 1971, 2: pp. 23-44.

Redfield, Robert. *The Little Community and Peasant Society and Culture.* University of Chicago Press, 1956.

Richards, J.F. (ed.). *Kingship and Authority in South Asia.* Oxford University Press, New Delhi, 1998.

Robertson, Roland. *Sociology of Religion.* Penguin, U.K., 1969.

Rose, H.A., *A Glossary of the Tribes and Castes of the Panjab and North West Frontier Province,* 3 vols., 1883. Reprint, Patiala, 1970.

——. "Hinduism in the Himalayas", *Indian Antiquary* XXXVI, 1907.

Rustomji, N.K. and Charles Ramble. *Himalayan Environment and Culture.* Indian Institute of Advanced Study, Shimla, 1990.

Sankrityayana, Rahul. *Himachal: Ek Sanskritik Yatra* (in Hindi).Vani Prakashan, Delhi, 1994.

Saraswati, Baidyanath. *Kashi: Myth and Reality of Classical Cultural Tradition.* Indian Institute of Advanced Study, Shimla, 1975.

Sarbdial, Dewan. *Tarikh-i Rajgan-*i *Zillah Kangra* (in Urdu).

Sax, William S. *Mountain Goddess: Gender and Politics in a Himalayan Pilgrimage*. Oxford University Press, New York, 1991.

——. *Dancing the Self: Personhood and Performance in the Pandav Lila of Garhwal*. Oxford University Press, New York, 2002.

——. *The Gods at Play: Lila in South Asia*. Oxford University Press, New York, 1995.

——. "Introduction: Divine Kingship in the Western Himalayas", *European Bulletin of Himalayan Research*, Vol. 29-30.

Schechner, R. *The Future of Ritual: Writings on Culture and Performance*. Routledge, London, 1993.

Shabab, Dilaram. *Kulu: Himaalyan Abode of the Divine*. Indus Publication Company, New Delhi, 1996.

Schnepel, Burkhard. "Kings and Rebel Kings: Rituals of Incorporation and Dissent in South Orissa" in Kulke and Schnepel, *Jagannath Revisited: Studying Society, Religion and the State in Orissa*.

——. *Twinned Beings: Kings and Effigies in Southern Sudan, East India and Renaissance France*. Institute for Advaced Studies in Social Anthropology, Gothenburg, 1995.

Sharma, B.R. and M.R. Thakur. *Himachal Pradesh: Lok Jiwan aur Paramparayein* (in Hindi). Shimla, 1987.

Sharma, Bansi Ram. *Himachal Lok Sanskriti ke Srota* (in Hindi). Arya Prakashan Mandal, New Delhi, 1986.

Sharma, Gautam 'Vyathit'. *Folklore of Himachal*. National Book Trust, New Delhi, 1984.

Sharma, Jagdish. *Himachal Pradesh ki Lok-gathaein* (in Hindi), Somsi Vishesank. Academy of Language and Culture, Shimla.

Sharma, Kamal Kishore. *Kuluvi Lok Natya Parampara: Ek Adhyayan* (in Hindi). M. Phil Dissertation, Himachal Pradesh University (mimeo).

Sharma, Mahesh. *The Realm of Faith: Subversion, Appropriation and Dominance in the Western Himalaya*. Indian Institute of Advanced Study, Shimla, 2001.

——. *Western Himalayan Temple Records: State, Pilgrimage, Ritual and Legality in Chamba*. Brill: Leiden/Boston, 2009.

——. "State Formation and Cultural Complex in Western Himalayas: Chamba Genealogy and Epigraphs – 700-1650 CE", *The Indian Economic and Social History Review*, 41, 4 (2004).

Sharma, Narendra Kumar. *Malana: Puratan Sanskriti ka Prateek* (in Hindi). Delhi, 1988

Sharma, Vidya. *Dev Bhumi Kulu Ke Parmukh Dev-Sthal*, District Languages Office, Kulu, n.d.

——. *Kulanta Darpan* (in Hindi). Kulu, 2001

Singer, Milton. *When a Great Tradition Modernizes: An Anthropological Approach to Indian Civilization*. Praeger Publishers, London, 1972.

Singer, Wendy. *Creating Histories: Oral Narratives and the Polities of History Making*. Oxford University Press, New Delhi, 1997.

Singh, G.P. *Political Thought in Ancient India*. D.K. Printworld, Delhi, 1993.

Sontheimer, Gunther-Dietz. *Folk Culture, Folk Religion and Oral Traditions as a Component in Maharashtrian Culture*. Manohar, Delhi, 1995.

——. *King of Hunters, Warriors and Shepherds: Essays on Khandoba*. Manohar, Delhi, 1997.

Srinivas, M.N. (ed.). *India's Villages*. Asia Publishing House, Bombay, 1955.

Srinivas, M.N. *Collected Essays*. Oxford University Press, New Delhi, 2002.

Stein, Burton. "The Segmentary State in South Indian History", in R.G. Fox (ed.), *Realm and Region in Traditional India*. Duke University, Durham, Monographs and Occasional Papers, no. 14.

Strenski, Ivan. *Four Theories of Myth in Twentieth Century History: Carrier, Eliade, Levi-Strauss and Malinowski*. Macmillan, London 1987.
Sukh Chain, "Legends of the Godlings of the Simla Hills", *Indian Antiquary*, LIV, 1925.
Sunder, Nandini. *Subalterns and Sovereigns*. Oxford University Press, New Delhi, 1997.
Sutherland, Peter. "T(r)opologies of Rule (Raj): Ritual Sovereignty and Theistic Subjection", *European Bulletin of Himalayan Research*, Vol. 29-30.
Tambiah, Stanley Jeyaraja. *Culture, Thought and Social Action: An anthropology Perspective*. Harvard University Press, 1985.
Tanaka, Masakazu. *Patrons, Devotees and Goddesses: Ritual Land Power among the Tamil Fishermen of Sri Lanka*. Manohar, Delhi, 1997.
Thakur, Laxman S. *The Architectural Heritage of Himachal: Origin and Development of Temple Styles*. Munshiram Manoharlal, Delhi, 1996.
——. (ed.) *Where Mortals and Mountain Gods Meet: Society and Culture in Himachal Pradesh*. Indian Institute of Advanced Study, Shimla, 2002.
——. *Visualizing a Buddhist Sutra: Text and Figure in Himalayan Art*. Oxford University Press, New Delhi, 2006.
Thakur, M.R. *Himachal Loka-natya aur Lokanuranjan* (in Hindi). Shimla, 1981.
——. *Myths, Rituals and Beliefs in Himachal Pradesh*. Delhi, 1997.
——. *Pahari Sanskriti Manjusha* (in Hindi). Delhi, n.d.
——. *Himachal mein Pujit Devi Devta* (in Hindi). Shimla, 1981.
Thakur, Surat (ed.). *Kulu ki Rishi Parampara* (in Hindi). Kulu, 2005.
——. *Himachal ki Dev Sanskriti: Mandir, Mele, Tyohar* (in Hindi). Delhi, 2004
Thakur, Vidya Chand. *Mandavya Prabha* (in Hindi). Puratatva Chetana Sangh, Mandi, 1990.
Thapar, Romila. *Cultural Pasts: Essays in Early Indian History*. Oxford University Press, New Delhi, 2000.
——. *From Lineage to State*. Oxford University Press, Delhi, 1984.
——. *Clan, Caste and Origin Myths in Early India*. Manohar, Delhi, 1992.
Turner, Bryan S. *Religion and Social Theory*. Sage Publications, New Delhi, 1983.
Turner, Victor. *Process, Performance and Pilgrimage*. Concept Publishing House, Delhi, 1979.
Vashisht, Sudarshan. *Himalaya mein Dev Sanskriti: Kulu Dev Parampara* (in Hindi). Delhi, n.d.
——. *Mandi Dev Milan* (in Hindi). 1997.
——. *Vyas ki Dhara* (in Hindi). Himachal Pustak Bhandar.
Vergatti, Anne. "Le Roi et les Deesses: La Fete de Navaratri et Dasahra en Rajasthan", in *Journal Asiatique*, Tome CCLXXXII. Paris, 1994.
Vidyarthi, L.P. and Makhan Jha. *Ecology, Economy and Religion of Himalayas*. Orient Publications, Ranchi, 1986.
——. *The Sacred Complex in Hindu Gaya*. Asia Publishing House, Bombay, 1961.
Village Directory Kulu, Census of India 1971.
Vogel, J. Ph. *India Antiqua*. Brill, Leiden, 1947.
Wolf, Eric R. *Religious Regimes and State Formation: Perspectives from European Ethnology*. State University of New York Press, New York, 1991.